PROFILE

OF

AMERICA

PROFILE

GROSSET & DUNLAP · PUBLISHERS · NEW YORK, N. Y.

OF

AMERICA

AN AUTOBIOGRAPHY OF THE U. S. A.

Text compiled by EMILY DAVIE

Foreword by CHARLES A. LINDBERGH

Introduction by LOUIS BROMFIELD

Picture Editor, BRYAN HOLME

ACKNOWLEDGMENTS

Grateful acknowledgment is made to the following publishers, authors, and copyright owners for permission to reproduce the copyrighted matter indicated below. The listing is alphabetical by author or subject.

ANTIN, MARY, *The Promised Land*, Houghton Mifflin Company.

BAILEY, THOMAS A., *A Diplomatic History of the American People*, copyright 1950 by Appleton-Century-Crofts, Inc. BENÉT, STEPHEN VINCENT, lines from Invocation to "John Brown's Body" in *Selected Works of Stephen Vincent Benét*, published by Rinehart & Company, Inc., copyright 1927, 1928 by Stephen Vincent Benét. BRADFORD, WILLIAM, *Of Plymouth Plantation*, edited by Samuel Eliot Morison, Alfred A. Knopf, Inc. BRADSTREET, ANNE, "Meditations Divine and Morall," from *Builders of the Bay Colony*, by Samuel Eliot Morison, Houghton Mifflin Company. BRADY, MATHEW B., photographs of General Grant and General Lee, from *Mr. Lincoln's Camera Man: Mathew B. Brady*, by Roy Meredith, copyright 1946 by Charles Scribner's Sons, by permission of the author. BROGAN, D. W., *The American Character*, by permission of Alfred A. Knopf, Inc., copyright 1944 by Denis W. Brogan. BUCHAN, JOHN, *Pilgrim's Way*, by permission of Houghton Mifflin Company and the Estate of Lord Tweedsmuir. BUNNELL, L. H., *The Discovery of the Yosemite and the Indian Wars of 1851*, Fleming H. Revell Company.

CABRILLO, JUAN RODRIGUEZ, extract from diary, from *The Missions and Missionaries of California*, James H. Barry Company, copyright 1920 by Fr. Zephyrin Engelhardt. CAMBA, JULIO, "Spaniard in a Barbershop," from *This Was America*, edited by Oscar Handlin, Harvard University Press. CARNEGIE, ANDREW, *The Empire of Business*, by permission of the Carnegie Corporation. CHARLEVOIX, PIERRE FRANÇOIS XAVIER DE, *Journal of a Voyage to North America*, edited by Louis Phelps Kellogg, The Caxton Club, Chicago.

DEWEY, JOHN, *School and Society*, The University of Chicago Press. DISNEY, WALT, story conference on "Fantasia," copyright 1942 by Walt Disney Productions.

FEININGER, ANDREAS, photograph on page 170. FORD, HENRY, AND CROWTHER, SAMUEL, *My Life and Work*, copyright 1922 by Doubleday & Company, Inc.

GARLAND, HAMLIN, *A Son of the Middle Border*, copyright 1945 by Hamlin Garland, by permission of The Macmillan Company. GEER, ELIZABETH DIXON, "Diary of a Woman on the Oregon

Trail," *Transactions of the Oregon Pioneer Association of 1908*, by permission of the Oregon Historical Society. GLASGOW, ELLEN, *Barren Ground*, copyright 1925, 1953 by Ellen Glasgow, used by permission of Harcourt, Brace and Company, Inc. GOMPERS, SAMUEL, *Seventy Years of Life and Labor*, copyright 1925 by E. P. Dutton & Co., Inc., renewed 1952 by Mrs. Gertrude Gleaves Gompers. GOOD, SARAH, witchcraft trial, from *Records of Salem Witchcraft*, courtesy New York Society Library. *Griffith, D. W., American Film Master*, by Iris Barry, by permission of The Museum of Modern Art, New York.

HARVARD COLLEGE, "Entrance Requirements, 1952," by permission of Harvard College. HOLMAN, EUGENE, "Our Inexhaustible Resources," copyright 1952 by The Atlantic Monthly Company, Boston 16, Massachusetts. HOOVER, HERBERT, "The Bill of Rights," by permission of Mr. Hoover. HUBNER, BARON VON, "An Austrian Views Us with Alarm," from *This Was America*, edited by Oscar Handlin, Harvard University Press. HUTCHINS, ROBERT, *The Higher Learning in America*, Yale University Press.

JAMES, WILLIAM, *The Varieties of Religious Experience*, copyright 1902 by Longmans, Green & Co., Inc. JEFFERSON, THOMAS, excerpts from *Jefferson Farm Book*, edited by Edwin Morris Betts, by permission of the American Philosophical Society.

KEYSERLING, HERMANN, *The Travel Diary of a Philosopher*, copyright 1925 by Hermann Keyserling, used by permission of Harcourt, Brace and Company, Inc.

LAFARGE, OLIVER, "To Set the Indians Free," *New Republic*, October 3, 1949. LAL, CHAMAN, *Inside America, A Political Survey of American Life and Manners*, New Book Company, Ltd., Bombay, India. LARDNER, RING, "Champion," reprinted from *How to Write Short Stories* by Ring Lardner; used by permission of the publishers, Charles Scribner's Sons. LEWIS, MERIWETHER, *The Journals of Lewis and Clark*, edited by Bernard De Voto, Houghton Mifflin Company, by permission of the American Philosophical Society. *Life* Magazine photographs, copyright by Time, Inc. LIN YUTANG, *The Importance of Living*, copyright 1937 by The John Day Company, Inc. LINCOLN-EVERETT letters, courtesy Massachusetts Historical Society. LINDBERGH, CHARLES A., *The Spirit of St. Louis*, used by permission of the publishers, Charles Scribner's Sons; *We*, copyright 1927 by Charles A. Lindbergh, by permission of G. P. Putnam's Sons.

"MARSHALL's Own Account of the Gold Discovery," by Charles B. Gillespie, *Century Magazine*, February 1891. MASTERS, EDGAR LEE, "Lucinda Matlock," from *Spoon River Anthology*, The Macmillan Company, by permission of the Estate of Edgar Lee Masters. MAUROIS, ANDRÉ, *The Miracle of America*, Harper & Brothers, copyright 1944 by André Maurois.

NOCK, ALBERT JAY, *Memoirs of a Superfluous Man*, Harper & Brothers, copyright 1943 by Albert Jay Nock.

OÑATE, JUAN DE, extracts from letter, from *Spanish Explorations in the Southwest*, edited by Herbert Eugene Bolton, Barnes & Noble, Inc. O'NEILL, EUGENE, *Ah, Wilderness!*, copyright 1933 by Eugene O'Neill, by permission of Random House, Inc. OSBORN, FAIRFIELD, *Our Plundered Planet*, copyright 1948 by Fairfield Osborn, by permission of Little, Brown & Company.

PALOU, FATHER FRANCISCO, extract from report, from *The Missions and Missionaries of California*, James H. Barry Company, copyright 1920 by Fr. Zephyrin Engelhardt. PEARY, ROBERT E., *The North Pole*, copyright 1910, 1937 by Josephine Peary, published by J. B. Lippincott Company. PINCHOT, GIFFORD, *The Fight for Conservation*, Doubleday and Company, Inc., by permission of the Estate of Gifford Pinchot. PRIESTLEY, J. B., *Midnight on the Desert*, Harper & Brothers, copyright 1937 by J. B. Priestley, reprinted by permission of Harold Matson.

ROCKEFELLER, JOHN D., *Random Reminiscences of Men and Events*, by permission of the Estate of John D. Rockefeller. ROSS, ALEXANDER, *Fur Hunters of the Far West*, Lakeside Press.

SPENDER, J. A., *Through British Eyes*, copyright 1928 by J. A. Spender, published by J. B. Lippincott Company, by permission of the Estate of J. A. Spender. STEINBECK, JOHN, *The Grapes of Wrath*, copyright 1939 by John Steinbeck, reprinted by permission of The Viking Press, Inc., New York. SULLIVAN, LOUIS, *Autobiography of an Idea*, American Institute of Architects.

by Charles A. Lindbergh

Here in America, on a continent recently rediscovered by European men, the cultures of diverse nations have impacted; a unique environment has developed; and a great power has been formed. *Profile of America* portrays, through concise examples of source material, the initiative, the thought, the courage and irresistible energy which so quickly transformed this country from a savage wilderness to the locus of world civilization.

Vikings describe New England's coast, a thousand years ago; John Hancock signs a call to revolution; Elizabeth Geer's diary pictures life on the Oregon Trail; the Wright Brothers relate experiences in flying. By skillful selection from fields almost unlimited in scope, and by a superb artistry of illustration, Emily Davie and Bryan Holme bring their readers into contact with the genetic stuff that has made us what we are today, and from which our future must evolve.

Here is the ancestral character of coming generations—mechanistic and humanistic; in concord and in contention. By a perception of the past, these pages assist an understanding of the present, and anticipate a pattern to emerge in years ahead; they help one to slough off the clutter of current news and propaganda, to gain a knowledge of America which both spreads across the surface and penetrates the core.

INTRODUCTION

by Louis Bromfield

Perhaps no question in the world is more difficult to answer than the one "*What is the United States?*" It is a question which is asked again and again by foreigners who have never visited this rich, powerful, and prosperous nation. It is asked by foreigners who have visited the United States and have left somewhat bewildered after a short stay. It is even asked by the thoughtful American who sometimes finds himself unable to see the forest for the trees.

There have been countless books written on the subject by foreign visitors from Mrs. Trollope and Dickens onward, some with years of experience in this country, some with only a few weeks. A few of these have been ecstatic, some controlled or critical and some actually abusive; but none of them have captured the whole substance of what the United States really is. A composite of them all might produce some sort of accurate and comprehensive picture but, taken separately, any or all of them have been unable to encompass the whole of the picture.

Perhaps the answer to "What is the United States?", like the Great American Novel, may never and can never be written, for the country itself is not only vast and greatly varied in terms of geography and climate but its people are, far more than any other people on earth, a blend of many races, nationalities, traditions, and even civilizations. The process of blending has been thorough and becomes increasingly so, and it has contributed to the nation vast resources of energy, ingenuity, variety, richness of tradition, and real biological force: and it has produced a wide diversity of opinion, thought, and philosophy which have tended to create in turn an extremely lively and varied and free-thinking political picture, in which the most intimate affairs of the nation are carried on in public, sometimes to a point which at times seems almost indecent to citizens of other nations. Yet this factor is the very essence of American life and indeed of true democratic theory and practice, all the way from government by acclamation in the public square to the formula of representative Republican government, which is perhaps the best system yet devised by man to permit people to live together in peace, in law, in freedom, and in prosperity.

One of the confusing elements in any effort to understand the United States is the fact that although, culturally and traditionally, the Americans are not really a new people but the inheritors of all the cultures of Europe, they exist within a political and an economic frame that was in the beginning a sharp departure from the forms of the old world and even today still remains largely new. It is this fact more than any other perhaps which determines what an American is, and defines the characteristics which tend to set him apart from most other peoples in terms of thought, character, and at times even action. The United States *is* a new country and one which differs very greatly from the countries of Europe, Asia, and even the Latin American nations of the new world.

Although the United States was established as a free nation before the actual outbreak of the French Revolution, the concept of liberty, equality, and brotherhood was the very essence of its revolutionary founding principles. The American form of government is essentially derived from the ideas of the French philosophers and revolutionists and our judiciary system from the long, slow-developing patterns and concepts of justice in England. From there on, one might say, the United States was on its own, to develop its own pattern of a free world which still felt from time to time the impact of European traditions and ideas that during nearly two centuries it has absorbed, interpreted, and modified to fit the basic American structure of government and free education. The total result has been to establish on a very solid foundation a nation and a people which in many fundamental aspects are quite different from Europeans or Asiatic governments and peoples.

In 1953 there was considerable discussion aroused in literary circles and magazines over the query of a young German girl who asked the recommendation of a novelist or a novel which would explain and interpret the United States. The discussion was a futile one because there is obviously no such book and no such novelist. The United States of Hemingway, Faulkner, or John Marquand are utterly different and diverse places, inhabited by characters which share almost nothing in common in terms of tradition, motives, and cultural background. And what of the writing and characters of Willa Cather or Edith Wharton or Henry James? The conception, fostered by Sinclair Lewis and H. L. Mencken, that Americans are completely standardized and mass-thinking was never a valid one, as any American or any foreigner knows who travels much in the United States. Few if any countries represent such a diversity of traditions, geographical background, climatic conditions, religious conceptions, and racial and national cultures. One might almost say with truth that various provincial areas of the United States exist on wholly different levels and even at different stages of civilization.

Indeed, it would be impossible for one writer to learn, understand, and present fairly in a clear and comprehensive form the immense diversity of background, growth, and tradition of the whole nation.

The editor of this volume has chosen quite a different method and a method with far greater possibilities of success in presenting the United States to the rest of the world. She has permitted a great number of Americans, possessed of different points of view and existing in different periods, to present and even interpret the phenomenon which is the United States and the sort of human being which this phenomenon has produced and is still producing. The task has involved an immense amount of reading and research, the cooperation of many living authorities and institutions, combined with great judgment and wise selectivity, in order to produce in the end a fair, comprehensible and at the same time readable volume of a reasonable size. In *Profile of America* it seems to me she has, through her efforts and judgment, succeeded in producing a volume which explains better than any other I know what is the United States and what is an American. Certainly its immense variety arrives at a total objectivity of presentation beyond that possible in any book written by a single author, however distinguished.

This is a book which one could put into the hands of any foreigner with confidence. But it is also a book which should be of the greatest value to almost all Americans, among whom there is a tendency to take for granted their country and their history, its living standards, its institutions, its traditions and above all the struggles, the wisdom, sometimes the suffering and tragedy which have gone into creating the United States and the American citizen of our time. Very often, conversely, these same Americans assume, thinking carelessly or not thinking at all, that virtually all other countries and especially European ones are quite like their own country. Few things could be less true. Only Canada among all nations bears a close resemblance to the form, the patterns, and the habits of thought of American life, and this is so, and becomes increasingly so, for much the same reasons which have gone into the making of the United States and its people.

For the German girl who wanted a book to explain to her the United States and its people, this one comes closer to answering her question than any I have encountered, partly at least, because it has been written by a great variety of Americans, from the founding fathers to many a citizen still living who has made great contributions to the form, the patterns, and the general welfare and character of the nation. It is a book written not by one writer, with the limitations from which no writer, however great, can escape, but in a sense by the American people themselves. Not the least interesting part of the book is the beauty of its physical production and the excellent and significant choice of the illustrations and photographs which it contains.

EDITOR'S NOTE FOR THE FOURTH EDITION

In *Profile of America* I have tried to give the reader an authentic picture of the United States through the words and deeds of those who made its history. It is the purpose of the book to reveal as much as possible of the evolving character of the nation through primary sources and pictures so that the reader, possessing the facts, may make his own interpretation.

In this era of uncertainty, conflicting ideologies, and false propaganda it is more and more difficult to evaluate what is happening in the world around us. New nations are being born, new alliances formed, and, all too often, new hostilities created. If young people are ill-versed in world and national history, they are unsure about their responsibilities as citizens. Often they fail to realize that the liberty they have inherited is in their keeping. Older people feel confused and lost in a nuclear-dominated world that is moving too fast. Though the search for understanding is one that each person must ultimately make for himself, perspective can be found by going back over history. Compiling *Profile of America* was for me just such a personal journey of discovery.

Since the book was first published I have been touched by letters I received from people all over the world telling of their wish to understand America and to share in the solution of common problems. A man in Israel wrote to express confidence in his nation's ability to achieve freedom because we did it in 1776; a woman in India said she never realized our women were once denied the vote; a man in Greece wrote to say he hadn't known that we, too, had been plagued by dust and erosion, and he wanted to know more about our dams and conservation.

It is particularly gratifying to have my book going into its fourth edition as this supports my belief that there is a continuing need for source material that cannot become obsolete or suspect of partisan interpretation.

My first debt of gratitude is to Bryan Holme, the editor of Studio Publications, who urged me to undertake this book. With admirable patience he gave me free rein throughout, and then stepped in and illustrated it with his fine selection of pictures that dramatize, support, and enliven the text.

To my father, Preston Davie, whose tremendous knowledge of history has been invaluable, I owe a special thanks.

To the late Louis Bromfield and to Charles A. Lindbergh, for their friendly help and encouragement no less than for the Introduction and Foreword, I am deeply grateful.

After the bulk of the text was gathered, I felt that some subjects needed developing or summarizing. This need was met with original articles by Louis Bromfield, Benjamin F. Fairless, Agnes de Mille, Edward V. Rickenbacker, and David Sarnoff, who interrupted their busy lives to impart their special knowledge of aspects of American life in which they are outstanding, indeed unique.

For guidance I have relied a great deal on the works of Charles A. Beard, Ludwig Lewisohn, and Samuel Eliot Morison. For primary source material which their labors uncovered I am indebted to Henry Steele Commager and Donald H. Sheehan.

For the generous gift of their suggestions, criticisms, and interest, my warmest thanks to R. Wesley Addy, Betsey Barton, Clarence W. Bartow, Eleanor Beckham, Henry Chafetz, Edward D. Churchill, Whitfield Cook, Douglas A. Fisher, Emily B. Fosdick, Gordon Grand, Jr., Richard D. Heffner, Philip G. Hodge, Moris T. Hoversten, Eugene Judge, Jean Kellogg, Christopher La Farge, Basil Langton, Anne M. Lindbergh, Mavis McIntosh, Bettina Sargeant, John E. Sattler, Stewart Shackne, Walter C. Teagle, Jr., Arthur B. Tourtellot, Louise M. Welch, William J. Welch.

In conclusion, the job would have been immeasurably more difficult were it not for the resources of the American Museum of Natural History, New York; the Library of Congress, Washington, D. C.; Massachusetts Historical Society, Boston; New York Society Library; New York Public Library; and the Smithsonian Institution, Washington, D. C.

New York, New York   EMILY DAVIE
May 1960

CONTENTS

SETTLING THE NEW LAND
Colonial settlement; to independence

1000 · Discoveries of Leif Ericsson — *Norse Saga* ... 27
1492 · Discoveries of Christopher Columbus — *Christopher Columbus* ... 29
1507 · The Naming of America — *Martin Waldseemüller* ... 30
1542 · Cabrillo Discovers San Diego Bay — *Juan Cabrillo* ... 30
1564 · First Painting: Jacques Le Moyne — ... 31
1565 · First Permanent Settlement: Florida — *Lopez de Mendoza* ... 34
1598 · The Spanish Take Possession of New Mexico — *Juan de Oñate* ... 34
1607 · Settlement of Virginia — *John Smith* ... 36
1620 · Settlement of New England — *William Bradford* ... 39
1620 · The Mayflower Compact* — ... 42
1621 · The First Thanksgiving — *Edward Winslow* ... 42
1632 · Tobacco in Maryland and Virginia — *Dankers; Sluyter* ... 42
1682 · A Quaker in Pennsylvania — *Richard Townsend* ... 44
1673 · From the St. Lawrence to the Gulf of Mexico — *Father Marquette* ... 45
1722 · From Natchez to New Orleans — *Father Charlevoix* ... 46
1773 · First Report on the California Missions — *Father Palou* ... 48
1641 · Reasons for Emigration — *William Castell* ... 50
1634 · Emigration Advice from an Englishman — *John Sadler* ... 50
1782 · Emigration Advice from an American — *Benjamin Franklin* ... 51
1775 · Battle of Lexington: American and British Versions — ... 52
1837 · "Concord Hymn"* — *Ralph Waldo Emerson* ... 55
1776 · Declaration of Independence* — *Thomas Jefferson* ... 55

GOVERNMENT
Birth of the United States; federal and state governments; foreign policy

THE STRUCTURE OF GOVERNMENT

Comments on the Constitution — ... 62
1789 · Excerpts from the Constitution — ... 62

* in contents indicates complete article. In the text excerpted articles not otherwise indicated are marked by a dagger (†).

1896 · Function of State Governments   *James Bryce* 66
1803 · The Supreme Court: Marbury v. Madison   *John Marshall* 68
1830 · On the Constitution   *Daniel Webster* 70
1935 · On the Bill of Rights   *Herbert Hoover* 71
1857 · "Your Constitution is all sail and no anchor"   *T. B. Macaulay* 72
1873 · James Garfield's Reply to Macaulay   *James Garfield* 73
1782 · What Is an American?   *de Crevecoeur* 75
1954 · Requirements for Citizenship   75
1789–1954 · List of Presidents*   76

MILESTONES IN FOREIGN POLICY

1796 · Washington's Farewell Address   *George Washington* 79
1823 · The Monroe Doctrine   *James Monroe* 80
1918 · Woodrow Wilson's Fourteen Points   82
1945 · Charter of the United Nations   84

[Constitution of the United States, see pages 401–407]

3

STRUGGLES: RELIGIOUS, MORAL, ECONOMIC

Establishing freedom of worship; issues that led to improved conditions or legislation; atomic age

1644 · "The Bloody Tenent of Persecution"   *Roger Williams* 88
1649 · The Maryland Act of Toleration   88
1663 · The Rhode Island Charter   90
1701 · Pennsylvania Charter of Privileges   *William Penn* 90
1786 · Virginia Statute of Religious Liberty   *Thomas Jefferson* 91
1688 · The First Protest Against Slavery   91
1692 · Salem Bewitched: Behavior of Witches   *Cotton Mather* 93
1691/2 · The Case of Sarah Good*   94
1736 · Fight for Freedom of the Press   *Peter Zenger* 95
      The American Indian: 97
1891 ·   "The Present Phase of the Indian Question"   *Thomas J. Morgan* 97
1805 ·   Seneca Chief   *Red Jacket* 98
1870 ·   Sioux Chief   *Red Cloud* 99
1855 ·   Dwamish Chief   *Chief Seattle* 100
1879 ·   Nez Percé Chief   *Chief Joseph* 109
1949 ·   "To Set the Indians Free"   *Oliver La Farge* 111
1846 · The Mormon Trek to Utah   *Brigham Young* 112
1859 · On Being Sentenced to Death*   *John Brown* 114
1859 · Eyewitness Account of the Execution of John Brown   *Thomas R. Preston* 115
1863 · Emancipation Proclamation*   *Abraham Lincoln* 118
1896 · "The American Standard"   *Booker T. Washington* 119
1954 · Segregation in Public Schools Ended   121
1873 · On Women's Right to Suffrage   *Susan B. Anthony* 121
1901 · "Hatchetation" and Prohibition   *Carry Nation* 124
1890 · The Sherman Anti-Trust Act   126

1890's . Gompers to the Socialists — Samuel Gompers............127
1925 . "Trade Union Creed" — Samuel Gompers............128
1937 . Address to the First C.I.O. Convention — John L. Lewis............129
1933 . U.S. Recognition of Soviet Russia:
Roosevelt-Litvinov Letters — 131
1940 . The Smith Act — 132
1954 . The Communist Control Act — 133
1953 . "To Help Solve the Fearful Atomic
Dilemma" — Dwight D. Eisenhower............133

SPANNING THE CONTINENT

Descriptions and reports by those who crossed the continent

1804 · Instructions to Lewis and Clark — Thomas Jefferson............140
1805 · "The gates of the rocky mountains" — Meriwether Lewis............142
1814 · "Fur Hunters of the Far West" — Alexander Ross............144
1817 · A Frontiersman Settles in Illinois — Morris Birkbeck............146
1843 · Buffalo Hunting on the Frémont Expedition — John C. Frémont............146
1848 · Diary of a Woman on the Oregon Trail — Elizabeth Geer............149
1848 · Discovery of Gold in California — James Marshall............151
1849 · The First Wagon Train into California — William G. Johnston............152
1849 · Life in the Diggings — Daniel B. Woods............156
1851 · Discovery and Naming of Yosemite — L. H. Bunnell............158
1851 · Clipper Ships: Log of the Flying Cloud — 159
1860's · The Pony Express — Mark Twain............162
1864–1869 · The Transcontinental Railroad: — 164
   "Across the Plains" — Robert Louis Stevenson............164
   Labor Troubles — Grenville M. Dodge............164
   General Dodge's Report to the Board
      of Directors — 164
   Driving of the Golden Spike — Grenville M. Dodge............165
1803–1916 · Territorial Growth of the United
      States* — 167
1790–1950 · United States Census Figures* — 169
1820–1950 · Immigration Figures* — 169

AGRICULTURE AND CONSERVATION

Comments on agriculture; aims and achievements of conservation

AGRICULTURE

1790–1809 · On Agriculture — Thomas Jefferson............172
1795–1796 · On Agriculture — George Washington............172

1954 · "Agriculture in the United States"*   *Louis Bromfield*................175

CONSERVATION—AGRICULTURAL AND INDUSTRIAL RESOURCES

1907 · "The Conservation of Natural Resources"   *Theodore Roosevelt*...........181
1910 · "The Fight for Conservation"   *Gifford Pinchot*...............182
1933 · Tennessee Valley Authority Act 183
1948 · "The Road to Survival"   *William Vogt*..................183
1939 · "The Grapes of Wrath"   *John Steinbeck*...............187
1949 · "Our Plundered Planet"   *Fairfield Osborn*..............189
1952 · "Our Inexhaustible Resources"   *Eugene Holman*...............193

6 ACHIEVEMENTS

Personal accounts of inventors, explorers, industrialists, and philanthropists

INVENTIONS, DISCOVERIES

1793 · The Cotton Gin   *Eli Whitney*..................198
1807 · "Mr. Fulton's Folly": New York-Al-
bany   *Robert Fulton*................199
1842–1846 · The Discovery of Anesthesia:
    Findings of Dr. William Welch 202
    Extracting a Tooth   *Dr. William Morton*...........203
    Removing a Tumor   *Dr. Crawford W. Long*........203
1878 · The Electric Light   *Thomas Edison*...............208
1900 · Conquest of Yellow Fever   *Dr. Walter Reed*..............210
1904–1914 · Building of the Panama Canal   *George W. Goethals*...........211
1909 · Discovering the North Pole   *Robert E. Peary*..............214
1903–1953 · Fifty Years of Flying:
    "How We Made the First
    Flight"   *Orville Wright*................216
    Early History of the Airplane   *Wright Brothers*..............217
    Barnstorming—1924   *Charles A. Lindbergh*..........218
    New York to Paris: First
    Account   *Charles A. Lindbergh*..........220
    "Commercial Aviation"*   *Edward V. Rickenbacker*.......223
1909–1945 · "The Father of Modern
    Rocketry": Dr. Goddard   *Harry F. Guggenheim*..........225
1926–1929 · First Tests of Liquid-Propellant
    Rockets   *Robert H. Goddard*............226
1954 · "Electronics—Today and Tomorrow"*   *David Sarnoff*................230

AMERICAN ENTERPRISE

1901 · "The Empire of Business"   *Andrew Carnegie*...............236
1954 · "Steel in the Twentieth Century"*   *Benjamin F. Fairless*...........240
1909 · Early Development of the Standard Oil
Company   *John D. Rockefeller*...........242

1903 · Henry Ford Puts the Nation on Wheels   247
1922 · "My Life and Work"   *Henry Ford* 247
1802–1954 · Story of an American Enterprise:
         The Du Pont Company*   254

       PHILANTHROPY

1889 · "The Gospel of Wealth"   *Andrew Carnegie* 259
1903 · "The Difficult Art of Giving"   *John D. Rockefeller* 262

7 WAR

War messages of the Presidents; speeches, letters, and accounts

1775–1953 · Principal Wars—Statistics   266
1775–1783 · Revolutionary War:
         "Declaration of the Causes and
           Necessity of Taking up Arms"   *John Hancock* 267
1812–1815 · War of 1812:
         President Madison's War Mes-
         sage   270
1846–1848 · Mexican War:
         President Polk's War Message   273
1861–1865 · Civil War:
         President Lincoln Calls Out the
         Militia   274
    1862 ·   Open Letter to the President   *Horace Greeley* 275
    1862 ·   Lincoln's Reply to Greeley's
         Letter   277
    1863 ·   Gettysburg—Decisive Battle:
         Southern Version of Pick-
           ett's Charge   *Joseph C. Mayo* 277
         Northern Version of Pick-
           ett's Charge   *Thomas Rafferty* 279
    1863 ·   Gettysburg Address*   *Abraham Lincoln* 280
    1863 ·   Lincoln-Everett Letters   280
    1865 ·   Lee's Surrender at Appomattox   *Ulysses S. Grant* 282
    1865 ·   Letter to Jefferson Davis   *Robert E. Lee* 286
    1865 ·   Lincoln's Second Inaugural
         Address   286
1898 · Spanish-American War:
         President McKinley's War Mes-
         sage   288
1917–1918 · World War I:
         President Wilson's War Message   291
1941–1945 · World War II:
         President Roosevelt's War
         Message*   294
    1945 ·   President Truman's Announce-
         ment of the Atomic Bomb   296

1950– · Korean War:
President Truman's War
Message 298
1951 · General MacArthur's Address
to Congress 299

8

EDUCATION

Aims and achievements; legislation; the McGuffey Reader; opinions of educators

ELEMENTARY EDUCATION

1647 · Massachusetts School Law* 305
1846 · On the Massachusetts School Law   Horace Mann.................305
1870's · Era of the Little Red Schoolhouse   Hamlin Garland..............306
1836 · Lessons from the McGuffy Reader* 308
1912 · An Immigrant Family Goes to School   Mary Antin...................312

HIGHER EDUCATION

1817 · On Education   Thomas Jefferson..............313
1862 · The Morrill Act 315
1642 · Rules and Precepts of Harvard University
sity 316
1952 · Entrance Requirements of Harvard
College 318
1943 · The Revolution in Education   Albert Jay Nock..............319

THE EDUCATORS SPEAK

1693 · "Some Fruits of Solitude"   William Penn.................320
1846 · "Thoughts of Horace Mann" 322
1869 · Inaugural Address as President of
Harvard   Charles W. Eliot..............322
1899 · "School and Society"   John Dewey...................322
1936 · "The Higher Learning in America"   Robert M. Hutchins...........323

9

THE AMERICAN EXPRESSION

Examples from the work of well-known artists, writers, and craftsmen

1612–1672 · "To my Dear and Loving Husband"*   Anne Bradstreet...............328
"Meditations Divine and
Morall" 328
1783–1859 · "Rip Van Winkle"   Washington Irving.............328

1804–1864 · "The House of the Seven Gables"   *Nathaniel Hawthorne*...........330
1807–1892 · "Ichabod"*   *John Greenleaf Whittier*.........331
1807–1882 · "Evangeline"   *Henry Wadsworth Longfellow*....332
1808–1849 · "Israfel"*   *Edgar Allan Poe*...............333
1803–1882 · "Self-Reliance"   *Ralph Waldo Emerson*.........334
1817–1862 · "Walden"   *Henry David Thoreau*.........337
1819–1892 · "When Lilacs Last in the Door-
          yard Bloom'd"   *Walt Whitman*.................338
1819–1891 · "Moby Dick"   *Herman Melville*...............339
1830–1886 · Selections*   *Emily Dickinson*..............340
1835–1910 · "Tom Sawyer"   *Mark Twain*..................341
1842–1910 · "The Varieties of Religious
          Experience"   *William James*.................344
1843–1916 · "The American"   *Henry James*..................348
1862–1937 · "The Age of Innocence"   *Edith Wharton*.................349
1874–1945 · "Barren Ground"   *Ellen Glasgow*.................351
1888–1954 · "Ah, Wilderness!"   *Eugene O'Neill*..............353
1885–1933 · "Champion"   *Ring Lardner*..................355
1896–1950 · "Lucinda Matlock"*   *Edgar Lee Masters*............357
1898–1943 · "John Brown's Body"   *Stephen Vincent Benét*.........357

ARCHITECTURE

1788 · "Architecture is worth great attention..."   *Thomas Jefferson*..............359
1924 · "Autobiography of an Idea"   *Louis Sullivan*.................360
1953 · "American Architecture"   *Frank Lloyd Wright*............360

JOURNALISM: THE SMALL-TOWN NEWSPAPER

1895 · "Entirely Personal"   *William Allen White*............364
1922 · "To an Anxious Friend"*   *William Allen White*............365
1935 · "Fifty Years of It"   *William Allen White*............366

MOTION PICTURE AND THE DANCE

1917 · Making "The Birth of a Nation"   *D. W. Griffith*.................368
1939 · Story Conference on "Fantasia"   *Walt Disney*...................372
1954 · "The Dance in America"*   *Agnes de Mille*...............373

10 AS OTHERS SEE US
Opinions from other countries

1769 · "... a race of convicts ..."   *Dr. Samuel Johnson*...........382
1835 · A Remarkable Prophecy   *Alexis de Tocqueville*..........382
1832 · "Domestic Manners of the Americans"   *Mrs. Trollope*.................382
1887 · "The American Man"   *Oscar Wilde*...................383
1928 · Business   *J. Alfred Spender*..............384
1873 · An Austrian Views Us with Alarm   *Baron von Hubner*..............386
1895 · Football As Seen by a Frenchman   *Paul Bourget*..................388

1927 · Spaniard in a Barbershop   *Julio Camba*...................389
1943 · Hindu in an Automat   *Chaman Lal*...................390
1925 · American Superficiality   *Hermann Keyserling*...........392
1931 · The American Temperament   *G. K. Chesterton*.............392
1937 · A Chinese Philosopher on American
         Vices   *Lin Yutang*...................393
1937 · Advertising and the American Woman *J. B. Priestley*.............394
1944 · "The American Character"   *D. W. Brogan*.................396
1940 · "The Miracle of America"   *André Maurois*...............397
1940 · The Future   *John Buchan*..................398
1944 · "... worthy of trust ..."   *Winston Churchill*...........399

CONSTITUTION OF THE UNITED STATES   401

INDEX   409

ONE

Settling

the New Land

"There is properly no history; only biography."

RALPH WALDO EMERSON

Settling the New Land

PRE-COLUMBIAN DISCOVERIES

Probably the first man to set foot on the continent of North America came across Bering Strait in search of game some twenty thousand years ago when the last ice age was receding. We know that migrations from Asia, which produced the American Indian, preceded European migrations by many centuries.

European man arrived when Eric the Red and the sea-straddling Vikings planted the first Norse colony in Greenland in 986. His son, Leif Ericsson, sailed up and down the coast of North America giving the names Helluland, Markland, *and* Vinland *to what are now called* Greenland, Nova Scotia, *and* New England. *Norse literature records these voyages in the Sagas—stories handed down orally to each generation until they were given permanent form in writing in the twelfth century.*

The excerpt that follows is taken from a translation of one of these early sagas. The original was reputedly written in the twelfth century, and this later version was found in a monastery on the island of Flatey, Iceland. The manuscript, beautifully preserved on parchment, is said to have been the work of priests between the years 1387–1395:

DISCOVERIES OF LEIF ERICSSON, c. 1000

"Here Beginneth the Narrative of the Greenlanders."

The next thing now to be related is, that Bjarni Herjulfson went out from Greenland, and visited Erik Jarl, and the Jarl received him well. Bjarni told about his voyages, that he had seen unknown lands, and people thought that he had shown no curiosity, when he had nothing to relate about these countries, and this became somewhat a matter of reproach to him. . . . There was now much talk about voyages of discovery. Leif, the son of Erik the Red, of Brattahlid, went to Bjarni Herjulfson, and bought the ship of him, and engaged men for it, so that there were thirty-five men in all. . . . Now prepared they their ship, and sailed out into the sea when they were ready, and then found that land first which Bjarni had found last. There sailed they to the land, and cast anchor, and put off boats, and went ashore, and saw there no grass. Great icebergs were over all up the country; but like a plain of flat stones was all from the sea to the mountains, and it appeared to them that this land had no good qualities. Then said Leif: "We have not done like Bjarni about this land, that we have not been upon it; now will I give the land a name, and call it HELLULAND." Then went they on board, and after that sailed out to sea, and found another land; they sailed again to the land, and cast anchor, then put off boats and went on shore. This land was flat, and covered with wood, and white sands were far around where they went, and the shore was low. Then said Leif: "This land shall be named after its qualities, and called MARKLAND" [woodland]. They then immediately returned to the ship. Now sailed they thence into the open sea with a northeast wind, and were two days at sea before they saw land, and they sailed thither and came to an island which lay to the eastward of the land, and went up there . . . and sailed into a sound, which lay between the island and a ness [promontory], which ran out to the eastward of the land; and then steered westwards past the ness . . . and there cast anchor, and brought up from the ship their skin cots, and made there booths. . . .

But when they had done with the house-building, Leif said to his comrades: "Now will I divide our men into two parts, and have the land explored; and the half of the men

27

Christopher Columbus. Engraving by Henri Lefort.

shall remain at home at the house, while the other half explore the land; but, however, not go further than that they can come home in the evening, and they should not separate." . . .

It happened one evening that a man of the party was missing, and this was Tyrker the German. . . . But when they had gotten a short way from the house, then came Tyrker towards them, and was joyfully received. . . . Then said Leif to him: "Why wert thou so late, my fosterer, and separated from the party?" He now spoke first, for a long time in German, and rolled his eyes about to different sides, and twisted his mouth; but they did not understand what he said. After a time he spoke Norse. "I have not been much further off, but still have something new to tell of; I found vines and grapes." "But is that true, my fosterer?" quoth Leif. "Surely it is true," replied he, "for I was bred up in a land where there is no want of either vines or grapes." They slept now for the night, but in the morning Leif said to his sailors: "We will now set about two things, in that the one day we gather grapes, and the other day cut vines and fell trees, so from thence will be a loading for my ship;" and that was the counsel taken, and it is said their long-boat was filled with grapes. Now was a cargo cut down for the ship, and when the spring came they got ready and sailed away; and Leif gave the land a name after its qualities, and called it VINLAND.

They sailed now into the open sea, and had a fair wind until they saw Greenland. . . .

DISCOVERIES OF CHRISTOPHER COLUMBUS, 1492

Columbus first told of his discoveries in the following letter, written on shipboard during his return voyage and dispatched March 14, 1493, to his friend Raphael Sanchez, Treasurer of Aragon:

"Knowing that it will afford you pleasure to learn that I have brought my undertaking to a successful termination, I have decided upon writing you this letter to acquaint you with all the events which have occurred in my voyage, and the discoveries which have resulted from it. Thirty-three days after my departure from Cadiz I reached the Indian sea, where I discovered many islands, thickly peopled, of which I took possession without resistance in the name of our most illustrious Monarch, by public proclamation and with unfurled banners. To the first of these islands . . . I gave the name of the blessed Saviour [San Salvador], relying upon whose protection I had reached this as well as the other islands. As soon as we arrived at . . . Juana [now Cuba], I proceeded along the coast a short distance westward, and I found it to be so large and apparently without termination, that I could not suppose it to be an island, but the continental province of Cathay. . . . In the meantime I had learned from some Indians whom I had seized, that the country was certainly an island: and therefore I sailed towards the east, coasting to the distance of three hundred and twenty-two miles, which brought us to the extremity of it; and from this point I saw lying eastwards another island, fifty-four miles distant from Juana, to which I gave the name of Espanola [now San Domingo]. . . . Thus it happened to me in the present instance, who have accomplished a task to which the powers of mortal men had never hitherto attained; for if there have been those who have anywhere written or spoken of these islands, they have done so with doubts and conjectures, and no one has ever asserted that he has seen them, on which account their writings have been looked upon as little else than fables. Therefore let the king and queen, our prince and their most happy kingdoms, and all other provinces of Christendom, render thanks to our Lord and Saviour Jesus Christ, who has granted us so great a victory and such prosperity. . . .

Contrary to widespread belief, in none of his four voyages did Columbus set foot on the continent of North America. He died in 1506 still believing the islands he had found were in the Indian Ocean off Cathay (China).

To the historian John Fiske is attributed the aphorism that when Columbus started out ". . . he did not know where he was going; when he arrived he did not know where he was; and when he returned he did not know where he had been." Nevertheless, the voyages of Columbus remain the most epochal in history, and his feats of navigation opened the way for Americus Vespucius, the Cabot brothers, and countless others who followed in his wake.

THE NAMING OF AMERICA, 1507
Martin Waldseemüller

Throughout the fifteenth century cartographers partitioned the world into three parts: Europe, Asia, and Africa. To this, in 1507, the German cartographer Martin Waldseemüller added a fourth part.

Much of Waldseemüller's information concerning this fourth part was derived from accounts of the voyages of Americus Vespucius along the coasts of what are today known as South and Central America, and Florida in North America.

Admiration of Vespucius led Waldseemüller, in his book Cosmographiae Introductio *(Introduction to World Geography) to suggest that this fourth part of the world be named after the explorer. The paragraph in which his suggestion appears, translated from the Latin, follows. This was the very first time the name "America" was used.*

But now these parts have been more extensively explored and another fourth part has been discovered by Americus Vespucius (as will appear in what follows): wherefore I do not see what is rightly to hinder us from calling it Amerige or America, i.e. the land of Americus, after its discoverer Americus, a man of sagacious mind, since both Europe and Asia have got their names from women. Its situation and the manners and customs of its people will be clearly understood from the twice two voyages of Americus which follow.

JUAN RODRIGUEZ CABRILLO DISCOVERS
SAN DIEGO BAY, 1542

The bay of San Diego was discovered in 1542 by the Portuguese navigator, Juan de Cabrillo, who gave it the name of San Miguel. The following is from the Diary of his voyage:

Having cast anchor in it, the men went ashore where there were people [Indians]. Three of these waited, but all the rest fled. To these three they gave some presents, and they said by signs that in the interior men like the Spaniards had passed. They gave signs of great fear. On the night of this day, they [the sailors] went ashore from the ships to fish with a net; and it appears that here there were some Indians, and that they began to shoot at them with arrows and wounded three men.

Next day, in the morning, they went with the boat farther into the port, which is large, and brought two boys, who understood nothing by signs. They gave shirts to both and sent them away immediately.

Next day, in the morning, three adult Indians came to the ships and said by signs that in the interior men like us were traveling about, bearded, clothed, and armed like those of the ships. They made signs that they carried crossbows and swords; and they made gestures with the right arm as if they were throwing lances, and ran around as if they were on horseback. They made signs that they were killing many native Indians, and that for

30

this reason they were afraid. These people are comely and large. They go about covered with skins of animals.

While they were in this port a heavy storm occurred; but since the port is good, they did not feel it at all. It was a violent storm from the west-southwest and south-southwest. This is the first storm which they have experienced. They remained in this port until the following Thursday. The people here called the Christians Guacamal. On the following Tuesday, October 3, they departed from this Port of San Miguel.

Collection: James Hazen Hyde

FIRST PAINTING: INDIANS IN FLORIDA, 1564
Jacques Le Moyne

The earliest white man to depict the people and land of the Western Hemisphere was a French-man, Jacques Le Moyne. He accompanied the second Laudonnière expedition, 1564, during which he made maps and paintings of Florida and its inhabitants. These paintings were subsequently engraved by Theodore de Bry to illustrate his famous work Grands Voyages.

The painting reproduced here is believed to be the only original work of Le Moyne that has survived. It depicts the Indian chief, Athore, showing Laudonnière the marble column erected by Jean Ribault two years earlier. This column, engraved with the arms of France, was all that remained of his ill-fated attempt to plant a colony there.

31

Castillo de San Marco, St. Augustine, Florida, oldest fort in the United States, started about 1638.

FIRST PERMANENT SETTLEMENT: FLORIDA, 1565

In 1513 the Spaniard, Ponce de Leon, landed near the site of St. Augustine in search of the "Fountain of Youth." This site, called Seloy *by the Indians, was a flat, sandy peninsula overgrown with palmetto scrub. Failing to find his "Fountain," de Leon re-embarked. In 1564 a French Huguenot colony under René de Laudonnière arrived at the same place but moved on to the St. John's River. Angered by a Protestant colony in his dominion, Philip II of Spain sent an expedition to exterminate it. This expedition, under Don Pedro Menéndez de Avilo, landed at* Seloy *on September 8, 1565, and erected the fort* San Augustin. *This was the first permanent settlement of Europeans on the continent of North America.*

In the text that follows, Fray Francisco Lopez de Mendoza, Chaplain of the expedition, describes the ceremonies following the landing of Menéndez. The name St. Augustine was given because the calendar day dedicated to that saint was the day of their arrival:

CEREMONIES AT ST. AUGUSTINE

Carrying a cross, I proceeded at the head, chanting the hymn *Te Deum Laudamus.* The General marched straight up to the cross, together with all those who accompanied him; and, kneeling, they all kissed the cross. A great number of Indians looked upon these ceremonies, and imitated whatever they saw done. Thereupon the General took possession of the country in the name of his Majesty. All the officers then took an oath of allegiance to him, as their general and as adelantado [overlord] of the whole country.

THE SPANISH TAKE POSSESSION OF NEW MEXICO, 1598

Juan de Oñate, Spanish explorer, entered into a contract with the Viceroy of Mexico to colonize New Mexico. His expedition, which he financed himself, consisted of four hundred settlers, a supply train of eighty-three wagons and carts, and seven thousand head of stock. On April 30, 1598, Oñate crossed the Rio Grande below El Paso del Norte and formally took possession of New Mexico in the name of the king. In the following letter written to the Viceroy, Oñate describes the land and the people:

There must be in this province . . . to make a conservative estimate, seventy thousand Indians, settled after our custom, house adjoining house, with square plazas. They have no streets, and in the pueblos, which contain many plazas or wards, one goes from one plaza to the other through alleys. They are of two and three stories . . .; and some houses are of four, five, six, and seven stories. Even whole pueblos dress in very highly colored cotton *mantas*, white or black, and some of thread—very good clothes. Others wear buffalo hides, of which there is a great abundance. They have most excellent wool, of whose value I am sending a small example.

It is a land abounding in flesh of buffalo, goats with hideous horns, and turkeys; and in Mohoce there is game of all kinds. There are many wild and ferocious beasts, lions, bears, wolves, tigers, *penicas*, ferrets, porcupines, and other animals, whose hides they tan and use. Towards the west there are bees and very white honey, of which I am sending a sample. Besides, there are vegetables, a great abundance of the best and greatest salines in the world, and a very great many kinds of very rich ores, as I stated above. Some discovered near here do not appear so, although we have hardly begun to see anything of the much there is to be seen. There are very fine grape vines, rivers, forests of many oaks, and some cork trees, fruits, melons, grapes, watermelons, Castilian plums, *capuli*, pine-nuts, acorns, ground-nuts, and *coralejo*, which is a delicious fruit, and other wild

Ansel Adams

Moonrise near Hernandez, old Spanish-American settlement in New Mexico. The Spanish took possession of New Mexico in 1598.

fruits. There are many and very good fish in this Rio del Norte, and in others. From the ores here are made all the colors which we use, and they are very fine.

The people are in general very comely; their color is like those of that land, and they are much like them in manner and dress, in their grinding in their food, dancing, singing, and many other things, except in their languages, which are many, and different from those there. Their religion consists in worshipping idols, of which they have many; and in their temples, after their own manner, they worship them with fire, painted reeds, feathers, and universal offering of almost everything they get, such as small animals, birds, vegetables, etc. In their government they are free, for although they have some petty captains, they obey them badly and in very few things. . . .

I should never cease were I to recount individually all of the many things which occur to me. I can only say that with God's help I shall see them all, and give new worlds, new, peaceful, and grand, to his Majesty, greater than the good Marquis* gave to him, although he did so much, if you, Illustrious Sir, will give to me the aid, the protection, and the help which I expect from such a hand. . . . And in order that you, Illustrious Sir, may be inclined to render them to me, I beg that you take note of the great increase which the royal crown and the rents of his Majesty have and will have in this land, with so many

* Cortés, the Marquis of the Valley.

35

and such a variety of things, each one of which promises very great treasures. I shall only note these four, omitting the rest as being well known and common:

First, the great wealth which the mines have begun to reveal and the great number of them in this land, whence proceed the royal fifths and profits. Second, the certainty of the proximity of the South Sea, whose trade with Pirú, New Spain, and China is not to be depreciated, for it will give birth in time to advantageous and continuous duties, because of its close proximity, particularly to China and to that land. And what I emphasize in this matter as worthy of esteem is the traffic in pearls, reports of which are so certain, as I have stated, and of which we have had ocular experience from the shells. Third, the increase of vassals and tributes, which will increase not only the rents, but his renown and dominion as well, if it be possible that for our king these can increase. Fourth, the wealth of the abundant salines, and of the mountains of brimstone, of which there is a greater quantity than in any other province. Salt is the universal article of traffic of all these barbarians and their regular food, for they even eat or suck it alone as we do sugar. These four things appear as if dedicated solely to his Majesty. I will not mention the founding of so many republics, the many offices, their quittances, vacancies, provisions, etc., the wealth of the wool and hides of buffalo, and many other things, clearly and well known, or, judging from the general nature of the land, the certainty of wines and oils.

In view, then, Illustrious Sir, of things of such honor, profit, and value, and of the great prudence, magnanimity, and nobility of your Lordship, . . . I humbly beg and supplicate, since it is of such importance to the service of God and of his Majesty, that the greatest aid possible be sent to me. . . .

SETTLEMENT OF VIRGINIA, 1607

In 1606 King James I granted charters to the London and Plymouth Companies to establish colonies in Virginia. In 1607, sponsored by the London Company, the first successful English colony was planted at Jamestown.

Captain John Smith, a resourceful and experienced soldier, played an important part in exploring and developing Virginia. His colorful tales, including his capture by the Indians and rescue by Pocahontas, daughter of the chieftain, often overshadowed his achievements. These included supervision of fortifications, explorations, obtaining food, and the invaluable reports he sent home picturing the true condition and needs of the new colony.

Immigrants sent by the London Company were too often inexperienced and unsuited for the stark realities they had to meet. Angrily Smith wrote demanding that they send: "carpenters, husbandmen, gardeners, fishermen, blacksmiths, masons, and diggers up of trees' roots," adding, "Nothing is to be expected thence, but by labor." In the following account Smith reviews some of the early difficulties encountered:

"THE GENERALL HISTORIE OF VIRGINIA, NEW ENGLAND, AND THE SUMMER ISLES," 1626*
Captain John Smith

Honorable Gentlemen, for so many fair and Navigable Rivers so near adjoining and piercing through so fair a natural Land. . . . I have not seen, read, nor heard of: And for the building of Cities, Towns, and Wharfage, if they will use the means. . . . Nature in few places affords any so convenient. . . .

* Spellings have been modernized.

Opposite: The tower of the 1676 Jamestown church, oldest relic of the first permanent English colony, Virginia.

Eliot Elisofon, courtesy "Life"

Being enjoined by our Commission not to unplant nor wrong the Savages, because the channel was so near the shore, where now is *James* Town, then a thick grove of trees; we cut them down, where the Savages pretending as much kindness as could be, they hurt and slew one and twenty of us in two hours: At this time our diet was for the most part water and bran, and three ounces of little better stuff in bread for five men a meal, and thus we lived near three months: our lodgings under boughs of trees, the Savages being our enemies, whom we neither knew nor understood; occasions I think sufficient to make men sick and die.

. . . In following the strict directions from *England* to do that was impossible at that time; So it happened, that neither we nor they had any thing to eat, but what the Country afforded naturally; yet of eighty who lived upon Oysters in June and July, with a pint of corn a week for a man lying under trees, and 120 for the most part living upon Sturgeon, which was dried till we pounded it to powder for meal, yet in ten weeks but seven died . . .

James town being burnt, we rebuilt it and three Forts more, besides the Church and Store-house, we had about forty or fifty several houses to keep us warm and dry. . . . We dug a fair well of fresh water in the Port . . . planted one hundred acres of corn. We had but six ships to transport and supply us, and but two hundred seventy men, boys, and women, by whose labors *Virginia* being brought to this kind of perfection, the most difficulties past, and the foundation thus laid by this small means; yet because we had

The only known likeness of Captain John Smith was engraved by Simon de Passe to illustrate Smith's *A Description of New England*, published in London, 1616. (New England was originally called North Virginia.)

done no more, they called in our Commission, took a new [one] in their own names, and appointed us near as many offices and Officers as I had Soldiers, that neither knew us nor we them, without our consents or knowledge; since there have gone more than one hundred ships of other proportions, and eight or ten thousand people. Now if you please to compare what hath been spent, sent, discovered and done this fifteen years, by that we did in the three first years, and every Governor that hath been there since, give you but such an account as this, you may easily find what hath been the cause of those disasters in *Virginia*. . . .†

SETTLEMENT OF NEW ENGLAND, 1620

William Bradford, Pilgrim leader on the Mayflower, *served as governor of the Plymouth colony for nearly thirty years. Bradford subtitled this account: "How They Passed the Sea, and of Their Safe Arrival at Cape Cod."*

"OF PLYMOUTH PLANTATION"
William Bradford

After they had enjoyed fair winds and weather for a season, they were encountered many times with cross winds and met with many fierce storms with which the ship was shroudly shaken, and her upper works made very leaky; and one of the main beams in the midships was bowed and cracked, which put them in some fear that the ship could not be able to perform the voyage. So some of the chief of the company, perceiving the mariners to fear the sufficiency of the ship as appeared by their mutterings, they entered into serious consultation with the master and other officers of the ship, to consider in time of the danger, and rather to return than to cast themselves into a desperate and inevitable peril. . . . But in examining of all opinions, the master and others affirmed they knew the ship to be strong and firm under water; . . . there would otherwise be no great danger, if they did not overpress her with sails. So they committed themselves to the will of God and resolved to proceed.

In sundry of these storms the winds were so fierce and the seas so high, as they could not bear a knot of sail, but were forced to hull for divers days together. . . .

But to omit other things (that I may be brief) after long beating at sea they fell with that land which is called Cape Cod; the which being made and certainly known to be it, they were not a little joyful. After some deliberation had amongst themselves and with the master of the ship, they tacked about and resolved to stand for the southward (the wind and weather being fair) to find some place about Hudson's River for their habitation. But after they had sailed that course about half the day, they fell amongst dangerous shoals and roaring breakers, and they were so far entangled therewith as they conceived themselves in great danger; and the wind shrinking upon them withal, they resolved to bear up again for the Cape and thought themselves happy to get out of those dangers before night overtook them, as by God's good providence they did. And the next day they got into the Cape Harbor where they rid in safety. . . .

Being thus arrived in a good harbor, and brought safe to land, they fell upon their knees and blessed the God of Heaven who had brought them from all the perils and miseries thereof, again to set their feet on the firm and stable earth, their proper element. . . .

But here I cannot but stay and make a pause, and stand half amazed at this poor people's present condition; . . . Being thus passed the vast ocean, and a sea of troubles before in their preparation (as may be remembered by that which went before), they had now no friends to welcome them nor inns to entertain or refresh their weatherbeaten bodies; no houses or much less towns to repair to, to seek for succour. . . . And for the season it was

New England settlers are symbolized by "The Puritan" statue in Salem, Massachusetts. *Above:* The *Mayflower*, painted by W. F. Halsall (detail). *Opposite:* Plymouth, Massachusetts.

winter, and they that know the winters of that country know them to be sharp and violent, and subject to cruel and fierce storms, dangerous to travel to known places, much more to search an unknown coast. Besides, what could they see but a hideous and desolate wilderness, full of wild beasts and wild men—and what multitudes there might be of them they knew not . . . for which way soever they turned their eyes (save upward to the heavens) they could have little solace or content in respect to any outward objects. For summer being done, all things stand upon them with a weatherbeaten face, and the whole country, full of woods and thickets, represented a wild and savage hue. If they looked behind them, there was the mighty ocean which they had passed and was now as a main bar and gulf to separate them from all the civil parts of the world. . . .

What could now sustain them but the Spirit of God and His grace? May not and ought not the children of these fathers rightly say: "Our fathers were Englishmen which came over this great ocean, and were ready to perish in this wilderness; but they cried unto the Lord, and He heard their voice and looked on their adversity," etc. "Let them therefore praise the Lord, because He is good: and His mercies endure forever." "Yea, let them which have been redeemed of the Lord, shew how He hath delivered them from the hand of the oppressor. . . ."†

THE MAYFLOWER COMPACT, 1620

An accident of navigation brought the Mayflower *to Cape Cod, outside the jurisdiction of the Virginia Company. Some of the voyagers, thus considering they were released from the conditions imposed by the Company, threatened to "use their own liberty," henceforth recognizing no government. Leaders among them, seeing the dangers of lawlessness in a new land, drew up and signed the following compact before landing:*

IN THE NAME OF GOD, AMEN.

We whose names are underwritten, the loyal subjects of our dread Sovereign Lord King James, by the Grace of God of Great Britain, France and Ireland, King, Defender of the Faith, etc.

Having undertaken, for the Glory of God and advancement of the Christian Faith and Honour of our King and Country, a Voyage to plant the First Colony in the Northern Parts of Virginia, do by these presents solemnly and mutually in the presence of God and one another, Covenant and Combine ourselves together into a Civil Body Politic, for our better ordering and preservation and furtherance of the ends aforesaid; and by virtue hereof to enact, constitute and frame such just and equal Laws, Ordinances, Acts, Constitutions and Offices, from time to time, as shall be thought most meet and convenient for the general good of the Colony, unto which we promise all due submission and obedience. In witness whereof we have hereunder subscribed our names at Cape Cod, the 11th of November, in the year of the reign of our Sovereign Lord King James, of England, France, and Ireland the eighteenth, and of Scotland the fifty-fourth. Anno Domini 1620.

THE FIRST THANKSGIVING, 1621

Edward Winslow, a founder of the Plymouth Colony in Massachusetts, describes the historic first Thanksgiving:

Our harvest being gotten in, our Governor sent four men on fowling, so that we might after a special manner rejoice together after we had gathered in the fruit of our labors. They four in one day killed as much fowl as served the company almost a week. At this time, among other recreations, we exercised our arms, many of the Indians coming among us, and with them their great King, Massasoit, with some ninety men, whom for three days we entertained and feasted, and they went out and killed five deer, which they brought to the plantation and bestowed on our Governor and upon the Captain and others.

TOBACCO IN MARYLAND AND VIRGINIA, 1632

Told by Jasper Dankers and Peter Sluyter. Dankers later became a
Labadist bishop and Sluyter was a Dutch wine-racker by trade.

. . . All of Maryland that we have seen, is high land, with few or no meadows, but possessing such a rich and fertile soil, as persons living there assured me, that they had raised tobacco off the same piece of land for thirty consecutive years. The inhabitants who are generally English, are mostly engaged in this production. It is their chief staple, and the means with which they must purchase every thing they require, which is brought to them from other English possessions in Europe, Africa and America. There is, nevertheless, sometimes a great want of these necessaries, owing to the tobacco market being low, or the shipments being prevented by some change of affairs in some quarter, particularly in

John James Audubon depicts America's Thanksgiving symbol, the turkey.

Europe, or to both causes, as was the case at this time, when a great scarcity of such articles existed there, as we saw. So large a quantity of tobacco is raised in Maryland and Virginia, that it is one of the greatest sources of revenue to the crown by reason of the taxes which it yields. Servants and negroes are employed in the culture of tobacco, who are brought from other places to be sold to the highest bidders, the servants for a term of years only, but the negroes forever, and may be sold by their masters to other planters as many times as their master choose, that is, the servants until their term is fulfilled, and the negroes for life. These men, one with another, each make, when they are able to work, from 2,500 pounds to 3,000 pounds, and even 3,500 pounds of tobacco a year, and some of the masters and their wives who pass their lives here in wretchedness, do the same. The servants and negroes after they have worn themselves down the whole day, and gone home to rest, have yet to grind and pound the grain, which is generally maize, for their masters and all their families as well as themselves, and all the negroes, to eat. Tobacco is the only production in which the planters employ themselves, as if there were nothing else in the world to plant but that, and while the land is capable of yielding all the productions that can be raised anywhere, so far as the climate of the place allows. As to articles of food, the only bread they have is that made of Turkish wheat or maize, and that is miserable. . . .

A QUAKER IN PENNSYLVANIA, 1682

Told by Richard Townsend, a Quaker who came from England in
the ship *Welcome* with William Penn.

At our arrival [in Pennsylvania], we found it a wilderness; the chief inhabitants were *Indians*, and some *Swedes;* who received us in a friendly manner: and though there was a great number of us, the good hand of *Providence* was seen in a particular manner; in that provisions were found for us, by the *Swedes*, and the *Indians*, at very reasonable rates, as well as brought from divers other parts that were inhabited before.

Our first concern was to keep up and maintain our *religious worship;* and, in order thereunto, we had several *meetings*, in the houses of the inhabitants; and one boarded meeting-house was set up, where the city was to be, near *Delaware;* and, as we had nothing but love and good-will, in our hearts, one to another, we had very comfortable meetings, from time to time; and after our meeting was over, we assisted each other, in building little houses, for our shelter. . . .

And, as our worthy Proprietor treated the *Indians* with extraordinary humanity, they became very civil and loving to us, and brought in abundance of venison. As, in other countries, the *Indians* were exasperated by hard treatment, which hath been the foundation of much bloodshed, so the contrary treatment here hath produced their love and affection.

About the time, in which *Germantown* was laid out, I settled upon my tract of land, which I had purchased of the Proprietor, in *England*, about a mile from thence; where I set up a house and a corn mill; — which was very useful to the country, for several miles round:— But there not being plenty of horses, people generally brought their corn on their backs many miles. . . .

As people began to spread, and improve their lands, the country became more fruitful; so that those, who came after us, were plentifully supplied; and with what we abounded we began a small trade abroad. And as *Philadelphia* increased, vessels were built, and many employed. Both country and trade have been wonderfully increasing to this day; so that, from a *wilderness*, the Lord, by his good hand of providence, hath made it a fruitful field. . . .

FROM THE ST. LAWRENCE TO THE GULF OF MEXICO, 1673
Father Marquette

Father Jacques Marquette (1637–1675), Jesuit missionary and explorer, arrived in New France in 1666. He lived among the Indians for several years, learning their languages and converting them to Christianity. In 1673 the governor of New France appointed him to accompany Louis Joliet on an expedition to trace a river the Indians said ran southward to the sea.

The expedition crossed Lake Michigan, reached the Mississippi, and descended it to the Arkansas, returning by way of the Illinois River, being the first to establish a water route from the St. Lawrence to the Gulf of Mexico. In the following selection Father Marquette describes part of the journey:

Having arrived about half a league from Arkansea, we saw two canoes coming towards us. The captain of one was standing up, holding the calumet in his hand, with which he made signs, according to the custom of the country. He afterwards joined us, inviting us to smoke, and singing pleasantly. He then gave us some sagamite and Indian bread to eat, and going before, made signs for us to follow him, which we did, but at some distance. They had in the meantime prepared a kind of scaffold to receive us, adorned with fine mats, upon which we sat down with the old men and warriors. We fortunately found among them a young man who spoke Illinois much better than the interpreter whom we brought with us from Mitchigamea [probably Helena, Arkansas]. We made them some small presents, which they received with great civility, and seemed to admire what I told them about God, the creation of the world, and the mysteries of our holy faith, telling us, by the interpreter, that they wished us to remain with them for the purpose of instructing them.

We then asked them what they knew of the sea, and they said we were within ten days' journey of it, but we might perform it in five. . . .

In the evening the chiefs held a secret council, wherein some proposed to kill us; but the great chief opposed this base design, and sent for us to dance the calumet, which he presented us with to seal our common friendship. M. Joliet and I held a council to deliberate upon what we should do—whether to proceed further, or return to Canada, content with the discoveries we had made.

Having satisfied ourselves that the Gulf of Mexico was in latitude 31° 40′, and that we could reach it in three or four days' journey from the Arkansea [Arkansas River], and that the Mississippi discharged itself into it, and not to the eastward of the Cape of Florida, nor into the California Sea, we resolved to return home. We considered that the advantage of our travels would be altogether lost to our nation if we fell into the hands of the Spaniards, from whom we could expect no other treatment than death or slavery; besides, we saw that we were not prepared to resist the Indians, the allies of the Europeans, who continually infested the lower part of this river; we therefore came to the conclusion to return, and make a report to those who had sent us. So that, having rested another day, we left the village of the Arkansea, on the seventeeth of July, 1673, having followed the Mississippi from the latitude of 42° to 34°, and preached the Gospel to the utmost of my power to the nations we visited. We then ascended the Mississippi, with great difficulty against the current, and left it in the latitude of 38° north, to enter another river [Illinois], which took us to the lake of the Illinois [Michigan], which is a much shorter way than through the river Mesconsin, by which we entered the Mississippi.

I never saw a more beautiful country than we found on this river. The prairies are covered with buffaloes, stags, goats, and the rivers and lakes with swans, ducks, geese, parrots, and beavers. The river upon which we sailed was wide, deep, and placid for sixty-five leagues, and navigable most all the year around. There is a portage of only half a league into the lake of the Illinois. We found on the banks of this river a village called Kuilka, consisting of seventy-four cabins. They received us very kindly, and we promised to return to instruct them. The chief, with most of the youth of this village, accompanied us to the lake, from whence we returned to the Bay of Puan [Green Bay], about the end of September. If my perilous journey had been attended with no other advantage than the salvation of one soul, I would think my perils sufficiently rewarded. I preached the Gospel to the Illinois of Perouarca for three days together. My instructions made such an impression upon this poor people, that as soon as we were about to depart they brought to me a dying child to baptize, which I did, about half an hour before he died, and which, by a special providence, God was pleased to save.

Nine years later the French trader and settler, René La Salle, reached the mouth of the Mississippi River and on April 9, 1682, took formal possession of the great valley for France, naming it Louisiana *in honor of the king.*

FROM NATCHEZ TO NEW ORLEANS, 1722
"DESCRIPTION OF THE COUNTRY AND OF SEVERAL INDIAN VILLAGES, WITH THAT OF THE CAPITAL OF LOUISIANA"
Father Pierre Francois Xavier de Charlevoix

Pierre de Charlevoix, 1682–1761, was a French Jesuit traveler and historian who voyaged up the St. Lawrence River, through the Great Lakes, down the Illinois river to the Mississippi, and thence to New Orleans. His detailed journal of this trip (from Histoire de la Nouvelle France) *is the only full account we have of the interior of America written at this early date. The excerpt that follows is from the thirty-first letter contained in this journal:*

New Orleans, January 10, 1722.
I am now at last arrived at this famous city of *Nouvelle Orleans*, New Orleans. Those who have given it this name, must have imagined Orleans was of the feminine gender. But of what consequence is this? Custom, which is superior to all the laws of grammar, has fixed it so.

This is the first city, which one of the greatest rivers in the world has seen erected on its banks. If the eight hundred fine houses and the five parishes, which our Mercury bestowed upon it two years ago, are at present reduced to a hundred barracks, placed in no very good order; to a large ware-house built of timber; to two or three houses which would be no ornament to a village in France; to one half of a sorry ware-house, formerly set apart for divine service, and was scarce appropriated for that purpose, when it was removed to a tent: what pleasure, on the other hand, must it give to see this future capital of an immense and beautiful country increasing insensibly, and to be able, not with a sigh like Virgil's hero, when speaking of his native country consumed by the flames, *et campus ubi Trojae fuit*, but full of the best grounded hopes to say, that this wild and desart place, at present almost entirely covered over with canes and trees, shall one day, and perhaps that day is not very far off, become the capital of a large and rich colony.

Your Grace will, perhaps, ask me upon what these hopes are founded? They are founded on the situation of this city on the banks of a navigable river, at the distance of thirty-three leagues from the sea, from which a vessel may come up in twenty-four hours; on the fertility of its soil; on the mildness and wholesomeness of the climate, in thirty degrees

Opposite: Early building in the old French Quarter, New Orleans. The city was founded in 1718.

Clarence John Laughlin

north latitude; on the industry of the inhabitants; on its neighborhood to Mexico, the Havanna, the finest islands of America, and lastly, to the English colonies. Can there be any thing more requisite to render a city flourishing? Rome and Paris had not such considerable beginnings, were not built under such happy auspices, and their founders met not with those advantages on the Seine and the Tiber, which we have found on the Mississippi, in comparison of which, these two rivers are no more than brooks. . . .

FIRST REPORT ON THE CALIFORNIA MISSIONS, 1773
Father Francisco Palou

The first California mission was dedicated and blessed by Father Junipero Serra, the Franciscan monk, on July 16, 1769. After High Mass the Spanish flag was raised over the mission which was named in honor of San Diego de Alcala. It is located in what is now San Diego, California.

Annual reports of the missions were requested by the viceroy and the Father Guardian of the College of San Fernando. In the following, Father Francisco Palou writes the viceroy of this first mission:

December 10, 1773

This mission was founded on July 16, 1769. It is situated on a high elevation (*loma* or bluff] about two gunshots from the beach [*playa*], looking toward Point Guijarros and the mouth of the port named San Diego, which is in thirty-two degrees and forty-two minutes north latitude. The beach, as also the vicinity of the mission, is well peopled by savages, since within a district of ten leagues there are more than twenty large rancherías, and one other adjoining the mission.

In the beginning, the Indians of this port showed themselves very haughty and arrogant, even daring to assault the camp when they noticed it left with only a small number of soldiers, the majority of whom were ill at the time when the expedition [Portola's] started out in search of Monterey Port; but they retired having learnt a good lesson when three or four of their number remained dead from gun-shots and many more were wounded, whereas only one servant of the camp and mission was killed, while two men were wounded, one of whom was a missionary at the mission; but their wounds are not dangerous. This frightened the Indians and for a long time they would not approach the camp and mission. However, by degrees, they came to join the mission, so that already eighty-three adults and children are baptized, seven of whom died recently, while twelve couples were married and are now living in the village composed of dwellings that are made of poles and tules. With them live also the catechumens, who assist punctually every day at the catechism. The pagans of other rancherías also frequent the mission and are present at the doctrina or catechism, attracted by their fondness for hearing the neophytes sing.

Within the stockade is the church or chapel, constructed of poles and roofed with tules, as also the habitation of the two missionaries, having the requisite rooms partly of adobe and partly of wood and roofed with tules.

Likewise, within the stockade, is a similar structure [*jacal*] that serves as the barracks for the soldier guards and as a storehouse for the supplies. For defensive purposes, within the stockade, are two cannon of bronze. One looks toward the port, and the other toward the Indian ranchería. On one side of the stockade, in the wall, is an opening for the foundations of a church thirty yards [*varas*] long. For this some stones and four thousand adobes have already been prepared. The foremen of the work are the Fathers, and the workmen are the neophytes, who labor with pleasure. The work has now stopped for want of provisions; the neophytes saw themselves obliged to retire in search of wild fruits, until the ship arrives.

As this mission lacks water for irrigating the extensive and fertile land which it possesses, the inmates must suffer want, unless the crops turn out well. The first two years have proved this. In the first year, the river rose so high (though it has running water near the mission only in the rainy season), that it carried away all that had been sown. In the second year, planting was done farther back of the stream. During the greater part of that season, however, the water was scarce so that the plants perished. Only five fanégas*

Ed Sievers

Mission San Diego de Alcala, first of the California missions, founded by the Spaniards, dedicated and blessed by Father Junipero Serra, 1769.

of wheat were secured, and these were used for sowing in the locality about two leagues from the mission, because from experience it was learned that in said place rain was more frequent. The country has been surveyed for a distance of ten leagues in every direction; but no running water for irrigation has been discovered. Only for the live stock is there in various places sufficient water and abundant pasture.

The savages subsist on the seeds of the *zacate* [wild grass] which they harvest in due season. From these they make sheaves as is the custom to do with wheat. They also live by fishing and by hunting hares and rabbits which are plentiful. The Missionary Fathers

* A fanéga is equal to one hundredweight.

have sent to San Blas for a canoe and a net so that the new Christians might subsist on fish. If this succeeds, it will, no doubt, be a great relief.

Of the cattle which came for these new missions from Lower California by order of Inspector-General José de Gálvez, this mission was allowed eighteen head, large and small. In the beginning of last October it had forty head. It then owned also seventy-four head of sheep, fifty-five goats, nineteen pigs, fifteen mares, four fillies, one colt, eight tame horses, one jackass, six donkeys, four riding mules, and eighteen pack mules with the necessary outfit.

The mission possesses twelve plowshares and other iron implements. There is also a sufficient supply of tools for carpenters and for masons, and a forge for the blacksmith, although there are no mechanics to teach these crafts.

REASONS FOR EMIGRATION, 1641

From a Petition by Reverend Wm. Castell to Parliament . . .
for Propagating of the Gospel in America

When a Kingdom beginneth to be over-burthened with a multitude of people (as *England* and *Scotland* now do) to have a convenient place where to send forth Colonies is no small benefit: And such are the North-east and North-west parts of *America*, betweene the degrees of 25. and 45. of the North latitude, which, at this time doe offer themselves unto us, to bee protected by us, against the knowne cruelty of the over-neare approaching Spaniard.

A very large tract of ground containing spacious, healthfull, pleasant, and fruitfull countries, not only apt, but already provided of all things necessary for mans sustenation, Corne, Grasse, and wholesome cattell in good competencie; but Fish, Fowle, Fruits and Herbes in abundant variety.

If wee should looke no further, than the South of *Virginia*, (which is our owne) wee shall find there all manner of provision for life; . . . and almost all things necessary for shipping, which if they shall bee employed that way; they who are sent away may (with God's blessing) within short time in due recompence of their setting forth, returne this Kingdome store of silver and gold, pearles and precious stones; for undoubtedly . . . such treasure is to bee had, if not there, yet in places not farre remote, where (as yet) the Spaniard hath nothing to doe. And in case the Spaniard bee troublesome to our Plantations, or shall (as it is generally conceived) bee found an Enemy to this Kingdome, there is no way more likely to secure *England*, then by having a strong Navie there; hereby wee may come to share, if not utterly to defeat him of that vaste Indian Treasure, wherewith hee setteth on fire so great a part of the Christian World, corrupteth many Counsellors of state, supporteth the Papacie, and generally perplexeth all reformed Churches. . . .

. . . And which is much more, our going with a generall consent in Gods cause, for the promoting of the Gospel, and inlarging of his church, may assure us of a more than ordinary protection and direction. . . .

EMIGRATION ADVICE FROM AN ENGLISHMAN, 1634
John Sadler, Emigration Broker in England

If it will please Sir Edmund and your ladyship to be ruled by my advice, your son should have with him 3 servants at least, which may be had here at a day's warning; if I were to send 40 servants I could have them here at a day's warning; . . . Every servant he sends over will stand him in 12. . . . After his coming into Virginia, I doubt not but by friends I have there he shall be well accommodated for his own person, and at a reasonable rate. . . . then the next year, if he shall like the country, and be minded to stay and settle a plantation him self, those servants will be seasoned, and be enabled to direct such others as shall be sent unto him from hence hereafter, or if he shall not like the country, then he may sell their time so they have to serve him unto other men that have need of servants, and make a good benefit of them. . . .

Now, for his own proper accommodation, I must entreat your ladyship that he may bring up with him a feather bed, bolster, pillow, blankets, rug, and 3 pair of sheets, unless you will please they shall be bought here, it is but a spare horse the more to bring them up. . .

Madam, the reason why I entreat your ladyship that he may have with him for his own particular use a feather bed, bolster, blankets, rug, curtains, and valence is, that, although many households in Virginia are so well provided as to entertain a stranger with all things necessary for the belly, yet few or none are better provided for the back as yet than to serve their own turns; therefore 'tis necessary that he be provided of that for more assurance. . . .*

EMIGRATION ADVICE FROM AN AMERICAN, 1782
Benjamin Franklin

Many persons in Europe having by letters expressed to the writer of this, who is well acquainted with North America, their desire of transporting and establishing themselves in that country, but who appear to have formed, through ignorance, mistaken ideas and expectations of what is to be obtained there, he thinks it may be useful, and prevent inconvenient, expensive, and fruitless removals and voyages of improper persons, if he gives some clearer and truer notions of that part of the world than appear to have hitherto prevailed.

He finds it is imagined by numbers that the inhabitants of North America are rich, capable of rewarding, and disposed to reward, all sorts of ingenuity; that they are at the same time ignorant of all the sciences, and, consequently, that strangers possessing talents in the belles-lettres, fine arts, etc., must be highly esteemed, and so well paid as to become easily rich themselves; that there are also abundance of profitable offices to be disposed of, which the natives are not qualified to fill; and that, having few persons of family among them, strangers of birth must be greatly respected, and of course easily obtain the best of those offices, which will make all their fortunes. . . . These are all wild imaginations; and those who go to America with expectations founded upon them will surely find themselves disappointed.

The truth is that though there are in that country few people so miserable as the poor of Europe, there are also very few that in Europe would be called rich; it is rather a general happy mediocrity that prevails. There are few great proprietors of the soil, and few tenants; most people cultivate their own lands, or follow some handicraft or merchandise; very few rich enough to live idly upon their rents or incomes. . . . Of civil officers or employments, there are few; no superfluous ones, as in Europe; and it is a rule established in some of the states that no office should be so profitable as to make it desirable. The thirty-sixth article of the Constitution of Pennsylvania runs expressly in these words: "As every freeman, to preserve his independence . . . ought to have some profession, calling, trade, or farm whereby he may honestly subsist, there can be no necessity for, nor use in establishing offices of profit, the usual effects of which are dependence and servility unbecoming freemen, . . . Wherefore, whenever an office, through increase of fees or otherwise, becomes so profitable as to occasion many to apply for it, the profits ought to be lessened by the legislature."

These ideas prevailing more or less in all the United States, it cannot be worth any man's while, who has a means of living at home, to expatriate himself in hopes of obtaining a profitable civil office in America; and, as to military offices, they are at an end with

* Spellings have been modernized.

the war, the armies being disbanded. Much less is it advisable for a person to go thither who has no other quality to recommend him but his birth. In Europe it has indeed its value; but it is a commodity that cannot be carried to a worse market than that of America, where people do not inquire concerning a stranger: *What is he?* but: *What can he do?* If he has any useful art, he is welcome; and if he exercises it, and behaves well, he will be respected by all that know him; but a mere man of quality, who on that account wants to live upon the public, by some office or salary, will be despised and disregarded. The husbandman is in honor there, and even the mechanic, because their employments are useful. . . .

. . . In short, America is the land of labor, and by no means what the English call *Lubberland*, and the French *Pays de Cocagne*, where the streets are said to be paved with half-peck loaves, the houses tiled with pancakes, and where fowls fly about ready roasted, crying: *Come eat me!*

THE BATTLE OF LEXINGTON, 1775
Official American and British Versions

Militarily the Battle of Lexington was little more than a skirmish that occurred when His Majesty's troops were sent by General Gage to capture the stores at Concord and arrest the "radicals" Samuel Adams and John Hancock. The mission failed when they met the resistance of the colonials. Politically the Battle of Lexington marked the beginning of American independence. Fifteen months later the Declaration of Independence was read from the steps of the State House in Philadelphia.

THE AMERICAN VERSION

Watertown, April 26th, 1775
In provincial congress of Massachusetts, to
     the inhabitants of Great Britain

Friends and fellow subjects—Hostilities are at length commenced in this colony by the troops under the command of general Gage, and it being of the greatest importance, that an early, true, and authentic account of this inhuman proceeding should be known to you, the congress of this colony have transmitted the same, and from want of a sesseion of the hon. continental congress, think it proper to address you on the alarming occasion.

By the clearest depositions relative to this transaction, it will appear that on the night preceding the nineteenth of April instant, a body of the king's troops, under the command of colonel Smith, were secretly landed at Cambridge, with an apparent design to take or destroy the military and other stores, provided for the defence of this colony, and deposited at Concord—that some inhabitants of the colony, on the night aforesaid, whilst travelling peaceably on the road, between Boston and Concord, were seized and greatly abused by armed men, who appeared to be officers of general Gage's army; that the town of Lexington, by these means, was alarmed, and a company of the inhabitants mustered on the occasion—that the regular troops on their way to Concord, marched into the said town of Lexington, and the said company, on their approach, began to disperse—that, notwithstanding this, the regulars rushed on with great violence and first began hostilities, by firing on said Lexington company, whereby they killed eight, and wounded several others—that the regulars continued their fire, until those of said company, who were

Opposite: Site of the Battle of Lexington where the first shot was fired in the Revolutionary War, 1775.

Eliot Elisofon, courtesy "Life"

LINE OF THE MINUTE MEN
APRIL 19 1775

STAND YOUR GROUND
DON'T FIRE UNLESS FIRED UPON
BUT IF THEY MEAN TO HAVE A WAR
LET IT BEGIN HERE

CAPTAIN PARKER

neither killed nor wounded, had made their escape—that colonel Smith, with the detachment then marched to Concord, where a number of provincials were again fired on by the troops, two of them killed and several wounded, before the provincials fired on them, and provincials were again fired on by the troops, produced an engagement that lasted through the day, in which many of the provincials and more of the regular troops were killed and wounded. . . .

These, brethren, are marks of ministerial vengeance against this colony, for refusing, with her sister colonies, a submission to slavery; but they have not yet detached us from our royal sovereign. We profess to be his loyal and dutiful subjects, and so hardly dealt with as we have been, are still ready, with our lives and fortunes, to defend his person, family, crown and dignity. Nevertheless, to the persecution and tyranny of his cruel ministry we will not tamely submit—appealing to Heaven for the justice of our cause, we determine to die or be free. . . .

By order,

JOSEPH WARREN, *President*

THE ENGLISH VERSION

Report of Lieutenant-Colonel Smith to Governor Gage, April 22, 1775

SIR,—In obedience to your Excellency's commands, I marched on the evening of the 18th inst. with the corps of grenadiers and light infantry for Concord, to execute your Excellency's orders with respect to destroying all ammunition, artillery, tents, &c, collected there, which was affected, having knocked off the trunnions of three pieces of iron ordnance, some new gun-carriages, a great number of carriage-wheels burnt, a considerable quantity of flour, some gun-powder and musquet-balls, with other small articles thrown into the river. Notwithstanding we marched with the utmost expedition and secrecy, we found the country had intelligence or strong suspicion of our coming, and fired many signal guns, and rung the alarm bells repeatedly; and were informed, when at Concord, that some cannon had been taken out of the town that day, that others, with some stores, had been carried three days before, which prevented our having an opportunity of destroying so much as might have been expected at our first setting off.

I think it proper to observe, that when I had got some miles on the march from Boston, I detached six light infantry companies to march with all expedition to seize the two bridges on different roads beyond Concord. On these companies' arrival at Lexington, I understand, from the report of Major Pitcairn, who was with them, and from many officers, that they found on a green close to the road a body of the country people drawn up in military order, with arms and accoutrement, and, as appeared after, loaded; and that they had posted some men in a dwelling and Meeting-house. Our troops advanced towards them, without any intention of injuring them, further than to inquire the reason of their being thus assembled, and, if not satisfactory, to have secured their arms; but they in confusion went off, principally to the left, only one of them fired before he went off, and three or four more jumped over a wall and fired from behind it among the soldiers; on which the troops returned it, and killed several of them. They likewise fired on the soldiers from the Meeting and dwelling-houses. . . . While at Concord we saw vast numbers assembling in many parts; at one of the bridges they marched down, with a very considerable body, on the light infantry posted there. On their coming pretty near, one of our men fired on them, which they returned; on which an action ensued, and some few were killed and wounded. . . . On our leaving Concord to return to Boston, they began to fire on us from behind the walls, ditches, trees, &c., which, as we marched, increased to a very great degree, and continued without intermission of five minutes altogether, for, I believe, upwards of eighteen miles; so that I can't think but it must have been a preconcerted scheme in them, to attack the King's troops the first favorable opportunity that offered, otherwise, I think they could not, in so short a time from our marching out, have raised such a numerous body, and for so great a space of ground. Notwithstanding the enemy's numbers, they did not make one gallant attempt during so long an action, though our men were so very much fatigued but kept under cover.

I have the honor, &c.,

F. SMITH, *Lieutenant-Colonel 10th Foot*

"CONCORD HYMN," 1837
Ralph Waldo Emerson

By the rude bridge that arched the flood,
Their flag to April's breeze unfurled,
Here once the embattled farmers stood
And fired the shot heard round the world.

The foe long since in silence slept;
Alike the conqueror silent sleeps;
And Time the ruined bridge has swept
Down the dark stream which seaward creeps.

On this green bank, by this soft stream,
We set to-day a votive stone;
That memory may their deed redeem,
When, like our sires, our sons are gone.

Spirit, that made those heroes dare
To die, and leave their children free,
But Time and Nature gently spare
The shaft we raise to them and thee.

THE DECLARATION OF INDEPENDENCE, JULY 4, 1776

By their Declaration of Independence the thirteen colonies, through their Continental Congress, renounced all allegiance to Great Britain. Thirteen years later, through ratification of the Constitution, the United States of America came into being as a sovereign nation.

WHEN in the Course of human events, it becomes necessary for one people to dissolve the political bands which have connected them with another, and to assume among the Powers of the earth, the separate and equal station to which the Laws of Nature and of Nature's God entitle them, a decent respect to the opinions of mankind requires that they should declare the causes which impel them to the separation.

We hold these truths to be self-evident, that all men are created equal, that they are endowed by their Creator with certain unalienable Rights, that among these are Life, Liberty and the pursuit of Happiness. That to secure these rights, Governments are instituted among Men, deriving their just powers from the consent of the governed, That whenever any Form of Government becomes destructive of these ends, it is the Right of the People to alter or to abolish it, and to institute new Government, laying its foundation on such principles and organizing its powers in such form, as to them shall seem most likely to effect their Safety and Happiness. Prudence, indeed, will dictate that Governments long established should not be changed for light and transient causes; and accordingly all experience hath shown, that mankind are more disposed to suffer, while evils are sufferable, than to right themselves by abolishing the forms to which they are accustomed. But when a long train of abuses and usurpations, pursuing invariably the same Object evinces a design to reduce them under absolute Despotism, it is their right, it is their duty, to throw off such Government, and to provide new Guards for their future security. — Such has been the patient sufferance of these Colonies; and such is now the necessity which constrains them to alter their former Systems of Government. The history of the present King of Great Britain is a history of repeated injuries and usurpations, all having in direct object the establishment of an absolute Tyranny over these States. To prove this, let Facts be submitted to a candid world.

He has refused his Assent to Laws, the most wholesome and necessary for the public good.

He has forbidden his Governors to pass Laws of immediate and pressing importance, unless suspended in their operation till his Assent should be obtained; and when so suspended, he has utterly neglected to attend to them.

He has refused to pass other Laws for the accommodation of large districts of people, unless those people would relinquish the right of Representation in the Legislature, a right inestimable to them and formidable to tyrants only.

He has called together legislative bodies at places unusual, uncomfortable, and distant from the depository of their Public Records, for the sole purpose of fatiguing them into compliance with his measures.

He has dissolved Representative Houses repeatedly, for opposing with manly firmness his invasions on the rights of the people.

He has refused for a long time, after such dissolutions, to cause others to be elected; whereby the Legislative Powers, incapable of Annihilation, have returned to the People at large for their exercise; the State remaining in the mean time exposed to all the dangers of invasion from without, and convulsions within.

He has endeavored to prevent the population of these States; for that purpose obstructing the Laws for Naturalization of Foreigners; refusing to pass others to encourage their migrations hither, and raising the conditions of new Appropriations of Lands.

He has obstructed the Administration of Justice, by refusing his Assent to Laws for establishing Judiciary Powers.

He has made Judges dependent on his Will alone, for the tenure of their offices, and the amount and payment of their salaries.

He has erected a multitude of New Offices, and sent hither swarms of Officers to harass our people, and eat out their substance.

He has kept among us, in times of peace, Standing Armies without the Consent of our legislatures.

He has affected to render the Military independent of and superior to the Civil Power.

He has combined with others to subject us to a jurisdiction foreign to our Constitution, and unacknowledged by our laws; giving his Assent to their acts of pretended Legislation:

For quartering large bodies of armed troops among us:

For protecting them, by a mock Trial, from Punishment for any Murders which they should commit on the Inhabitants of these States:

For cutting off our Trade with all parts of the world:

For imposing taxes on us without our Consent:

For depriving us in many cases, of the benefits of Trial by Jury:

For transporting us beyond Seas to be tried for pretended offences:

Thomas Jefferson, author of Declaration of
Independence. Painting by Rembrandt Peale.

For abolishing the free System of English Laws in a neighbouring Province, establishing therein an Arbitrary government, and enlarging its Boundaries so as to render it at once an example and fit instrument for introducing the same absolute rule into these Colonies:

For taking away our Charters, abolishing our most valuable Laws, and altering fundamentally the Forms of our Governments:

For suspending our own Legislatures, and declaring themselves invested with Power to legislate for us in all cases whatsoever.

He has abdicated Government here, by declaring us out of his Protection and waging War against us.

He has plundered our seas, ravaged our Coasts, burnt our towns, and destroyed the lives of our people.

He is at this time transporting large armies of foreign mercenaries to compleat the works of death, desolation and tyranny, already begun with circumstances of Cruelty & perfidy scarcely paralleled in the most barbarous ages, and totally unworthy the Head of a civilized nation.

He has constrained our fellow Citizens taken Captive on the high Seas to bear Arms against their Country, to become the executioners of their friends and Brethren, or to fall themselves by their Hands.

He has excited domestic insurrections amongst us, and has endeavored to bring on the inhabitants of our frontiers, the merciless Indian Savages, whose known rule of warfare, is an undistinguished destruction of all ages, sexes and conditions.

In every stage of these Oppressions We have Petitioned for Redress in the most humble terms: Our repeated Petitions have been answered only by repeated injury. A Prince, whose character is thus marked by every act which may define a Tyrant, is unfit to be the ruler of a free people.

Nor have We been wanting in attentions to our British brethren. We have warned them from time to time of attempts by their legislature to extend an unwarrantable jurisdiction over us. We have reminded them of the circumstances of our emigration and settlement here. We have appealed to their native justice and magnanimity, and we have conjured them by the ties of our common kindred to disavow these usurpations which, would inevitably interrupt our connections and correspondence. They too have been deaf to the voice of justice and of consanguinity. We must, therefore, acquiesce in the necessity, which denounces our Separation, and hold them, as we hold the rest of mankind, Enemies in War, in Peace Friends.

We, therefore, the Representatives of the United States of America, in General Congress, Assembled, appealing to the Supreme Judge of the world for the rectitude of our intentions, do, in the Name, and by authority of the good People of these Colonies, solemnly publish and declare, That these United Colonies are, and of Right ought to be Free and Independent States; that they are Absolved from all Allegiance to the British Crown, and that all political connection between them and the State of Great Britain, is and ought to be totally dissolved; and that as Free and Independent States, they have full power to levy War, conclude Peace, contract Alliances, establish Commerce, and to do all other Acts and Things which Independent States may of right do. And for the support of this Declaration, with a firm reliance on the Protection of Divine Providence, we mutually pledge to each other our Lives, our Fortunes and our sacred Honor.

Opposite: Independence Hall, Philadelphia, where the Declaration of Independence was adopted, July 4, 1776, and the Constitution of the United States was signed September 17, 1787.

Government

To one that advised him to set up a democracy in Sparta, "Pray,"
said Lycurgus, "do you first set up a democracy in your own house."

LYCURGUS IN PLUTARCH'S

"APOPHTHEGMS OF KINGS AND GREAT COMMANDERS"

The Structure of Government

The United States of America is a constitutional republic consisting of Federal and State governments. No powers of government can be exercised by any individual or group unless authorized by a written Constitution, Federal or State, or laws enacted thereunder. Ours is a "government of laws, not of men."

When the States created the Federal government they established a dual system by which all governmental powers are divided between the Federal and the individual State governments, each supreme within its respective sphere, none permitted to encroach upon the powers of the other. The Federal government functions solely under authority vested in it by the Constitution of the United States. Each State, on the other hand, is an independent sovereignty except for those powers specifically ceded by it to the Federal government; and State governments function under authority conferred upon them by their respective State Constitutions.

The full text of the Constitution of the United States is given in the appendix. The following selections include comments on this Constitution by great statesmen; the Preamble and excerpts from Articles I, II, and III, showing the three main divisions of government; Article X of the Bill of Rights; and a summary of the function of State governments, from James Bryce's American Commonwealth:

"The basis of our political system is the right of the people to make and alter their Constitutions of government; but the Constitution which at any times exists, till changed by an explicit and authentic act of the whole people, is sacredly obligatory upon all."

GEORGE WASHINGTON

"The American Constitution is, so far as I can see, the most wonderful work ever struck off at a given time by the brain and purpose of man."

WILLIAM GLADSTONE

"The Constitution of 1789 deserves the veneration with which Americans have been accustomed to regard it . . . it ranks above every other written constitution for the excellence of its scheme, its adaptation to the circumstances of the people, the simplicity, brevity, and precision of its language, its judicious mixture of definiteness in principle with elasticity in details."

JAMES BRYCE

THE CONSTITUTION OF THE UNITED STATES OF AMERICA

Adopted September 17, 1787

Ratified June 21, 1788

In Effect March 4, 1789

PREAMBLE

We the People of the United States, in Order to form a more perfect Union, establish Justice, insure domestic Tranquillity, provide for the common defense, promote the general Welfare, and secure the Blessings of Liberty to ourselves and our Posterity, do ordain and establish this CONSTITUTION for the United States of America.

The Capitol, Washington, D.C., seat of the legislative branch of the federal government, contains the Senate and House of Representatives.

ARTICLE I

Section 1. All legislative Powers herein granted shall be vested in a Congress of the United States, which shall consist of a Senate and House of Representatives.

The White House, seat of the executive branch of the federal government and residence of the President.

ARTICLE II

Section I. The executive Power shall be vested in a President of the United States of America. . . .

ARTICLE III

Section I. The judicial Power of the United States, shall be vested in one supreme Court, and in such inferior Courts as the Congress may from time to time ordain and establish. . . .

The Supreme Court, seat of the judicial branch of the federal government.

The powers not delegated to the United States by the Constitution nor prohibited by it to the States, are reserved to the States respectively, or to the people.

Opposite: Town meeting, Bow, New Hampshire. A typical example of local self-government in which residents meet to discuss and decide local affairs by majority vote. Probably the earliest form of democratic government, these meetings had their origin in the early days of Greece; they evolved in England after the Roman occupation and were brought to America, where they were held in New England at Plymouth as early as 1621. Generally speaking the purposes of these meetings are to elect local officials, enact ordinances, determine taxes and expenditures, and voice complaints.

THE STATE GOVERNMENTS

"THE AMERICAN COMMONWEALTH," 1896

James Bryce

"The American State is a peculiar organism, unlike anything in modern Europe or in the ancient world. . . ."

"No State can, as a commonwealth, politically deal with or act upon any other State . . . no coercion can be exercised by one upon another. And although the government of the Union can act on a State, it rarely does act, and then only in certain strictly limited directions, which do not touch the inner political life of the commonwealth."

"Each State makes its own Constitution; that is, the people agree on their form of government for themselves, with no interference from the other States or from the Union. . . ."

"Each State has its own—

Constitution.

Executive, consisting of a governor and various other officials.

Legislature of two Houses.

System of local government in counties, cities, townships, and school districts.

System of State and local taxation.

Debts, which it may repudiate at its own pleasure.

Body of private law, including the whole law of real and personal property, of contracts, of torts, and of family relations.

System of procedure, civil and criminal.

Court, from which no appeal lies (except in cases touching Federal legislation or the Federal Constitution) to any Federal court.

Citizenship, which may admit persons (*e. g.,* recent immigrants) to be citizens at times, or on conditions, wholly different from those prescribed by other States."†

"The American State is a peculiar organism, unlike anything in modern Europe or in the ancient world. . ." Governor's Mansion and State Capitol at Charleston, West Virginia, one of the forty-eight state capitals.

JOHN MARSHALL ON THE SUPREME COURT, 1803

John Marshall was Chief Justice of the United States for thirty-four years, during which time his decisions did much to establish the position of the Court as a vital factor in our constitutional system of checks and balances in government.

In the famous Marbury v. Madison case Marshall's opinion established the important judicial precedent that the Court had the right to review Congressional legislation. An excerpt from this case follows:

MARBURY v. MADISON

It is, emphatically, the province and duty of the judicial department to say what the law is. Those who apply the rule to particular cases must of necessity expound and interpret that rule. If two laws conflict with each other, the courts must decide on the operation of each.

So if a law be in opposition to the Constitution, if both the law and the Constitution apply to a particular case, so that the court must either decide that case conformably to the law, disregarding the Constitution, or conformably to the Constitution, disregarding the law, the court must determine which of these conflicting rules governs the case. This is of the very essence of judicial duty. If, then, the courts are to regard the Constitution, and

68

the Constitution is superior to any ordinary act of the legislature, the Constitution, and not such ordinary act, must govern the case to which they both apply.

Those, then, who controvert the principle that the Constitution is to be considered, in court, as a paramount law are reduced to the necessity of maintaining that courts must close their eyes on the Constitution and see only the law.

This doctrine would subvert the very foundation of all written constitutions. It would declare that an act which, according to the principles and theory of our government, is entirely void, is yet, in practice, completely obligatory. It would declare that if the legislature shall do what is expressly forbidden, such act, notwithstanding the express prohibition, is in reality effectual. It would be giving to the legislature a practical and real omnipotence, with the same breath which professes to restrict their powers within narrow limits. It is prescribing limits and declaring that those limits may be passed at pleasure.

That it thus reduces to nothing what we have deemed the greatest improvement on political institutions, a written constitution would of itself be sufficient, in America, where written constitutions have been viewed with so much reverence, for rejecting the construction. But the peculiar expressions of the Constitution of the United States furnish additional arguments in favor of its rejection.

The judicial power of the United States is extended to all cases arising under the Constitution. Could it be the intention of those who gave this power to say that, in using it, the Constitution should not be looked into? That a case arising under the Constitution should be decided without examining the instrument under which it arises?

This is too extravagant to be maintained.

In some cases, then, the Constitution must be looked into by the judges. And if they can open it at all, what part of it are they forbidden to read or to obey?

There are many other parts of the Constitution which serve to illustrate this subject. It is declared that "no tax or duty shall be laid on articles exported from any state." Suppose a duty on the export of cotton, or tobacco, or of flour; and a suit instituted to recover it. Ought judgment to be rendered in such a case? Ought the judges to close their eyes on the Constitution and only see the law?

The Constitution declares that "no bill of attainder or *ex post facto* law shall be passed." If, however, such a bill should be passed and a person should be prosecuted under it, must the court condemn to death those victims whom the Constitution endeavors to preserve?

"No person," says the Constitution, "shall be convicted of treason, unless on the testimony of two witnesses to the same *overt* act, or on confession in open court." Here the language of the Constitution is addressed especially to the courts. It prescribes, directly for them, a rule of evidence not to be departed from. If the legislature should change that rule and declare one witness, or a confession out of court, sufficient for conviction, must the constitutional principle yield to the legislative act?

From these, and many other selections which might be made, it is apparent that the framers of the Constitution contemplated that instrument as a rule for the government of *courts* as well as of the legislature.

Why otherwise does it direct the judges to take an oath to support it? This oath certainly applies, in an especial manner, to their conduct in their official character. How immoral to impose it on them, if they were to be used as the instruments, and the knowing instruments, for violating what they swear to support!

The oath of office, too, imposed by the legislature is completely demonstrative of the legislative opinion on this subject. It is in these words: "I do solemnly swear that I will administer justice, without respect to persons, and do equal right to the poor and to the rich; and that I will faithfully and impartially discharge all the duties incumbent on me as, according to the best of my abilities and understanding, agreeably to the Constitution, and laws of the United States."

Why does a judge swear to discharge his duties agreeably to the Constitution of the United States if that Constitution forms no rule for his government? If it is closed upon him, and cannot be inspected by him? If such be the real state of things, this is worse than solemn mockery. To prescribe, or to take this oath, becomes equally a crime.

It is also not entirely unworthy of observation that, in declaring what shall be the supreme law of the land, the Constitution itself is first mentioned; and not the laws of the United States generally, but those only which shall be made in pursuance of the Constitution have that rank.

Thus, the particular phraseology of the Constitution of the United States confirms and strengthens the principle, supposed to be essential to all written constitutions, that a law repugnant to the Constitution is void and that courts, as well as other departments, are bound by that instrument.

The rule must be discharged.†

DANIEL WEBSTER ON THE CONSTITUTION

Speech delivered in the Senate, January 26, 1830

If anything be found in the national constitution, either by original provision, or subsequent interpretation, which ought not to be in it, the people know how to get rid of it. If any construction be established, unacceptable to them, so as to become, practically, a part of the constitution, they will amend it, at their own sovereign pleasure: but while the people choose to maintain it, as it is; while they are satisfied with it, and refuse to change it, who has given, or who can give, to the State legislatures a right to alter it, either by interference, construction, or otherwise? Gentlemen do not seem to recollect that the people have any power to do anything for themselves; they imagine there is no safety for them, any longer than they are under the close guardianship of the State legislatures. Sir, the people have not trusted their safety, in regard to the general constitution, to these hands. They have required other security, and taken other bonds. They have chosen to trust themselves, first, to the plain words of the instrument, and to such construction as the government itself, in doubtful cases, should put on its own powers, under their oaths of office, and subject to their responsibility to them: just as the people of a State trust their own State governments with a similar power. Secondly, they have reposed their trust in the efficacy of frequent elections, and in their own power to remove their own servants and agents, whenever they see cause. Thirdly, they have reposed trust in the judicial power, which, in order that it might be trustworthy, they have made as respectable, as disinterested, and as independent as was practicable. Fourthly, they have seen fit to rely, in case of necessity, or high expediency, on their known and admitted power, to alter or amend the constitution, peaceably and quietly, whenever experience shall point out defects or imperfections. And, finally, the people of the United States have, at no time, in no way, directly or indirectly, authorized any State legislature to construe or interpret their high instrument of government; much less to interfere, by their own power, to arrest its course and operation.

If, sir, the people in these respects, had done otherwise than they have done, their constitution could neither have been preserved, nor would it have been worth preserving. And, if its plain provisions shall now be disregarded, and these new doctrines interpolated in it, it will become as feeble and helpless a being, as its enemies, whether early or more recent, could possibly desire. . . .

. . . The people have preserved this, their own chosen constitution, for forty years, and have seen their happiness, prosperity, and renown, grow with its growth, and strengthen with its strength. They are now, generally, strongly attached to it. Overthrown by direct assault, it cannot be; evaded, undermined, nullified, it will not be, if we, and those who shall succeed us here, as agents and representatives of the people, shall conscientiously and vigilantly discharge the two great branches of our public trust—faithfully to preserve, and wisely to administer it.†

HERBERT HOOVER ON THE BILL OF RIGHTS

Constitution Day address, delivered at San Diego, California, September 17, 1935

Our Constitution is not alone the working plan of a great Federation of States under representative government. There is embedded in it also the vital principles of the American system of liberty. That system is based upon certain inalienable freedoms and protections which not even the government may infringe and which we call the Bill of Rights. It does not require a lawyer to interpret these provisions. They are as clear as the Ten Commandments. . . .

These rights were no sudden discovery, no over-night inspiration. They were established by centuries of struggle in which men died fighting bitterly for their recognition. Their beginnings lie in the Magna Charta at Runnymede five hundred and seventy years before the Constitution was written. . . . Our forefathers migrated to America that they might attain them more fully. When they wrote the Declaration of Independence they boldly extended these rights. Before the Constitution could be ratified patriotic men who feared a return to tyranny, whose chains had been thrown off only after years of toil and bloody war, insisted that these hard-won rights should be incorporated in black and white within the Constitution—and so came the American Bill of Rights.

In the hurricane of revolutions which have swept the world since the Great War, men, struggling with the wreckage and poverty of that great catastrophe and the complications of the machine age, are in despair surrendering their freedom for false promises of economic security. Whether it be Fascist Italy, Nazi Germany, Communist Russia, or their lesser followers, the result is the same. Every day they repudiate every principle of the Bill of Rights. . . .

Here is the most fundamental clash known to mankind—that is, free men and women, co-operating under orderly liberty, as contrasted with human beings made pawns of dictatorial government; men who are slaves of despotism, as against free men who are the masters of the State.

Even in America, where liberty blazed brightest and by its glow shed light on all the others, it is besieged from without and challenged from within. Many, in honest belief, hold that we cannot longer accommodate the growth of science, technology and mechanical power to the Bill of Rights and our form of government. With that I do not agree. Men's inventions cannot be of more value than men themselves. But it would be better that we sacrifice something of economic efficiency than to surrender these primary liberties. In them lies a spiritual right of men. Behind them is the conception which is the highest development of the Christian faith—the conception of individual freedom with brotherhood. From them is the fullest flowering of individual human personality.

Those who proclaim that by the Machine Age there is created an irreconcilable conflict in which Liberty must be sacrificed should not forget the battles for these rights over the centuries, for let it be remembered that in the end these are undying principles which spring from the souls of men. We imagine conflict not because the principles of Liberty are unworkable in a machine age, but because we have not worked them conscientiously or have forgotten their true meaning. . . .

Down through a century and a half this American concept of human freedom has enriched the whole world. From the release of the spirit, the initiative, the co-operation, and the courage of men, which alone comes of these freedoms, has been builded this very machine age with all its additions of comfort, its reductions of sweat. Wherever in the world the system of individual liberty has been sustained, mankind has been better clothed, better fed, better housed, has had more leisure. Above all, men and women have had more self-respect. They have been more generous and of finer spirit. Those who scoff that liberty is of no consequence to the underprivileged and the unemployed are grossly ignorant of the primary fact that it is through the creative and the productive impulses of free men that the redemption of those sufferers and their economic security must come. Any system which curtails these freedoms and stimulants to men destroys the possibility of the full production from which economic security can alone come. . . .

Liberty comes alone and lives alone where the hard-won rights of men are held inalienable, where governments themselves may not infringe, where governments are indeed but the mechanisms to protect and sustain these principles. It was this concept for which America's sons have died on a hundred battlefields. . . .†

"YOUR CONSTITUTION IS ALL SAIL AND NO ANCHOR"
Lord Macaulay, 1857

Thomas Babington Macaulay, historian, author, and Member of Parliament, wrote the following much quoted letter to the Hon. H. S. Randall of New York in acknowledgement of the latter's Life of Thomas Jefferson. *Sixteen years later (and eight years before he became President) James A. Garfield replied to Macaulay's letter in an address entitled "The Future of the Republic." Excerpts from both pieces follow.*

Holly Lodge, Kensington,
London, May 23, 1857.

Dear Sir,
. . . I have long been convinced that institutions purely democratic must, sooner or later, destroy liberty, or civilisation, or both. In Europe, where the population is dense, the effect of such institutions would be almost instantaneous. What happened lately in France is an example. In 1848 a pure democracy was established there. During a short time there was reason to expect a general spoliation, a national bankruptcy, a new partition of the soil, a maximum of prices, a ruinous load of taxation laid on the rich for the purpose of supporting the poor in idleness. Such a system would, in twenty years, have made France as poor and barbarous as the France of the Carlovingians. Happily the danger was averted; and now there is despotism, a silent tribune, an enslaved press. Liberty is gone, but civilisation has been saved. I have not the smallest doubt that, if we had a purely democratic government here, the effect would be the same. Either the poor would plunder the rich, and civilisation would perish, or order and property would be saved by a strong military government, and liberty would perish. You may think that your country enjoys an exemption from these evils. I will frankly own to you that I am of a very different opinion. Your fate I believe to be certain, though it is deferred by a physical cause. As long as you have a boundless extent of fertile and unoccupied land, your labouring population will be far more at ease than the labouring population of the old world; and, while that is the case, the Jeffersonian polity may continue to exist without causing any fatal calamity. But the time will come when New England will be as thickly peopled as old England. Wages will be as low, and will fluctuate as much with you as with us. You will have your Manchesters and Birminghams, and in those Manchesters and Birminghams, hundreds of thousands of artisans will assuredly be sometimes out of work. Then your institutions will be fairly

brought to the test. Distress every where makes the labourer mutinous and discontented, and inclines him to listen with eagerness to agitators who tell him that is a monstrous iniquity that one man should have a million while another cannot get a full meal. In bad years there is plenty of grumbling here, and sometimes a little rioting. But it matters little. For here the sufferers are not the rulers. The supreme power is in the hands of a class, numerous indeed, but select; of an educated class, of a class which is, and knows itself to be, deeply interested in the security of property and the maintenance of order. Accordingly, the malcontents are firmly, yet gently, restrained. The bad time is got over without robbing the wealthy to relieve the indigent. The springs of national prosperity soon begin to flow again: work is plentiful: wages rise; and all is tranquillity and cheerfulness. I have seen England pass three or four times through such critical seasons as I have described. Through such seasons the United States will have to pass, in the course of the next century, if not of this. How will you pass through them. I heartily wish you a good deliverance. But my reason and my wishes are at war; and I cannot help foreboding the worst. It is quite plain that your government will never be able to restrain a distressed and discontented majority. For with you the majority is the government, and has the rich, who are always a minority, absolutely at its mercy. The day will come when, in the State of New York, a multitude of people, none of whom has had more than half a breakfast, or expects to have more than half a dinner, will choose a Legislature. Is it possible to doubt what sort of a Legislature will be chosen? On one side is a statesman preaching patience, respect for vested rights, strict observance of public faith. On the other is a demagogue ranting about the tyranny of capitalists and usurers, and asking why anybody should be permitted to drink Champagne and to ride in a carriage, while thousands of honest folks are in want of necessaries. Which of the two candidates is likely to be preferred by a working man who hears his children cry for more bread? I seriously apprehend that you will, in some such season of adversity as I have described, do things which will prevent prosperity from returning; that you will act like people who should in a year of scarcity, devour all the seed corn, and thus make the next year a year, not of scarcity, but of absolute famine. There will be, I fear, spoliation. The spoliation will increase the distress. The distress will produce fresh spoliation. There is nothing to stop you. Your Constitution is all sail and no anchor. As I said before, when a society has entered on this downward progress, either civilisation or liberty must perish. Either some Caesar or Napoleon will seize the reins of government with a strong hand; or your republic will be as fearfully plundered and laid waste by barbarians in the twentieth Century as the Roman Empire was in the fifth; — with this difference, that the Huns and Vandals who ravaged the Roman Empire came from without, and that your Huns and Vandals will have been engendered within your own country by your own institutions. . . .

I have the honor to be, dear Sir, your faithful servant,

T. B. MACAULAY

H. S. Randall, Esq., etc., etc., etc.

JAMES A. GARFIELD'S ANSWER TO MACAULAY, 1873

Address entitled "The Future of the Republic," delivered to the Literary Societies of Western Reserve College, Hudson, Ohio, July 2, 1873

. . . I venture the declaration, that this opinion of Macaulay's is vulnerable on several grounds.

In the first place, it is based upon a belief from which few if any British writers have been able to emancipate themselves; namely, the belief that mankind are born into permanent classes, and that in the main they must live, work, and die in the fixed class or condition in which they are born. It is hardly possible for a man reared in an aristocracy like that of England to eliminate this conviction from his mind, for the British empire is built upon it. Their theory of national stability is, that there must be a permanent class who shall hold in their own hands so much of the wealth, the privilege, and the political power of the kingdom, that they can compel the admiration and obedience of all other classes. . . . The great voiceless class of day-laborers have made but little headway against the doctrine. The editor of a leading British magazine told me, a few years ago, that in twenty-five years of observation he had never known a mere farm-laborer in England to rise above his class. Some, he said, have done so in manufactures, some in trade, but in mere farm labor not one. The government of a country where such a fact is possible has much to answer for.

We deny the justice or the necessity of keeping ninety-nine of the population in perpetual poverty and obscurity, in order that the hundredth may be rich and powerful enough to hold the ninety-nine in subjection. Where such permanent classes exist, the conflict of which Macaulay speaks is inevitable. And why? Not that men are inclined to fight the class above them, but that they fight against any artificial barrier which makes it impossible for them to enter that higher class and become a part of it. We point to the fact, that in this country there are no classes in the British sense of that word, — no impassable barriers of caste. . . . Our society resembles rather the waves of the ocean, whose every drop may move freely among its fellows, and may rise toward the light until it flashes on the crest of the highest wave.

Again, in depicting the dangers of universal suffrage, Macaulay leaves wholly out of the account the great counterbalancing force of universal education. He contemplates a government delivered over to a vast multitude of ignorant, vicious men, who have learned no self-control, who have never comprehended the national life, and who wield the ballot solely for personal and selfish ends. If this were indeed the necessary condition of democratic communities, it would be difficult, perhaps impossible, to escape the logic of Macaulay's letter. And here is a real peril, — the danger that we shall rely upon the mere extent of the suffrage as a national safeguard. We cannot safely, even for a moment, lose sight of the quality of the suffrage, which is more important than its quantity.

We are apt to be deluded into false security by political catch-words, devised to flatter rather than instruct. We have happily escaped the dogma of the divine right of kings. Let us not fall into the equally pernicious error that multitude is divine because it is a multitude. The words of our great publicist, the late Dr. Lieber, whose faith in republican liberty was undoubted, should never be forgotten. In discussing the doctrine of *Vox populi, vox Dei*, he said, "Woe to the country in which political hypocrisy first calls the people almighty, then teaches that the voice of the people is divine, then pretends to take a mere clamor for the true voice of the people, and lastly gets up the desired clamor."*
This sentence ought to be read in every political caucus. It would make an interesting and significant preamble to most of our political platforms. It is only when the people speak truth and justice that their voice can be called "the voice of God." Our faith in the democratic principle rests upon the belief that intelligent men will see that their highest political good is in liberty, regulated by just and equal laws; and that, in the distribution of political power, it is safe to follow the maxim, "Each for all, and all for each." We confront the dangers of suffrage by the blessings of universal education. We believe that the strength of the state is the aggregate strength of its individual citizens; and that the suffrage is the link that binds, in a bond of mutual interest and responsibility, the fortunes of the citizen to the fortunes of the state. Hence, as popular suffrage is the broadest base, so, when coupled with intelligence and virtue, it becomes the strongest, the most enduring base on which to build the superstructure of government. . . .†

* Civil Liberty and Self-Government (Philadelphia, 1859), p. 415.

WHAT IS AN AMERICAN?

"LETTERS FROM AN AMERICAN FARMER"
Hector St.-Jean de Crevecoeur (1735–1813)

In this great American asylum, the poor of Europe have by some means met together, and in consequence of various causes; to what purpose should they ask one another what countrymen they are? Alas, two thirds of them had no country. Can a wretch who wanders about, who works and starves, whose life is a continual scene of sore affliction or pinching penury; can that man call England or any other kingdom his country? A country that had no bread for him, whose fields procured him no harvest, who met with nothing but the frowns of the rich, the severity of the laws, with jails and punishments; who owned not a single foot of the extensive surface of this planet? No! urged by a variety of motives, here they came. Every thing has tended to regenerate them; new laws, a new mode of living, a new social system; here they are become men: in Europe they were as so many useless plants, wanting vegetative mould, and refreshing showers; they withered, and were mowed down by want, hunger, and war; but now by the power of transplantation, like all other plants they have taken root and flourished! Formerly they were not numbered in any civil lists of their country, except in those of the poor; here they rank as citizens. By what invisible power has this surprising metamorphosis been performed? By that of the laws and that of their industry. The laws, the indulgent laws, protect them as they arrive, stamping on them the symbol of adoption; they receive ample rewards for their labours; these accumulated rewards procure them lands; those lands confer on them the title of freemen, and to that title every benefit is affixed which men can possibly require. This is the great operation daily performed by our laws. From whence proceed these laws? From our government. Whence the government? It is derived from the original genius and strong desire of the people. . . .

What then is the American, this new man? . . . *He* is an American, who leaving behind him all his ancient prejudices and manners, receives new ones from the new mode of life he has embraced, the new government he obeys, and the new rank he holds. He becomes an American by being received in the broad lap of our great *Alma Mater*. Here individuals of all nations are melted into a new race of men, whose labours and posterity will one day cause great changes in the world. . . . The American is a new man, who acts upon new principles; he must therefore entertain new ideas, and form new opinions. From involuntary idleness, servile dependence, penury, and useless labour, he has passed to toils of a very different nature, rewarded by ample subsistence. — This is an American.†

REQUIREMENTS FOR UNITED STATES CITIZENSHIP

Source: Department of Justice
Immigration and Naturalization Service

The right of a person to become a naturalized citizen of the United States shall not be abridged because of race, of sex, or because that person is married.

Generally an applicant for naturalization must have been lawfully admitted to the United States for permanent residence. Further, he must have resided continuously in the United States for the number of years required by law.

Every person who files a petition for naturalization must:

(1) Sign the petition in his own handwriting, if physically able to write:

(2) Demonstrate an understanding of the English language, including an ability to read, write, and speak words in ordinary usage in the English language (persons physically unable to do so, and persons who were on September 23, 1950, over fifty years of age and

who had on that date been residing in the United States for periods totalling twenty years are excepted from this requirement):

(3) Have been a person of good moral character, attached to the principles of the Constitution, and well disposed to the good order and happiness of the United States for the five years just before filing the petition or for whatever other period of residence is required in his case and continue to be such a person until admitted to citizenship: and

(4) Demonstrate a knowledge and understanding of the fundamentals of the history, and the principles and form of government, of the United States.

The petitioner is also obliged to have two witnesses who are persons of good moral character and citizens. These witnesses must have personal knowledge of the applicant's character, residence, loyalty, and other qualifications.

After he has made his preliminary application, and filed his petition for naturalization, he will be notified by the Immigration and Naturalization Service when and where to appear with his witness for preliminary interrogation. The applicant and his witnesses are questioned by an examiner, and if he meets the requirements, the examiner assists him in filing a petition for naturalization. This petition must be filed by the petitioner with the clerk of the court in the jurisdiction in which he resides. The fee is $10. The cost of the certificate of naturalization is included in this fee. After the filing of the petition and after further examination, the petitioner is told that he will be notified by mail when to appear in the naturalization court for final hearing.

If the court grants a petition for naturalization the petitioner must renounce allegiance to any foreign state of which he is a citizen or subject and take an oath of allegiance to the United States.†

PRESIDENTS OF THE UNITED STATES

No.	Name	Inauguration	Age at Inauguration	Age at Death
1	George Washington	1789	57	67
2	John Adams	1797	61	90
3	Thomas Jefferson	1801	57	83
4	James Madison	1809	57	85
5	James Monroe	1817	58	73
6	John Quincy Adams	1825	57	80
7	Andrew Jackson	1829	61	78
8	Martin Van Buren	1837	54	79
9	William Henry Harrison	1841	68	68
10	John Tyler	1841	51	71
11	James Knox Polk	1845	49	53
12	Zachary Taylor	1849	64	65
13	Millard Fillmore	1850	50	74
14	Franklin Pierce	1853	48	64
15	James Buchanan	1857	65	77
16	Abraham Lincoln	1861	52	56
17	Andrew Johnson	1865	56	66
18	Ulysses Simpson Grant	1869	46	63
19	Rutherford Birchard Hayes	1877	54	70
20	James Abram Garfield	1881	49	49
21	Chester Alan Arthur	1881	50	56
22	Grover Cleveland	1885	47	71
23	Benjamin Harrison	1889	55	67

Immigrant studying for citizenship.

George Washington. Painting by Joseph Wright.

24	Grover Cleveland	1893	55	71
25	William McKinley	1897	54	58
26	Theodore Roosevelt	1901	42	60
27	William Howard Taft	1909	51	72
28	Woodrow Wilson	1913	56	67
29	Warren Gamaliel Harding	1921	55	57
30	Calvin Coolidge	1923	51	60
31	Herbert Clark Hoover	1929	54	
32	Franklin Delano Roosevelt	1933	51	63
33	Harry S. Truman	1945	60	
34	Dwight D. Eisenhower	1953	62	
35	JOHN F KENNEDY	1960	44	

Milestones in Foreign Policy

George Washington, retiring after having served two terms, delivered his memorable "Farewell Address" to the Congress, 1796. In it he suggested principles for future guidance of the nation, and that portion of it dealing with our foreign relations is generally regarded as the corner-stone of America's foreign policy. Excerpts from this follow:

GEORGE WASHINGTON'S FAREWELL ADDRESS, 1796

Observe good faith and justice towards all nations; cultivate peace and harmony with all. Religion and morality enjoin this conduct. . . .

. . . nothing is more essential than that permanent, inveterate antipathies against particular nations, and passionate attachments for others, should be excluded; and that in place of them, just and amicable feelings towards all should be cultivated. The nation, which indulges towards another an habitual hatred, or an habitual fondness, is in some degree a slave. It is a slave to its animosity or to its affection, either of which is sufficient to lead it astray from its duty and its interest. Antipathy in one nation against another, disposes each more readily to offer insult and injury, to lay hold of slight causes of umbrage, and to be haughty and intractable, when accidental or trifling occasions of dispute occur. . . .

So, likewise, a passionate attachment of one nation for another produces a variety of evils. Sympathy for the favorite nation facilitating the illusion of an imaginary common interest in cases where no real common interest exists, and infusing into one the enmities of the other, betrays the former into a participation in the quarrels and wars of the latter, without adequate inducement or justification. It leads also to concessions to the favorite nation of privileges denied to others, which is apt doubly to injure the nation making the concessions; by unnecessarily parting with what ought to have been retained; and by exciting jealousy, ill-will, and a disposition to retaliate, in the parties from whom equal privileges are withheld; and it gives to ambitious, corrupted, or deluded citizens (who devote themselves to the favorite nation) facility to betray, or sacrifice the interests of their own country, without odium, sometimes even with popularity; gilding, with the appearances of a virtuous sense of obligation, a commendable deference for public opinion, or laudable zeal for public good the base or foolish compliances of ambition, corruption, or infatuation. . . .

Against the insidious wiles of foreign influence (I conjure you to believe me, fellow-citizens), the jealousy of a free people ought to be constantly awake; since history and experience prove, that foreign influence is one of the most baneful foes of republican government. . . . Excessive partiality for one foreign nation, and excessive dislike of another, cause those whom they actuate, to see danger only on one side; and serve to veil and even second the arts of influence on the other. . . .

The great rule of conduct for us, in regard to foreign nations is, in extending our commercial relations, to have with them as little political connection as possible. So far as we have already formed engagements, let them be fulfilled with perfect good faith. Here let us stop.

Europe has a set of primary interests, which to us have none, or a very remote relation. Hence she must be engaged in frequent controversies, the causes of which are essentially foreign to our concerns. Hence, therefore, it must be unwise in us to implicate ourselves, by artificial ties, in the ordinary vicissitudes of her politics, or the ordinary combinations and collisions of her friendships and enmities. . . .

'Tis our true policy to steer clear of permanent alliances with any portion of the foreign world; so far, I mean, as we are now at liberty to do it; for let me not be understood as capable of patronizing infidelity to existing engagements. I hold the maxim no less applicable to public than to private affairs, that honesty is always the best policy. I repeat it, therefore, let those engagements be observed in their genuine sense. But, in my opinion, it is unnecessary, and would be unwise, to extend them.

Taking care always to keep ourselves, by suitable establishments, in a respectable defensive posture, we may safely trust to temporary alliances for extraordinary emergencies.

Harmony, and a liberal intercourse with all nations, are recommended by policy, humanity, and interest. But even our commercial policy should hold an equal and impartial hand; neither seeking nor granting exclusive favors or preferences; consulting the natural course of things; diffusing and diversifying, by gentle means, the streams of commerce, but forcing nothing; establishing, with powers so disposed, in order to give trade a stable course, to define the rights of our merchants, and to enable the government to support them, conventional rules of intercourse, the best that present circumstances and mutual opinion will permit, but temporary, and liable to be, from time to time, abandoned or varied, as experience and circumstances shall dictate; constantly keeping in view, that it is folly in one nation to look for disinterested favors from another; that it must pay, with a portion of its independence, for whatever it may accept under that character; that, by such acceptance, it may place itself in the condition of having given equivalents for nominal favors, and yet of being reproached with ingratitude for not giving more. There can be no greater error than to expect to calculate upon real favors from nation to nation. It is an illusion, which experience must cure, which a just pride ought to discard.†

THE MONROE DOCTRINE, 1823

Threats of European expansion and exploitation in the western hemisphere by Russia, France, and Spain made it necessary in 1823 for the United States to set forth her principles of foreign policy.

England was fearful that France might acquire former Spanish colonies which would threaten British trade. To prevent this she proposed joint action between Great Britain and America. But the United States would not "come in as a cock-boat in the wake of a British man-of-war," declared Secretary of State John Quincy Adams. With the help of Adams, President Monroe drafted and announced our policy, since known as the Monroe Doctrine:

. . . At the proposal of the Russian Imperial Government, made through the minister of the Emperor residing here, a full power and instructions have been transmitted to the minister of the United States at St. Petersburg to arrange by amicable negotiation the respective rights and interests of the two nations on the northwest coast of this continent. A similar proposal had been made by His Imperial Majesty to the Government of Great Britain, which has likewise been acceded to. The government of the United States has been desirous by this friendly proceeding of manifesting the great value which they have invariably attached to the friendship of the Emperor and their solicitude to cultivate the best understanding with his Government. In the discussions to which this interest has given rise and in the arrangements by which they may terminate the occasion has been judged proper for asserting, as a principle in which the rights and interests of the United States are involved, that the American continents, by the free and independent condition which they have assumed and maintain, are henceforth not to be considered as subjects for future colonization by any European powers. . . .

It was stated at the commencement of the last session that a great effort was then making in Spain and Portugal to improve the condition of the people of those countries, and that it appeared to be conducted with extraordinary moderation. It need scarcely be remarked that the result has been so far very different from what was then anticipated. Of events in that quarter of the globe, with which we have so much intercourse and from which we derive our origin, we have always been anxious and interested spectators. The citizens of the United States cherish sentiments the most friendly in favor of the liberty and happiness of their fellow-men on the side of the Atlantic. In the wars of the European powers in matters relating to themselves we have never taken any part, nor does it comport with our policy so to do. It is only when our rights are invaded or seriously menaced that we resent injuries or make preparations for our defense. With the movements in this hemisphere we are of necessity more immediately connected, and by causes which must be obvious to all enlightened and impartial observers. The political system of the allied powers is essentially different in this respect from that of America. This difference proceeds from that which exists in their respective Governments; and to the defense of our own, which has been achieved by the loss of so much blood and treasure, and matured by the wisdom of their most enlightened citizens, and under which we have enjoyed unexampled felicity, this whole nation is devoted. We owe it, therefore, to candor and to the amicable relations existing between the United States and those powers to declare that we should consider any attempt on their part to extend their system to any portion of this hemisphere as dangerous to our peace and safety. With the existing colonies or dependencies of any European power we have not interfered and shall not interfere. But with the Governments who have declared their independence and maintained it, and whose independence we have, on great consideration and on just principles, acknowledged, we could not view any interposition for the purpose of oppressing them, or controlling in any other manner their destiny, by any European power in any other light than as the manifestation of an unfriendly disposition toward the United States. In the war between those new Governments and Spain we declared our neutrality at the time of their recognition, and to this we have adhered, and shall continue to adhere, provided no change shall occur which, in the judgment of the competent authorities of this Government, shall make a corresponding change on the part of the United States indispensable to their security.

The late events in Spain and Portugal shew that Europe is still unsettled. Of this important fact no stronger proof can be adduced than that the allied powers should have thought it proper, on any principle satisfactory to themselves, to have interposed by force in the internal concerns of Spain. To what extent such interposition may be carried, on the same principle, is a question in which all independent powers whose governments differ from theirs are interested, even those most remote, and surely none more so than the United States. Our policy in regard to Europe, which was adopted at an early stage of the wars which have so long agitated that quarter of the globe, nevertheless remains the same, which is, not to interfere in the internal concerns of any of its powers; to consider the government *de facto* as the legitimate government for us; to cultivate friendly relations with it, and to preserve those relations by a frank, firm, and manly policy, meeting in all instances the just claims of every power, submitting to injuries from none. But in regard to these continents circumstances are eminently and conspicuously different. It is impossible that the allied powers should extend their political system to any portion of either continent without endangering our peace and happiness; nor can anyone believe that our southern brethren, if left to themselves, would adopt it of their own accord. It is equally impossible, therefore, that we should behold such interposition in any form with indifference. If we look to the comparative strength and resources of Spain and those new Governments, and their distance from each other, it must be obvious that she can never subdue them. It is still the true policy of the United States to leave the parties to themselves, in the hope that other powers will pursue the same course.†

WOODROW WILSON'S FOURTEEN POINTS, 1918

In proposing his Fourteen Points Woodrow Wilson set forth the principles on which he hoped a "peace of justice" could be based. They formed, in fact, the basis for the armistice with Germany. At the Paris Peace Conference, 1919, where the Treaty of Versailles was drafted, President Wilson succeeded in having Point XIV, the formation of a league of nations, incorporated into the Treaty. The Covenant of the League of Nations was subsequently drawn up, but Wilson did not succeed in getting Senatorial approval and America did not join the League.

Wilson's idealism in calling for a "peace without victory" foundered on the rock of European power politics, and the Treaty was ultimately based on secret agreements made during the war and on division of spoils after the war. French Premier Clemenceau neatly expressed Europe's cynicism when he said, "Mr. Wilson bores me with his Fourteen Points; why, God Almighty has only ten!"

But Wilson's idealism did succeed in setting up a world tribunal. "I would rather fail in a cause that I know will some day triumph," he said, "than win in a cause that I know will some day fail."

On April 18, 1946, the League of Nations voted itself out of existence and turned over its physical properties to the United Nations.

I. Open covenants of peace, openly arrived at, after which there shall be no private international understandings of any kind but diplomacy shall proceed always frankly and in the public view.

II. Absolute freedom of navigation upon the seas, outside territorial waters, alike in peace and in war, except as the seas may be closed in whole or in part by international action for the enforcement of international covenants.

III. The removal, so far as possible, of all economic barriers and the establishment of an equality of trade conditions among all the nations consenting to the peace and associating themselves for its maintenance.

IV. Adequate guarantees given and taken that national armaments will be reduced to the lowest point consistent with domestic safety.

V. A free, open-minded, and absolutely impartial adjustment of all colonial claims, based upon a strict observance of the principle that in determining all such questions of sovereignty the interests of the populations concerned must have equal weight with the equitable claims of the government whose title is to be determined.

VI. The evacuation of all Russian territory and such a settlement of all questions affecting Russia as will secure the best and freest cooperation of the other nations of the

Council of Four: Lloyd George, Orlando, Clemenceau, and Woodrow
Wilson, principals at the Paris Peace Conference where Wilson's
Fourteen Points were incorporated into the Treaty of Versailles.

world in obtaining for her an unhampered and unembarrassed opportunity for the independent determination of her own political development and national policy and assure
her of a sincere welcome into the society of free nations under institutions of her own
choosing; and, more than a welcome, assistance also of every kind that she may need
and may herself desire. The treatment accorded Russia by her sister nations in the months
to come will be the acid test of their good will, of their comprehension of her needs as
distinguished from their own interests, and of their intelligent and unselfish sympathy.

VII. Belgium, the whole world will agree, must be evacuated and restored, without any
attempt to limit the sovereignty which she enjoys in common with all other free nations.
No other single act will serve as this will serve to restore confidence among the nations
in the laws which they have themselves set and determined for the government of their
relations with one another. Without this healing act the whole structure and validity of
international law is forever impaired.

VIII. All French territory should be freed and the invaded portions restored, and the
wrong done to France by Prussia in 1871 in the matter of Alsace-Lorraine, which has

83

unsettled the peace of the world for nearly fifty years, should be righted, in order that peace may once more be made secure in the interest of all.

IX. A readjustment of the frontiers of Italy should be effected along clearly recognizable lines of nationality.

X. The peoples of Austria-Hungary, whose place among the nations we wish to see safeguarded and assured, should be accorded the freest opportunity of autonomous development.

XI. Rumania, Serbia, and Montenegro should be evacuated; occupied territories restored; Serbia accorded free and secure access to the sea; and the relations of the several Balkan states to one another determined by friendly counsel along historically established lines of allegiance and nationality; and international guarantees of the political and economic independence and territorial integrity of the several Balkan states should be entered into.

XII. The Turkish portions of the present Ottoman Empire should be assured a secure sovereignty, but the other nationalities which are now under Turkish rule should be assured an undoubted security of life and an absolutely unmolested opportunity of autonomous development, and the Dardanelles should be permanently opened as a free passage to the ships and commerce of all nations under international guarantees.

XIII. An independent Polish state should be erected which should include the territories inhabited by indisputably Polish populations, which should be assured a free and secure access to the sea, and whose political and economic independence and territorial integrity should be guaranteed by international covenant.

XIV. A general association of nations must be formed under specific covenants for the purpose of affording mutual guarantees of political independence and territorial integrity to great and small states alike. . . .

CHARTER OF THE UNITED NATIONS, 1945

We, the peoples of the United Nations

Determined to save succeeding generations from the scourge of war, which twice in our lifetime has brought untold sorrow to mankind, and

To reaffirm faith in fundamental human rights, in the dignity and worth of the human person, in the equal right of men and women and of nations large and small, and

To establish conditions under which justice and respect for the obligations arising from treaties and other sources of international law can be maintained, and

To promote social progress and better standards of life in larger freedom, and for these ends

To practice tolerance and live together in peace with one another as good neighbors, and

To unite our strength to maintain international peace and security, and

To insure, by the acceptance of principles and the institution of methods, that armed force shall not be used, save in the common interest, and

To employ international machinery for the promotion of the economic and social advancement of all people, have resolved to combine our efforts to accomplish these aims.

Accordingly, our respective governments, through representatives assembled in the city of San Francisco, who have exhibited their full powers found to be in good and due form, have agreed to the present Charter of the United Nations and do hereby establish an international organization to be known as the United Nations.

General Assembly of the United Nations, established 1945.

CHAPTER I

Purposes

Article 1—The purposes of the United Nations are:

1. To maintain international peace and security, and to that end: to take effective collective measures for the prevention and removal of threats to the peace and for the suppression of acts of aggression or other breaches of the peace, and to bring about by peaceful means, and in conformity with the principles of justice and international law, adjustment or settlement of international disputes or situations which might lead to a breach of the peace;

2. To develop friendly relations among nations based on respect for the principle of equal rights and self-determination of peoples, and to take other appropriate measures to strengthen universal peace;

3. To achieve international cooperation in solving international problems of an economic, social, cultural or humanitarian character, and in promoting and encouraging respect for human rights and for the fundamental freedoms for all without distinction as to race, sex, language or religion; and

4. To be a center for harmonizing the actions of nations in the attainments of these common ends.†

THREE

Struggles:

Religious, Moral, Economic

"Be not deceived; God is not mocked:
for whatsoever a man soweth, that shall he also reap."

GALATIANS, VI, 7

Struggles: Religious, Moral, Economic

America was founded by men who sought freedom from tyranny in all its forms. Mindful of religious persecution in the lands from which they came, many of the founding fathers wrote into their earliest laws "Charters," "Acts," and "Orders" establishing freedom of worship. Excerpts from a few of these follow. The first selection is from the writings of Roger Williams, clergyman and founder of Rhode Island, who advocated complete separation of Church and State. His fiery refusal to recant his views before the Massachusetts General Court caused him to be banished from the Massachusetts Bay Colony in 1635. Subsequently he obtained a charter (from England) for the Providence settlement that contained the grant of absolute liberty of conscience in religion.

"THE BLOODY TENENT OF PERSECUTION," 1644
Roger Williams
PREFACE

First, that the blood of so many hundred thousand souls of Protestants and Papists, spilt in the wars of present and former ages for their respective consciences, is not required nor accepted by Jesus Christ the Prince of Peace.

Secondly, pregnant scriptures and arguments are throughout the work proposed against the doctrine of persecution for the cause of conscience.

Fourth, the doctrine of persecution for cause of conscience is proved guilty of all the blood of the souls crying for vengeance under the altar.

Seventhly, the state of the land of Israel, the kings and people thereof, in peace and war, is proved figurative and ceremonial, and no pattern nor precedent for any kingdom or civil state in the world to follow.

Eighthly, God requireth not a uniformity of religion to be enacted and enforced in any civil state; which enforced uniformity (sooner or later) is the great occasion of civil war, ravishing of conscience, persecution of Christ Jesus in his servants, and of the hypocrisy and destruction of millions of souls.

Ninthly, in holding an enforced uniformity of religion in a civil state, we must necessarily disclaim our desires and hopes of the Jews' conversion to Christ.

Tenthly, an enforced uniformity of religion throughout a nation or civil state confounds the civil and religious, denies the principles of Christianity and civility, and that Jesus Christ is come in the flesh.

Twelfthly, lastly, true civility and Christianity may both flourish in a state or kingdom, notwithstanding the permission of divers and contrary consciences, either of Jew or Gentile.†

MARYLAND ACT OF TOLERATION, 1649

Passed in accordance with instructions from Lord Baltimore to clear Maryland, a largely Catholic community, of the charge of intolerance toward Protestantism.

Foreasmuch as in a well governed and Christian Common Wealth matters concerning Religion and the honor of God ought in the first place to bee taken, into serious consideration and endeavored to bee settled. Be it therefore . . . enacted. . . . That whatsoever person or persons within this Province . . . shall from henceforth blaspheme God, . . . or deny the holy Trinity the father sonne and holy Ghost, or the Godhead of any of the

Opposite: Church at Litchfield, Connecticut

Andre de Dienes

said Three persons of the Trinity or the Unity of the Godhead . . . shall be punished with death and confiscation or forfeiture of all his or her lands. . . .

. . . And whereas the inforceing of the conscience in matters of Religion hath frequently fallen out to be of dangerous Consequence in those commonwealthes where it hath been practised, and for the more quiett and peaceable government of this Province, and the better to preserve mutuall Love and amity amongst the Inhabitants thereof. Be it Therefore . . . enacted (except as in this present Act is before Declared and sett forth) that noe person or persons whatsoever within this Province, or the Islands, Ports, Harbors, Creekes, or havens thereunto belonging professing to believe in Jesus Christ, shall from henceforth bee any waies troubled, Molested or discountenanced for or in respect of his or her religion nor in the free exercise thereof within this Province or the Islands thereunto belonging nor any way compelled to the beliefe or exercise of any other Religion against his or her consent, soe as they be not unfaithful to the Lord Proprietary, or molest or conspire against the civill Government established or to bee established in this Province under him or his heires. And that all & every person and persons that shall presume Contrary to this Act and the true intent and meaning thereof directly or indirectly either in person or estate willfully to wronge disturbe trouble or molest any person whatsoever within this Province professing to believe in Jesus Christ for or in respect of his or her religion or the free exercise thereof within this Province other than is provided for in this Act that such person or persons soe offending, shalbe compelled to pay trebble damages to the party soe wronged or molested. . . .†

CHARTER OF RHODE ISLAND, 1663

. . . That our loyall will and pleasure is, that noe person within the said colonye, at any tyme hereafter shall be any wise molested, punished, disquieted or called in question for any differences in opinion in matters of religion and doe not actually disturb the civill peace of sayd colony, but that all and every person and persons may from tyme to tyme and at all tymes hereafter freelye and fullye enjoye his and their own judgements and consciences in matters of religious concernments, they behaving themselves peaceably and quietly, and not using this libertie to lycentiousness and profanenesse, nor to the civill injurye or outward disturbance of other.†

PENNSYLVANIA CHARTER OF PRIVILEGES, 1701
William Penn

FIRST

BECAUSE no People can be truly happy, though under the greatest Enjoyment of Civil Liberties, if abridged of the Freedom of their Consciences, as to their Religious Profession and Worship: And almighty God being the only Lord of Conscience, Father of Lights and Spirits; and the Author as well as Object of all divine Knowledge, Faith and Worship, who only doth enlighten the Minds, and persuade and convince the Understandings of People, I do hereby grant and declare, That no Person or Persons, inhabiting in this province or Territories, who shall confess and acknowledge One almighty God, the Creator, upholder and Ruler of the World: and profess him or themselves obliged to live quietly under the Civil Government, shall be in any Case molested or prejudiced, in his or their Person or Estate, because of his or their conscientious Persuasion or Practice, nor be compelled to frequent or maintain any religious Worship, Place of Ministry, contrary to his or their Mind, or to do or suffer any other Act or Thing, contrary to their religious Persuasion.

AND that all Persons who also profess to believe in *Jesus Christ*, the Saviour of the

World, shall be capable (notwithstanding their other Persuasions and Practices in Point of Conscience and Religion) to serve this Government in any Capacity, both legislatively and executively, he or they solemnly promising, when lawfully required, Allegiance to the King as Sovereign, and Fidelity to the Proprietary and Governor. . . .†

VIRGINIA STATUTE OF RELIGIOUS LIBERTY, 1786

The aim of this document was, as Jefferson said: "To comprehend, within the mantle of its protection, the Jew and the Gentile, the Christian and the Mohametan, the Hindoo and the infidel of every denomination."

Section II. *Be it enacted by the General Assembly*, that no man shall be compelled to frequent or support any religious worship, place or ministry whatsoever, nor shall be enforced, restrained, molested, or burthened in his body or goods, nor shall otherwise suffer on account of his religious opinions or belief; but that all men shall be free to profess, and by argument to maintain, their opinion in matters of religion, and that the same shall in no wise diminish, enlarge, or affect their civil capacities.

Section III. . . . the rights hereby asserted are of the natural rights of mankind, and that if any act shall hereafter be passed to repeal the present, or to narrow its operation, such act will be an infringement of natural right.†

THE EARLIEST PROTEST AGAINST SLAVERY
RESOLUTIONS OF GERMANTOWN MENNONITES
FEBRUARY 18, 1688

In 1619 slavery was first introduced to the English colonies in America. Among the most vigorous to protest were the Quakers and Mennonites.

This is the monthly meeting held at Richard Worrell's:

These are the reasons why we are against the traffic of men-body, as followeth: Is there any that would be done or handled at this manner? viz., to be sold or made a slave for all the time of his life? How fearful and faint-hearted are many at sea, when they see a strange vessel, being afraid it should be a Turk, and they should be taken, and sold for slaves into Turkey. Now, what is *this* better done, than Turks do? Yea, rather is it worse for them, which they say are Christians; for we do hear that the most part of such negers are brought hither against their will and consent, and that many of them are stolen. Now, though they be black, we cannot conceive there is more liberty to have them slaves, as it is to have other white ones. There is a saying, that we should do all men like as we will be done ourselves; making no difference of what generation, descent, or colour they are. And those who steal or rob men, and those who buy or purchase them, are they not all alike? Here is liberty of conscience, which is right and reasonable; here ought to be likewise liberty of the body, except of evil-doers, which is another case. But to bring men hither, or to rob or sell them against their will, we stand against. . . . Ah, do consider well this thing, you who do it, if you would be done at this manner—and if it is done according to Christianity! . . . Pray, what thing in the world can be done worse towards us, than if men should rob or steal us away, and sell us for slaves to strange countries; separating husbands from wives and children. Being now this is not done in the manner we would be done at; therefore, we contradict, and are against this traffic of men-body. And we who profess that it is not lawful to steal, must likewise, avoid to purchase such things as are stolen, but rather help to stop this robbing and stealing. . . .

Now consider well this thing, if it is good or bad. And in case you find it to be good to handel these blacks in that manner, we desire and require you hereby lovingly, that you

91

Douglas Grundy

Gallows Hill, Salem, Massachusetts, where nineteen
people accused of "witchcraft" were executed in 1692

may inform us herein, which at this time was never done, viz., that Christians have such a liberty to do so. To the end we shall be satisfied on this point. . . .

This is from our meeting at Germantown, held ye 18th of the 2nd month, 1688, to be delivered to the monthly meeting at Richard Worrell's.†

GARRET HENDERICH
DERICK OP DE GRAEFF
FRANCIS DANIEL PASTORIUS
ABRAM OP DE GRAEFF

SALEM BEWITCHED, 1692

The superstition of witchcraft, under various names, has existed since the dawn of history. In Europe, from 1450 to 1650, punishment of supposed witches became rampant; thousands were stoned to death, burned at the stake, or hanged. This phenomenon spread to the American colonies in the seventeenth century, lodging with peculiar virulence in New England. In the year 1692, in Salem, Massachusetts, nineteen persons, convicted of witchcraft, were executed.

In the first selection to follow, Cotton Mather, noted New England clergyman and author, describes the behavior of "witches." The second selection is the court record of the case of Sarah Good.

THE BEHAVIOR OF WITCHES

"Memorable Providences, Relating to Witchcrafts and Possessions"

Cotton Mather

On Lords Day, the Twentieth of March, There were sundry of the afflicted Persons at Meeting. . . . They had several sore Fits in the time of Publick Worship, which did something interrupt me in my first Prayer, being so unusual. . . .

In Sermon time, when Goodwife C. was present in the Meeting-House, Ab. W. called out, *Look where Goodwife C. sits on the beam suckling her Yellow Bird betwixt her fingers! Ann Putnam,* another Girlie afflicted, said, *There was a Yellow Bird sat on my Hat as it hung on the Pin in the Pulpit;* but those that were by, restrained her from speaking loud about it.

On Monday the 21st of March, the Magistrates of Salem appointed to come to Examination of Goodwife C. And about Twelve of the Clock they went into the Meeting-House, which was thronged with Spectators . . . there were three Girls from 9 to 12 Years of Age, each of them, or thereabouts . . . did vehemently Accuse her in the Assembly of Afflicting them, by *Biting, Pinching, Strangling,* etc. And that they in their Fits see her Likeness coming to them, and bringing a *Book* to them; she said, she had no *Book;* . . . Ann Putnam did there affirm, that one day when Lieutenant *Fuller* was at Prayer at her Father's House, she saw the shape of Goodwife C. and she thought Goodwife N. Praying at the same time to the Devil; she was not sure it was Goodwife N. she thought it was; but very sure she saw the shape of Goodwife C. The said C. said, they were poor distracted Children, and no heed to be given to what they said. Mr. *Hathorne* and Mr. *Noyes* replyed, It was the Judgment of all that were present, they were *Bewitched,* and only she the Accused Person said, they were *Distracted.* It was observed several times, that if she did but bite her under lip in time of Examination, the Persons afflicted were bitten on their Arms and Wrists, and produced the *Marks* before the Magistrates, Ministers, and others. Ann being watched for that, if she did but *Pinch* her Fingers, or *Grasp* one Hand hard in another, they were Pinched, and produced the *Marks* before the Magistrates, and Spectators . . . Particularly Mrs. *Pope* complained of grievous Torment in her *Bowels,* as if they were torn out. She vehemently accused the said C. as the Instrument, and first threw her Muff at her; but that flying not home, she got off her *shoe*, and hit Goodwife C. on the Head with it. After these Postures were watched, if the said C. did but stir her Feet, they were afflicted in their *Feet*, and stamped fearfully. The afflicted Persons asked her, why she did not go to the Company of Witches which were before the Meeting-House Mustering? Did she not hear the *Drum* beat? They accused her of having Familiarity with the *Devil*, in the time of Examination, in the shape of a Black *Man* whispering in her *Ear;* . . .

They told her, she had Covenanted with the *Devil* for ten Years, six of them were gone, and four more to come . . . she denied all that was charged upon her, and said; *They could not prove a Witch;* she was that Afternoon Committed to *Salem* Prison. . . .†

THE CASE OF SARAH GOOD

Indictment vs. Sarah Good, No. 2.
Dated Salem, Feb^r 29th 1691/2

Anno Regis et Regine Willm et Mariae nunce Anglice & Quarto

Essex. ss.

The Juro^s for our Sovereigne Lord and Lady the King and Queen, presents That Sarah Good Wife of William Good of Salem Village in the County of Essex husbandman, the first Day of March in the forth year of the Reigne of our Sovereigne Lord and Lady, William and Mary by the Grace of God of England, Scottland, Ffrance and Ireland, Defenders of the faith &c and divers other Days and times as well before as after, certaine Detestable artes called witchcrafts and sorceries, wickedly and ffeloniously hath used, Practised & Exercised at and within the Towne Ship of Salem in the County of Essex aforesaid in upon and against one Elizabeth Hubbard of Salem aforesaid Singlewoman, by wch said wicked arts the said Elizabeth Hubbard, the said first Day of March in the fourth year aforesaid, and at Divers other Days and times as well before as after was and is tortured, afflicted, Pined, wasted and Tormented, as also for Sundry other acts of witchcraft by s^d Sarah Good committed and done before and since that time ag^t the Peace of our Sovereign Lord and Lady King and Queen of England and ag^t the forme of the Statute in that case made and Provided.

Witnesses Elizabeth Hubbard. Mary Walcott Jurat in luria June 28 1692. Anne Putman. jurat Abigaill Williams Jurat.
Examination of Sarah Good.
The examination of Sarah Good before the Worshipfull Assts John Harthorn Jonathan Curran

    (H)   Sarah Good what evil spirt have you familiarity with
    (SG) None
    (H)   Have you made no contracte with the devil
           Good answered no.
    (H)   Why doe you hurt these children
    (g)   I doe not hurt them. I scorn it.
    (H)   Who doe you imploy then to doe it.
    (g)   I employ no body
    (H)   What creature do you imploy then.
    (g)   no creature but I am falsely accused.
    (H)   Why did you go away muttering from Mr Parris his house.
    (g)   I did not mutter but I thanked him for what he gave my child.
    (H)   have you made no contract with the devil.
    (g)   no.

(H)   Desired the children all of them to look upon her and see if this were the person that had hurt them and so they all did looke upon her, and said this was one of the persons that did torment them—presently they were all tormented.

(H)   Sarah Good do you not see now what you have done, why doe you not tell us the truth, why doe you thus torment these poor children

(g)   I doe not torment them.

(H)   Who doe you imploy then.

(g)   I imploy nobody I scorn it.

(H)   How came they thus tormented

(g)   What doe I know you bring others here and now you charge me with it

(H)   Why who was it.

(g)   I doe not know but it was some you brought into the meeting house with you.

(H)   wee brought you into the meeting house.

(g)   but you brought in two more.

(H)   who was it then that tormented the children.

(g)   it was osburn

(H)   what is it you say when you go muttering away from persons houses

(g)   if I must tell I will tell.

(H)   doe tell us then

(g)   if I must tell, I will tell, it is the commandments. I may say my command-ments I hope.

(H)   what commandment is it.

(g)   if I must tell I will tell, it is a psalm

(H)   what psalm.

(g)   after a long time shee muttered over some part of a psalm.

(H)   who doe you serve

(g)   I serve God

(H)   What God doe you serve.

(g)   the God that made heaven and earth. though shee was not willing to mention the word God. her answers were in a very wicked spitfull manner. reflecting and retorting against the authority with base and abusive words and many lies shee was taken in. it was here said that her husband had said that he was afraid that she either was a witch or would be one very quickly. the worsh. Mr. Harthon asked him his reason why he said so of her, whether he had ever seen any thing by her, he answered no, not in this nature, but it was her bad carriage to him, and indeed said he I may say with tears that shee is an enemy to all good.

A death warrant was issued July 19, 1692, and Sarah Good was duly executed.

FIGHT FOR FREEDOM OF THE PRESS, 1736

Colonial editors were not permitted to criticize local administrations or report anything unfavorable to the Crown. In 1690 Publick Occurrances, *the first newspaper in the English colonies, was suppressed after one issue for reporting that the English forces were allying themselves with "miserable" savages.*

In 1734 John Peter Zenger, a German immigrant who published the New York Weekly Journal, *was jailed for attacking the highhanded actions of Governor William Cosby. Unable to pay the excessive bail demanded, Zenger, during his ten months' imprisonment awaiting trial, managed to have the paper appear every Monday, giving instructions to his wife "through the Hole in the Door of the Prison."*

Zenger was brought to trial for criminal libel in April, 1735. His counsel, Smith and Alexander, accused the judges of bias and were promptly disbarred. Andrew Hamilton then appeared for the prisoner and pleaded for a new interpretation of the law for seditious libel. He successfully withstood a hostile court and the jury found Zenger not guilty. This verdict first established that in trials for seditious libel it was the right of the jury, not the court, to judge the truth of the matter published.

The following excerpt is taken from Zenger's report of the trial:

"A BRIEF NARRATIVE OF THE CASE AND TRYAL OF JOHN PETER ZENGER," NEW YORK, 1736

Mr. Attorney: The case before the court is whether Mr. Zenger is guilty of libeling His Excellency the Governor of New York, and indeed the whole administration of the government. Mr. Hamilton has confessed the printing and publishing, and I think nothing is plainer than that the words in the information are *scandalous, and tend to sedition, and to disquiet the minds of the people of this province.* And if such papers are not libels, I think it may be said there can be no such thing as a libel.

Mr. Hamilton: May it please Your Honor; I cannot agree with Mr. Attorney: for though I freely acknowledge that there are such things as libels, yet I must insist at the same time that what my client is charged with is not a libel; and I observed just now that Mr. Attorney, in defining a libel, made use of the words *scandalous, seditious and tend to disquiet the people;* but (whether with design or not I will not say) he omitted the word *false. . . .*

Mr. Chief Justice: Mr. Hamilton, the court is of opinion you ought not to be permitted to prove the facts in the papers; these are the words of the book, "*It is far from being a justification of a libel that the contents thereof are true, or that the person upon whom it is made had a bad reputation, since the greater appearance there is of truth in any malicious invective so much the more provoking it is.*"

Mr. Hamilton: These are Star Chamber cases, and I was in hopes that practice had been dead with the court.

Mr. Chief Justice: Mr. Hamilton, the court have delivered their opinion, and we expect you will use us with good manners; you are not to be permitted to argue against the opinion of the court. . . .

Mr. Hamilton: I thank Your Honor. Then, gentlemen of the jury, it is to you we must now appeal, for witnesses to the truth of the facts we have offered, and are denied the liberty to prove; . . . You are citizens of New York; you are really what the law supposes you to be, *honest and lawful men;* and, according to my brief, the facts which we offer to prove were not committed in a corner; *they are notoriously known to be true;* and therefore in your justice lies our safety. And as we are denied the liberty of giving evidence, to prove the truth of what we have published, I will beg leave to lay it down as a standing rule in such cases *that the suppressing of evidence ought always to be taken for the strongest evidence;* and I hope it will have that weight with you. . . .

The question before the court and you, gentlemen of the jury, is not of small nor private concern, it is not the cause of a poor printer, nor of New York alone, which you are now trying. No! It may in its consequence affect every freeman that lives under a British government on the Main of America. It is the best cause. It is the cause of liberty; and I make no doubt but your upright conduct this day will not only entitle you to the love and esteem of your fellow citizens; but every man who prefers freedom to a life of slavery will bless and honor you as men who have baffled the attempt of tyranny, and, by an impartial and uncorrupt verdict, have laid a noble foundation for securing to ourselves, our posterity, and our neighbors that to which nature and the laws of our country have given us a right—the liberty both of exposing and opposing arbitrary power (in these parts of the world, at least) by speaking and writing truth.

Mr. Chief Justice: Gentlemen of the jury. The great pains Mr. Hamilton has taken to show how little regard juries are to pay to the opinion of the judges, and his insisting so much upon the conduct of some judges in trials of this kind, is done, no doubt, with a design that you should take but very little notice of what I may say upon this occasion. I shall therefore only observe to you that, as the facts or words in the information are confessed: the only thing that can come in question before you is whether the words, as set forth in the information, make a libel. And that is a matter of law, no doubt, and which you may leave to the court. But I shall trouble you no further with anything more of my own, but read to you the words of a learned and upright judge in a case of the like nature.

"To say that corrupt officers are appointed to administer affairs is certainly a reflection on the government. If people should not be called to account for possessing the people with an ill opinion of the government, no government can subsist. For it is necessary for all governments that the people should have a good opinion of it. And nothing can be worse to any government than to endeavor to procure animosities; as to the management of it, this has been always looked upon as a crime, and no government can be safe without it be punished."

. . . . .

The jury withdrew, and in a small time returned, and being asked by the clerk whether they were agreed of their verdict, and whether John Peter Zenger was guilty of printing and publishing the libels in the information mentioned, they answered by Thomas Hunt, their foreman: *Not Guilty.* Upon which there were three huzzas in the hall, which was crowded with people, and the next day I was discharged from my imprisonment.†

THE AMERICAN INDIAN

Estimates of the Indian population by the Bureau of the Census:

1492	846,000
1865	294,574
1890	248,253
1900	237,196
1910	265,683
1920	244,437
1930	332,397
1940	333,969

1950 estimated 400,000 (exact figures not available)

In 1887 Indian land holdings were 137,000,000 acres. In 1949 Indian land holdings were 56,000,000 acres.

"THE PRESENT PHASE OF THE INDIAN QUESTION," 1891
Thomas J. Morgan, Commissioner of Indian Affairs

. . . There are certain things which the people of the United States will do well to remember.

First.—The people of this country during the past hundred years have spent enormous sums of money in Indian wars. These wars have cost us vast quantities of treasure and multitudes of valuable lives, besides greatly hindering the development of the country, have destroyed great numbers of Indians, and have wrought upon them incalculable disaster. The record which the nation has made for itself in this sanguinary conflict is not one to be proud of.

Fifth.—The only possible solution of our Indian troubles lies in the suitable education of the rising generation. So long as the Indians remain among us aliens, speaking foreign languages, unable to communicate with us except through the uncertain and often misleading medium of interpreters, so long as they are ignorant of our ways, are superstitious and fanatical, they will remain handicapped in the struggle for existence, will be an easy prey to the medicine men and false prophet, and will be easily induced, by reason of real or imaginary wrongs, to go upon the war-path. An education that will give them the mastery of the English language, train their hands to useful industries, waken within them ambition for civilized ways, and develop a consciousness of power to achieve honorable places for themselves, and that arouses within them an earnest and abiding patriotism, will make of them American citizens, and render future conflicts between them and the Government impossible.

Eighth.—In our judgment of the Indians and of the difficulties of the Indian question, we should remember that the most perplexing element in the problem is not the Indian, but the white man. The white man furnishes the Indians with arms and ammunition; the white man provides him with whiskey; the white man encroaches upon his reservation, robs him of his stock, defrauds him of his property, invades the sanctity of his home, and treats him with contempt, thus arousing within the Indian's breast those feelings of a sense of wrong, and dishonor, and wounded manhood that prepares him to vindicate his honor and avenge his wrongs. . . .

Ninth.—We should not forget that the prime object to be aimed at is the civilization of the Indians and their absorption into our national life, and that the agencies for the accomplishment of this work are not bayonets, but books. A school-house will do vastly more for the Indians than a fort. It is better to teach the Indian to farm than to teach him to fight. . . .

Tenth.—Finally . . . let us keep our faith with the Indian; protect him in his rights to life, liberty, and the pursuit of happiness; provide for all his children a suitable English and industrial education; throw upon them the responsibilities of citizenship, and welcome them to all the privileges of American freemen.

The end at which we aim is that the American Indians shall become as speedily as possible Indian-Americans. . . .†

RED JACKET, SENECA CHIEF

Address made at a council with missionaries held in Buffalo in 1805

Brother, you say there is but one way to worship and serve the Great Spirit. If there is but one religion, why do you white people differ so much about it? Why not all agreed, as you can all read the Book?

Brother, we do not understand these things. We are told that your religion was given to your forefather and has been handed down from father to son. We also have a religion which was given to our forefathers and has been handed down to us, their children. We worship in that way. It teaches us to be thankful for all the favors we receive, to love each other, and to be united. We never quarrel about religion.

Brother, the Great Spirit has made us all, but He has made a great difference between His white and His red children. He has given us different complexions and different customs. To you He has given the arts. To these He has not opened our eyes. We know these things to be true. Since He has made so great a difference between us in other things, why may we not conclude that He has given us a different religion according to our understanding? The Great Spirit does right. He knows what is best for His children; we are satisfied.

Brother, we do not wish to destroy your religion or take it from you. We only want to enjoy our own. . . .

Brother, we are told that you have been preaching to the white people in this place. These people are our neighbors. We are acquainted with them. We will wait a little while and see what effect your preaching has upon them. If we find it does them good, makes them honest, and less disposed to cheat Indians, we will then consider again of what you have said. . . .†

RED CLOUD, SIOUX CHIEF

Speech made at a reception held in his honor at Cooper Institute, July 17, 1870

My brethren and my friends who are here before me this day, God Almighty has made us all, and he is here to bless what I have to say to you today. The Good Spirit made us both; He gave you lands and He gave us lands; He gave us these lands; you came in here and we respected you as brothers. God Almighty made you, but made you all white and clothed you; when He made us He made us with red skins and poor; now you have come. When you first came we were very many, and you were few, now you are many, and we are getting very few, and we are poor. You do not know who appears before you today to speak. I am a representative of the original American race the first people of this continent. We are good and not bad. The reports that you hear concerning us are all on one side. We are always well-disposed to them. You are here told that we are traders and thieves, and it is not so. We have given you nearly all our lands, and if we had any more land to give we would be very glad to give it. We have nothing more. We are driven into a very little land, and we want you now, as our dear friends, to help us with the government of the United States. The Great Father made us poor and ignorant—made you rich and wise, and more skillful in these things that we know nothing about. The Great Father, the Good Father in heaven, made you all to eat tame food—made us to eat wild food—gives us the wild food. You ask anybody who has gone through our country to California; ask those who have settled there and in Utah, and you will find that we have treated them always well. You have children; we have children. You want to raise your children and make them happy and prosperous; we want to raise and make them happy and prosperous. We ask you to help us to do it. At the mouth of the Horse Creek, in 1852, the Great Father made a treaty with us by which we agreed to let all that country open for 55 years for the transit of those who were going through. We kept this treaty; we never treated any man wrong; we never committed any murder or depredation until afterward the troops were sent into that country, and the troops killed our people and ill-treated them, and thus war and trouble arose; but before the troops were sent there we were quiet and peaceable, and there was no disturbance. Since that time there have been various goods sent from time to time to us, the only ones that ever reached us, and then after they reached us (very soon after) the Government took them away. You, as good men, ought to help us to these goods. Col. Fitzpatrick of the Government said we must all go to farm, and some of the people went to Fort Laramie and were badly treated. I only want to do that which is peaceful, and the Great Fathers know it, and also the Great Father who made us both. I came to Washington to see the Great Father in order to have peace, and in order to have peace continue. That is all we want, and that is the reason why we are here now.

In 1868 men came out and brought papers. We are ignorant and do not read papers, and they did not tell us right what was in these papers. We wanted them to take away their forts, leave our country, would not make war, and give our traders something. They said we had bound ourselves to trade on the Missouri, and we said, No, we did not want that.

The interpreters deceived us. When I went to Washington I saw the great Father. The Great Father showed me what the treaties were; he showed me all these points, and showed me that the interpreters had deceived me, and did not let me know what the right side of the treaty was. All I want is right and justice. . . . I represent the Sioux nation; they will be governed by what I say and what I represent. . . . Look at me. I am poor and naked, but I am the chief of the nation. We do not want riches, we do not ask for riches, but we want our children properly trained and brought up. We look to you for your sympathy. Our riches will not do us no good; we cannot take away into the other world anything we have—we want to have love and peace . . . we would like to know why commissioners are sent out there to do nothing but rob them and get the riches of this world away from us? I was brought up among the traders and those who came out there in those early times. I had a good time for they treated us nicely and well. They taught me how to wear clothes and use tobacco, and to use fire-arms and ammunition, and all went on very well until the Great Father sent out another kind of men—men who drank whisky. He sent out whiskymen, men who drank and quarreled, men who were so bad that he could not keep them at home, and so he sent them out there. I have sent a great many words to the Great Father, but I don't know that they ever reach the Great Father. They were drowned on the way, therefore I was a little offended with it. The words I told the Great Father lately would never come to him, so I thought I would come and tell you myself. And I am going to leave you today, and I am going back to my home. I want to tell the people that we cannot trust his agents and superintendents. I don't want strange people that we know nothing about. I am very glad that you belong to us. I am very glad that we have come here and found you and that we can understand one another. I don't want any more such men sent out there, who are so poor that when they come out there their first thoughts are how they can fill their own pockets. We want preserves in our reserves. We want honest men and we want you to help to keep us in the lands that belong to us so that we may not be a prey to those who are viciously disposed. I am going back home. I am very glad that you have listened to me, and I wish you good bye and give you an affectionate farewell.†

CHIEF SEATTLE, DWAMISH CHIEF

Speech made before signing the Treaty of 1855

. . . We are two distinct races with separate origins and separate destinies. There is little in common between us. To us the ashes of our ancestors are sacred and their resting place is hallowed ground. You wander far from the graves of your ancestors and seemingly without regret. Your religion was written on tables of stone by the iron finger of your God so that you could not forget. The Red Man could never comprehend nor remember it. Our religion is the traditions of our ancestors—the dreams of our old men, given them in the solemn hours of night by the great spirit, and the visions of our sachems, and is written in the hearts of our people.

Your dead cease to love you and the land of their nativity as soon as they pass the portals of the tomb and wander away beyond the stars. They are soon forgotten and never return. Our dead never forget the beautiful world that gave them being—they still love its verdant valleys, its murmuring rivers, its magnificent mountains, sequestered vales and verdant-lined lakes and bays, and ever yearn in tender, fond affection over the lonely hearted living, and often return from the happy hunting ground to visit, guide, console and comfort them.

(Continued, page 109)

Opposite: "White House," Arizona.   Cliff dwellings of Pueblo tribes, eleventh and twelfth centuries.

Ansel Adams

Left: Red Cloud, Sioux Chief (1822-1909). "I am a representative of th original American race, the first peo ple of this continent . . . . I am poo and naked, but I am the chief o the nation."

Above: Pretty Hail, Sioux, in cere monial dress, 1890's.

Opposite: Three Feathers, Nez Perce "Words do not pay for my dead peo ple."—Chief Joseph (Nez Perce)

Cheyenne tepees.   Photograph, 1867–1874.

Plains Indian answering smoke signal—end of nineteenth century.

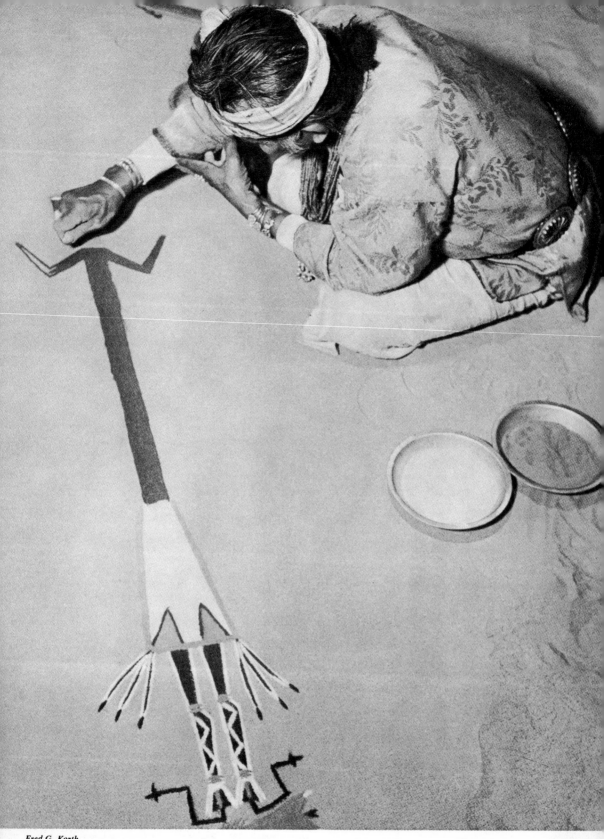

Present day Navajo singer or medicine man preparing a sand painting representing one of the Holy People, in order to effect a cure.

Ray Atkeson

Navajos in Monument Valley, Arizona, 1950's.

Maurice Terrell, courtesy "Look"

Indian school, Shiprock, New Mexico, 1950's.

"The only possible solution of our Indian troubles lies in the suitable education of the rising generation"—Thomas J. Morgan

Day and night cannot dwell together. The red man has ever fled the approach of the white man as the morning mist flees before the rising sun. However, your proposition seems fair and I think that my folks will accept it and will retire to the reservation you offer them. . . . It matters little where we pass the remnant of our days. They will not be many. . . . A few more moons. A few more winters—and not one of the descendants of the mighty hosts that once moved over this broad land or lived in happy homes, protected by the Great Spirit, will remain to mourn over the graves of a people—once more powerful than yours. But why should I mourn at the untimely fate of my people? Tribe follows tribe, and nation follows nation, and regret is useless. Your time of decay may be distant— but it will surely come, for even the white man whose God walked and talked with him as friend with friend, can not be exempt from the common destiny. We may be brothers after all. We will see.

We will ponder your proposition and when we decide we will let you know. But should we accept it, I here and now make this condition—that we will not be denied the privilege without molestation, of visiting at any time the tombs of our ancestors. . . . Every part of this soil is sacred. In the estimation of many people, every hillside, every valley, every plain and grove, has been hallowed by some sad or happy event in days long vanished. Even the rocks, which seem to be dumb and dead as they swelter in the sun along the silent shore thrill with memories of stirring events connected with the lives of my people, and the very dust upon which you now stand responds more lovingly to their footsteps than to yours, because it is rich with the dust of our ancestors and our bare feet are conscious of the sympathetic touch. . . . And when the last red man shall have become a myth among the white man . . . when your children's children think themselves alone in the field, the store, the shop, upon the highway, or on the silence of the pathless woods, they will not be alone. In all the earth there is no place dedicated to solitude. At night when the streets of your cities and villages are silent and you think them deserted, they will throng with the returning hosts that once filled them and still love this beautiful land. The white man will never be alone.

Let him be just and deal kindly with my people, for the dead are not powerless. Dead— I say? There is no death. Only a change of worlds.†

CHIEF JOSEPH, NEZ PERCE CHIEF

"An Indian's View of Indian Affairs," 1879

My friends, I have been asked to show you my heart. I am glad to have a chance to do so. I want the white people to understand my people. Some of you think an Indian is like a wild animal. This is a great mistake. I will tell you all about our people, and then you can judge whether an Indian is a man or not. I believe much trouble and blood would be saved if we opened our hearts more. I will tell you in my way how the Indian sees things. The white man has more words to tell you how they look to him, but it does not require many words to speak the truth. What I have to say will come from my heart, and I will speak with a straight tongue. Ah-cum-kin-i-ma-me-hut (the Great Spirit) is looking at me, and will hear me.

My name is In-mut-too-yah-lat-lat [Thunder traveling over the Mountains]. I am chief of the Wal-lam-wat-kin band of Chute-pa-lu, or Nez Perces (nose-pierced Indians). I was born in eastern Oregon, thirty-eight winters ago. My father was chief before me. When a young man, he was called Joseph by Mr. Spaulding, a missionary. He died a few years ago. There was no stain on his hands of the blood of a white man. He left a good name on the earth. He advised me well for my people.

Our fathers gave us many laws, which they had learned from their fathers. These laws were good. They told us to treat all men as they treated us; that we should never be the first to break a bargain; that it was a disgrace to tell a lie; that we should speak only the truth; that it was a shame for one man to take from another his wife, or his property without paying for it. We were taught to believe that the Great Spirit sees and hears everything, and that he never forgets; that hereafter he will give every man a spirit-home according to his deserts: if he has been a good man, he will have a good home; if he has been a bad man, he will have a bad home. This I believe, and all my people believe the same.†

CHIEF JOSEPH CALLS ON PRESIDENT HAYES

At last I was granted permission to come to Washington and bring my friend Yellow Bull and our interpreter with me. I am glad I came. I have shaken hands with a good many friends, but there are some things I want to know which no one seems able to explain. I cannot understand how the Government sends a man out to fight us, as it did General Miles, and then breaks his word. Such a government has something wrong about it. I cannot understand why so many chiefs are allowed to talk so many different ways, and promise so many different things. I have seen the Great Father Chief [President Hayes]; the Next Great Chief [Secretary of the Interior]; the Commissioner Chief [Hoyt]; the Law Chief [General Butler]; and many other law chiefs [Congressmen] and they all say they are my friends, and that I shall have justice, but while all their mouths talk right I do not understand why nothing is done for my people. I have heard talk and talk but nothing is done. Good words do not last long unless they amount to something. Words do not pay for my dead people. They do not pay for my country now overrun by white men. They do not protect my father's grave. They do not pay for my horses and cattle. Good words do not give me back my children. Good words will not make good the promise of your war chief, General Miles. Good words will not give my people good health and stop them from dying. Good words will not get my people a home where they can live in peace and take care of themselves. I am tired of talk that comes to nothing. It makes my heart sick when I remember all the good words and all the broken promises. There has been too much talking by men who had no right to talk. Too many misinterpretations have been made; too many misunderstandings have come up between the white men and the Indians. If the white man wants to live in peace with the Indian he can live in peace. There need be no trouble. Treat all men alike. Give them the same laws. Give them all an even chance to live and grow. All men were made by the same Great Spirit Chief. They are all brothers. The earth is the mother of all people, and all people should have equal rights upon it. You might as well expect all rivers to run backward as that any man who was born a free man should be contented penned up and denied liberty to go where he pleases. If you tie a horse to a stake, do you expect he will grow fat? If you pen an Indian up on a small spot of earth and compel him to stay there, he will not be contented nor will he grow and prosper. I have asked some of the Great White Chiefs where they get their authority to say to the Indian that he shall stay in one place, while he sees white men going where they please. They cannot tell me.

I only ask of the Government to be treated as all other men are treated. If I cannot go to my own home, let me have a home in a country where my people will not die so fast. I would like to go to Bitter Root Valley. There my people would be happy; where they are now they are dying. Three have died since I left my camp to come to Washington.

When I think of our condition, my heart is heavy. I see men of my own race treated as outlaws and driven from country to country, or shot down like animals.

I know that my race must change. We cannot hold our own with the white men as we are. We only ask an even chance to live as other men live. We ask to be recognized as men.

We ask that the same law shall work alike on all men. If an Indian breaks the law, punish him by the law. If a white man breaks the law, punish him also.

Let me be a free man, free to travel, free to stop, free to work, free to trade where I choose, free to choose my own teachers, free to follow the religion of my fathers, free to talk, think and act for myself—and I will obey every law or submit to the penalty.

Whenever the white man treats the Indian as they treat each other then we shall have no more wars. We shall be all alike—brothers of one father and mother, with one sky above us and one country around us and one government for all. Then the Great Spirit Chief who rules above will smile upon this land and send rain to wash out the bloody spots made by brothers' hands upon the face of the earth. For this time the Indian race is waiting and praying. I hope no more groans of wounded men and women will ever go to the ear of the Great Spirit Chief above, and that all people may be one people.†

"TO SET THE INDIANS FREE," 1949
Oliver La Farge, Anthropologist, Author, President of the Association on American-Indian Affairs

Human affairs are always complex, Indian affairs perhaps a little more so than usual, because of special dilemmas and the conflict between cultures. The complexity can be illustrated by considering a proposal to remove wardship and Indian Bureau control from an average tribe. (An "average tribe" is, of course, a fiction, but the type is fairly clear.) Here is a group of a few thousand people, of whom the oldest speak no English; the rest are semi-educated by white standards. None has gone to college; none has become a technician.

Tuberculosis is endemic and the general disease rate is high, but the population is increasing. The tribe owns a reservation, mostly semi-arid, with some farming land and a little timber. About two-thirds of the tribe can earn a living from this area, chiefly by grazing cattle; the others depend upon occasional labor, and relief. The tribe is organized, has a tribal council and governs itself moderately well.

These people are citizens *and wards* of the United States. "Citizens" means just that, although a few recalcitrant states, notably Arizona and New Mexico, still struggle valiantly to deny them their full rights; the meaning of "ward" requires more explanation.

The tribe's oldest, basic asset is real estate, a reservation, set aside for its exclusive use because its people are Indians. This hereditary property, unique in American law, is held in trust for the tribe by the United States, and is tax-exempt. It, and certain revenues derived from it, may not be disposed of or alienated in any way without the consent of both the trustee and the Indians, except that Congress may, and too often does, appropriate from tribal moneys "for the benefit" of the tribes, without their consent. Further, the federal government is obligated to furnish its wards with schools, hospitals and many other services which communities ordinarily provide for themselves. State law and police power stop at the reservation boundary; the territory within is subject only to federal law and the ordinances passed by the tribe itself. That is the extent of wardship. It cannot be emphasized too strongly that there is no restriction upon the individual, that he may go and come as he chooses, live where he chooses. It is well worth remembering that the late Charles Curtis was a ward Indian when he was Vice President of the United States....

When we plan to terminate a tribe's wardship, two conditions must be met: the Indians must be culturally and economically ready to fend for themselves; the surrounding community, both the local community and the state as a whole, must be ready to accept them....

If wardship ends, the Indians' property must be taxed. The tribe is barely getting by; the extra burden of a property tax would probably ruin its shaky economy. The land is so poor, and the improvements so slight, that state and county would lose money if they imposed a tax and took over the services that are now being rendered by the federal government. Even prosperous tribes are naturally reluctant to give up this exemption. Hence among both Indians and the Indian states there is a wide-spread opposition to abolishing wardship. . . .

Most reflective Indians know very well that they are not yet ready to fend for themselves in our culture. For this they blame the Indian Bureau's failure to educate them. They might also blame themselves for past resistance to education. We must not forget the strong influence of an ancient, deep-seated culture, based upon premises entirely unlike ours. Indian culture is remarkably non-competitive. Ours, equally ancient, is based upon competition and highly individual effort to survive in a general free-for-all. . . .

If the hand of the federal government were removed, if the Indians had to look to the surrounding community for the group services required for survival in today's world, what would they find? They know that they are a few thousands surrounded by millions. . . . They may have a thousand criticisms of the Bureau of Indian Affairs, but they know that it exists to serve them and that, with all its faults, they are safer with it than they would be as a tiny minority in a population which mainly regards Indians as legitimate objects of exploitation. . . .

One of the essential difficulties of the Indian problem is that so many laws, procedures and ordinances which we establish for ourselves locally are set up for the Indians by a distant Congress preoccupied with much greater matters. The only way in which the Indians can go free is to obtain the only real security, the comprehension and sympathy of the white world, which will enable them to fend for themselves and face down local bigotries. It is in the lack of this, and not in their special legal status, that Indians today are not free. . . .

The Indian problem is national. Its solution begins with the people—including the Indians. These "wards" of ours have great innate ability; given an even chance, they will soon enough override local prejudices and discriminations. When they are solidly self-supporting, masters of our techniques and devices, sound in health, the Indians themselves will abolish the Indian Bureau by rendering it superfluous.†

THE MORMON TREK TO UTAH, 1846

"THE DISCOURSES OF BRIGHAM YOUNG"

The term Mormon *is applied to a religious sect founded by Joseph Smith in New York state in 1830. The Angel Moroni appeared to Smith in a series of visions, predicting the second coming of Christ, and giving directions for finding an ancient record preserved on plates of gold. This record Smith translated (1827) into the* Book of Mormon.

Early in their history the Mormons' religious beliefs brought them into conflict with other religious faiths and with established political institutions, including differences over Constitutional limitations. (In 1852 their sanction of polygamy caused violent opposition.) Joseph Smith was jailed and killed by a mob in Illinois in 1844. Two years later Brigham Young led the Mormons westward to establish their own settlement. Today Utah stands a symbol to Mormon foresight, industry, and ability. Young's account follows:

. . . We lived in the State of Illinois a few years; and here, as elsewhere, persecution overtook us. It came from Missouri, centering itself upon Joseph [Smith], and fastened itself upon others. We lived in Illinois from 1839 to 1844, by which time they again succeeded in kindling the spirit of persecution against Joseph and the Latter-day Saints. Treason! Treason! they cried, calling us murderers, thieves, liars, adulterers, and the worst people on the earth. And this was done by the priests, those pious dispensers of the Christian religion whose charity was supposed to be extended to all men, Christian and heathen; they were joined by drunkards, gamblers, thieves, liars, in crying against the Latter-day Saints. They took Joseph and Hyrum, and as a guarantee for their safety, Governor Thomas Ford pledged the faith of the State of Illinois. They were imprisoned, on the pretense of safe keeping, because the mob was so enraged and violent. The Governor left them in the hands of the mob, who entered the prison and shot them dead. John Taylor, who is present with us today, was in prison too, and was also shot, and was confined to his bed for several months afterwards. After the mob had committed these murders, they came upon us and burned our houses and grain. When the brethren would go out to put out the fire, the mob would lie concealed under fences, and in the darkness of the night, they would shoot them. At last they succeeded in driving us from the state of Illinois. . . .

We left Nauvoo in February, 1846. There remained behind a few of the very poor, the sick and the aged, who suffered again from the violence of the mob; they were whipped and beaten, and had their houses burned. We travelled west, stopping in places, building settlements, where we left the poor who could not travel any farther with the company. Exactly thirty years today myself, with others, came out of what we named Emigration Canyon; we crossed the Big and Little mountains, and came down the valley about three quarters of a mile south of this. We located, and we looked about, and finally we came and camped between the two forks of City Creek, one of which ran south-west and the other west. Here we planted our standard on this temple block and the one above it; here we pitched our camps and determined that here we would settle and stop. . . .

We wish strangers to understand that we did not come here out of choice, but because we were obliged to go somewhere, and this was the best place we could find. It was impossible for any person to live here unless he labored hard and battled and fought against the elements, but it was a first-rate place to raise Latter-day Saints, and we shall be blessed in living here, and shall yet make it like the Garden of Eden; and the Lord Almighty will hedge about his Saints and defend and preserve them if they will do his will. The only fear I have is that we will not do right; if we do we will be like a city set on a hill, our light will not be hid. . . .

Mark our settlements for six hundred miles in these mountains and then mark the path that we made coming here, building the bridges and making the roads across the prairies, mountains and canyons! We came here penniless in old wagons, our friends back telling us to "take all the provisions you can: for you can get no more! Take all the seed grain you can, for you can get none there!" We did this, and in addition to all this we have gathered all the poor we could, and the Lord has planted us in these valleys, promising that he would hide us up for a little season until his wrath and indignation passed over the nations. Will we trust in the Lord? Yes.†

JOHN BROWN (1800–1859)

John Brown, the famous abolitionist, was one of the most colorful characters in American history. Believing in the immediate and forceful liberation of slaves, he succeeded in arming and helping many to escape to free territory via the "underground railway." Unfortunately, Brown was a fanatic who took the law into his own hands. In Pottawatamie, Kansas, on the night of May 24, 1856, in order "to cause a restraining fear," Brown, with four of his sons and two other men, dragged five pro-slavery men from their beds and deliberately murdered them. In this act he claimed he was an instrument in the hands of God.

In 1859 Brown's raid on Harper's Ferry ended in his capture, trial, and execution. The popularity of his cause and his courage during the trial and execution made Brown a hero to many in the North but increased the friction between North and South. A year and a half later the nation exploded into civil war.

Brown's extemporaneous speech, delivered in the court when his sentence was passed, is the first selection that follows. The second is an eyewitness account of the execution written by Major Thomas Randolph Preston, commander of the Virginia Military Institute cadets, who was appointed by Governor Wise to protect the sheriff assigned to execute Brown. This account was contained in a letter Preston wrote to his wife, Margaret Junkin Preston.

ON BEING SENTENCED TO DEATH, NOVEMBER 30, 1859
John Brown

I have, may it please the Court, a few words to say.

In the first place, I deny everything but what I have all along admitted: of a design on my part to free slaves. I intended certainly to have made a clean thing of that matter, as I did last winter, when I went into Missouri and there took slaves without the snapping of a gun on either side, moving them through the country, and finally leaving them in Canada. I designed to have done the same thing again on a larger scale. That was all I intended. I never did intend murder, or treason, or the destruction of property, or to exercise or incite slaves to rebellion, or to make insurrection.

I have another objection, and that is that it is unjust that I should suffer such a penalty. Had I interfered in the manner which I admit, and which I admit has been fairly proved—for I admire the truthfulness and candor of the greater portion of the witnesses who have testified in this case—Had I so interfered in behalf of the rich, the powerful, the intelligent, the so-called great, or in behalf of any of their friends, either father, mother, brother, sister, wife or children, or any of that class, and suffered and sacrificed what I have in this interference, it would have been all right. Every man in this Court would have deemed it an act worthy of reward rather than punishment.

This Court acknowledges, too, as I suppose, the validity of the law of God. I see a book kissed, which I suppose to be the Bible, or at least the New Testament, which teaches me that all things whatsoever I would that men should do to me, I should do even so to them. It teaches me, further, to remember them that are in bonds as bound with them. I endeavored to act up to that instruction. I say I am yet too young to understand that God is any respecter of persons. I believe that to have interfered as I have done, as I have always freely admitted I have done, in behalf of His despised poor, I did no wrong, but right. Now, if it is deemed necessary that I should forfeit my life for the furtherance of the ends of justice, and mingle my blood further with the blood of my children and with the blood of millions in this slave country whose rights are disregarded by wicked, cruel, and unjust enactments, I say, let it be done.

Let me say one word further. I feel entirely satisfied with the treatment I have received on my trial. Considering all the circumstances, it has been more generous than I expected. But I feel no consciousness of guilt. I have stated from the first what was my intention, and what was not. I never had any design against the liberty of any person, nor any disposition to commit treason or incite slaves to rebel or make any general insurrection. I never encouraged any man to do so, but always discouraged any idea of that kind.

Let me say, also, in regard to the statements made by some of those who were connected with me, I hear it has been stated by some of them that I have induced them to join me. But the contrary is true. I do not say this to injure them, but as regretting their weakness. Not one but joined me of his own accord, and the greater part at their own expense. A number of them I never saw, and never had a word of conversation with, till the day they came to me, and that was for the purpose I have stated.

Now, I have done.

EYEWITNESS ACCOUNT OF THE EXECUTION OF JOHN BROWN

Thomas Randolph Preston

Charlestown, December 2, 1859

. . . The execution is over. We have just returned from the field, and I sit down to give you some account of it. . . . Between eight and nine o'clock the troops began to put themselves in motion to occupy the position assigned to them on the field. To Colonel Smith had been assigned the superintendence of the execution, and he and his staff were the only mounted officers on the ground, until the major-general and his staff appeared. By ten o'clock all was arrayed. . . .

The whole enclosure was lined by cavalry troops, posted as sentinels, with their officers. . . . Outside this enclosure were other companies acting as rangers and scouts. . . . The military force was about 1500. . . . The jail was guarded by several companies of infantry, and pieces of artillery were put in position for defense.

Shortly before eleven o'clock, the prisoner was taken from the jail and the funeral cortege was put in motion. First came three companies—then the criminal's wagon, drawn by two large white horses. John Brown was seated on his coffin, accompanied by the sheriff and two other persons. The wagon drove to the foot of the gallows, and Brown descended with alacrity, and without assistance, and ascended the steep steps to the platform. He made no speech; had he desired it, it would not have been permitted. Any speech of his must of necessity have been unlawful, as being directed against the peace and dignity of the Commonwealth, and, as such, could not be allowed by those who were then engaged in the most solemn and extreme vindication of the Law. His manner was free from trepidation, but his countenance was not without concern, and it seemed to me to have a little cast of wildness. He stood upon the scaffold but a short time giving brief adieus to those about him, when he was properly pinioned, the white cap drawn over his face, the noose adjusted and attached to the hook above, and he was moved blindfold a few steps forward. It was curious to note how the instincts of nature operated to make him careful in putting out his feet, as if afraid he would walk off the scaffold. The man who stood unblenched on the brink of eternity was afraid of falling a few feet to the ground!

He was now all ready. The sheriff asked him if he should give him a private signal before the fatal moment. He replied in a voice that sounded to me unnaturally natural—so composed was its tone and so distinct its articulation—that "it did not matter to him, if only they would not keep him waiting too long." He *was* kept waiting, however. The troops that had formed his escort had to be put in their proper position, and while this was going on, he stood for ten or fifteen minutes blindfold, the rope around his neck, and his feet on the treacherous platform, expecting instantly the fatal act. But he stood for this comparatively long time upright as a soldier in position, and motionless. I was close to him, and watched him narrowly, to see if I could perceive any signs of shrinking or trembling in his person. Once I thought I saw his knees tremble, but it was only the wind blowing his loose trousers. His firmness was subjected to still further trial by hearing Colonel Smith announce to the sheriff, "We are all ready, Mr. Campbell." The sheriff did not hear, or did not comprehend, and in a louder tone the announcement was made. But the culprit still stood steady, until the sheriff, descending the flight of steps, with a well directed blow of a hatchet, severed the rope that held up the trap door, which instantly sank sheer beneath him, and he fell about three feet. And the man of strong and bloody hand, of fierce passions, of iron will, of wonderful vicissitudes—the terrible partisan of Kansas—the capturer of the United States Arsenal at Harper's Ferry—the would-be

Catiline of the South—the demi-God of the Abolitionists—the man execrated and lauded—damned and prayed for—the man who in his motives, his means, his plans, and his successes must ever be a wonder, a puzzle and a mystery—John Brown was hanging between heaven and earth.

There was profoundest stillness during the time his struggles continued, growing feebler and feebler at each abortive attempt to breathe. His knees were scarcely bent, his arms were drawn up to a right angle at the elbow, with the hands clenched; but there was no writhing of the body, no violent heaving of the chest. At each feebler effort at respiration, the arms sank lower, and the legs hung more relaxed, until at last, straight and lank he dangled, swayed slightly to and fro by the wind.

It was a moment of deep solemnity, and suggestive of thoughts that made the bosom swell. The field of execution was a rising ground that commanded the outstretching valley from mountain to mountain, and their still grandeur gave sublimity to the outline. . . . Before us the greatest array of disciplined forces ever seen in Virginia, infantry, cavalry, and artillery combined, composed of the old Commonwealth's choicest sons, and commanded by her best officers, and the great canopy of the sky, overarching all, came to add its sublimity—ever present, but only realized when great things are occurring beneath it.

But the moral scene was the great point. A sovereign State had been assailed, and she had uttered but a hint, and her sons had hastened to show that they were ready to defend her. Law had been violated by actual murder and attempted treason, and that gibbet was erected by Law, and to uphold Law was this military force assembled. But greater still, God's holy law and righteous will was vindicated. "Thou shalt not kill." "Whoso sheddeth man's blood, by man shall his blood be shed." And here the gray-haired man of violence meets his fate, after he has seen his two sons cut down before him earlier in the same career of violence into which he had introduced them. So perish all such enemies of Virginia! all such enemies of Union! all such foes of the human race! So I felt, and so I said, without a shade of animosity, as I turned to break the silence, to those around me. Yet the mystery was awful—to see the human form thus treated by man—to see life suddenly stopped in its current, and to ask one's self the question without answer, "And what then?"

In all that array there was not, I suppose, one throb of sympathy for the offender. All felt in the depths of their hearts that it was right. On the other hand there was not one word of exultation or insult. From the beginning to the end, all was marked by the most absolute decorum and solemnity. There was no military music, no saluting of troops as they passed one another, nor anything done for show. The criminal hung upon the gallows for nearly forty minutes, and after being examined by a whole staff of surgeons, was deposited in a neat coffin, to be delivered to his friends, and transported to Harper's Ferry, where his wife awaited it. . . .

Brown would not have the assistance of any minister in the jail, during his last days, nor their presence with him on the scaffold. In going from the prison to the place of execution, he said very little, only assuring those who were with him that he had no fear, nor had he at any time of his life known what fear was. When he entered the gate of the enclosure, he expressed his admiration of the beauty of the surrounding country, and pointing to different residences, asked who were the owners of them.

There was a very small crowd to witness the execution. Governor Wise and General Taliaferro both issued proclamations exhorting the citizens to remain at home and guard their property, and warning them of possible danger. . . .

There is but one opinion as to the completeness of the arrangements made on the occasion, and the absolute success with which they were carried out . . . the excellence of it is that everything was arranged solely with a view to efficiency, and not for the effect upon the eye. Had it been intended for a mere spectacle, it could not have been more imposing; had actual need occurred, it was the best possible arrangement. . . .

116

John Brown. Painting by John Steuart Curry.

THE EMANCIPATION PROCLAMATION, JANUARY 1, 1863

Abraham Lincoln

Whereas, on the twenty-second day of September, in the year of our Lord one thousand eight hundred and sixty-two, a proclamation was issued by the President of the United States, containing, among other things, the following, to wit:

That on the first day of January, in the year of our Lord one thousand eight hundred and sixty-three, all persons held as slaves within any State, or designated part of a State, the people whereof shall then be in rebellion against the United States, shall be then, thenceforward, and forever free; and the Executive Government of the United States, including the military and naval authority thereof, will recognize and maintain the freedom of such persons, and will do no act or acts to repress such persons, or any of them, in any efforts they may make for their actual freedom.

That the Executive will, on the first day of January aforesaid, by proclamation, designate the States and parts of States, if any, in which the people thereof respectively shall then be in rebellion against the United States; and the fact that any State, or the people thereof, shall on that day be in good faith represented in the Congress of the United States by members chosen thereto at elections wherein a majority of the qualified voters of such State shall have participated, shall in the absence of strong countervailing testimony be deemed conclusive evidence that such State and the people thereof are not then in rebellion against the United States.

Now, therefore, I, Abraham Lincoln, President of the United States, by virtue of the power in me vested as Commander-in-Chief of the Army and Navy of the United States, in time of actual armed rebellion against the authority and government of the United States, and as a fit and necessary war measure for suppressing said rebellion, do, on this first day of January, in the year of our Lord one thousand eight hundred and sixty-three, and in accordance with my purpose so to do, publicly proclaimed for the full period of 100 days from the days first above mentioned, order and designate as the States and parts of States wherein the people thereof, respectively, are this day in rebellion against the United States, the following to wit:

Arkansas, Texas, Louisiana (except the parishes of St. Bernard, Plaquemines, Jefferson, St. John, St. Charles, St. James, Ascension, Assumption, Terre Bonne, Lafourche, St. Mary, St. Martin, and Orleans, including the city of New Orleans), Mississippi, Alabama, Florida, Georgia, South Carolina, North Carolina, and Virginia (except the forty-eight counties designated as West Virginia, and also the counties of Berkeley, Accomac, Northampton, Elizabeth City, York, Princess Anne, and Norfolk, including the cities of Norfolk and Portsmouth), and which excepted parts are for the present left precisely as if this proclamation were not issued.

And by virtue of the power and for the purpose aforesaid, I do order and declare that all persons held as slaves within said designated States and parts of States are, and henceforward shall be, free; and that the Executive Government of the United States, including the military and naval authorities thereof, shall recognize and maintain the freedom of said persons.

And I hereby enjoin upon the people so declared to be free to abstain from all violence, unless in necessary self-defense; and I recommend to them that, in all cases where allowed, they labor faithfully for reasonable wages.

And I further declare and make known that such persons of suitable condition will be received into the armed service of the United States to garrison forts, positions, stations, and other places, and to man vessels of all sorts in said service.

And upon this act, sincerely believed to be an act of justice, warranted by the Consti-

A rare photograph of slaves. Sweet potato planting on James
Hopkinson's plantation, Edisto Island, South Carolina, 1862.

tution upon military necessity, I invoke the considerate judgment of mankind and the
gracious favor of Almighty God.

In witness whereof, I have hereunto set my hand and caused the seal of the United
States to be affixed.

*Done at the city of Washington, the first day of January, in the year of our Lord one
thousand eight hundred and sixty-three, and of the independence of the United States of
America the eighty-seventh.*

By the President: ABRAHAM LINCOLN
WILLIAM H. SEWARD, *Secretary of State*

"THE AMERICAN STANDARD"
Booker T. Washington (1856–1915)

*Born a slave in Franklin County, Virginia, Booker T. Washington rose to become the great
educational leader of the Negro people in the United States. In 1881 he founded Tuskegee
Institute in Alabama.*

*The following excerpt is taken from an address Washington gave before the Harvard Alumni
in 1896, after receiving an honorary degree of Master of Arts from Harvard University:*

119

. . . If my life in the past has meant anything in the lifting up of my people and the bringing about of better relations between your race and mine, I assure you from this day it will mean doubly more. In the economy of God, there is but one standard by which an individual can succeed—there is but one for a race. This country demands that every race measure itself by the American standard. By it a race must rise or fall, succeed or fail, and in the last analysis mere sentiment counts for little. During the next half century or more my race must continue passing through the severe American crucible. We are to be tested in our patience, our forbearance, our perseverance, our power to endure wrong, to withstand

Booker T. Washington.

temptations, to economize, to acquire and use skill; our ability to compete, to succeed in commerce, to disregard the superficial for the real, the appearance for the substance, to be great and yet small, learned and yet simple, high and yet the servant of all. This, this is the passport to all that is best in the life of our Republic, and the Negro must possess it, or be debarred.

While we are thus being tested, I beg of you to remember that wherever our life touches yours, we help or hinder. Wherever your life touches ours, you make us stronger or weaker. No member of your race in any part of our country can harm the meanest member of mine, without the proudest and bluest blood in Massachusetts being degraded. When Mississippi commits crime, New England commits crime, and in so much lowers the standard of your civilization. There is not escape—man drags man down, or man lifts man up.

In working out our destiny, while the main burden and center of activity must be with us, we shall need in a large measure in the years that are to come as we have in the past, the help, the encouragement, the guidance that the strong can give the weak. Thus helped, we of both races in the South soon shall throw off the shackles of racial and sectional prejudices and rise as Harvard University has risen and as we all should rise, above the clouds of ignorance, narrowness, and selfishness, into that atmosphere, that pure sunshine, where it will be our highest ambition to serve man, our brother, regardless of race or previous condition.†

SEGREGATION IN PUBLIC SCHOOLS ENDED

UNANIMOUS DECISION, SUPREME COURT OF THE UNITED STATES, MAY 17, 1954*

Today, education is perhaps the most important function of state and local governments. Compulsory school attendance laws and the great expenditures for education both demonstrate our recognition of the importance of education to our democratic society . . . it is doubtful that any child may reasonably be expected to succeed in life if he is denied the opportunity of an education. Such an opportunity, where the state has undertaken to provide it, is a right which must be made available to all on equal terms.

We then come to the question presented: Does segregation of children in public schools solely on the basis of race, even though the physical facilities and other "tangible" factors may be equal, deprive the children of the minority group of equal educational opportunities? We believe that it does. . . . To separate them from others of similar age and qualifications solely because of their race generates a feeling of inferiority as to their status in the community that may affect their hearts and minds in a way unlikely ever to be undone . . .

We conclude that in the field of public education the doctrine of "separate but equal" has no place. Separate educational facilities are inherently unequal. Therefore, we hold that the plaintiffs and others simularly situated for whom actions have been brought are, by reason of the segregation complained of, deprived of the equal protection of the laws guaranteed by the Fourteenth Amendment . . .†

* Brown *v.* Board of Education.

SUSAN B. ANTHONY

ON WOMEN'S RIGHT TO SUFFRAGE, 1873

"All men and women are created equal" was the battle cry of women when they made their Declaration of Sentiments and Resolutions at Seneca Falls, New York, 1848. Wyoming was the first to enfranchise women in 1869, but it was not until August 26, 1920, that all women were enfranchised by passage of the nineteenth amendment to the Constitution.

Susan B. Anthony was arrested in 1872 for casting a vote in the presidential election. The speech that follows was made by this famous suffragist in 1873:

Friends and Fellow Citizens:—I stand before you to-night under indictment for the alleged crime of having voted at the last presidential election, without having a lawful right to vote. It shall be my work this evening to prove to you that in thus voting, I not only committed no crime, but, instead, simply exercised my *citizen's rights*, guaranteed to me and all United States citizens by the National Constitution, beyond the power of any State to deny.

The preamble of the Federal Consititution says:

"We, the people of the United States, in order to form a more perfect union, establish justice, insure *domestic* tranquility, provide for the common defense, promote the general welfare, and secure the blessings of liberty to ourselves and our posterity, do ordain and establish this Constitution for the United States of America."

It was we, the people; not we, the white male citizens; nor yet we, the male citizens; but we, the whole people, who formed the Union. And we formed it, not to give the blessings of liberty, but to secure them; not to the half of ourselves and the half of our posterity, but to the whole people—women as well as men. And it is a downright mockery to talk to women of their enjoyment of the blessings of liberty while they are denied the use of the only means of securing them provided by this democratic-republican government—the ballot.

For any State to make sex a qualification that must ever result in the disfranchisement of one entire half of the people is to pass a bill of attainder, or an *ex post facto* law, and is therefore a violation of the supreme law of the land. By it the blessings of liberty are for

Suffragists in New York canvassing for recruits.

A woman casts her vote, 1948.

ever withheld from women and their female posterity. To them this government has no just powers derived from the consent of the governed. To them this government is not a democracy. It is not a republic. It is an odious aristocracy; a hateful oligarchy of sex; the most hateful aristocracy ever established on the face of the globe; an oligarchy of wealth, where the rich govern the poor. An oligarchy of learning, where the educated govern the ignorant, or even an oligarchy of race, where the Saxon rules the African, might be endured; but this oligarchy of sex, which makes father, brothers, husband, sons, the oligarchs over the mother and sisters, the wife and daughters of every household—which ordains all men sovereigns, all women subjects, carries dissension, discord and rebellion into every home of the nation.

Webster, Worcester and Bouvier all define a citizen to be a person in the United States, entitled to vote and hold office.

The only question left to be settled now is: Are women persons? And I hardly believe any of our opponents will have the hardihood to say they are not. Being persons, then, women are citizens; and no State has a right to make any law, or to enforce any old law, that shall abridge their privileges or immunities. Hence, every discrimination against women in the constitutions and laws of the several States is to-day null and void, precisely as is every one against negroes.

123

"HATCHETATION" AND PROHIBITION, 1901

Prohibition proved a failure in the United States and so the Prohibition Amendment, ratified in 1919, was repealed in 1933. Hailed by the "drys" as a great moral victory, the actual effect of this law was to promote bootlegging, hi-jacking, large-scale gangsterism, and innumerable speakeasies resulting in many poisonings from bad liquor.

The most picturesque of the temperance agitators was Carry Nation, whose first husband died of delirium tremens and whose second divorced her on the grounds of desertion. Mrs. Nation, a squat, determined little figure in a poke bonnet, lectured, preached, and fought her way through the bars of the nation from Wichita, Kansas, to New York. In her organized crusade against drink she and her feminine followers armed themselves with shiny little hatchets which they wielded with great effect. This gentle art of demolition she called "Hatchetation," and when the breakage was sufficient it often landed her in local jails, from which she issued enthusiastic statements about the need to attract attention "against the selling of that hell-broth."

Below is the New York World's *account, August 29, 1901, of Mrs. Nation's first invasion of New York:*

Here is what Carry Nation did during her six-hour stay on Manhattan Island yesterday:

Gave Police Commissioner Murphy the most uncomfortable quarter of an hour in his life.

Scared Chief Devery into dodging her.

Gave John L. Sullivan a bad attack of the frights.

Kept Acting Mayor Guggenheimer in a state of nervous agitation. . . .

With a two-foot hatchet strapped to the girdle under her linen jacket, her beaded black poke bonnet pushed down firmly on her head, her broad jaw set at its most pugnacious angle, the Smasher strode into Colonel Murphy's room at Headquarters at eleven A.M., plumped into a chair close to him, and in ringing tones demanded:

"Don't you think New York is an awful bad place?"

"I don't think anything of the kind," testily said the Colonel.

"Yes, it is," insisted the Smasher. "It's full of hellholes and murder factories."

"Stop right there. I don't want to listen to you or to hear that kind of talk in this place," almost shouted the Commissioner.

"You won't listen to me?" queried the Smasher in surprise. "Why, I came here a-purpose to discuss these matters with you. Do you mean to say you won't discuss these murder shops, these hellholes, these sinks of depravity of New York?"

"That's just what I mean". . . .

Mrs. Nation laid a pudgy forefinger on the Colonel's arm. He angrily brushed it away, but in her sweetest tones the Smasher went on:

"I only came here to do New York good. I want to do good for humanity. I want to do something for you."

"You don't know what you're talking about," said the Colonel in a rage. "Go back to Kansas. If you want to do something, why don't you do it for your husband?"

"I have no husband now," said the Smasher in a tone of regret. "I supposed you knew all about it."

"Oh, yes," said the Commissioner, with a grin. "All I have to say is that I congratulate Mr. Nation. He ought to be a happy man now."

Unabashed, the Smasher took hold of the saloon question again. . . .

Murphy beckoned to Detective Linden to eject Mrs. Nation. Linden hesitated, and the Joint Smasher, undaunted, added new misery by saying:

"Now, father, be calm. I want to talk with you without quarreling."

"Don't call me father," said Murphy in a voice of agony.

arry Nation.

"I will call you father. You are old enough to be my father. I'm only fifty-four and you are at least eighty, and I'll call you father anyway. Now, father, do you think a little 'hatcheta-tion' would do a lot of good in New York?"

"If you violate the law I'll have you locked up," shouted the Commissioner.

The Smasher kept a crafty eye on Linden, and as she saw the detective had got his nerve up to the ejecting point she bounced out of her chair. . . .

"Now take me to see John L. Sullivan," said the Smasher to her manager. "He once said some mean things about me."

Up to the Forty-second Street saloon formerly owned by the ex-champion the Smasher went. The saloon was recently closed, but John L. still had a room on the upper floor. A messenger took up word to the pugilist, who said:

"Not on your life. Tell her I'm sick in bed."

GOVERNMENT REGULATION OF INDUSTRY:
THE SHERMAN ANTI-TRUST ACT, 1890

During the 1870's a tremendous economic growth began in America, which, despite cycles of depression and two world wars still continues, dwarfing any similar development in recorded history. Its magnitude can be seen in the fact that although the United States contains only 6% of the world's population it produces about half of the world's staple goods.

Accompanying this spectacular growth was a process of economic integration. In industry larger and larger units were created to achieve greater productivity and efficiency. In transportation the same process took place, with railroads amalgamating into great systems. Inevitably this led to restraints of trade and monopolies. Railroads, competing for freight, gave secret rebates to favored shippers. Giant industries frequently swallowed up or destroyed smaller rivals. In order to protect the public from such abuses it became necessary for federal and state legislation to be enacted.

In 1887 the Interstate Commerce Act was passed requiring railroads to publish and adhere to freight tariffs, thus eliminating "rebates." Similar state laws affecting intrastate commerce quickly followed.

In 1890 the Sherman Anti-Trust Act was passed to regulate "big business." Its failure to define what were illegal restraints of trade, monopoly and trusts has led to confusion on the part of both business and government which the Courts have attempted to remedy by judicial interpretation. Excerpts from the Sherman Anti-Trust Act follow:

An ACT to protect trade and commerce against unlawful restraints and monopolies . . .
Be it enacted

Sec. 1. Every contract, combination in the form of trust or otherwise, or conspiracy, in restraint of trade or commerce among the several States, or with foreign nations, is hereby declared to be illegal. Every person who shall make any such contract or engage in any such combination or conspiracy, shall be deemed guilty of a misdemeanor, and, on conviction thereof, shall be punished by fine not exceeding five thousand dollars, or by imprisonment not exceeding one year, or by both said punishments, in the discretion of the court.

Sec. 2. Every person who shall monopolize, or attempt to monopolize, or combine or conspire with any other person or persons, to monopolize any part of the trade or commerce among the several States, or with foreign nations shall be deemed guilty of a misdemeanor, and, on conviction thereof, shall be punished by fine not exceeding five thousand dollars, or by imprisonment not exceeding one year, or by both said punishments, in the discretion of the court.

Sec. 4. The several circuit courts of the United States are hereby invested with jurisdiction to prevent and restrain violations of this act; and it shall be the duty of the several district attorneys of the United States in their respective districts, under the direction of the Attorney-General, to institute proceedings in equity to prevent and restrain such violations. Such proceedings may be by way of petition setting forth the case and praying that such violation shall be enjoined or otherwise prohibited. When the parties complained of shall have been duly notified of such petition the courts shall proceed, as soon as may be, to the hearing and determination of the case; and pending such petition and before final decrees, the court may at any time make such temporary restraining order or prohibition as shall be deemed just in the premises.

Sec. 6. Any property owned under any contract or by any combination, or pursuant to any conspiracy (and being the subject thereof) mentioned in section one of this act, and being in the course of transportation from one State to another, or to a foreign country, shall be forfeited to the United States, and may be seized and condemned by like proceedings as those provided by law for the forfeiture, seizure, and condemnation of property imported into the United States contrary to law.†

GROWTH OF LABOR UNIONS IN AMERICA

The growth of labor unions to their present importance in the nation is a stormy chapter in American history marked by strikes, lockouts, and riots, often necessitating government intervention in the public interest.

Historically the shift from an agrarian to a mixed agarian-industrial economy, known as the "Industrial Revolution," took place in Great Britain, 1750–1850. A corresponding movement occurred in the United States in the mid-nineteenth century. In our country rapid growth of industry often crowded workers into inadequate factories and housing areas. There were frequent clashes between employer and employee over wages, hours, and conditions of labor in the course of which labor unions were formed to enable workers to negotiate on more equal footing with employers.

The earliest effort on the part of labor to organize was that of the Philadelphia shoemakers. In 1794 they formed the Federal Society of Journeymen Cordwainers, and in 1799 they effected a craft union contract between employers and organized labor. After a ten-week strike the employers acceded to their demands. Other efforts to federate labor unions included the formation of the National Labor Union, 1866; the Noble Order of the Knights of Labor, 1869; and the Federation of Trades and Labor Unions of the United States and Canada, 1881. From these beginnings grew today's powerful nationwide unions, of which the two largest are the American Federation of Labor, 1881, and the Congress of Industrial Orangizations, 1938.

Prior to 1913 the Federal government handled Federal labor problems through bureaus placed in different departments, such as Commerce, and Interior. As labor problems became more numerous, complex, and nationwide, affecting the general public through tie-ups in transportation and halts in production of such basic materials as coal and steel, a Department of Labor was created by Act of Congress, March 4, 1913. An important function of this department has been to establish standard procedures for adjusting disputes between labor and capital. Recent legislation to perfect these procedures includes the National Labor Relations Act, 1937 (also known as the Wagner Act), and the Taft-Hartley Labor Act, 1947.

Selections that follow are excerpts from speeches by Samuel Gompers, founder and first president of the A. F. of L., and John L. Lewis, founder and first president of the C.I.O.

GOMPERS ON SOCIALISM

"Seventy Years of Life and Labor," 1925

Samuel Gompers

I want to tell you, Socialists, that I have studied your philosophy; read your works upon economics . . . studied your standard works, both in English and German . . . I have heard your orators and watched the work of your movement the world over, I have kept close watch upon your doctrines for thirty years; have been closely associated with many of you and know how you think and what you propose. I know, too, what you have up your sleeve. And I want to say that I am entirely at variance with your philosophy. . . . Economically, you are unsound; socially you are wrong; industrially you are an impossibility.†

"TRADE UNION CREED"
Samuel Gompers

Speech delivered at an A. F. of L. conference, El Paso, 1925

Forty-four years ago in the city of Pittsburgh a group of labor men met to bring to fruition an effort extending over a period of years—to organize a national labor movement. We were a group of labor men with little experience in a national labor movement. We had to find our problems and devise ways of meeting them. There was little to guide us. . . . Industrialism growing out of constantly increasing invention of machinery . . . was making the need of economic protection for the workers increasingly imperative. . . .

. . . in 1886 a national labor conference was called . . . it was designated a trade union conference. The deliberations of that conference resulted in the formation of our present American Federation of Labor. . . . This new federation recognized only the trade union card as a credential and proposed to deal primarily with economic problems. It was an organization that had no power and no authority except of a voluntary character. It was a voluntary coming together of unions with common needs and common aims. That feeling

John L. Lewis, President of the United Mine Workers of America, founder of the C.I.

Karsh

of mutuality has been a stronger bond of union than could be welded by any autocratic authority. Guided by voluntary principles our Federation has grown from a weakling into the strongest, best organized labor movement of all the world.

But the very success of our organization has brought additional and serious dangers. Office in the labor movement now offers opportunity . . . for the self seeker who sees an instrumentality for personal advancement, both in the economic and in the political field. . . .

Men and women of our American trade union movement . . . I want to urge devotion to the fundamentals of human liberty—the principles of voluntarism. No lasting gain has ever come from compulsion. If we seek to force, we but tear apart that which, united, is invincible. There is no way whereby our labor movement may be assured sustained progress in determining its policies and plans other than sincere democratic deliberation until a unanimous decision is reached. This may seem a cumbrous, slow method to the impatient, but the impatient are more concerned for immediate triumph than for the education of constructive development.

Understanding, patience, high-minded service, the compelling power of voluntarism have in America made what was but a rope of sand, a united, purposeful, integrated organization, potent for human welfare, material and spiritual.

As I review the events of my sixty years of contact with the labor movement and as I survey the problems of today and study the opportunities of the future, I want to say to you, men and women of the American labor movement, do not reject the cornerstone upon which labor's structure has been builded—but base your all upon voluntary principles. . . . We have tried and proved these principles in economic, political, social and international relations. They have been tried and not found wanting. Where we have tried other ways, we have failed. . . . As we move upward to higher levels, a wider vision of service and responsibility will unfold itself. Let us keep the faith. There is no other way.†

JOHN L. LEWIS TO THE C. I. O.

Address to the C.I.O., First Constitutional Convention,
November 14, 1937

. . . I profoundly appreciate the opportunity of opening this convention. . . . Why these greetings? Why this interest? Why this enthusiasm? Why this acclaim? Because there has been born in America a new, modern labor movement dedicated to the proposition that all who labor are entitled to equality of opportunity, the right to organize, the right to participate in the bounties and the blessings of this country and our government, the right to aspire to an equality of position and the right to express views, objectives and rights on a parity with any other citizen, whatever may be his place, his condition of servitude, or the degree of world's goods which he may possess.

So that is the greeting of the Committee for Industrial Organization, assembled here and about to formalize its own internal affairs and make permanent its form of organization.

It is perhaps an interesting coincidence that 57 years ago almost to the day the great Gompers founded in this city the labor movement of his generation. That labor movement served that generation in a period where the skills in American trade and industry were the skills of handicraft and not the skills of the machine age and of mass production. But time moves on and the old order changes, and as the changes become obvious it was more and more apparent that the labor movement and the type of organization founded in Pittsburgh 57 years ago was not equal to the task of organizing or rendering service to the teeming millions who labor in American industries in this generation of our life.

Perhaps it will be illustrative to say that in 54 years of existence and advocation and administration of its affairs the American Federation of Labor failed to bring to the hundreds of thousands of workers in the industries in the Pittsburgh area the blessings of collective bargaining, and during all those years the Pittsburgh industrial district was the citadel of non-unionism in America, the citadel of labor exploitation, and the recognized fortress of those financial interests and industrial interests in America who preferred to exploit and debase and degrade labor rather than recognize its existence or concede its right to fair treatment. The old order changes, and what the American Federation of Labor could not do in 54 years of agitation the Committee for Industrial Organization has done in less than three years. . . .

But why should there be opposition and criticism of a movement that stands for orderly procedure and for a rational working out of the problems of modern industrial relationships, of an organization that is dedicated to the proposition of maintaining and supporting our democratic form of government, of an organization that is dedicated to the proposition of the right of investors to have a profit on their investment, and an organization that maintains the right to the freedom of contract relations between citizens of our republic, that is willing to lend its strength and its resources and its young men at any time to support and maintain that form of government, asking only in return that the safeguards of the Constitution and the Bill of Rights be extended to cover the most lowly, humble worker, as a right, as a privilege for an American.

These are troublous times in the world of affairs. Great and sinister forces are moving throughout the world, and he is optimistic indeed who believes that those forces will not affect Americans and will not have their impact and repercussions upon the peoples of the Western Hemisphere. Democracy is on trial in the world and in the United States. We want to preserve democracy. We cannot preserve democracy here in our country if we encourage as a people the overwhelming tidal wave of criticism, slander and abuse for an American institution like the CIO that stands for the protection of the privileges of all Americans, whether they be gentiles or Jews or of any creed or religion, or any school of thought that maintains its self-respect for our institutions. . . .

We must not forget that we have 12 million more or less unemployed people in America who have a right to work, but who have not been given work; that there are dependent upon those 12,000,000 many more millions who are underprivileged, ill-provided for and who are asking for a participation and are looking to this convention to devise policies, to state objectives, to lay out procedures that will cause them to have hope for the future.

I am sure that every man and woman here recognizes the great weight of responsibility upon them in their representative capacities, and that each will contribute toward the successful foundation and the final completion of this great, new, modern labor movement of the CIO. †

MEMBERSHIP OF LABOR UNIONS, 1897–1950

Source: United States Department of Labor, *Handbook of Labor Statistics*, 1950 Edition

Year	Total Membership All Unions
1897	440,000
1900	791,000
1910	2,116,000
1920	5,034,000
1930	3,632,000
1940	8,944,000
1950	14,000,000–16,000,000*

* Includes Canadian members of labor unions with headquarters in the United States.

COMMUNIST ACTIVITIES IN THE UNITED STATES

Soviet Russia has always used subversive propaganda and activities to spread Communism throughout the world. This was a contributing factor in the refusal by the United States formally to recognize the Soviet Union after the Russian Revolution of 1917.

In 1933, with the advent of the New Deal, President Franklin D. Roosevelt advocated a more liberal policy toward the U.S.S.R. In an exchange of letters between Roosevelt and Maxim Litvinov, the President negotiated formal recognition of Soviet Russia by the United States. In the following letters President Roosevelt notifies Mr. Litvinov of our formal recognition; and Mr. Litvinov states the terms agreed to by the U.S.S.R.

UNITED STATES' RECOGNITION OF SOVIET RUSSIA, 1933

The White House,
Washington, D.C.,
November 16, 1933

My dear Mr. Litvinov:

I am very happy to inform you that as a result of our conversations the Government of the United States has decided to establish normal diplomatic relations with the Government of the Union of Soviet Socialist Republics and to exchange ambassadors.

I trust that the relations now established between our peoples may forever remain normal and friendly, and that our Nations henceforth may cooperate for their mutual benefit and for the preservation of the peace of the world.

I am, my dear Mr. Litvinov,

Very sincerely yours,
FRANKLIN D. ROOSEVELT

Washington, November 16, 1933

My dear Mr. President:

I have the honor to inform you that coincident with the establishment of diplomatic relations between our two Governments it will be the fixed policy of the Government of the Union of Soviet Socialist Republics:

1. To respect scrupulously the indisputable right of the United States to order its own life within its own jurisdiction in its own way and to refrain from interfering in any manner in the internal affairs of the United States, its territories or possessions.

2. To refrain, and to restrain all persons in Government service and all organizations of the Government or under its direct or indirect control, including organizations in receipt of any financial assistance from it, from any act overt or covert liable in any way whatsoever to injure the tranquility, prosperity, order, or security of the whole or any part of the United States, its territories or possessions, and, in particular, from any act tending to incite or encourage armed intervention, or any agitation or propaganda having as an aim, the violation of the territorial integrity of the United States, its territories or possessions, or the bringing about by force of a change in the political or social order of the whole or any part of the United States, its territories or possessions.

3. Not to permit the formation or residence on its territory of any organization or group— and to prevent the activity on its territory of any organization or group, or of representatives or officials of any organization or group—which makes claim to be the Government of, or makes attempt upon the territorial integrity of, the United States, its territories or possessions; not to form, subsidize, support or permit on its territory military organizations or groups having the aim of armed struggle against the United States, its territories or possessions, and to prevent any recruiting on behalf of such organizations and groups.

131

4. Not to permit the formation or residence on its territory of any organization or group—and to prevent the activity on its territory of any organization or group, or of representatives or officials of any organization or group—which has as an aim the overthrow or the preparation for the overthrow of, or the bringing about by force of a change in, the political or social order of the whole or any part of the United States, its territories or possessions

I am, my dear Mr. President,

Very sincerely yours,
MAXIM LITVINOV
People's Commissar for Foreign Affairs,
Union of Soviet Socialist Republics

Despite the agreements made at the time of our recognition of Russia, the Soviet Union carried on widespread subversive activities in the United States. By 1940 the extent of these activities resulted in Congress' enacting legislation to clarify and strengthen our laws relating to treason, sedition, and subversive activities. This was done through enactment of the Alien Registration Act (known as the Smith Act), excerpts from which follow:

THE SMITH ACT, 1940

(Public Law No. 670, 76th Congress)

AN ACT

To prohibit certain subversive activities; to amend certain provisions of law with respect to the admission and deportation of aliens; to require the fingerprinting and registration of aliens; and for other purposes.

*Be it enacted by the Senate and House of Representatives of
the United States of America in Congress Assembled*

TITLE I

SEC. 2. (a) It shall be unlawful for any person—

(1) to knowingly or willfully advocate, abet, advise, or teach the duty, necessity, desirability, or propriety of overthrowing or destroying any government in the United States by force or violence, or by the assassination of any officer of any such government;

(2) with the intent to cause the overthrow or destruction of any government in the United States, to print, publish, edit, issue, circulate, sell, distribute, or publicly display any written or printed matter advocating, advising, or teaching the duty, necessity, desirability, or propriety of overthrowing or destroying any government in the United States by force or violence;

(3) to organize or help to organize any society, group, or assembly of persons who teach, advocate, or encourage the overthrow or destruction of any government in the United States by force or violence; or to be or become a member of, of affiliate with, any such society, group, or assembly of persons, knowing the purposes thereof.

(b) For the purposes of this section, the term "government in the United States" means the Government of the United States, the government of any State, Territory, or possession of the United States, the government of the District of Columbia, or the government of any political subdivision of any of them.

SEC. 3. It shall be unlawful for any person to attempt to commit, or to conspire to commit, any of the acts prohibited by the provisions of this title.

SEC. 4. Any written or printed matter of the character described in section 1 or section 2 of this Act, which is intended for use in violation of this Act, may be taken from any house or other place in which it may be found, or from any person in whose possession it may be, under a search warrant issued pursuant to the provisions of title XI of the Act entitled "An Act to punish acts of interference with the foreign relations, the neutrality and the foreign commerce of the United States, to punish espionage, and better to enforce the criminal laws of the United States, and for other purposes," approved June 15, 1917 (40 Stat. 228; U.S.C., title 18, ch. 18).

SEC. 5. (a) Any person who violates any of the provisions of this title shall, upon conviction thereof, be fined not more than $10,000 or imprisonment for not more than ten years, or both.

(b) No person convicted of violating any of the provisions of this title shall, during the five years next following his conviction, be eligible for employment by the United States, or by any department or agency thereof (including any corporation the stock of which is wholly owned by the United States).†

The world-wide Communist conspiracy continued unabated in the United States, with the agents of the Soviet international organization infiltrating key positions in the federal government. During and after World War II Congressional committees in both Houses carried out numerous investigations, examining the record in order to enact legislation against subversion, in the course of which they determined and exposed the extent of this infiltration. In 1953 it was the unanimous finding of the Internal Security Subcommittee of the U.S. Senate that the Soviet conspiracy constituted "a continuing hazard to our national security." In 1954 Congress passed and the President signed Public Law 637, excerpts from which follow:

THE COMMUNIST CONTROL ACT, 1954

(Public Law No. 637, 83rd Congress)

AN ACT

*Be it enacted by the Senate and House of Representatives of
the United States of America in Congress Assembled*

That this Act may be cited as the "Communist Control Act of 1954."

SECT. 2. The Congress hereby finds and declares that the Communist Party of the United States, although purportedly a political party, is in fact an instrumentality of a conspiracy to overthrow the Government of the United States . . . . Therefore, the Communist Party should be outlawed.

SECT. 3. The Communist Party of the United States, or any successors of such party . . . are not entitled to any of the rights, privileges, and immunities attendant upon legal bodies created under the jurisdiction of the laws of the United States or any political subdivision thereof; and whatever rights, privileges, and immunities which have heretofore been granted to said party or any subsidiary organization by reason of the laws of the United States or any political subdivision thereof, are hereby terminated. . . .

SEC. 4. Whoever knowingly and willfully becomes or remains a member of (1) the Communist Party . . . shall be subject to all the provisions and penalties of the Internal Security Act of 1950. . . .

"TO HELP SOLVE THE FEARFUL ATOMIC DILEMMA"
President Dwight D. Eisenhower

Address delivered before the General Assembly of the United Nations, December 8, 1953

I know that the American people share my deep belief that if a danger exists in the world, it is a danger shared by all—and equally that if a hope exists in the mind of one nation, that hope should be shared by all. . . .

I feel impelled to speak today in a language that in a sense is new—one which I, who have spent so much of my life in the military profession, would have preferred never to use.

That new language is the language of atomic warfare.

The atomic age has moved forward at such a pace that every citizen of the world should have some comprehension . . . of the extent of this development. . . . Clearly, if the peoples of the world are to conduct an intelligent search for peace, they must be armed with the significant facts of today's existence. . . .

Atomic bombs today are more than 25 times as powerful as the weapons with which the atomic age dawned, while hydrogen weapons are in the ranges of millions of tons of TNT equivalent.

Today, the United States' stockpile of atomic weapons, which, of course, increases daily, exceeds by many times the total equivalent of the total of all bombs and all shells that came from every plane and every gun in every theatre of war through all the years of World War II.

A single air group, whether afloat or land based, can now deliver to any reachable target, a destructive cargo exceeding in power all of the bombs that fell on Britain in all of World War II.

In size and variety the development of atomic weapons has been no less remarkable. This development has been such that atomic weapons have virtually achieved conventional status within our armed services. In the United States, the Army, the Navy, the Air Force, and the Marine Corps are all capable of putting this weapon to military use.

But the dread secret and the fearful engines of atomic might are not ours alone.

In the first place, the secret is possessed by our friends and allies, Great Britain and Canada, whose scientific genius made a tremendous contribution to our original discoveries and the designs of atomic bombs.

The secret is also known by the Soviet Union. . . .

If at one time the United States possessed what might have been called a monopoly of atomic power, that monopoly ceased to exist several years ago. Therefore, although our earlier start has permitted us to accumulate what is today a great quantitative advantage, the atomic realities of today comprehend two facts of even greater significance.

First, the knowledge now possessed by several nations will eventually be shared by others, possibly all of them.

Second, even a vast superiority in numbers of weapons, and a consequent capability of devastating retaliation, is no preventive, of itself, against the fearful material damage and toll of human lives that would be inflicted by surprise aggression.

The free world, at least dimly aware of the facts, has naturally embarked on a large program of warning and defense systems. That program will be accelerated and expanded.

But let no one think that the expenditure of vast sums for weapons and systems of defense can guarantee absolute safety for the cities and citizens of any nation. The awful arithmetic of the atomic bomb does not permit of any such easy solution. Even against the most powerful defense, an aggressor in possession of the effective minimum number of atomic bombs for a surprise attack could probably place a sufficient number of his bombs on the chosen targets to cause hideous damage.

Should such an atomic attack be launched against the United States, our reactions would be swift and resolute. But for me to say that the defense capabilities of the United States are such that they could inflict terrible losses upon an aggressor—for me to say that the retaliation capabilities of the United States are so great that such an aggressor's land would be laid waste—all this while fact, is not the true expression of the purpose and the hope of the United States.

To pause there would be to confirm the hopeless finality of a belief that two atomic collossi are doomed malevolently to eye each other indefinitely across a trembling world. To stop there would be to accept helplessly the probability of civilization destroyed—the

134

annihilation of the irreplaceable heritage of mankind handed down to us from generation to generation—and the condemnation of mankind to begin all over again the age-old struggle upward from savagery toward decency, right, and justice.

Surely no sane member of the human race could discover victory in such desolation. Could anyone wish his name to be coupled by history with such human degradation and destruction?

Occasional pages of history do record the faces of the "Great Destroyers" but the whole book of history reveals mankind's never-ending quest for peace and mankind's God-given capacity to build.

It is with the book of history, and not with isolated pages, that the United States will ever wish to be identified. My country wants to be constructive, not destructive. It wants agreements, not wars, among nations. It wants itself to live in freedom and in the confidence that the people of every other nation enjoy equally the right of choosing their own way of life.

So my country's purpose is to help us move out of this dark chamber of horrors into the light, to find a way by which the minds of men, the hopes of men, the souls of men everywhere, can move forward toward peace and happiness and well being.

In this quest, I know that we must not lack patience.

I know that in a world divided, such as ours today, salvation cannot be attained by one dramatic act.

I know that many steps will have to be taken over many months before the world can look at itself one day and truly realize that a new climate of mutually peaceful confidence is abroad in the world.

But I know, above all else, that we must start to take these steps—NOW. . . .

The gravity of the time is such that every new avenue of peace, no matter how dimly discernible, should be explored.

There is at least one new avenue of peace which has not yet been well explored—an avenue now laid out by the General Assembly of the United Nations.

In its resolution of November 18, 1953, this General Assembly suggested—and I quote— "that the Disarmament Commission study the desirability of establishing a sub-committee consisting of representatives of the powers principally involved, which should seek, in private, an acceptable solution—and report such a solution to the General Assembly and to the Security Council not later than 1 September 1954."

The United States, heeding the suggestion of the General Assembly of the United Nations, is instantly prepared to meet privately with such other countries as may be "principally involved," to seek "an acceptable solution" to the atomic armaments race which overshadows not only the peace, but the very life, of the world. . . .

To hasten the day when fear of the atom will begin to disappear from the minds of the people and the governments of the East and West, there are certain steps that can be taken now.

I therefore make the following proposal:

The Governments principally involved, to the extent permitted by elementary prudence, to begin now and continue to make joint contributions from their stock-piles of normal uranium and fissionable materials to an International Atomic Energy Agency. We would expect that such an agency would be set up under the aegis of the United Nations. . . .

The United States is prepared to undertake these explorations in good faith. Any partner of the United States acting in the same good faith will find the United States a not unreasonable or ungenerous associate.

Undoubtedly initial and early contributions to this plan would be small in quantity. However, the proposal has the great virtue that it can be undertaken without irritations and mutual suspicions incident to any attempt to set up a completely acceptable system of world-wide inspection and control.

The Atomic Energy Agency could be made responsible for the impounding, storage and protection of the contributed fissionable and other materials. The ingenuity of our scientists will provide special safe conditions under which such a bank of fissionable material can be made essentially immune to surprise seizure.

The more important responsibility of this Atomic Energy Agency would be to devise methods whereby this fissionable material would be allocated to serve the peaceful pursuits of mankind. Experts would be mobilized to apply atomic energy to the needs of agriculture, medicine, and other peaceful activities. A special purpose would be to provide abundant electrical energy in the power-starved areas of the world. Thus the contributing powers would be dedicating some of their strength to serve the needs rather than the fears of mankind.

The United States would be more than willing—it would be proud to take up with others "principally involved" the development of plans whereby such peaceful use of atomic energy would be expedited.

Of those "principally involved" the Soviet Union must, of course, be one.

I would be prepared to submit to the Congress of the United States, and with every expectation of approval, any such plan that would:

First—encourage world-wide investigation into the most effective peacetime uses of fissionable material, and with the certainty that they had all the material needed for the conduct of all experiments that were appropriate;

Second—begin to diminish the potential destructive power of the world's atomic stockpiles;

Third—allow all peoples of all nations to see that, in this enlightened age, the great powers of the earth, both of the East and of the West, are interested in human aspirations first rather than in building up the armaments of war;

Fourth—open up a new channel for peaceful discussion and initiate at least a new approach to the many difficult problems that must be solved in both private and public conversations if the world is to shake off the inertia imposed by fear and make positive progress toward peace.

Against the dark background of the atomic bomb, the United States does not wish merely to present strength, but also the desire and hope for peace.

The coming months will be fraught with fateful decisions. In this Assembly; in the capitals and military headquarters of the world, in the hearts of men everywhere, be they governed or governors, may they be the decisions which will lead this world out of fear and into peace.

To the making of these fateful decisions, the United States pledges before you—and therefore before the world—its determination to help solve the fearful atomic dilemma—to devote its entire heart and mind to find the way by which the miraculous inventiveness of man shall not be dedicated to his death, but consecrated to his life.†

FOUR

Spanning

the Continent

All the past we leave behind,
We debouch upon a newer, mightier world, varied world,
Fresh and strong the world we seize, world of labor
and the march,
Pioneers! O Pioneers!

We primeval forests felling
We the rivers stemming, vexing we and piercing deep
the mines within,
We the surface broad surveying, we the
virgin soil upheaving,
Pioneers! O Pioneers!

WALT WHITMAN

"Daniel Boone's First View of Kentucky." Painting by William Ranney. *Opposite:* Recent photograph of the Cumberland Gap through which Boone guided the pioneers in 1769.

Spanning the Continent

The spanning of the continent of North America is one of the great epics of the world.

During the first century and a quarter, starting in 1609, the Virginia settlers moved westward, up the rivers that empty into the Chesapeake Bay until, by 1727, they reached the Blue Ridge Mountains and began to spill over into the great Valley of Virginia.

Hunters and trappers, in the vanguard of civilization, found their way across the Alleghenies, to the Mississippi and Missouri Rivers; on into the far northwest. After them came the pioneers and settlers led by such men as Daniel Boone, who by 1769 was taking parties through the Cumberland Gap and on into Kentucky.

At the time of the Revolutionary War soldiers were given land bonuses in lieu of money and many settled in the area of the Ohio Valley. Then began the great migrations: the Northwest

Ordinance Act of 1787 opened up the territory north of the Ohio River. Government surveys and maps made it possible for pioneers to locate and buy land sight unseen, often for $1.25 an acre. Expansion by the southern route was made possible when the 1795 Treaty with Spain opened navigation on the Mississippi. In 1803 Napoleon, fearful of losing his American possessions in a war with Great Britain, negotiated the sale of the Louisiana Territory for $15,000,000. Known as the Louisiana Purchase, this transaction more than doubled the area of the United States from 900,000 square miles to over 1,800,000.

History records these facts, but it is through the letters, diaries and reports of the pioneers themselves that we can best realize the magnitude of their accomplishments. In the following selections we set out with Lewis and Clark on their famous expedition; follow a fur trapper as he works his way down the Columbia River; join Kit Carson on a buffalo hunt; cross the wilderness in an ox-drawn prairie schooner; sail around Cape Horn on a clipper ship; join the California Gold Rush; and watch the ceremony as the Golden Spike is driven in, symbolizing the joining of east and west as the Transcontinental Railroad spans the continent:

THE LEWIS AND CLARK EXPEDITION, 1804–1806

No sooner had the Louisiana Purchase been completed than President Jefferson sent Captains Meriwether Lewis and William Clark into the new territory ostensibly to determine whether there was a water route to the Pacific via the Missouri and Columbia Rivers; but also to secure the Columbia for the United States and to establish a Pacific trading base.

In 1526 Cabeza de Vaca made a transcontinental crossing north of Mexico to the Pacific, and in 1793 the Canadian explorer Alexander Mackenzie succeeded in reaching the Pacific north of Vancouver Island by a spectacular but commercially impossible route. In his account Voyages from Montreal *Mackenzie wrote: "The entire command of the fur trade of North America might be obtained from 48° North to the Pole. . . . Then would this country begin to be remunerated for the expenses it has sustained in discovering and surveying the coast of the Pacific Ocean, which is at present left to American adventurers. . . . Such adventurers, and many of them, as I have been informed, have been very successful, would instantly disappear before a well-regulated trade."*

In 1803 Congress appropriated $2,500 for the expedition, and in 1804 Lewis and Clark ascended the Missouri River, crossed the Rockies, descended the Columbia River and first sighted the Pacific on November 15, 1805. Their expedition was probably the most important in the history of the United States, for they succeeded in giving final and documented proof that America was a single vast continent stretched between two oceans. The way was now open, the stage now set for what Theodore Roosevelt later described as "The Winning of the West." The following is an excerpt from Thomas Jefferson's long and detailed letter of instructions to Lewis and Clark:

THOMAS JEFFERSON'S LETTER OF INSTRUCTIONS
JUNE 20, 1803

The object of your mission is to explore the Missouri river, and such principal streams of it as, by its course and communication with the waters of the Pacific Ocean . . . may offer the most direct and practicable water communication across the continent, for the purposes of commerce. . . .

Your observations are to be taken with great pains and accuracy; . . . and are to be rendered to the war-office, for the purpose of having the calculations made concurrently by

"I called it the *gates of the rocky mountains*." Captain Lewis first saw
the Rockies in July, 1805. Painting by Albert Bierstadt (detail).

proper persons within the United States. . . . [Here Jefferson gives a long list of the things
they are to observe and record: "tribes and nations," their food, clothing, traditions, occupations, diseases and remedies, etc. "Other objects worthy of notice will be" the country,
its soil, vegetation, animals, minerals, climate, etc.]

   In all your intercourse with the natives, treat them in the most friendly and conciliatory
manner which their own conduct will admit . . . make them acquainted with the position,

141

extent, character, peaceable and commercial dispositions of the United States; of our wish to be neighborly, friendly and useful to them; confer with them on the points most convenient as mutual emporiums, and the articles of most desirable interchange for them and us. . . . If any of them should wish to have some of their young people brought up with us, and taught such arts as may be useful to them, we will receive, instruct, and take care of them. . . .

As it is impossible for us to foresee in what manner you will be received by these people, whether with hospitality or hostility, so it is impossible to prescribe the exact degree of perseverance with which you are to pursue your journey. We value too much the lives of citizens to offer them to probable destruction. . . . To your own discretion, therefore, must be left the degree of danger you may risk, and the point at which you should decline, only saying, we wish you to err on the side of your safety, and to bring back your party safe, even if it be with less information. . . .†

THOMAS JEFFERSON
President of the United States of America

CAPTAIN LEWIS DESCRIBES THE GATES OF THE ROCKY MOUNTAINS

Friday, July 19th, 1805

This morning we set out early and proceeded on very well tho' the water appears to encrease in velocity as we advance. the current has been strong all day and obstructed with some rapids, tho' these are but little broken by rocks and are perfectly safe. the river deep and from 100 to 150 yds. wide. I walked along shore today and killed an Antelope. wh[en]ever we get a view of the lofty summits of the mountains the snow presents itself, altho' we are almost suffocated in this confined valley with heat. this evening we entered much the most remarkable clifts that we have yet seen. these clifts rise from the waters edge on either side perpendicularly to the hight of 1200 feet. every object here wears a dark and gloomy aspect. the tow[er]ing and projecting rocks in many places seem ready to tumble on us. the river appears to have forced it's way through this immence body of solid rock for the distance of 5¾ Miles and where it makes it's exit below has th[r]own on either side vast collumns of rocks mountains high.

the river appears to have woarn a passage just the width of it's channel or 150 yds. it is deep from side to side nor is there in the 1st 3 Miles of this distance a spot except one of a few yards in extent on which a man could rest the soal of his foot. several fine springs burst out at the waters edge from the interstices of the rocks. it happens fortunately that altho' the current is strong it is not so much so but what it may be overcome with the oars for their is hear no possibility of using either the cord or Setting pole. it was late in the evening before I entered this place and was obliged to continue my rout untill sometime after dark before I found a place sufficiently large to encamp my small party; at length such an one occurred on the lard. side where we found plenty of lightwood and pich pine. this rock is a black grannite below and appears to be of a much lighter colour above and from the fragments I take it to be flint of a yellowish brown and light creem-coloured yellow. from the singular appearance of this place I called it the *gates of the rocky mountains.*

Opposite: The Columbia River, whose source Lewis and Clark traced.

Lewis and Clark reached the Oregon coast in November, 1805.

"FUR HUNTERS OF THE FAR WEST"

Alexander Ross

The fur trade was one of the chief incentives for exploration of the Northwest. It caused intense rivalry between the English, French, and Spanish and did much to increase friction between Indians and whites.

Alexander Ross, a Scotsman, was originally a trapper with John Jacob Astor's Pacific Fur Company. When it was disbanded in 1813, Ross moved to the North West Fur Company, from which he wrote the following account, describing how a large fur-trapping party worked among the Indians:

A safe and secure spot, near wood and water, is first selected for the camp. Here the chief of the party resides with the property. It is often exposed to danger or sudden attack, in the absence of the trappers, and requires a vigilant eye to guard against the lurking savages. The camp is called headquarters. From hence all the trappers, some on foot, some on horseback, according to the distance they have to go, start every morning in small parties in all directions ranging the distance of some twenty miles around. Six traps is the allowance for each hunter, but to guard against wear and tear, the complement is more frequently ten. These he sets every night and visits again in the morning, sometimes oftener, according to the distance or other circumstances. The beaver taken in the traps are always conveyed to the camp, skinned, stretched, dried, folded up with the hair in the inside, laid by, and the flesh

144

used for food. No sooner, therefore, has a hunter visited his traps, set them again, and looked out for some other place, than he returns to the camp to feast and enjoy the pleasures of an idle day.

There is, however, much anxiety and danger in going through the ordinary routine of a trapper's duty. For as the enemy is generally lurking about among the rocks and hiding-places, watching an opportunity, the hunter has to keep a constant lookout, and the gun is often in one hand while the trap is in the other. But when several are together, which is often the case in suspicious places, one-half set the traps and the other half keep guard over them. Yet notwithstanding all their precautions some of them fall victims to Indian treachery.

The camp remains stationary while two-thirds of the trappers find beaver in the vicinity, but whenever the beaver become scarce the camp is removed to some more favorable spot. In this manner the party keeps moving from place to place during the whole season of hunting. Whenever serious danger is apprehended, all the trappers make for the camp. Were we, however, to calculate according to numbers, the prospects from such an expedition would be truly dazzling: say seventy-five men with each six traps, to be successfully employed during five months; that is, two in the spring, and three in the fall, equal to 131 working days, the result would be 58,950 beaver! Practically, however, the case is very different. The apprehension of danger at all times is so great that three-fourths of their time is lost in the necessary steps taken for their own safety. There is also another serious drawback unavoidably accompanying every large party. The beaver is a timid animal. The least noise, therefore, made about its haunt will keep it from coming out for nights together, and noise is unavoidable when the party is large. But when the party is small the hunter has a chance of being more or less successful. Indeed, were the nature of the ground such as to admit of the trappers moving about in safety at all times, and alone, six men with six traps each would in the same space of time and at the same rate kill as many beaver— say 4,716—as the whole seventy-five could be expected to do! And yet the evil is without a remedy, for no small party can exist in these parts. Hence the reason why beaver are so numerous.†

"The Trappers." Painting by William Ranney.

A FRONTIERSMAN SETTLES IN ILLINOIS, 1817

MORRIS BIRBECK'S "LETTERS FROM ILLINOIS," LONDON, 1818

. . . I am now going to take you to the prairies, to show you the very beginning of our settlement. Having fixed on the north-western portion of our prairie for our future residence and farm, the first act was building a cabin, about two hundred yards from the spot where the house is to stand. This cabin is built of round straight logs, about a foot in diameter, lying each upon the other, and notched in at the corners, forming a room eighteen feet long by sixteen; the intervals between the logs "chunked," that is, filled in with slips of wood; and "mudded," that is, daubed with a plaister of mud: a spacious chimney, built also of logs, stands like a bastion at one end: the roof is well covered with four hundred "clap boards" of cleft oak, very much like the pales used in England for fencing parks. A hole is cut through the side, called, very properly, the "door," (the through) for which there is a "shutter," made also of cleft oak, and hung on wooden hinges. All this has been executed by contract, and well executed, for twenty dollars. I have since added ten dollars to the cost, for the luxury of a floor and ceiling of sawn boards, and it is now a comfortable habitation.

. . . We arrived in the evening, our horses heavily laden with our guns, and provisions, and cooking utensils, and blankets, not forgetting the all-important axe. This was immediately put in requisition, and we soon kindled a famous fire, before which we spread our pallets, and, after a hearty supper, soon forgot that besides ourselves, our horses and our dogs, the wild animals of the forest were the only inhabitants of our wide domain. Our cabin stands at the edge of the prairie, just within the wood, so as to be concealed from the view until you are at the very door. Thirty paces to the east the prospect opens from a commanding eminence over the prairie, which extends four miles to the south and south-east, and over the woods beyond to a great distance; whilst the high timber behind, and on each side, to the west, north, and east, forms a sheltered cove about five hundred and fifty yards from the wood each way, but open to the south, that we propose building our house.

There are many other prairies, or natural meadows, of various dimensions and qualities, scattered over this surface, which consists of about two hundred square miles, containing perhaps twelve human habitations, all erected, I believe, within one year of our first visit—most of them within three months. . . .

There are no very good mill-seats on the streams in our neighborhood, but our prairie affords a most eligible site for a windmill; we are therefore going to erect one immediately: the materials are in great forwardness, and we hope to have it in order to grind the fruits of the ensuing harvest.

By the first of May I hope to have two ploughs at work, and may possibly put in 100 acres of corn this spring. Early in May, I think, we shall be settled in a convenient temporary dwelling, formed of a range of cabins of ten rooms, until we can accomplish our purpose of building a more substantial house. . . .†

BUFFALO HUNTING ON THE FRÉMONT EXPEDITION, 1843

Under Congressional authority, John C. Frémont, explorer, army officer, led three expeditions into the Oregon territory and through the Rocky Mountains, mapping (1842) the famous Oregon Trail. When California entered the Union in 1850, Frémont was one of its first two senators and, in 1856, was nominated for President by the newly formed Republican Party, but was defeated by James Buchanan. In the following, Frémont describes a buffalo hunt with his frontiersman guide, Kit Carson:

146

"The first act was building a cabin." A
Currier & Ives print of frontier life, 1867.

A few miles brought us into the midst of the buffalo, swarming in immense numbers over
the plains, where they had left scarcely a blade of grass standing. Mr. Preuss, who was
sketching at a distance in the rear, had at first noted them as large groves of timber. In the
sight of such a mass of life, the traveler feels a strange emotion of grandeur. We had heard
from a distance a dull and confused murmuring, and, when we came in view of their dark
masses, there was not one among us who did not feel his heart beat quicker. It was the early
part of the day, when the herds were feeding; and everywhere they were in motion. Here
and there a huge old bull was rolling in the grass, and clouds of dust rose in the air from
various parts of the bands, each the scene of some obstinate fight. . . . The wind was favorable; the coolness of the morning invited to exercise; the ground was apparently good, and
the distance across the prairie (two or three miles) gave us a fine opportunity to charge them
before they could get among the river hills. It was too fine a prospect for a chase to be lost;
and, halting for a few moments, the hunters were brought up and saddled, and Kit Carson,
Maxwell and I started together. They were now somewhat less than half a mile distant, and
we rode easily along until within about three hundred yards, when a sudden agitation, a
wavering in the band, and a galloping to and fro of some which were scattered along the
skirts, gave us the intimation that we were discovered. We started together at a hand gallop,
riding steadily abreast of each other, and here the interest of the chase became so engrossing-

147

ly intense that we were sensible of nothing else. We were now closing upon them rapidly, and the front of the mass was already in rapid motion for the hills, and in a few seconds the movement had communicated itself to the whole herd.

A crowd of bulls, as usual, brought up the rear, and every now and then some of them faced about, and then dashed on after the band a short distance, and turned and looked again, as if more than half inclined to stand and fight. In a few moments, however, during which we had been quickening our pace, the rout was universal, and we were going over the ground like a hurricane. When at about thirty yards, we gave the usual shout (the hunter's

"Buffalo, swarming in immense number over the plains." Painting by George Catlin (detail).

battle cry) and broke into the herd. We entered on the side, the mass giving way in every direction in their heedless course. Many of the bulls, less active and less fleet than the cows, paying no attention to the ground, and occupied solely with the hunter, were precipitated to the ground with great force, rolling over and over with the violence of the shock, and hardly distinguishable in the dust. We separated on entering, each singling out his game.

My horse was a trained hunter, famous in the West under the name of Proveau, and, with his eyes flashing and the foam flying from his mouth, sprang on after the cow like a tiger. In a few moments he brought me alongside of her, and, rising in the stirrups, I fired at the distance of a yard, the ball entering at the termination of the long hair, and passing near the heart. She fell headlong at the report of the gun, and checking my horse, I looked around for my companions. At a little distance, Kit was on the ground, engaged in tying his horse to the horns of a cow which he was preparing to cut up. Among the scattered bands, at some distance below, I caught a glimpse of Maxwell; and while I was looking, a light wreath of white smoke curled away from his gun, from which I was too far to hear the report.

Nearer, and between me and the hills, toward which they were directing their course, was the body of the herd, and giving my horse the rein, we dashed after them. A thick cloud of dust hung upon their rear, which filled my mouth and eyes, and nearly smothered me. In the midst of this I could see nothing, and the buffalo were not distinguishable until within thirty feet. They crowded together more densely still as I come upon them, and rushed along in such a compact body, that I could not obtain an entrance—the horse almost leaping after them. In a few minutes the mass divided to the right and left, the horns clattering with a noise heard above everything else, and my horse darted into the opening. Five or six bulls charged on us and we dashed along the line, but were left far behind; singling out a cow, I gave her my fire, but struck too high. She gave me a tremendous leap, and scoured on swifter than before. I reined up my horse, and the band swept on like a torrent, and left the place quiet and clear.

Our chase had led us into dangerous ground. A prairie-dog village, so thickly settled that there were three or four holes in every twenty yards square, occupied the whole bottom for nearly two miles length. Looking around, I saw one of the hunters, nearly out of sight, and the long dark line of our caravan crawling along, at three or four miles distance.

DIARY OF A WOMAN ON THE OREGON TRAIL, 1848

Mrs. Elizabeth Dixon Smith Geer

June 3. Passed through St. Joseph on the bank of the Missouri. Laid in our flour, cheese and crackers and medicine, for no one should travel this road without medicine, for they are almost sure to have the summer complaint. Each family should have a box of physicking pills, a quart of castor oil, a quart of the best rum, and a large vial of peppermint essence. We traveled 4 miles by the river and encamped. Here we found nine wagons bound for Oregon.

June 5. Made 9 miles. At present 22 wagons.

June 6. Made 18 miles. Passed 70 Oregon wagons as they were encamped.

June 12. Laid by to wash. Had 2 horses stolen by the Indians last night out of the company.

June 23. Made 18 miles. At present there is one hundred and forty persons in our company. We see thousands of buffalo and have to use their dung for fuel. A man will gather a bushel in a minute; three bushels make a good fire. We call the stuff "buffalo chips."

Aug. 1. Passed over the Rocky Mountains, the backbone of America . . . made 18 miles. Had rain and hail today which made it disagreeably cold.

Aug. 29. Made 16 miles. Camped on Snake River. Plenty of grass and willows. Very dusty roads. You in "The States" know nothing about dust. It will fly so that you can hardly see the horns of your tongue yoke of oxen. It often seems that the cattle must die for the want of breath, and then in our wagons, such a spectacle—beds, clothes, victuals and children, all completely covered.

Sept. 16. Saw a boiling hot spring. Clear and good tasting water. Made 18 miles. Camped at Barrel Camp. Good grass by driving up the stream a mile or so where two cattle were shot with arrows by Indians, but not mortally wounded.

Sept. 24. Laid by to dry our things which got wet crossing the river. Mr. Kimball's oldest son died of typhus fever.

A prairie schooner on the Oregon Trail, 1886.

Oct. 9. Doubled teams on another mountain. Made 15 miles. Camped at Pine Camp. Good feed and water. My husband and I are both sick with the summer complaint.

Oct. 17. Cold and windy. We made a fire of a little wood that we carried all day yesterday. Made a bite to eat. Our cattle ran off in search of water which hindered us till late. Made 4 miles. Camped without wood, except a small shrub called greasewood. It burns like greased weeds. I used to wonder why it was said that men must be dressed in buckskin to come to this country, but now I know. Everything we travel through is thorny and rough. There is no chance of saving your clothes. Here we found a great hole of water 12 or 15 feet across. Had to water a hundred and fifty head of cattle with pails. Had to stand out all night in the rain to keep the cattle from drowning each other— after water in this hole.

Oct. 28 (On the Columbia River). Here are a great many immigrants encamped, some making rafts, others going down in boats which have been sent up by speculators.†

THE CALIFORNIA GOLD RUSH, 1849

John Augustus Sutter, having secured an immense tract of land near the Sacramento River, was developing it into a principality. On January 24, 1848, while working on the trailrace of a sawmill, Sutter's foreman, James W. Marshall, discovered gold. This discovery touched off one of the most exciting migrations in the history of the country.

Across prairies, deserts and mountains, through Texas and Mexico, over the deadly Isthmus of Panama and around Cape Horn, by 1852 over 200,000 people had swarmed into California. Sutter's principality was devastated; mining camps sprang up having such picturesque names as Red Dog, Poker Flat, and Grub Gulch. In the best year, 1852, the washings yielded $81-294,270, and Eldredge's history records the larest nugget as weighing one hundred and forty-one pounds four ounces of almost pure gold, found in 1854. As the fever waned some prospectors left but many stayed to farm the fertile valleys of California.

The selections that follow include Marshall's description of his discovery; an account from the diary of William G. Johnston, who accompanied the first wagon train into California; and a description by Daniel B. Woods, a Philadelphia schoolteacher, of his adventures as a gold miner:

150

JAMES MARSHALL TELLS HOW HE DISCOVERED GOLD IN CALIFORNIA, 1848

One morning in January [definitely established as January 24, 1848], it was a clear cold morning; I shall never forget that morning, as I was taking my usual walk along the race, after shutting off the water, my eye was caught by a glimpse of something shining in the bottom of the ditch. There was about a foot of water running there. I reached my hand down and picked it up; it made my heart thump for I felt certain it was gold. The piece was about half the size and of the shape of a pea. Then I saw another piece in the water. After taking it out, I sat down and began to think right hard. I thought it was gold, and yet it did not seem to be of the right color; all the gold coin I had seen was of a reddish tinge; this looked more like brass. I recalled to mind all the metals I had ever seen or heard of, but I could find none that resembled this. Suddenly the idea flashed across my mind that it might be iron pyrites. I trembled to think of it! This question could soon be determined. Putting one of the pieces on hard river stone, I took another and commenced hammering it. It was soft and didn't break; it therefore must be gold, but largely mixed with some other metal, very likely silver; for pure gold, I thought, would certainly have a brighter color.

When I returned to our cabin for breakfast I showed the two pieces to my men. They were all a good deal excited, and had they not thought that the gold only existed in small quantities they would have abandoned everything and left me to finish the job alone. However, to satisfy them, I told them that as soon as we had the mill finished we would devote a week or two to gold hunting and see what we could make out of it.

Sutter's mill, site of James Marshall's discovery of gold.

Deane Dickason

While we were looking in the race after this discovery, we always kept a sharp lookout, and in the course of three or four days we had picked up about three ounces—our work still progressing as lively as ever, for none of us imagined at that time that the whole country was sowed with gold.

About a week's time after the discovery I had to take another trip to the fort; and to gain what information I could respecting the real value of the metal, took all we had collected with me and showed it to Mr. Sutter, who at once declared it was gold, but thought with me, it was greatly mixed with some other metal. It puzzled us a great deal to hit upon the means of telling the exact quantity contained in the alloy; however, we at last stumbled on an old American cyclopedia where we saw the specific gravity of all the metals, and rules given to find the quantity of each in a given bulk. After hunting over the whole fort and borrowing from some of the men, we got three dollars and a half in silver, and with a small pair of scales we soon cyphered it out that there was no silver nor copper in the gold, but that it was entirely pure.

This fact being ascertained, we thought it our best policy to keep it as quiet as possible till we should have finished our mill, but there was a great number of disbanded Mormon soldiers in and about the fort, and when they came to hear of it, why, it just spread like wildfire, and soon the whole country was in a bustle. I had scarcely arrived at the mill again till several persons appeared with pans, shovels and hoes, and those that had not iron picks had wooden ones, all anxious to fall to work and dig up our mill; but this we would not permit. As fast as one party disappeared another would arrive, and sometimes I had the greatest kind of trouble to get rid of them. I sent them all off in different directions, telling them about such and such places, where I was certain there was plenty of gold if they would only take the trouble of looking for it. At that time I never imagined the gold was so abundant. I told them to go to such and such places, because it appeared that they would dig nowhere but in such places as I pointed out, and I believe such was their confidence in me that they would have dug on the very top of yon mountain if I had told them to do so.

So there, stranger, is the entire history of the gold discovery in California—a discovery that hasn't as yet been of much benefit to me.

THE FIRST WAGON TRAIN INTO CALIFORNIA, 1849

William G. Johnston

On Sunday, March 11th, 1849, destined for the little frontier town of Independence, we left St. Louis and were soon steaming up the great Missouri. Four days later we reached a diminutive village glorying in the name of Wayne City, the landing place for Independence, four miles inland.

It soon became evident that it would be several weeks before we could proceed on the long journey westward. We had yet to purchase mules and numerous things needed on the plains, and time would be required for the grass to grow upon which the animals must subsist. . . .

April 17th. The tide of emigrants westward increases, and almost hourly wagon after wagon, some drawn by oxen and some by mules, roll past. Our guide, Jim Stewart, tells us to be in no haste. He says the parties starting this early are making woeful mistakes and that when once we take up the line of march, he will engage to pass every mother's son of them. . . .

April 28th. At ten o'clock the first two wagons of our train took the lead, and we got started about an hour later. Our mules bothered us greatly. A few rods from the camp they came to a dead halt. Neither mild persuasion nor severe drubbing had the effect of making

Wagon train en route to the gold fields.

them pull together, but when our patience had oozed out and our strength was about gone, they started off as though nothing had happened.

At six o'clock we reached the frontier line of Missouri, which marks the separation of civilized from uncivilized life. Beyond us are the vast plains as yet but little known to the white man. Here alongside a farm we encamped and used the enclosure near the barn for our animals, the last opportunity of this kind it would be possible to enjoy. . . .

May 9th. Our daily task for a time to come will be to get past those in advance of us, and to so travel that no trains shall overtake us. In this way only can we hope properly to maintain our animals. The locusts of Egypt could scarcely be a greater scourge than these great caravans, as grass and whatever else is green vanish completely before them. . . .

May 14th. A word as to our meals. All are alike, or at least there is scarce any variety, and we rarely have more than two in a day. The dishes comprise oatmeal mush, bacon sides with pilot bread fried in the fat, and coffee; these repeated ad infinitum. We had for a brief time sugar and molasses but these were luxuries of which but a limited supply could be carried and we soon ran out. . . .

June 21st. The real troubles of mountain climbing began with this day. From Weber River the road led over a succession of elevations and our struggles were without cessation. The trail led up a ravine, narrow and precipitous, down which coursed a stream of no great proportions but sufficient to occasion difficulties which at times seemed impossible to overcome. The mire in places was of ascertained depth, in others it appeared fathomless. Occasionally the river was confined to a narrow space, but again it overspread the entire pass and it had washed out the earth and left bare rocks and boulders which clogged our way over which mules and wagon wheels had to be pulled or lifted constantly. Thus in labors inconceivable and altogether indescribable we toiled up the well nigh inaccessible heights of the Wahsatch range while the day wore on and night found both men and beasts weary and exhausted. . . .

June 22nd. Towards evening we saw at a distance of perhaps twenty miles, having the resemblance of a sea of molten silver—the American Dead Sea—Salt Lake. . . .

June 23rd. Shortly after sunrise we made camp a mile from Salt Lake, where, in addition to having much needed repairs done to our wagons, both men and mules were to enjoy two days of relaxation from our recent severe toils and to recruit strength for others yet in store.

The good people of the town made our coming an occasion for a holiday. The accounts previously received concerning the Mormons had not led to favorable opinions in our minds, but from the contacts of our brief stay it would be only just to say we found ample reason to doubt the truth of much that has been said against them. That their leaders are bad, unprincipled men there can be no question, but the masses, their victims, are to be pitied rather than denounced. Their carefully cultivated farms and gardens, and the neatness of their cottages, bore evidence of industry and thrift. . . .

June 24th. Near ten o'clock a deep-toned bell began to ring, calling the worshippers together. About the center of the village, in an open lot, we found a large congregation sitting on rough benches, altogether unprotected from the intense heat of the sun. . . .

Brigham Young, Orson Pratt and other holy apostles were seated on the platform, below which were ranged a great row of musicians who played with skill upon brass instruments. They were playing when we entered and continued for some time. Although anxious to see more I found the heat so unendurable that I felt obliged to withdraw to camp where under an awning I found some comfort. . . .

July 16th. At four we were jogging along. The early air was pleasant but by nine o'clock the sun blazed fiercely upon us. Brinish as it was, we drank water gratefully from our canteens. . . . At every step we sank in the deep sand and were compelled often to seek rest by sitting down on the desolate wayside. . . . As if in cruel mockery to torture us while already

154

suffering sufficiently, again and again mirages arose, deceiving with their pleasing enchantments. . . .

July 20th. Entering a valley between high mountains we began the ascent of the Sierras. The road was frightfully steep, quite narrow and beset with rocks. . . . Within this gap the sun never enters and the air had the chill of an ice house. Our night camp was made alongside the mountain torrent. Grass was scarce and the mules had to subsist on the recollection of excellent pasturage enjoyed in the morning.

July 21st. Following the course of the little mountain stream; twice crossing it, where rocks well nigh choking it presented barriers almost impassable, we continued climbing upwards. Some large trees, uprooted by storms, lay across the path which we were obliged to go over, lifting the wheels of the wagons, for the doing of which all our latent energies were pressed into service. . . . To make this ascent with loaded wagons was not to be thought of. It was sufficiently difficult by the doubling of teams in addition to the use of ropes, to lift empty wagons. The air was blue with oaths while all this was in progress. Then packs had to be made for the backs of the mules to carry up the contents of the wagons. The amount of labor required in this task was beyond conception. I doubt if so fine an example of immense muscular energy could be found anywhere as was exhibited on this difficult pass of the Sierra by these struggling toilers, the Spanish mules. . . .

July 23rd. A succession of mountain ridges. Again we passed over beds of hard packed snow whose surfaces, sheltered from the sun, never melt.

July 24th. A short way from camp we realized that we no longer had mountains to climb. Our route lay over the foothills at the western base of the Sierra. We had reached California, the first train with wagons to enter California. Our journey had reached its consummation, having been accomplished in 88 days, a total of nineteen hundred and seventy-four miles.

Across the Continent." Print by Currier & Ives, 1868.

Ewing Galloway

Miners paying for supplies with gold du

LIFE IN THE DIGGINGS, 1849
Daniel B. Woods

July 9th

Today we made $20 each. One of the conclusions at which we are rapidly arriving is that the chances of our making a fortune in the gold mines are about the same as those in favor of our drawing a prize in a lottery. No kind of work is so uncertain. A miner may happen upon a good location in his very first attempt and in a very few days make hundreds or thousands, while the experienced miners about him may do nothing. An instance of this kind happened recently when two men who had been some time in the mines started a dispute as to a small space between their claims. As they could not amicably settle the dispute they agreed to leave it to a newcomer who happened by who had not yet done an hour's work in the mines. He measured off ten feet—the amount allowed by custom—to each of the claimants, taking for his trouble the narrow strip of land between them. In a few hours the larger claims belonging to the older miners were abandoned as useless while the newcomer discovered a deposit which yielded him $7,435.

July 10th

We made $3.00 each today. This life of hardships and exposure has affected my health. Our diet consists of hard tack, flour we eat half cooked, and salt pork, with occasionally a salmon which we purchase from the Indians. Vegetables are not to be procured. Our feet are wet all day, while a hot sun shines down upon our heads and the very air parches the skin like the hot air of an oven. Our drinking water comes down to us thoroughly impreg-

156

nated with the mineral substances washed through the thousand cradles above us. After our days of labor, exhausted and faint, we retire—if this word may be applied to the simple act of lying down in our clothes—robbing our feet of their boots to make a pillow of them, and wrapping our blankets about us, on a bed of pine boughs, or on the ground beneath the clear, bright stars of the night. Near morning there is always a change in the temperature and several blankets become necessary. The feet and the hands of a novice in this business become blistered and lame, and the limbs are stiff. Besides all these causes of sickness, the anxieties and cares which wear away the lives of so many men who leave their families to come to this land of gold, contribute, in no small degree, to the same result.

ld prospector in California.

Bodie, California, one of the many ghost towns left after the gold ru

DISCOVERY AND NAMING OF YOSEMITE, 1851
L. H. Bunnell

Lafayette Houghton Bunnell, a doctor who spoke several Indian languages, migrated to California in '49 where he became a successful gold miner. When Indian troubles broke out, he volunteered with the Mariposa Battalion to help subdue the Indians. In the following he tells of his first view of Yosemite and the naming of this famous valley:

. . . we suddenly came in full view of the valley in which was the village, or rather the encampment of the Yosemites. The immensity of the rock I had seen in my vision on the Old Bear Valley trail was here presented to my astonished gaze. The mystery of that glimpse was here disclosed and my awe was increased by this nearer view of that stupendous cliff, now known as El Capitan. None but those who have visited this wonderful valley can even imagine the feelings with which I looked upon the view that was there presented. The grandeur of the scene was but softened by the haze that hung over the valley—light as gossamer—and by the clouds which partially dimmed the higher cliffs and mountains. An exalted sensation seemed to fill my whole being and I found my eyes in tears with emotion. . . .

I suggested that the valley should have an appropriate name. Different names were proposed but none were satisfactory to a majority about the circle. Some romantic and foreign names were offered and a large number canonical and scriptural, from which I inferred that I was not the only one in whom religious emotions or thoughts had been aroused by the mysterious power of the surrounding scenery.

I did not like any of the names proposed and suggested that it would be better to give the valley an Indian name than to import a strange and inexpressive one; and that the name of the tribe who had occupied it would be more appropriate than any which I had heard suggested. I then proposed that we give the valley the name of Yosemite, that by so doing the name of the tribe of Indians which we met leaving their homes in the valley, perhaps never to return, would be perpetuated.

I was here interrupted by Mr. Tunnehill with: "Devil take the Indians and their names! Why should we honor these vagabond murderers by perpetuating their name?"

158

"Damn the Indians and their names," said another. "Let's call this Paradise Valley."

Before an opportunity was given for any others to object to the name, John O'Neil, a rollicking Texan, vociferously announced: "Hear ye! Hear ye! Hear ye! A vote will now be taken to decide what name shall be given to this valley." A *viva voce* vote was taken and the name of Yosemite was almost unanimously adopted. The name that was there and thus adopted by us, while seated around our camp fire, on the first visit of a white man to this remarkable locality, is the name by which it is now known to the world. At the time its significance—grizzly bear—was not generally known to our battalion. Neither was it pronounced with uniformity. Savage, who could speak the dialects of most of the mountain tribes in this part of California, told us that the correct pronunciation was Yo-sem-i-ty and that it signified a full grown grizzly; and that the name was given to old Tenieya's band because of their lawless and predatory character.

The date of our discovery and entrance into the Yosemite Valley was about the 21st of March, 1851. We were afterwards assured by Tenieya and others of his band that this was the first visit ever made to this valley by white men. . . .

CLIPPER SHIPS—THE FLYING CLOUD, 1851

America has always built fine ships. With expanding trade the emphasis shifted from seaworthiness and tonnage capacity to speed. The clipper ship was the answer. Long, narrow, with the greatest beam aft of center, clippers were usually full-rigged, with three raking masts and extra sails known as moonrakers and skysails. The first true clipper ship was the Ann McKim, *built in Baltimore in 1832. Donald McKay built the* Flying Cloud *in 1851 and her 89-day record under sail from New York to San Francisco still stands today. An excerpt from the log of this voyage follows:*

THE LOG OF THE "FLYING CLOUD"

June 6th (three days out from New York). Lost main and mizen topgallant masts, and maintopsail yard.—June 7th. Sent up main and mizen topgallant masts and yards.—June 8th. Sent up maintopsail yard.—June 14th. Discovered mainmast badly sprung about a foot from the hounds, and fished it.—July 11th. Very severe thunder and lightning, double reefed topsails, split fore and maintopmast stay sails. At 1 P.M. discovered mainmast had sprung, sent down royal and topgallant yards and studding sail booms off lower and topsail yards to relieve strain.—July 13th. Let men out of irons in consequence of wanting their services, with the understanding that they would be taken care of on arriving in San Francisco. At 6 P.M., carried away the maintopsail tye and band round mainmast.—July 23d. Cape Horn north five miles. The whole coast covered with snow.—July 31st. Fresh breezes, fine weather, all sail set. At 2 P.M. wind southeast. At 6 squally; in lower and topgallant studding sails; 7, in royals; at 2 A.M. in foretopmast studding sail. Latter part, strong gales and high sea running. Ship very wet fore and aft. Distance run this day by observation is 374 miles. During the squalls 18 knots of line was not sufficient to measure the rate of speed. Topgallantsails set.—Aug. 3d. At 3 P.M. suspended first officer from duty, in consequence of his arrogating to himself the privilege of cutting up rigging, contrary to my orders, and long continued neglect of duty.—Aug. 25th. Spoke barque *Amelia Packet*, 180 days from London for San Francisco.—Aug. 29th. Lost foretopgallant mast.—Aug. 30th. Sent up foretopgallant mast. Night strong and squally. Six A.M. made South Farallones bearing northeast ½ east; took a pilot at 7; anchored in San Francisco harbor at 11:30 A.M. after a passage of 89 days, 21 hours.†

Pages 160–161: The Yosemite Valley.

Ansel Adams

The Flying Cloud's *abstract log on this passage is as follows:*

Sandy Hook to the equator	21 days
Equator to 50° S.	25 "
50° S. in the Atlantic to 50° S. in Pacific	7 "
50° S. to equator	17 "
Equator to San Francisco	19 "
Total	89 "

Clipper ship *Flying Cloud.* Print by Currier & Ives 1852.

Old Print Shop

MARK TWAIN TELLS OF THE PONY EXPRESS, 1860's

The Pioneer mail route, known as the Pony Express Trail, was nearly 2,000 miles long and ran from St. Joseph, Missouri, westward over the Oregon Trail through Nebraska and Wyoming to Fort Bridger, continuing on the Mormon or Overland Trail to Salt Lake City, through Nevada and ended at Sacramento, California. There were 180 express stations en route at which horses and riders were changed. In a passage from Roughing It *Mark Twain tells of a meeting on the Trail:*

In a little while all interest was taken up in stretching our necks and watching for the pony, rider—the fleet messenger who sped across the continent from St. Joe to Sacramento-carrying letters nineteen hundred miles in eight days! Think of that for perishable horse and human flesh and blood to do! The pony-rider was usually a little bit of a man, brimful of spirit and endurance. No matter what time of the day or night his watch came on, and no matter whether it was winter or summer, raining, snowing, hailing, or sleeting, or whether his "beat" was a level straight road or a crazy trail over mountain crags and precipices, or whether it led through peaceful regions or regions that swarmed with hostile Indians, he must be always ready to leap into the saddle and be off like the wind! There was no idling-time for a pony-rider on duty. He rode fifty miles without stopping, by daylight, moonlight, starlight, or through the blackness of darkness—just as it happened. He rode a splendid

162

horse that was born for a racer and fed and lodged like a gentleman; kept him at his utmost speed for ten miles, and then, as he came crashing up to the station where stood two men holding fast a fresh, impatient steed, the transfer of rider and mail-bag was made in the twinkling of an eye, and away flew the eager pair and were out of sight before the spectator could get hardly the ghost of a look. Both rider and horse went "flying light." The rider's dress was thin, and fitted close; he wore a "round-about," and a skull-cap, and tucked his pantaloons into his boot-tops like a race-rider. He carried no arms—he carried nothing that was not absolutely necessary, for even the postage on his literary freight was worth *five dollars a letter*. He got but little frivolous correspondence to carry—his bag had business letters in it, mostly. His horse was stripped of all unnecessary weight, too. He wore a little wafer of a racing-saddle, and no visible blanket. He wore light shoes, or none at all. The little flat mail-pockets strapped under the rider's thighs would each hold about the bulk of a child's primer. They held many and many an important business chapter and newspaper letter, but these were written on paper as airy and thin as gold-leaf, nearly, and thus bulk and weight were economized. The stage-coach travelled about a hundred to a hundred and twenty-five miles a day (twenty-four hours), the pony-riders about two hundred and fifty.

'The Pony Express attacked by Indians." Painting by Frederic Remington.

There were about eighty pony-riders in the saddle all the time, night and day, stretching in a long, scattering procession from Missouri to California, forty flying eastward, and forty toward the west, and among them making four hundred gallant horses earn a stirring livelihood and see a great deal of scenery every single day in the year. . . .

Away across the endless dead level of the prairie a black speck appears against the sky, and it is plain that it moves. Well, I should think so! In a second or two it becomes a horse and rider, rising and falling—sweeping toward us nearer and nearer—growing more and more distinct, more and more sharply defined—nearer and still nearer, and the flutter of the hoofs comes faintly to the ear—another instant a whoop and a hurrah from our upper deck, a wave of the rider's hand, but no reply, and man and horse burst past our excited faces, and go winging away like a belated fragment of a storm!

So sudden is it all, and so like a flash of unreal fancy, that but for the flake of white foam left quivering and perishing on a mail-sack after the vision had flashed by and disappeared, we might have doubted whether we had seen any actual horse and man at all, maybe.

BUILDING OF THE TRANSCONTINENTAL RAILROAD, 1864–1869

The Herculean task of spanning the continent by rail began when President Lincoln signed the first Pacific Railway Bill, July 1, 1862. This task was entrusted to two corporations: the Union Pacific, which was to build westward from Council Bluffs, Iowa, and the Central Pacific, to build eastward from Sacramento, California. In Across the Plains, *Robert Louis Stevenson gives a picture of this epic:*

When I think of how the railroad has been pushed through this unwatered wilderness and haunt of savage tribes . . . ; how at each stage of construction, roaring, impromptu cities full of gold and lust and death sprang up and then died away again, and are now but way-side stations in the desert; how in these uncouth places pigtailed Chinese pirates worked side by side with border ruffians and broken men from Europe, talking together in a mixed dialect mostly oaths, . . . how the plumed hereditary lord of all America heard in this last fastness the scream of the "bad medicine wagon" charioting his foes; and then when I go on to remember that all this epical turmoil was conducted by gentlemen in frocked coats, and to nothing more extraordinary than a fortune and a subsequent visit to Paris, it seems to me . . . as if this railway were the one typical achievement of the age in which we live. . . . If it be romance, if it be contrast, if it be heroism that we require, what was Troytown to this.

LABOR TROUBLES

In his book How We Built the Union Pacific Railway, *General Grenville M. Dodge, chief engineer of the Union Pacific describes one of many problems:*

Between Ogden and Promontory each company graded a line, running side by side, and in some places one line was right above the other. The laborers upon the Central Pacific were Chinamen, while ours were Irishmen, and there was much ill-feeling between them. Our Irishmen were in the habit of firing their blasts in the cuts without giving warning to the Chinamen on the Central Pacific working right above them. From this cause several Chinamen were severely hurt. Complaint was made to me by the Central Pacific people, and I endeavored to have the contractors bring all hostilities to a close, but, for some reason or other, they failed to do so. One day the Chinamen, appreciating the situation, put in what is called a "grave" on their work, and when the Irishmen right under them were all at work let go their blast and buried several of our men. This brought about a truce at once. From that time the Irish laborers showed due respect for the Chinamen, and there was no further trouble.

GENERAL DODGE'S LAST REPORT TO THE BOARD OF DIRECTORS

In 1863 and 1864 surveys were inaugurated, but in 1866 the country was systematically occupied; and day and night, summer and winter the explorations were pushed forward through dangers and hardships that very few at this day appreciate, for every mile had to be run within range of the musket, as there was not a moment's security. In making the surveys numbers of our men, some of them the ablest and most promising, were killed; and during the construction our stock was run off by the hundred, I might say by the thousand, and as one difficulty after another arose and was overcome, both in the engineering, running and constructing departments, a new era in railroad building was inaugurated.

Each day taught us lessons by which we profited for the next, and our advances and improvements in the art of railway construction were marked by the progress of the work, forty miles of track having been laid in 1865, 260 in 1866, 240 in 1867, including the ascent to the summit of the Rocky mountains, at an elevation of 8235 feet above the ocean; and during 1868 and to May 10, 1869, 555 miles all exclusive of side and temporary tracks, of which over 180 miles were built in addition.

The first grading was done in the autumn of 1864, and the first rail laid in July, 1865. When you look back to the beginning at the Missouri river, with no railroad communication from the east, and 500 miles of the country in advance without timber, fuel or any material whatever from which to build or maintain a road, except the sand for the bare roadbed itself with everything to be transported, and that by teams or at best by streamboats, for hundreds and thousands of miles; everything to be created, with labor scarce and high, you can all look back upon the work with satisfaction and ask, under such circumstances, could we have done more or better?

The country is evidently satisfied that you accomplished wonders and have achieved a work that will be a monument to your energy, your ability, and to your devotion to the enterprise through all its gloomy as well as its bright periods; for it is notorious that, notwithstanding the aid of the Government, there was so little faith in the enterprise that its dark days—when your private fortunes and your all was staked on the success of the project—far exceeded those of sunshine, faith and confidence.

This lack of confidence in the project, even in the West, in those localities where the benefits of its construction were manifest, was excessive, and it will be remembered that laborers even demanded their pay before they would perform their day's work, so little faith had they in the payment of their wages, or in the ability of the company to succeed in their efforts. Probably no enterprise in the world has been so maligned, misrepresented and criticized as this; but now, after the calm judgment of the American people is brought to bear upon it, unprejudiced and biased, it is almost without exception pronounced the best new road in the United States. . . .

Its future is fraught with great good. It will develop a waste, will bind together the two extremes of the nation as one, will stimulate intercourse and trade, and bring harmony, prosperity and wealth to the two coasts. A proper policy, systematically and perisistently followed, will bring to the road the trade of two oceans, and will give it all the business it can accommodate; while the local trade will increase gradually until the mining, grazing and agricultural regions through which it passes will build up and create a business that will be a lasting and permanent support to the country.†

DRIVING OF THE GOLDEN SPIKE, 1869

"How We Built the Union Pacific Railway"

General Grenville M. Dodge

On the morning of May 10, 1869, Hon. Leland Stanford, Governor of California and President of the Central Pacific, accompanied by Messrs. Huntington, Hopkins, Crocker and trainloads of California's distinguished citizens, arrived from the west. During the forenoon Vice President T. C. Durant and Directors John R. Duff and Sidney Dillon and Consulting Engineer Silas A. Seymour of the Union Pacific, with other prominent men, including a delegation of Mormons from Salt Lake City, came in on a train from the east. The National Government was represented by a detachment of "regulars" from Fort Douglass, Utah, accompanied by a band, and 600 others, including Chinese, Mexicans, Indians, half-breeds, negroes and laborers, suggesting an air of cosmopolitanism, all gathered around the open space where the tracks were to be joined. The Chinese laid the rails from the west end, and the Irish laborers laid them from the east end, until they met and joined.

Telegraphic wires were so connected that each blow of the descending sledge could be reported instantly to all parts of the United States. Corresponding blows were struck on the bell of the City Hall in San Francisco, and with the last blow of the sledge a cannon was fired at Fort Point. General Stafford presented a spike of gold, silver and iron as the offering of the Territory of Arizona. Governor Tuttle of Nevada persented a spike of silver from his state. The connecting tie was of California laurel, and California presented the last spike of gold in behalf of that state. A silver sledge had also been presented for the occasion. A prayer was offered. Governor Stanford of California made a few appropriate remarks on behalf of the Central Pacific and the chief engineer responded for the Union Pacific. Then the telegraphic inquiry from the Omaha office, from which the circuit was to be started, was answered: "To everybody: Keep quiet. When the last spike is driven at Promontory Point we will say 'Done.' Don't break the circuit, but watch for the signals of the blows of the hammer. The spike will soon be driven. The signal will be three dots for the commencement of the blows." The magnet tapped one—two—three—then paused—"Done." The spike was given its first blow by President Stanford and Vice President Durant followed. Neither hit the spike the first time, but hit the rail, and were greeted by the lusty cheers of the onlookers, accompanied by the screams of the locomotives and the music of the military band. Many other spikes were driven on the last rail by some of the distinguished persons present, but it was seldom that they first hit the spike. The original spike, after being tapped

The Golden Spike ceremony, symbolizing the spanning of the continent, 1869

Union Pacific Railroad

Spanning the continent, 1954.

by the officials of the companies, was driven home by the chief engineers of the two roads. Then the two trains were run together, the two locomotives touching at the point of junction, and the engineers of the two locomotives each broke a bottle of champagne on the other's engine. Then it was declared that the connection was made and the Atlantic and Pacific were joined together never to be parted.†

TERRITORIAL GROWTH OF THE UNITED STATES

Source: "A Diplomatic History of the American People" by Thomas A. Bailey

The original territory of the United States after ratification of the Constitution, 1789, was 892,135 square miles. Today its area is 3,639,990 square miles. Acquisition of this territory was achieved in the following ways:

DATE*	ACQUISITION	AREA (sq. mi.)	HOW ACQUIRED	PRICE
1803	Louisiana	827,987	Purchase from France	$15,000,000 in cash and assumed claims
1819	Floridas	72,101	Treaty with Spain	$5,000,000 in assumed claims and relinquishment of Texas claim
1845	Texas	389,166	Independent republic, annexed	
1846	Oregon	286,541	Treaty with Great Britain	

1848	Mexican Cession	529,189	Conquest from Mexico	$15,000,000 plus maximum claims of $3,250,000
1853	Gadsden Purchase	29,670	Purchase from Mexico	$10,000,000
1867	Alaska	586,400	Purchase from Russia	$7,200,000
1867	Midway Islands	1½	Occupation	
1898	Hawaiian Islands	6,407	Independent republic, annexed	
1898	Philippine Islands	114,400	Conquest from Spain	$20,000,000
1898	Puerto Rico	3,435	Conquest from Spain	
1898	Guam	206	Conquest from Spain	
1899	Wake Island	3	Occupation	
1899	American Samoa	76	Division with Germany and Great Britain	
1903	Panama Canal Zone	549	Treaty with Panama	$10,000,000 annual payment of $250,000 beginning 9 years after ratification
1916	Virgin Islands	133	Purchase from Denmark	$25,000,000

* If treaty, date of signing.

MAP OF THE
UNITED STATES
showing
ACQUISITION OF TERRITORY

Oklahoma Land Rush.   At the firing of the gun these homesteaders raced to stake their claims, 1889.

UNITED STATES CENSUS FIGURES 1790–1950

1790	3,929,214	1870	39,818,449
1800	5,308,483	1880	50,155,783
1810	7,239,881	1890	62,947,714
1820	9,638,453	1900	75,995,575
1830	12,866,020	1910	91,972,266
1840	17,069,453	1920	105,710,620
1850	23,191,876	1930	122,775,046
1860	31,443,321	1940	131,669,275
	1950	150,697,361	

IMMIGRANTS ADMITTED FROM ALL COUNTRIES: BY DECADES 1820–1950

1820	8,385	1890	455,302
1830	23,322	1900	448,572
1840	84,066	1910	1,041,570
1850	369,980	1920	430,001
1860	153,640	1930	241,700
1870	387,203	1940	70,756
1880	457,257	1950	249,187

Source: The World Almanac, 1953

FIVE

Agriculture

and Conservation

"Man must recognize the necessity of co-operating with nature. He must temper his demands and use and conserve the natural living resources of this earth in a manner that alone can provide for the continuation of his civilization."

FAIRFIELD OSBORN

Opposite: "The oldest living things."   Sequoias (California redwood trees).

Agriculture

Throughout their lives George Washington and Thomas Jefferson were intensely interested in agriculture, devoting much time to their respective farms at Mount Vernon and Monticello. In the following observations and letters they discuss agriculture and their experiments:

THOMAS JEFFERSON, 1809

I trust the good sense of our country will see that its greatest prosperity depends on a due balance between agriculture, manufactures and commerce.

GEORGE WASHINGTON, 1796
LETTER TO ALEXANDER HAMILTON

November 2, 1796

It must be obvious to every man who considers the agriculture of this country (even in the best improved parts of it), and compares the produce of our lands with those of other countries no ways superior to them in *natural fertility*, how miserably defective we are in the management of them; and that if we do not fall on a better mode of treating them, how ruinous it will prove to the landed interest. Ages will not produce a systematic change without public attention and encouragement, but a few years more of increased sterility will drive the inhabitants of the Atlantic states westwardly for support, whereas if they were taught how to improve the old instead of going in pursuit of new and productive soils, they would make those acres which now scarcely yield them anything turn out beneficial to themselves; to the mechanics by supplying them with the staff of life on much cheaper terms, to the merchants by increasing their commerce and exportation, and to the community generally by the influx of wealth resulting therefrom.†

THOMAS JEFFERSON TO GEORGE WASHINGTON, 1790

Monticello Sep. 12. 1790

. . . I propose to sow and plant the next spring 2. acres at each of my farms, for the maintenance of 8. plough-horses (4. to the acre) and I count on it's feeding them thro' the whole summer without anything else, my plough horses have this summer (from April) had nothing but clover, & have gone through the summer's work as well as then they were crammed with corn. it is a great step towards recruiting our lands, to abate the culture of corn. . . . the field pea of Europe & their winter vetch I find to be great desiderata in the farm. the former to cultivate in such of our fallows as will not yield clover; as while we are keeping our ground clean for the next wheat sowing, the pea will shade it, and give us a valuable crop both of grain & fodder. the winter vetch down on our fall fallows for corn, will give a fine crop of green fodder in the spring, which may be cut in time to prepare the ground or corn, this will cost us not a single ploughing. I have taken two or three chances of getting these things from Europe, in time as I hope to try them the next season. I expect to take both these articles into the regular course of my husbandry thus. 1. wheat. followed by winter vetch. 2. corn followed by winter vetch. 3. a fallow of pease. 4. wheat. 5.6.7. three years of clover. a very decisive experiment has banished rye from my rotation. I mix potatoes with my corn, on your plan. You shall know the result of my trials of European pea & vetch, and be furnished with seed, they prove worth your notices. we have had this year such rains as never came I believe since Noah's flood. our clear profits will not repay the damage done our lands. . . .

A farm in the Shenandoah Valley, Virginia.

GEORGE WASHINGTON TO THOMAS JEFFERSON, 1795

Mount Vernon 4th. Octr. 1795

. . . I am much pleased with the account you have given of the Succory. This, like all other things of the sort with me, since my absence from home, have come to nothing; for neither my Overseers nor Manager, will attend properly to anything but the crops they have usually cultivated: and in spite of all I can say, if there is the smallest discretionary power allowed them, they will fill the land with Indian corn; altho' they have demonstrable proof, at every step they take, of its destructive effects. I am resolved however, as soon as it shall be in my power to attend a little more closely to my own concerns, to make this crop yield, in a great degree to other grain; to pulses, and to grasses. I am beginning again with Chiccory from a handful of seed given me by Mr. Strickland; which, though flourishing at present has no appearance of seeding this year. Lucern has not succeeded better with me than with you; but I will give it another, and a fairer trial before it is abandoned altogether. Clover, when I can dress lots well, succeeds with me to my full expectation; but not on the fields in

173

Mount Vernon, home of George Washington.

rotation; although I have been at much cost in seeding them. This has greatly disconcerted the system of rotation on which I had decided. I wish you may succeed in getting good seed of the winter Vetch: I have often imported it, but the seed never vegetated, or in so small a proportion as to be destroyed by weeds. I believe it would be an acquisition if it was once introduced properly in our farm. The Albany Pea, which is the same as the field Pea of Europe, I have tried, and found it grew well; but it is subject to the same bug that perforates the garden pea, & eats out the kernel; so it will happen, I fear, with the pea that you propose to import. I had great expectation from a green dressing with Buck wheat, as a preparatory fallow for a crop of wheat; but it has not answered my expectation yet. I ascribe this however, more to mismanagement in the times of seeding and ploughing in, than to any defect in the system. The first ought to be so ordered, in point of time, as to meet a convenient season for ploughing it in while the plant is in its most succulent state; but this has never been done on my farms, & consequently has drawn as much *from*, as it has given *to* the earth.

It has always appeared to me that there were two modes in which Buck Wheat might be used advantageously as a manure. One, to sow early; and as soon as a sufficiency of seed ripened to stock the ground a second time, to turn the whole in; and when the succeeding growth is getting in full bloom to turn that in also before the seed begins to ripen: and when the fermentation and putrefaction cease, to show the ground in that state, & plough in the Wheat. The other mode is, to sow the Buck Wheat so late as that it shall be generally, about a foot high at the usual seeding of Wheat; then turn it in, and sow thereon immediately, as on a clover lay; harrowing in the seed lightly to avoid disturbing the buried Buck Wheat.

174

The last method I have never tried, but see no reason why it should not succeed. The other as I have observed before, I have practiced but the Buck Wheat has always stood too long, & consequently had become too dry and sticky, to answer the end of a succulent plant. But of all the improving and ameliorating crops, none, in my opinion, is equal to Potatoes on stiff, & hard bound land as mine. From a variety of instances I am satisfied that on such land, a crop of Potatoes is equal to an ordinary dressing. In *no* instance have I failed of good Wheat, Oats, or clover that followed potatoes. And I concede they give the soil a darker hue.

I shall thank you for the result of your proposed experiments relatively to the winter vetch & Pea, when they are made.

I am sorry to hear of the depredation committed by the weevil in your parts. It is a great calamity at all times, and this year, when the demand for wheat is so great, and the price so high, must be a mortifying one to the farmer. . . .

THOMAS JEFFERSON, 1798

It has been said that no rotation of crops will keep the earth in the same degree of fertility without the aid of manure. But it is well known here that a space of rest greater or less in spontaneous herbage, will restore the exhaustion of a single crop. This then is a rotation: and as it is not to be believed that spontaneous herbage is the only or best covering during rest, so may we expect that a substitute for it may be found which will yield profitable crops. Such perhaps are clover, peas, vetches, &c. A rotation then may be found, which by giving time for the slow influence of the atmosphere, will keep the soil in a constant and equal state of fertility. But the advantage of manuring is that it will do more in one than the atmosphere would require several years to do, and consequently enables you so much the oftener to take exhausting crops from the soil, a circumstance of importance where there is much more labor than land.

AGRICULTURE IN THE UNITED STATES*
Louis Bromfield, Writer, Farmer, Economist

The history of agriculture in the United States until a generation ago followed very largely the historical pattern of agriculture in new countries everywhere in the world, a history of quick and frequently reckless exploitation of the soil and water resources in a world in which these things *seemed* for a long period to be inexhaustible. The pattern is as old as time. It had been worked out centuries ago to a disastrous end in such countries as India, China, the whole of the Middle East and North Africa. To some extent in regions of the Western Hemisphere and elsewhere its destructive results are still in progress.

The thought and reasoning behind such an agriculture and such a pattern are understandable from the point of view of the pioneer agriculturist. In the beginning a man claimed land in the Atlantic coastal area and when that was worn out he could go west and get new, rich virgin land for the taking or for a dollar an acre. Virtually all he needed for a start was a team, a plow, a harrow, good health, energy and ambition. This, in brief, has been until quite recently the pattern of American agriculture.

But out of this pattern there arose a curious philosophy—that the land owed the farmer a living, and that therefore it was not necessary for the farmer to make any effort toward the maintenance, let alone an increase, in the fertility of the soil he owned. The operation of such a philosophy was possible for the first generation. In the second generation, crop yields began to diminish. If the third generation followed the same philosophy, actual disaster was visible on the horizon and more often than not the sons and daughters migrated westward to begin a new life on new virgin land. In other words a good deal of our agriculture in the

* Original article.

past produced something resembling the result of a plague of locusts moving acoss the nation from the Atlantic to the Pacific Coast, until at last about a couple of generations ago, the migrants reached the Pacific Coast and there was no longer any free land to be had.

To be sure there existed here and there in the nation individual good farmers and even colonies of good farmers, such as those living in the so-called "Pennsylvania Dutch" regions, farmers who practiced a sound and permanent agriculture based upon proper treatment of the land which maintained and even increased the natural fertility; but these individuals and colonies were rare indeed.

Many factors entered into the ruin of millions of acres of once good agriculture land. Soil erosion, both by wind and water, ruined or damaged badly thousands of farms. The business of replacing organic material, vital to all sound agriculture, was neglected or wholly ignored, but there was one basic element which contributed enormously to wholesale destruction. This was the fact that most of our farmers came from northern and central Europe and they brought with them an agriculture, sound enough in those areas, but un-suited in many respects to the violence of the climate and to the soils and crops raised in the New World. In northern and central Europe, open cultivated row crops, such as corn and cotton, which kept the soil constantly under cultivation and frequently left bare to the ravages of a violent climate, were almost unknown. The careless and greedy exploitation of American soils through a bad corn and cotton agriculture (as well as perpetual exploitation of soils by quick cash crops) produced in many areas such as the deep South and the Middle West a destruction by erosion and depletion which could only be described as disastrous.

But these direct evils also spawned a crop of secondary evils, costly to the nation in terms of prices, profits, taxes and other economic factors. By stripping millions of acres of good land of its forest or grass cover and putting it to the plow under a careless agriculture, the volume and violence of floods and runoff water on rivers and streams everywhere was greatly increased and problems of siltation produced damaging effects upon the general economy. Hundreds of millions of dollars had to be spent upon confining dykes and levees and upon the removal of silt and gravel from channels and harbors.

Trillions of gallons of water which once was held and diverted *into* the earth by the forest and grass covers were diverted *off* the bare land, creating floods and eventually ending in the ocean. In the long run this began to make itself felt in falling water tables, sources of surface water supplies and in ground moisture for the production of crops. This condition was also greatly aggravated by the increasing use of water as great cities developed and industries moved into large areas which were once almost wholly agricultural. Today the increasing shortage of water for agriculture, for industry and for domestic uses in large cities has become one of the vital problems of the whole nation.

Not all of the picture, however, is a dark one. Beginning with Theodore Roosevelt and Gifford Pinchot, more and more enlightened and intelligent citizens and leaders began to understand that the great wealth and power of the United States was very largely founded upon the nation's immense supply of natural resources of all kinds, and that as these became gradually exhausted and the population steadily increased, there might well come a day when this fabulously rich nation would reach the level of many overpopulated nations poor in natural resources which were forced to import not only raw materials for their industries but actually food, in order to maintain even a low standard of diet for their citizens. Roose-velt and Pinchot chose the word "conservation" to cover the whole movement that was designed to maintain and even increase natural resources. They placed their initial emphasis upon forests.

The policy of conservation of soils and a better agriculture came a little later and the great figure in this movement was and still is Dr. Hugh H. Bennett, who brought about the establishment of the Soil Conservation Service set up to aid and instruct farmers everywhere regarding the means of preventing erosion by wind and water, the conservation of water

"Farmers who practice a sound and permanent
agriculture." A Pennsylvania Dutch farm.

and in general agricultural practices which maintained and even increased the fertility of soils.

The Soil Conservation Service under Dr. Bennett was compelled to discover or invent a whole new system of agriculture, very different from that in common practice in northern and central Europe. This included the establishment and use of terraces, strip cropping, contour plowing (around a hill rather than up or down the hill), the increased use of grasses and leguminous plants and in general an increase in organic material and the intelligent and selective use of commercial fertilizers.

The establishment of the Soil Conservation Service and of a new kind of agriculture has proven to be one of the most remarkable developments in all history for a number of reasons, (1) because it is probably the first example in all history of a nation checking disastrous land practice before disaster actually became a reality as it did in the Near East, in some Asiatic nations and in North Africa, which once very nearly fed the Roman Empire and today is very largely desert; (2) because of the speed with which the reform was accomplished; (3) because of the intelligent reaction of the American farmer himself and his willingness to adopt new and revolutionary methods to which he was unaccustomed and which in many cases ran exactly counter to the agricultural tradition in which he had been brought up. The general practice of soil conservation and of new agricultural methods and concepts has been virtually accomplished within little more than a generation.

At the same time the operation of economics has exerted a significant force in the whole of this revolution. As the areas of free virgin land diminished or ceased to exist and the pressures of a growing population began to be felt, as agricultural labor shortages developed in times of prosperity, and mechanization of agriculture in the United States became the most thorough in the world, land values and the general costs of farming increased greatly. These factors, together with the educational and working program of the Soil Conservation Service, the state agricultural colleges and the whole Department of Agriculture, brought about a veritable revolution in which the old, wasteful, pioneer, frontier agriculture was doomed.

In the United States there began to come into being for the first time a generally good, intelligent and scientific agriculture instead of an agriculture in which only a comparatively few individuals or groups practiced really sound farming methods. The agriculture of the nation is rapidly becoming both a mature and a permanent agriculture in which, in most areas, crop yields per acre are steadily increasing rather than decreasing. All this serves more and more to diminish any possibility of real food shortages for the whole nation within the next two or three hundred years, despite the rapid increase in population.

It is quite possible under a really modern and efficient agriculture for the soils of the nation now actually under cultivation, to feed three times our present population at its present level of diet. Dr. Firmin Bear, of Rutgers University, one of the great authorities in the field of agriculture and food, believes that by utilizing properly all our land as well as the resources of lakes, rivers, ponds and seafood, we could in the United States support a population of one billion at a good dietary level.

Indeed, the trend of top level agriculture in the United States is steadily in the direction of a more intensive and concentrated agriculture, of producing more and more per acre at greatly reduced costs. This is in exact contradiction to the old pioneer, frontier school which, if an increase in production was desired, undertook simply to plant more and more acres, while the production *per acre* on their land constantly declined. There are in the United States still too many farmers who are farming five acres to produce what they should produce on one acre, with the result that whatever they raise costs them, in general, five times as much in taxes, interest, gasoline, labor and seed as it does the farmer who is producing the same amount on one acre.

With regard to information and education the American farmer is the most fortunate man in the world, not only because of the wide variety of information and the great amounts of money spent upon research and experiment, but because so much of this information and education costs him nothing or very little indeed. In Washington the Department of Agriculture, in buildings covering acres of ground, spends immense sums each year in the farmers' behalf on everything from subsidy payments and price support purchasing, through departments of experiment and research and the publication of free bulletins of information on virtually every subject concerned with agriculture, horticulture, soils and livestock breeding. In all the individual states exist agricultural colleges, offering education, without tuition payments, to the citizens of those states. These colleges in turn maintain stations for experiment and research which are open to every farmer and which provide him on request with information upon every subject remotely related to agriculture.

In addition to all these sources of information and education, there exist dozens of excellent agricultural magazines and publications, some national in scope, others regional and concerned largely with the specialized problems, the crops, climates and soils of a given area. Radio maintains excellent "farm hours" and television has recently entered the field with farm programs. All of this mass of information and education in modern agriculture largely costs the farmer nothing and in the case where payments are necessary, they come at bargain prices. It could be said that no element of our citizenry is so well provided for and that there is little or no excuse today for any farmer being a bad farmer.

The significance of all of this bears evidence in the fact that while nearly all the other countries of the world are plagued constantly with food shortages or are forced to import large amounts of food to provide a passable diet for their populations, the United States is constantly plagued by problems of over-production and surplus. This embarrassment of riches lies at the root of the *political* problem represented by the whole range of devices set up to maintain farm prices at a level that will provide the farmer with profits which in turn can be spent in purchasing the products of our vast industries. This particular economic aspect of the farm supports program has been frequently overlooked.

In general both the citizens of the United States and of the world think of the United States as a nation whose power and wealth is almost wholly based upon industry. This is

J. T. Mitchell

Contour farming: "around a hill rather than up and down the hill."   Aerial view of six farms in Texas.

logical in view of the fact that the United States produces more of many industrial commodities than the rest of the world put together. It is largely unknown or unrecognized that the total investment in agriculture in terms of land, building, livestock, machinery, etc. in the United States is larger than the total investment in industry. It is also unrecognized that agriculture provides in one way or another the wages, salaries, and consequently the purchasing power for industrial commodities of around fifty per cent of our population. This

179

Normal equipment needed to run an average 400-acre farm.   Photographed in Ohio

includes by far the greater part of the small towns and villages whose economy is almost entirely based upon agricultural purchasing power and many larger cities such as Omaha, Kansas City, Minneapolis, Des Moines, Memphis and others whose insurance companies, real estate values and general markets are largely based upon livestock and agriculture. There is the whole of the vast meat and food processing industries, the huge agriculture machinery industry and large segments of the automobile, steel, rubber industries and other industries which are dependent for prosperity and employment upon agricultural purchasing power.

Indeed, perhaps the very keystone of American prosperity, high living and dietary standards is the remarkable balance between agriculture and industry which is unique in the United States among all the nations of the world. American food producers feed the country with an ample diet, create industrial employment and in turn, out of their income, purchase the commodities manufactured by industry while the industrial worker in turn buys the food the farmer produces, without any need for the nation as a whole to import food of any kind. In the whole of this picture lies another factor . . . that the United States has the best, the most varied diet and the cleanest, high quality food of any nation in the world and at the same time it has the cheapest food in terms of the percentages of the family budget spent upon food or the number of work hours required to purchase that food. In time of almost universal inflation of currencies, these are the only standards by which the costs of food can be measured.

Toward this end (the production of abundant, high quality, reasonably priced food) countless Americans, from the farmer himself through the educator, the government agent, the scientist, the home economics teacher and many others, have made contributions. Moreover, in the field of agricultural research and experiment, and especially in the whole field of the new agriculture based upon soil and water conservation, the United States has become the world's leader and the services of American experts in the various fields related to agriculture are sought in almost all the countries of the world. This is a long way indeed from the primitive frontier, pioneer agriculture which once moved across the nation from Atlantic to Pacific destroying as it went.

Conservation—Agricultural Resources

THE CONSERVATION OF NATURAL RESOURCES
President Theodore Roosevelt's Seventh Annual Message to Congress, 1907

. . . The conservation of our natural resources and their proper use constitute the fundamental problem which underlies almost every other problem of our national life. . . . As a nation we not only enjoy a wonderful measure of present prosperity but if this prosperity is used aright it is an earnest of future success such as no other nation will have. The reward of foresight for this nation is great and easily foretold. But there must be the look ahead, there must be a realization of the fact that to waste, to destroy, our natural resources, to skin and exhaust the land instead of using it so as to increase its usefulness, will result in undermining in the days of our children the very prosperity which we ought by right to hand down to them amplified and developed. . . .

. . . We are prone to speak of the resources of this country as inexhaustible; this is not so. The mineral wealth of the country, the coal, iron, oil, gas, and the like, does not reproduce itself, and therefore is certain to be exhausted ultimately; and wastefulness in dealing with it today means that our descendants will feel the exhaustion a generation or two before they otherwise would. But there are certain other forms, of waste which could be entirely stopped—the waste of soil by washing, for instance, which is among the most dangerous of all wastes now in progress in the United States, is easily preventable, so that this present enormous loss of fertility is entirely unnecessary. The preservation or replacement of the forests is one of the most important means of preventing this loss. We have made a beginning in forest preservation, but . . . so rapid has been the rate of exhaustion of timber in the United States in the past, and so rapidly is the remainder being exhausted, that the country is unquestionably on the verge of a timber famine which will be felt in every household in the land. . . . The present annual consumption of lumber is certainly three times as great as the annual growth; and if the consumption and growth continue unchanged, practically all our lumber will be exhausted in another generation, while long before the limit to complete exhaustion is reached the growing scarcity will make itself felt in many blighting ways upon our national welfare. About twenty per cent of our forested territory is now reserved in national forests; but these do not include the most valuable timberlands, and in any event the proportion is too small to expect that the reserves can accomplish more than a mitigation of the trouble which is ahead for the nation. . . .†

"THE FIGHT FOR CONSERVATION," 1910

Gifford Pinchot, Chief, Division of Forestry, U.S. Government

The principles which govern the conservation movement, like all great and effective things, are simple and easily understood. . . .

The first principle of conservation is development, the use of the natural resources now existing on this continent for the benefit of the people who live here now. There may be just as much waste in neglecting the development and use of certain natural resources as there is in their destruction. . . .

. . . In every case and in every direction the conservation movement has development for its first principle, and at the very beginning of its work. The development of our natural resources and the fullest use of them for the present generation is the first duty of this generation. . . .

In the second place conservation stands for the prevention of waste. There has come gradually in this country an understanding that waste is not a good thing and that the attack on waste is an industrial necessity. I recall very well indeed how, in the early days of forest fires, they were considered simply and solely as acts of God, against which any opposition was hopeless and any attempt to control them not merely hopeless but child-ish. . . . To-day we understand that forest fires are wholly within the control of men. So we are coming in like manner to understand that the prevention of waste in all other directions is a simple matter of good business. The first duty of the human race is to control the earth it lives upon.

We are in a position more and more completely to say how far the waste and destruction of natural resources are to be allowed to go no and where they are to stop. It is curious that the effort to stop waste, like the effort to stop forest fires, has often been considered as a matter controlled wholly by economic law. I think there could be no greater mistake. Forest fires were allowed to burn long after the people had means to stop them. . . . When at length we came to see that the control of logging in certain directions was profitable, we found it had long been possible. In all these matters of waste of natural resources, the ed-ucation of the people to understand that they can stop the leakage comes before the actual stopping and after the means of stopping it have long been ready at our hands.

In addition to the principles of development and preservation of our resources there is a third principle. It is this: The natural resources must be developed and preserved for the benefit of the many, and not merely for the profit of a few. We are coming to understand in this country that public action for public benefit has a very much wider field to cover and a much larger part to play than was the case when there were resources enough for every one. . . .

The conservation idea covers a wider range than the field of natural resources alone. Conservation means the greatest good to the greatest number for the longest time. . . .

The principles of conservation thus described—development, preservation, the common good—have a general application which is growing rapidly wider. The development of resources and the prevention of waste and loss, the protection of the public interests, by foresight, prudence, and the ordinary business and home-making virtues, all these apply to other things as well as to the natural resources. There is, in fact, no interest of the people to which the principles of conservation do not apply.

. . . In other words, and that is the burden of the message, we are coming to see the logical and inevitable outcome that these principles, which arose in forestry and have their bloom in the conservation of natural resources, will have their fruit in the increase and promotion of national efficiency along other lines of national life.

182

The outgrowth of conservation, the inevitable result, is national efficiency. In the great commercial struggle between nations which is eventually to determine the welfare of all, national efficiency will be the deciding factor. So from every point of view conservation is a good thing for the American people.†

THE TENNESSEE VALLEY AUTHORITY ACT, May 18, 1933

Public vs. private ownership of utilities is an extremely controversial subject in the United States, the pros and cons of which are outside the scope of this book. Following is an excerpt from the Tennessee Valley Authority Act, which brought into being the government's largest power project:

AN ACT to improve the navigability and to provide for the flood control of the Tennessee River; to provide for reforestation and the proper use of marginal lands in the Tennessee Valley; to provide for the agricultural and industrial development of said valley; to provide for the national defense by the creation of a corporation for the operation of Government properties at and near Muscle Shoals in the State of Alabama, and for other purposes. . . .

Be it enacted, That for the purpose of maintaining and operating the properties now owned by the United States . . . there is hereby created a body corporate by the name of the "Tennessee Valley Authority." . . .

SEC. 23. The President shall, from time to time . . . recommend to Congress such legislation as he deems proper to carry out the general purposes stated . . . and for the especial purpose of bringing about in said Tennessee drainage basin and adjoining territory . . . (1) the maximum amount of flood control; (2) the maximum development of said Tennessee River for navigation purposes; (3) the maximum generation of electric power consistent with flood control and navigation; (4) the proper use of marginal lands; . . . and (6) the economic and social well-being of the people living in said river basin. . . .

T.V.A. has succeeded in controlling floods, improving navigation channels and creating hydroelectric power within an area known as the Tennessee River Valley, an area embracing seven states. Today giant turbines produce electrical energy, marketed at low cost, serving 80 per cent of the farms within its domain as compared to 3 per cent twenty years ago. The 627 miles of navigation channels created by T.V.A. have made possible low water-freight rates, resulting in greatly increased shipment of raw materials, aiding industrial growth.

"THE ROAD TO SURVIVAL," 1948
William Vogt

The floods of our Middle West and the almost hysterical demands for flood control through engineering methods are a by-product of misuse of the land. People who have settled on the flood plains of the Missouri, Mississippi, and their tributaries, and then wail that the rest of the country must bail them out, remind one of the man who jumped off the Empire State Building—and changed his mind. The land on which they have built and the fields they till have obviously been deposited by past floods. Simply because human beings occupy the flood plain is no reason why there should not be further floods.

To reduce temporary floods by building a series of dams that would permanently submerge some of the richest land in the world—the project of the U. S. Army Engineers—

Tennessee Valley. *Above:* Construction work on the Fontana T.V.A. dam in North Carolina. *Opposite:* Fort Loudon Dam, Tennessee.

Navigation channels created by T.V.A.

Forsythe

"The floods of our Middle West"—from the Missouri River

would seem to compound the foolishness. Yet an inquiry addressed to the Army Engineers on July 7, 1947, brought forth the information that they had no idea how many acres their reservoirs would cover. How much good land would be forever removed from use by the American people under a Missouri Valley Authority has never been calculated. Unless this is done, and any MVA development adjusted to this factor, the MVA plan may well be a national liability. We no longer can afford to waste fertile fields beneath hydroelectric reservoirs. Nor can we afford to sacrifice many of them to protect downstream urban areas against floods. . . . We are far from ending the erosion loss of the good land we have left; and both world and domestic drains on it are increasing.

The concept of resource management on the basis of watersheds is one of the most promising and soundest of modern times. But, like many human activities, it is plagued by Aristotelian identifications. Unless we start with the premise that every watershed is unique, the Valley Authority concept may lead to destructive and costly mistakes. The Missouri Valley is *not* the Tennessee Valley; even were the TVA an unqualified success, it should be profoundly modified before it is transferred to other regions. Mistakes made in the Tennessee Valley, such as flooding productive land and neglecting the watershed, might be far graver elsewhere; the Missouri Valley is, to a considerable extent, a region of light, extremely erodible soils that are extensively and intensively cultivated.

An especial danger is that the engineers will be turned loose before adequate studies have been made. Some of our foremost scientists gave a brilliant exposition, in MVA hearings, of the complexity of the problem of sound land-use development, and especially of irrigation, in the Missouri Valley; this testimony made it clear that there are vast gaps in our

186

understanding of the region. Satisfactory studies cannot be made overnight, and to locate dams without them—as the U.S. Army Engineers and Bureau of Reclamation have been doing—seems like irresponsible abuse of both the land and the taxpayer.

The hundreds of millions of dollars that we are asked to spend to prevent destruction of cities and avert loss of life are an enormous burden on the taxpayer. At a time when our school system threatens to break down because we cannot pay teachers a decent wage, or support hospitals to care for the sick, we are urged to spend billions on people too stupid to stay off flood plains, and on damming rivers that have got out of hand largely because of destruction of forests and grasslands. The Okies who flocked into California in 1936 and 1937 were products of ignorance and abuse of nature's laws and resources. A period of favorable rainfall has brought many of these people back to the danger zone; it is certain that within a few years drifts to topsoil will once more be overwhelming farmhouses—and the Okies will be on the move again. People who overgraze and deforest watersheds and plant themselves in the path of the floods are as much of a national liability as the Okies.

. . . The present living standards for 145,000,000 people is being maintained only by living on our resource capital. Within about a hundred and fifty years we have lost one-third of our topsoil, more than half of our high-grade timber, an unknown proportion of reserve waters, and a large but unmeasured part of our wild-life. As we reduce our capital, our income from interest naturally fails; so we use still more capital.

Obviously, this cannot continue indefinitely. In terms of lost productive capacity and the cost of patching up the damage we have already inflicted on the continent, we have heavily mortgaged the welfare of our children and grandchildren—as our ancestors put ours in pawn.

Without an abundant and balanced diet, without resources of water, timber, minerals, without dependable supplies of food from good soils, freedom from floods, dust storms, clogging reservoirs, our nation can remain neither strong, great—nor, in this overpeopled world, safe from aggression.

I am not suggesting that such decadence lies in store for the United States. It need not. . . . The future of our country is within our control. But a few more decades of such abuse as we have subjected it to will wrest the control out of our hands. We shall be slipping toward the oblivion of Ur, of Timgad, or Angkor Wat, of the North Chinese, the ancient Mayans, and at a speed too great to check.

The greatest danger may lie in lack of time to apply the brakes.†

"THE GRAPES OF WRATH," 1939
John Steinbeck

The surface of the earth crusted, a thin hard crust, and as the sky became pale, so the earth became pale, . . .

. . . And as the sharp sun struck day after day, the leaves of the young corn became less stiff and erect; they bent in a curve at first, and then, as the central ribs of strength grew weak, each leaf tilted downward. Then it was June, and the sun shone more fiercely. The brown lines on the corn leaves widened and moved in on the central ribs. The weeds frayed and edged back toward their roots. The air was thin and the sky more pale; and every day the earth paled.

In the roads where the teams moved, where the wheels milled the ground and the hooves of the horses beat the ground, the dirt crust broke and the dust formed. Every moving thing lifted the dust into the air; a walking man lifted a thin layer as high as his waist, and a wagon lifted the dust as high as the fence tops, and an automobile boiled a cloud behind it. . . .

". . . every moving thing lifted the dust into the air."   Dust storm in Colorad

. . . The dust from the roads fluffed up and spread out and fell on the weeds beside the fields, and fell into the fields a little way. Now the wind grew strong and hard and it worked at the rain crust in the corn fields. Little by little the sky was darkened by the mixing dust, and the wind thus over the earth, loosened the dust, and carried it away. The wind grew stronger. The rain crust broke and the dust lifted up out of the fields and drove gray plumes into the air like sluggish smoke. The corn threshed the wind and made a dry, rushing sound. The finest dust did not settle back to earth now, but disappeared into the darkening sky.

The wind grew stronger, whisked under stones, carried up straws and old leaves, and even little clods, marking its course as it sailed across the fields. The air and the sky darkened and through them the sun shone redly, and there was a raw sting in the air. During a night the wind raced faster over the land, dug cunningly among the rootlets of the corn, and the corn fought the wind with its weakened leaves until the roots were freed by the prying wind and then each stalk settled wearily sideways toward the earth and pointed the direction of the wind.

The dawn came, but no day. In the gray sky a red sun appeared, a dim red circle that gave a little light, like dusk; and as that day advanced, the dusk slipped back toward darkness, and the wind cried and whimpered over the fallen corn.

Men and women huddled in their houses, and they tied handkerchiefs over their noses when they went out, and wore goggles to protect their eyes.

When the night came again it was black night, for the stars could not pierce the dust to get down, and the window lights could not even spread beyond their own yards. Now the dust was evenly mixed with the air, an emulsion of dust and air. Houses were shut tight and cloth wedged around doors and windows, but the dust came in so thinly that it could not be seen in the air, and it settled like pollen on the chairs and tables, on the dishes. The people brushed it from their shoulders. Little lines of dust lay at the door sills.

188

In the middle of that night the wind passed on and left the land quiet. The dust-filled air muffled sound more completely than fog does. The people, lying in their beds, heard the wind stop. They awakened when the rushing wind was gone. They lay quietly and listened deep into the stillness. Then the roosters crowed, and their voices were muffled, and the people stirred restlessly in their beds and wanted the morning. They knew it would take a long time for the dust to settle out of the air. In the morning the dust hung like fog, and the sun was as red as ripe new blood. All day the dust sifted down from the sky, and the next day it sifted down. An even blanket covered the earth. It settled on the corn, piled up on the tops of the fence posts, piled up on the wires; it settled on roofs, blanketed the weeds and trees.†

"OUR PLUNDERED PLANET," 1949
Fairfield Osborn

There is beauty in the sound of the words "good earth." They suggest a picture of the elements and forces of nature working in harmony. The imagination of men through all ages has been fired by the concept of an "earth-symphony." Today we know the concept of poets and philosophers in earlier times is a reality. Nature may be a thing of beauty and is indeed a symphony, but above and below and within its own immutable essences, its distances, its apparent quietness and changelessness it is an active, purposeful, co-ordinated machine. Each part is dependent upon another, all are related to the movement of the whole. Forest, grasslands, soils, water, animal life—without one of these the earth will die—will become dead as the moon. This is provable beyond questioning. Parts of the earth,

Soils . . . will become dead as the moon." Abandoned farm in Oklahoma.

Aaron G. Fryer

Dairy farm in New Hampshire.

mbining wheat in South Dakota.

Parker

le World

Roundup in Wyoming.

once living and productive, have thus died at the hand of man. Others are now dying. If we cause more to die, nature will compensate for this in her own way, inexorably, as already she has begun to do.

The story of our nation in the last century as regards the use of forests, grasslands, wildlife and water sources is the most violent and the most destructive of any written in the long history of civilization. The velocity of events is unparalleled and we today are still so near to it that it is almost impossible to realize what has happened, or, far more important, what is still happening. Actually it is the story of human energy unthinking and uncontrolled. . . .

. . . Our people came to a country of unique natural advantages, of varying yet favorable climates, where the earth's resources were apparently limitless. Incredible energy marked the effort of a young nation to hack new homes for freedom-loving people out of the vast wilderness of forests that extended interminably to the grassland areas of the Midwest. Inevitably the quickest methods were used in putting the land to cultivation, not the desirable methods. Great areas of forest were completely denuded by ax or fire, without thought of the relationship of forests to water sources, or to the soil itself. . . . Today a large proportion . . . of the land originally put to productive use . . . has become wasteland and has had to be abandoned.

Finally, when will the truth come out into the light in international affairs? When will it be openly recognized that one of the principal causes of the aggressive attitudes of individual nations and of much of the present discord among groups of nations is traceable to diminishing productive lands and to increasing population pressures? Every country, all the world, is met with the threat of an oncoming crisis. . . . The tide of the earth's population is rising, the reservoir of the earth's living resources is falling. Technologists may outdo themselves in the creation of artificial substitutes for natural subsistence, and new areas, such as those in tropical or subtropical regions, may be adapted to human use, but even such resources or developments cannot be expected to offset the present terrific attack upon the natural life-giving elements of the earth. There is only one solution: Man must recognize the necessity of co-operating with nature. He must temper his demands and use and conserve the natural living resources of this earth in a manner that alone can provide for the continuation of his civilization. The final answer is to be found only through comprehension of the enduring processes of nature. The time for defiance is at an end.†

Conservation—Industrial Resources

"OUR INEXHAUSTIBLE RESOURCES"
Eugene Holman
President, Standard Oil (New Jersey), 1944–1954

All of us who are in any way connected with natural resources industries—geologists, engineers, executives, investors—are even more concerned than most people about how fast we are using up our natural resources. These materials have a vitally important place in the pattern of human existence, and people frequently fear that we are going to run out

Opposite: "Research and ingenuity have been great multipliers of our natural resources." Coal mine. Mechanical miner.

Andreas Feininger

of one or another of them. We worry about "wasting" our resources and "exhausting" them. But I suggest that the viewpoint expressed in those terms "wasting" and "exhausting" is a partial viewpoint. I think that under certain circumstances we can forget our fears and entertain the notion of inexhaustible resources.

Let's look at the record. It shows that from earliest times men have used minerals drawn from the earth. And we see that the availability of larger numbers of minerals, in greater quantities, has progressed by a kind of steplike process. . . .

The Stone age developed both the instruments and the knowledge which enabled men to use certain of the softer metals, especially copper and tin. Humanity then stepped up to the Bronze age. . . . As men equipped with bronze tools learned more and more about the world, humanity stepped up again—this time to an age of Iron. Now man began fashioning a really formidable array of tools. He had a new power to cut, grind, hammer, and otherwise work materials. . . . In modern times the age of Iron has given way to the Steel age. And within our own lifetimes there has been superimposed on the Steel age what we may call the age of lightweight metals, plastics, and atomic fission.

From the Stone age to the present so great a wealth of scientific information has been amassed—most of it in the past hundred years—that we now have tools and instruments of a power and precision beyond all previous imagination. . . .

A notable feature of the steplike pattern of material progress is that it has proceeded at a geometric rate. Each successive age has been shorter than the one before it. The Stone age lasted several hundred thousand years; the Bronze age, 4000 years; the Iron age, 2500 years. Steel was first made in commercial quantities 95 years ago; and the past 20 years have seen material developments that are almost incredible. . . . Another outstanding feature in the history of material progress is that each step has been dependent on the one before it. The use of materials available in one period—and I emphasize the word "use"—has supported societies in which men could accumulate knowledge. Such knowledge then made new quantities and new kinds of material available.

I emphasize the fact that people used the materials available in any period so that a fallacy one sometimes finds in connection with the conservation of natural resources will be crystal-clear. This fallacy is the concept of conservation as nonuse. I am convinced that nonuse results only in hobbling progress. It will not result in more natural resources for men to use but less, because it retards the march of scientific knowledge.

Increasing knowledge operates in a number of ways to expand the natural resources available to us. It helps us to discover new sources of materials which we are already using and in the raw form that is currently useful to us. For example, new techniques like the use of the airborne magnetometer help us to locate oil fields. New knowledge also enables us to extract a material we are already using from raw forms which we were previously unable to process, such as iron from taconite. . . .

MINERALS

A great many new sources of oil have been discovered in just the past several years. To mention only a few . . . in North Dakota, Utah, Canada, and Texas, in addition to fields in central Sumatra, southern Iraq, and the Cretaceous fields of western Venezuela. In some of these areas, geologic explorations had gone on for years without any oil ever having been found before. In others, oil had been produced before, production had subsequently fallen off, then new horizons were tapped.

By producing and using oil we have built a dynamic oil industry and have developed the means, both financial and technical, to find more oil. . . . As a result, in the United States alone, there has been produced since 1938 as much oil as was known to exist in the country at that time. And despite that great withdrawal, the domestic industry's proved reserves are at an all-time high level. It's as though we started out with a tank of oil, used it all up, and had a bigger tankful left. . . .

Besides learning more about finding underground reservoirs of crude, oilmen are also learning how to get more of the oil out of the reservoir after it has been located. We are discovering how to get maximum yield from large, highly porous reservoirs of the Middle East type, where the water table is important, as we are also learning how to get maximum yield from tricky, tight reservoirs. . . .

New developments in the science of refining make possible better products. This fact, coupled with improvements in consuming devices, means that we can get more work from a barrel of oil today, than we could previously. And I think we've only begun to use the energy potential in a barrel of oil. . . .

Finally, our present use of oil and coal supports an industrial and scientific structure in which men are already learning how to apply atomic power to constructive work and may learn how to harness solar energy. Such developments, of course, would probably displace the fossil fuels in some applications, thus making them available for other use. The over-all effect would be to increase still more the total amount of energy available to humanity. . . .

METALS

. . . Now let us look at the picture for metals. There are 45 metallic elements and some 8000 alloys of those metals now in commercial use. . . . The world in general, and the United States in particular, is using metals at a rate never seen before. . . . The metals we use most— iron and aluminum—are second only to the elements of oxygen and silicon in their abundance on our planet. It has been estimated that there are at least 5000 times as much iron ore, bauxite, and alunite in the earth's crust as the world now uses annually. Furthermore, unlike fossil fuels, most metals can be reclaimed after use and used again. In the meantime, the discovery of new sources of metal supplies and the development of techniques for making them economically available go on at a rapid pace. . .

Rich deposits of iron ore have been found in a number of countries outside the United States and are now being developed, in many cases by American capital. Labrador, Venezuela, and Brazil, for example, are the scenes of some truly epic engineering projects. A 358-mile railroad is being cut through wilderness and wasteland to haul ore from the Ungava area in Labrador to water. At Steep Rock Lake, Ontario, 70 million tons of lake bed are being removed in a four-year dredging operation to get at an iron deposit underneath. In El Pao, Venezuela, one of two projects in that country has been completed after fourteen years of work. Ore has been shipped by a railroad built through jungles, and by barge to the sea on a river whose water level at the loading point fluctuates 42 feet at different seasons.

We take aluminum for granted these days. It costs currently about 18 cents a pound. Yet when the Civil War started, it sold for $545 a pound. United States production now amounts to about 800,000 tons per year. . . . If it becomes necessary to find substitutes for bauxite or alunite ores, chemists seem confident they will be able to produce aluminum oxide from aluminum-bearing clays.

The first plant to extract magnesium from sea-water went into operation only eleven years ago with a capacity of 9000 tons a year. . . . As for the future—there's a lot of water in the sea. . . .

With almost every metal the story is repeated—of widening use, of the discovery of new sources and better methods of extraction. Here, as in other fields, research and ingenuity have been great multipliers of our natural resources. . . .

For many years, I believe, people have tended to think of natural resources as so many stacks of raw material piled up in a storehouse. A person with this sort of picture in his mind logically assumes that the more you use of any natural resource, the sooner you get to the bottom of the pile. Now I think we are beginning to discover that the idea of a storehouse—or, at least, a single-room storehouse—does not correspond with reality. Instead, the fact seems to be that the first storehouse in which man found himself was only one of a series. As he used up what was piled in that first room, he found he could fashion a key to open a door into a much larger room. And as he used the contents of this larger room, he discovered there was another room beyond, larger still. The room in which we stand at the middle of the twentieth century is so vast that its walls are beyond sight. Yet it is probably still quite near the beginning of the whole series of storehouses. It is not inconceivable that the entire globe—earth, ocean, and air—represents raw materials for mankind to utilize with more and more ingenuity and skill. . . .

I should like to point out a corollary to this thesis. It is that the concept of unlimited raw materials does not mean that progress is simple and that Utopia is at hand. On the contrary, raw materials, no matter how vast in amount, do not become available resources until human thought and effort are applied to them. In a very real sense raw materials do not exist, they are created. We know, for example, that in a region of great mineral wealth, people can grind out their lives in poverty and misery if they do not realize the wealth that exists or if they do not know how to get at it. It is use that makes it valuable. Even when the wealth is made available through technical means, the accelerating growth of populations and the enormous wastage of war are additional complications to consider.

So the march up the steps of material progress, or from storehouse to storehouse—according to which figure of speech you prefer—depends not alone on the continued expansion of scientific knowledge and on industrial daring and managerial skill, but also on political and social conditions. Those conditions in many parts of the world today are not conducive to progress. In fact, extreme nationalism, government controls and monopolies, currency restrictions, abnormal tariffs, threats of expropriation, wars and revolutions, have sealed the doors to many storehouses of useful raw materials.

The basic requirement for progress is freedom—freedom to inquire, to think, to communicate, to venture. Without these conditions, the human mind and spirit will be so shackled that the availability of natural resources will be limited and we may exhaust the known sources of some needed material and find nothing to replace it. To the free man, all things are possible. Opportunity is the wand which can change the useless into the useful, waste into raw materials of great value, exhaustible resources into inexhaustible resources. It is the key that unlocks the greatest energy source of all—the infinite power of the human individual.

The longer I live, the more convinced I am that material progress is not only valueless without spiritual progress: it is, in the long term, impossible.†

Achievements: Inventions, Discoveries, Enterprise

"Where there is an open mind, there will always be a frontier."

CHARLES F. KETTERING

Achievements: Inventions, Discoveries, Enterprise

In listing the world's 338 most important inventions, no less than 187 are accredited, by the World Almanac of 1953, to Americans. Ranging in size from the safety pin to the submarine, many of these inventions and improvements brought about revolutionary changes throughout the world. Space permits mention of only a few:

In 1793 Eli Whitney's cotton gin made it possible for one man to clean fifty pounds of cotton a day as against a single pound by hand. Later, when the machine was improved and run by water or steam power, one operator's daily output ran to 1000 pounds. The annual export of cotton in 1791 was 200,000 pounds; by 1807 it had jumped to 63,000,000 pounds. In 1831 the agricultural methods of the nation were changed by Cyrus McCormick's reaper; Elias Howe's sewing machine, 1846, revolutionized the making of clothes; Mergenthaler's Linotype, 1880, speeded the processes of typesetting that made possible today's modern press. It was the invention of the safety device on passenger elevators by Elisha Otis, in 1854, that led to the construction of skyscrapers, encouraged metropolitan growth, and gave New York its spectacular skyline.

"What hath God wrought?" were the immortal words tapped out by Samuel Morse on his telegraph key in 1837.

"Mr. Watson, come here; I want you," was the first sentence ever spoken on a telephone by its inventor, Alexander Graham Bell, in 1876.

"Mary had a little lamb," were the somewhat less than immortal words recorded by Thomas Edison on his gramophone in 1887. Edison, often called the Napoleon of inventors, had been granted 1,097 patents by the United States Patent Office at the time of his death and among his inventions were the dictaphone, incandescent lamp, alkaline accumulator battery, and motion-picture machine. He might have spoken for all inventors when he said: "Genius is one per cent inspiration and ninety-nine per cent perspiration." In the selections which follow, some outstanding Americans tell of their efforts:

THE COTTON GIN, 1793

ELI WHITNEY WRITES TO HIS FATHER

New Haven, Sept. 11th, 1793

Dear Parent,

. . . . I presume, sir, you are desirous to hear how I have spent my time since I left College. This I conceive you have a right to know and time it is my duty to inform you and should have done it before this time. . . .

I went from N. York with the family of the late Major General Greene to Georgia. I went immediately with the family to their Plantation about twelve miles from Savannah with an expectation of spending four or five days and then proceed into Carolina to take the school as I have mentioned in former letters.* During this time I heard much said of the extreme difficulty of ginning Cotton, that is, separating it from its seeds. There were a number of very respectable Gentlemen at Mrs. Greene's who all agreed that if a machine could be invented which would clean the cotton with expedition, it would be a great thing both to the Country and to the inventor. I involuntarily happened to be thinking on the subject and struck out a plan of a Machine in my mind, which I communicated to Miller, (who is agent to the Executors of Genl. Greene and resides in the family, a man of respectibility and property) he was pleased with the Plan and said if I would pursue it and try an experi-

* Whitney tutored the Greene children and was seeking employment as a school teacher.

ment to see if it would answer, he would be at the whole expense, I should loose nothing but my time, and if I succeeded we would share the profits. Previous to this I found I was like to be disappointed in my school, that is, instead of a hundred, I found I could get only fifty Guineas a year. I however held the refusal of the school untill I tried some experiments. In about ten Days I made a little model, for which I was offered, if I would give up all right and title to it, a Hundred Guineas. I concluded to relinquish my school and turn my attention to perfecting the Machine. I made one before I came away which required the labor of one man to turn it and with which one man will clean ten times as much cotton as he can in any other way before known and also cleanse it much better than in the usual mode. This machine may be turned by water or with a horse, with the greatest ease, and one man and a horse will do more than fifty men with the old machines. It makes the labor fifty times less, without throwing any class of People out of business.

I returned to the Northward for the purpose of having a machine made on a large scale and obtaining a Patent for the invention. I went to Philadelphia soon after I arrived, made myself acquainted with the steps necessary to obtain a Patent, took several of the steps and the Secretary of State Mr. Jefferson agreed to send the Patent to me as soon as it could be made out—so that I apprehended no difficulty in obtaining the Patent—Since I have been here I have employed several workmen in making machines and as soon as my business is such that I can leave it a few days, I shall come to Westboro'. . . . I am certain I can obtain a patent in England. As soon as I have got a Patent in America I shall go with the machine which I am now making, to Georgia, where I shall stay a few weeks to see it at work. From thence I expect to go to England, where I shall probably continue two or three years. How advantageous this business will eventually prove to me, I cannot say. It is generally said by those who know anything about it, that I shall make a Fortune by it. I have no expectation that I shall make an independent fortune by it, but think I had better pursue it than any other business into which I can enter. Something which cannot be foreseen may frustrate my expectations and defeat my Plan; but I am now so sure of success that ten thousand dollars, if I saw the money counted out to me, would not tempt me to give up my right and relinquish the object. I wish you, sir, not to show this letter nor communicate anything of its contents to any body except My Brothers and Sister, *enjoining* it on them to keep the whole a *profound secret*. . . .

> With respects to Mama I am,
> kind Parent, your most obt. Son
> ELI WHITNEY, Junr.

ROBERT FULTON AND THE STEAMBOAT, 1807

Inventors and engineers in France, Scotland, and the United States were experimenting with steamboats in the 1780's. In 1787 steamboats were being operated by James Rumsey on the Potomac and John Fitch on the Delaware. But to Robert Fulton, inventor, engineer, and artist, goes the credit for being the first to apply steam to navigation with practical results.

Work on Fulton's boat, the Clermont, *was completed in 1807 at a shipyard on the East River in New York. She was 133 feet long, 18 feet wide, 9 feet in depth, and was fueled with pine wood. In the following selections Fulton describes the public's attitude toward his efforts, and he tells of the historic first trip from New York to Albany and back:*

"MR. FULTON'S FOLLY"
Robert Fulton

When I was about to build my first steamboat, the public of New York in part regarded it with indifference, in part with contempt, as an entirely foolish undertaking. My friends were polite, but they were shy of me. They listened with patience to my explanations but, with a decided expression of disbelief in their countenances. As I went daily to and from the place where my boat was building, I oftened lingered unknown near the idle groups of strangers who were collected there, and listened to their remarks respecting the new locomotive. Their language was always that of scorn and persecution. People laughed aloud, and made jokes at my expense; and reckoned up the fallacy and loss of money on "Mr. Fulton's Folly," as the undertaking was constantly called. Never did I meet with an encouraging remark, an animating hope, or a warm wish.

At length came the day when the experiment was to be tried. To me it was a moment of the utmost importance. I had invited many of my friends to go on board and witness the first successful voyage. Many of these did so reluctantly, and in the belief that they should become the witnesses of my humiliation, and not of my triumph; and I know very well that there was sufficient reason to doubt of my success. The machinery was new and ill made. A great portion of it was prepared by artisans unaccustomed to such work; and difficulties might easily arise, also, from other causes. The hour arrived at which the boat was to begin to move. My friends stood in groups on deck. Their looks indicated uneasiness, mingled with fear; they were silent and dejected. The signal was given, and the boat was put in motion; it advanced a short distance, then stopped, and became immovable. The former silence now gave place to murmurs, and displeasure, and disquiet whisperings and shrugging of shoulders. I heard on all sides "I said it would be so"; "It is a foolish undertaking"; "I wish we were all well out of it."

I mounted on the platform, and told my friends that I did not know what was the cause of the stoppage, but that if they would be calm, and give me half an hour's time, I would either continue the voyage or give it up entirely. I went down to the engine, and very soon discovered an unimportant oversight in the arrangement: this was put to rights. The boat began to move once more. We left New York; we passed through the Highlands; we arrived at Albany! But even then was mistrust stronger than positive proof. It was doubted whether the thing could be carried through, and if so, whether it would ever lead to any great advantage.†

NEW YORK—ALBANY

Letter written by Robert Fulton to the *American Citizen*,
September, 1807

I arrived this afternoon at four o'clock in the steamboat from Albany. As the success of my experiment gives me great hopes that such boats may be rendered of great importance to my country, to prevent erroneous opinions and give some satisfaction to my friends of useful improvements, you will have the goodness to publish the following statement of facts:

I left New York on Monday at one o'clock and arrived at Clermont, the seat of Chancellor Livingston, at one o'clock on Tuesday: time, twenty four hours; distance, one hundred and ten miles. On Wednesday I departed from the Chancellor's at nine in the morning, and arrived at Albany at five in the afternoon: distance, forty miles; time, eight hours. The sum is one hundred and fifty miles in thirty-two hours, equal to near five miles an hour.

On Thursday, at nine o'clock in the morning, I left Albany, and arrived at the Chancellor's at six in the evening. I started from thence at seven, and arrived at New York at four in the afternoon: time, thirty hours; space ran through, one hundred and fifty miles, equal to five miles an hour. Throughout my whole way, both going and returning, the wind was ahead. No advantage could be derived from my sails. The whole has therefore been performed by the power of the steam-engine.†

The *Clermont*, Robert Fulton's steamboat, passing West Point.   Lithograph by de F. Berthaux.

THE DISCOVERY OF ANESTHESIA, 1842–1846

In the following texts Dr. William Welch, the eminent medical historian and pathologist from Johns Hopkins University, tells of the controversy surrounding the discovery of anesthesia. And Dr. William Morton and Dr. Crawford W. Long describe early experiments with ether.

"A CONSIDERATION OF THE INTRODUCTION OF SURGICAL ANESTHESIA"
Dr. William Welch

Address delivered, 1909, at the annual "Ether Day" ceremony at the Massachusetts General Hospital

The boon of painless surgery is the greatest gift of American medicine to mankind and one of the most beneficent ever conferred. . . .

The approach to a great discovery is long and devious and marked by the capture of a barrier here and an outpost there. . . . The final assault is often made by more than one person, and the victor stands upon the shoulders of many who have preceded him. . . . Every effort should be made to determine the share and the credit belonging to each contributor to the discovery and the introduction of surgical anaesthesia . . . to give honor where honor is due.

The attendant circumstances were such as to make the operation performed on October 16, 1846 [in the surgical amphitheater of the Massachusetts General Hospital], by John Collins Warren, upon the patient, Gilbert Abbott, placed in the sleep of ether anaesthesia by William Morton, the decisive event from which date the first convincing, public demonstration of surgical anaesthesia, the continuous, orderly, historical development of the subject, and the promulgation to the world of the glad tidings of this conquest of pain. . . .

[Charles T.] Jackson . . . was a highly trained and eminent chemist and geologist. . . . The evidence seems conclusive that Morton was indebted to Jackson for valuable information which the latter had acquired by personal experience four years earlier concerning properties of ether, strongly suggesting its availability for surgical anaesthesia . . . and for apparatus for administering ether. There is, however, good evidence that Morton . . . acted independently and conducted experiments and tests with ether upon his own initiative and in accordance with his own ideas. . . .

I deem it . . . fitting and only historical justice to say that in my judgment, after careful study of the evidence, the greater share of the honor belongs to Morton. This was the prevailing opinion of those most competent to judge and best acquainted with the facts . . .

The honor of making the first trial of anaesthesia inhalation in surgical operations belongs to Dr. Crawford W. Long, a respected and honorable country doctor, then living in Jefferson County, Georgia, who, in March, 1842, removed painlessly a small tumor from the neck of James M. Venable, anaesthetized by ether. He seems to have performed at least eight minor surgical operations during the next four years upon patients under influence of ether. Dr. Long is necessarily deprived of the larger honor which would have been his due had he not delayed publication of his experiments with ether until several years after the universal acceptance of surgical anaesthesia. It is also to be regretted that his published details of the mode of administering the ether and the depth of the anaesthesia are so meager and unsatisfactory. While the accepted rule that scientific discovery dates from publication is a wise one, we need not in this instance withhold from Dr. Long the credit of independent and prior experiment and discovery, but we cannot assign to him any influence upon the historical development of our knowledge of surgical anaesthesia or any share in the introduction to the world at large of the blessings of this matchless discovery.†

DR. WILLIAM MORTON EXTRACTS A TOOTH

Dr. Morton's "Memoir to the Academy of Arts and Sciences," Paris, 1847

Taking the tube and flask, I shut myself up in my room, seated myself in the operating chair, and commenced inhaling. I found the ether so strong that it partially suffocated me, but produced no decided effect. I then saturated my handkerchief and inhaled it from that. I looked at my watch, and soon lost consciousness. As I recovered, I felt a numbness in my limbs, with a sensation like nightmare, and would have given the world for someone to come and arouse me. I thought for a moment I should die in that state, and the world would only pity or ridicule my folly. At length I felt a slight tingling of the blood in the end of my third finger, and made an effort to touch it with my thumb, but without success. At a second effort, I touched it, but there seemed to be no sensation. I gradually raised my arm and pinched my thigh but I could see that sensation was imperfect. I attempted to rise from my chair, but fell back. Gradually I regained power over my limbs and found that I had been insensible between seven and eight minutes.

Delighted with the success of this experiment, I immediately announced the result to the persons employed in my establishment, and awaited impatiently for some one upon whom I could make a further trial. Toward evening, a man residing in Boston came in. suffering great pain, and wishing to have a tooth extracted. He was afraid of the operation, and asked if he could be mesmerized. I told him I had something better, and saturated my handkerchief, gave it to him to inhale. He became unconscious almost immediately. It was dark, and Dr. Hayden held the lamp while I extracted a firmly-rooted bicuspid tooth. There was not much alteration in the pulse and no relaxing of the muscles. He recovered in a minute and knew nothing of what had been done for him. He remained for some time talking about the experiment. This was on the 30th of September, 1846.†

DR. CRAWFORD W. LONG REMOVES A TUMOR*

On numerous occasions I inhaled ether for its exhilarating properties, and would frequently at some short time subsequent to its inhalation, discover bruised or painful spots on my person which I had no recollection of causing and which I felt satisfied were received while under the influence of ether. I noticed my friends, while etherized, received falls and blows which I believed were sufficient to produce pain on a person not in a state of anesthesia, and on questioning them they uniformly assured me that they did not feel the least pain from these accidents. Observing these facts, I was led to believe that anesthesia was produced by the inhalation of ether and that its use would be applicable in surgical operations.

The first patient to whom I administered ether in a surgical operation was James M. Venable, who then resided within two miles of Jefferson. He consulted me on several occasions in regard to the propriety of removing two small tumors on the back of his neck, but would postpone from time to time having the operation performed, from dread of pain. At length I mentioned to him the fact of my receiving bruises while under the influence of the vapor of ether without suffering and as I knew him to be fond of and accustomed to inhaling ether, I suggested to him the probability that the operation might be performed without pain. He consented to have one tumor removed, and the operation was performed the same evening. The ether was given on a towel, and when he was fully under its influence I extirpated the tumor.

It was encysted and about half an inch in diameter. The patient continued to inhale ether during the time of the operation, and when informed it was over, seemed incredulous until the tumor was shown him. He gave no evidence of suffering during the operation, and assured me, after it was over, that he did not experience the least degree of pain . . .†

* From "This Is America, My Country," edited by Donald H. Sheehan.

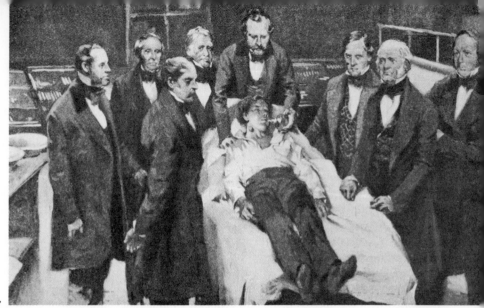

Bettmann Archive

Metropolitan Museum of Art

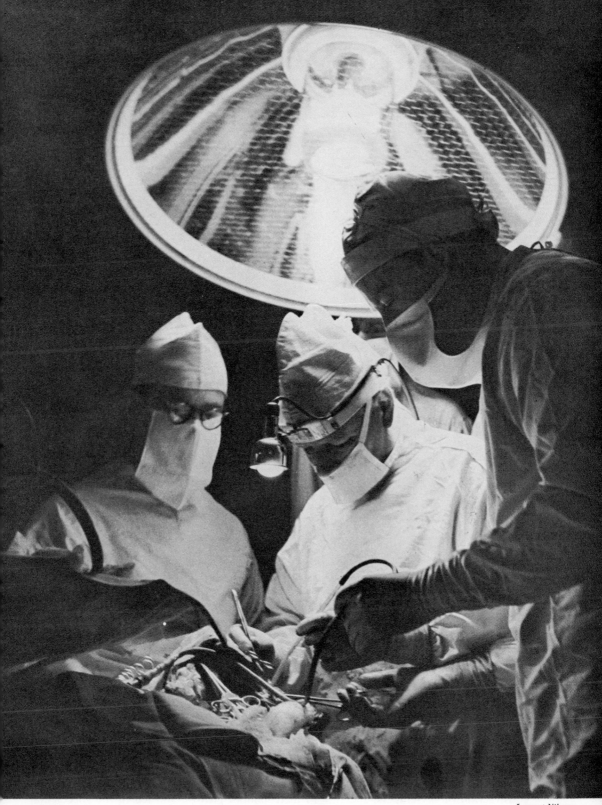

Opposite, top: Dr. William Morton gives the first demonstration of ether anesthesia at the Massachusetts General Hospital, Boston, October 16, 1846. *Opposite, bottom:* Early surgery. "The Gross Clinic." Painting by Thomas Eakins. *Above:* Modern surgery.

A SAFETY DEVICE FOR ELEVATORS: 1854. ELISHA OTIS

"All's safe, gentlemen, all's safe," said Elisha Otis in 1854 when he first demonstrated his safety device on elevators. It was the invention of this device that made possible the construction of skyscrapers, encouraged metropolitan growth, and led to the spectacular skylines of New York and other cities. *Above:* Chicago. *Right:* New York.

When this picture was taken, Edison had just completed five days and nights of continuous work on the improvement of the phonograph, in 1888.

THE ELECTRIC LIGHT, 1878
Thomas Edison
"TALKS WITH EDISON," BY GEORGE PARSONS LATHROP

To the question: "Which invention caused you the most study?" Thomas Edison replied: . . . The electric light. For, although I was never myself discouraged, or inclined to be hopeless of success, I cannot say the same for all of my associates. And yet, through all those years of experimenting and research, I never once made a discovery. All my work was deductive, and the results I achieved were those of invention pure and simple. I would construct a theory and work on its lines until I found it was untenable. Then it would be discarded at once, and another theory evolved. This was the only possible way for me to work out the problem, for the conditions under which the incandescent electric light exists are peculiar and unsatisfactory for close investigation. Just consider this: we have an almost infinitesmal filament heated to a degree which it is difficult for us to comprehend, and it is in a vacuum, under conditions of which we are wholly ignorant. You cannot use your eyes to help you in the investigation, and you really know nothing of what is going on in that tiny bulb. I speak without exaggeration when I say that I have constructed *three thousand* different theories in connection with the electric light, each one of them reasonable and apparently likely to be true. Yet only in two cases did my experiments prove the truth of my theory.†

Opposite: Model of the first electric light bulb, invented by Edison, 187[

DR. REED TELLS OF THE CONQUEST OF YELLOW FEVER, 1900

Address delivered at a medical meeting in Baltimore, Maryland, 1901

Until 1900 yellow fever took a steady toll of human life in the United States as well as in the tropics. In that year Dr. Walter Reed, American army surgeon, headed a mission to Cuba (including Aristides Agramonte, James Carroll, and Jesse Lazear) to investigate the cause and transmission of this scourge. At Camp Lazear, by controlled experiments on courageous men who volunteered as human guinea pigs, it was proved that yellow fever is caused and transmitted by the mosquito Aedes aegypti. *These findings led to eradicating the disease by destroying the carrier. This knowledge was later used to clear Panama of yellow fever, thus making possible the building of the Canal. In the following account Dr. Reed tells of some of these controlled experiments.*

Let us now present to you, as succinctly as possible, our observations at this camp, prefacing what I shall have to say with the remark that here we proposed to attempt the infection of nonimmune individuals in three ways, viz, first, by the bites of mosquitoes that had previously bitten cases of yellow fever; secondly, by the injection of blood taken during the early stages from the general circulation of those suffering with the disease; and, thirdly, by exposure to the most intimate contact with fomites. For this purpose, in addition to the seven tents provided for the quartering of the detachment, two frame buildings, each 14 by 20-feet in size, were constructed. . . . These houses were placed on opposite sides of a small valley, about 80 yards apart, and each 75 yards distant from the camp proper. Both houses were provided with wire-screen windows and double wire-screen doors, so that mosquitoes could be kept without or within the buildings, as the experimenter might desire. . . .

On the fifteenth day of our encampment therefore (Dec. 5, at 2 P.M.) we concentrated our insects, so to speak, on one of those nonimmunes—Kissinger by name—selecting 5 of our most promising mosquitoes for the purpose. These had been contaminated as follows: Two, 15 days; 1, 19 days; and 2, 21 days previously . . . at the expiration of 3 days and 9½ hours the subject, who had been under strict quarantine during 15 days, was suddenly seized with a chill about midnight, December 8, which was the beginning of a well-marked attack of yellow fever.

I can not let this opportunity pass without expressing my admiration of the conduct of this young Ohio soldier, who volunteered for this experiment, as he expressed it, "solely in the interest of humanity and the cause of science," and with the only proviso that he should receive no pecuniary reward. In my opinion this exhibition of moral courage has never been surpassed in the annals of the Army of the United States.

The following morning (Sunday, Dec. 9, at 10.30 A.M.) we selected from those insects that had bitten Case I, one mosquito that seemed to us to possess the best record of contamination, as it had bitten a fatal case of yellow fever, on the second day of the disease, 19 days before. The insect was applied to a Spanish immigrant, who had been strictly quarantined at our station for 19 days. At the expiration of 3 days and 11 hours (Dec. 9, 9.30 P.M.) this individual was also seized with an attack of yellow fever.

In the meantime, on December 8, 1900, at 4 o'clock P.M., we had applied to a young Spaniard three of the mosquitoes that had, three days previously, bitten Case I, together with an additional mosquito contaminated 17 days before. At the end of 4 days and 20 hours (Dec. 13, noon) this Spaniard suddenly lost his vivacity and took to his bed. The following morning at 9 A.M. his febrile paroxysm began. His case, which was the mildest of our series, was also marked by a long period of incubation, viz, 5 days and 17 hours. He had been in quarantine 9 days.

December 11, at 4.30 P.M., the identical 4 insects which had bitten Case III were fed on a Spanish immigrant who had been in quarantine for the past 21 days. At the expiration of 3 days and 19½ hours (Dec. 15, noon) he was likewise seized with yellow fever.

Thus within the period of one week—December 9 to 15—we had succeeded in producing an attack of yellow fever in each of the 4 individuals whom we had caused contaminated insects to bite, and in all save 1 of the 5 nonimmunes whom we had originally selected for experimentation.

It can readily be imagined that the concurrence of 4 cases of yellow fever in our small command of 12 nonimmunes within the space of 1 week, while giving rise to feelings of exultation in the hearts of the experimenters, in view of the vast importance attaching to these results, might inspire quite other sentiments in the bosoms of those who had previously consented to submit themselves to the mosquito's bite. In fact, several of our good-natured Spanish friends who had jokingly compared our mosquitoes to "the little flies that buzzed harmlessly about their tables," suddenly appeared to lose all interest in the progress of science, and, forgetting for the moment even their own personal aggrandizement, incontinently severed their connection with Camp Lazear. Personally, while lamenting to some extent their departure, I could not but feel that in placing themselves beyond our control they were exercising the soundest judgment. . . .

. . . at 11.55 A.M., December 21, 1900, 15 mosquitoes were freed in the larger room of the "infected mosquito building," which, as I have said, was divided into two compartments by a wire-screen partition. . . . At noon on the same day, 5 minutes after the mosquitoes had been placed therein, a plucky Ohio boy, Moran by name, clad only in his nightshirt, and fresh from a bath, entered the room containing the mosquitoes, where he lay down for a period of 30 minutes. On the opposite of the screen were the two "controls" and one other nonimmune. Within 2 minutes from Moran's entrance he was being bitten about the face and hands by the insects that had promptly settled down upon him. Seven in all bit him at this visit. At 4.30 P.M., the same day, he again entered and remained 20 minutes, during which time 5 others bit him. The following day at 4.30 P.M., he again entered and remained 15 minutes, during which time 3 insects bit him, making the number 15 that had fed at these three visits. The building was then closed, except that the two nonimmune "controls" continued to occupy the beds on the noninfected side of the screen. On Christmas morning, at 11 A.M., this brave lad was stricken with yellow fever, and had a sharp attack, which he bore without a murmur. . . . The two "controls" who had slept each night in this house, only protected by the wire screen, but breathing the common atmosphere of the building, had remained in good health. They continued to so remain, although required to sleep here for 13 additional nights. As Moran had remained in strict quarantine for the period of 32 days prior to his attack, the source of his infection must be found within this house. . . .†

BUILDING OF THE PANAMA CANAL, 1904–1914

As told by General George W. Goethals in an account appearing in
Scribner's Magazine, 1915

The Panama Canal, connecting the Atlantic and Pacific, was built by the United States, 1904–1914, on land leased by it in perpetuity from the Republic of Panama.

The French, in 1881, under Ferdinand de Lesseps, had attempted this same task, but appalling mortality from malaria and yellow fever defeated their effort, and by 1889 the company became bankrupt.

Of the ten years required to build the Canal, the first three were devoted to preliminary preparations including control of yellow fever and malaria, adequate housing, and assembling material; actual construction was completed in seven years. The total cost was $366,650,000.

In 1907 General George W. Goethals was appointed engineer in chief and given complete civil and military power in the Zone, a postion he held until the work was completed. In the following account General Goethals describes some of the problems encountered:

The general impression prevailed from the beginning that the building of the Panama Canal comprised one of the world's greatest engineering feats, and the tremendous scope of the work as it developed during the construction period served to mold this impression into a fixed belief; yet Mr. Stevens, who, for nearly two years had control on the Isthmus, not only of all construction, but of those various coordinate branches which were essential adjuncts to the building of the Canal, expressed the opinion that the engineering features were the least difficult, describing them as "of magnitude and not of intricacy." On the other hand, his experience convinced him that the administrative problems were the greater. . . .

In every undertaking of an engineering character there must necessarily be a greater or less amount of administrative details resulting from problems of supply, labor, policy, and considerations arising out of them. In the case of the Panama Canal, not only were those problems present, but, as compared with those of engineering, they made the latter appear relatively small.

The very magnitude of the work imposed difficulties which would have existed even had it been undertaken in any portion of the United States, but these difficulties were increased materially by reason of having to carry on the work in a tropical country, sparsely populated, non-productive, affording no skilled and very little efficient common labor, with customs and modes of living as different as the civilizations of North and Central America have been since the settlement of these portions of the western hemisphere, with a heavy rainfall during the greater portion of the year, and with a reputation for unhealthfulness which place Panama in the category of one of the worst pest-holes of the earth. . . .

The forces of the United States were fortunate . . . for before the transfer of the work to them preventive medicine had made such advances as to make possible the conversion of the pest-hole into a habitat where most white men would live and work. The diseases which sapped the energy and vitality of the men and struck terror to their souls were malaria and yellow fever. The cause of the former had been discovered by Sir Ronald Ross, of the British army, who formulated rules by which an infected locality could be rid of its influences. Not only were his theory and practices known, but we had the benefit of his advice and experience, for he visited the Isthmus on invitation of the commission at the instigation of the health authorities in order that we might have his assistance. After Sir Ronald Ross's discovery, Doctors Reed, Lazear and Carroll, in Cuba, with Aristides Agramonte, a Cuban immune, proved the correctness of the theory advanced by Doctor Carlos Finlay, of Havana, that yellow fever was transmitted only by the mosquito, and prescribed the methods that resulted in ridding Cuba of that dread disease; it naturally followed that the Isthmus could be freed in the same way. Finally, great advances had been made in construction machinery of all kinds, making the equipment used by the French obsolete, though this was continued in use by the Americans until it could be replaced by the more modern and up-to-date appliances that experience had shown would accomplish the results. . . .

The Panama Railroad, constructed in 1850–55 by Americans with American capital, constituted a part of one of the through routes between the east and west; its commercial interests had to be continued, and, in addition, it must assist in the construction of the Canal. The roadbed, equipment, and facilities were scarcely adequate for the former alone, and, with the immense quantities required for the Canal, they became totally inadequate. The road was double-tracked and rebuilt to suit the heavier equipment that had been ordered, round-houses were constructed, docks erected, and yards built at the terminals and at various places along the line for the handling of freight of all kinds and spoil from the Canal.

Panama Canal.   U. S. Navy carrier passing through Miraflores Locks.

All of these various branches of the work came directly under the control of the chief engineer; and it was necessary to co-ordinate them with the construction of the Canal. Under these circumstances, it can readily be seen that Mr. Stevens' conclusions, that the administrative problems were greater than those of engineering, were correct. . . .

The engineering side of the enterprise was necessarily of very great importance, for the success of the undertaking was dependent upon the proper solutions of the problems involved, both theoretically and practically. The construction of the locks presented no new problems, though some novel features were introduced in the operating machinery for the locks and spillways; neither did the dams, dredging, or dry excavation; the methods adopted had been in use elsewhere. The difficulties were due to size and were sufficiently great in themselves; there is no desire or intent to detract from them or to belittle their importance. There were also questions concerning the plans of the Canal and methods of construction that required administrative action, and to these were added the problems or questions which arose in all the other departments and divisions, so that on the whole the administrative side of the work, including the co-ordination of its various parts, was the greater. This is more especially true if there be embraced under administration, where it properly belongs, the problem caused by the "human element."

In any line of endeavor this is always the uncertain factor. It can be told with a great degree of accuracy what a particular piece of machinery will do under specified conditions, or, knowing a man, what that man will do under normal circumstances, but take 40,000 men gathered from all parts of the world, place them in a tropical country, many miles away from home and away from the ties and associations which have more or less guided and restrained them, and the "human element" straightway becomes a problem heavily charged with uncertainties and difficulties. I have been asked frequently what part of the work I considered the most difficult, and the reply was, invariably, the human problem; it extended from the highest to the lowest. . . .

ADMIRAL PEARY DISCOVERS THE NORTH POLE, APRIL 6, 1909

The first explorers of the Arctic regions were the Vikings, c. 870 A.D., who discovered Iceland, Greenland, and the northern shores of America. As early as 1576 explorations were made to try and find a northeast or northwest passage to the Orient. Roald Amundsen of Norway finally negotiated the Northwest Passage in 1903–1905.

Robert Edwin Peary first started his polar explorations in 1886, making a trip to the interior of Greenland. From 1891 to 1902 he made expeditions into the Arctic, some of which took him further north than any white man had ever been.

In order to secure for the United States the honor of being the first to reach the North Pole, Peary set out on his epic voyage in 1908. The expedition was financed by members and friends of the Peary Arctic Club of New York City. The Roosevelt *took them through the waters between Greenland and Ellesmere Island, where Peary and his aides wintered on the coast at a spot 82 degrees and 30 minutes north. On March 1, 1909, they started forward across the ice for the North Pole.*

Accompanying Peary were six white men, one Negro, and seventeen Eskimos, with 133 dogs and nineteen sledges, but the men were gradually sent back as the supplies diminished. On April 6, with only his Negro servant, Matthew Hensen, four Eskimos, five sledges and thirty-eight dogs, Peary achieved his goal.

Peary's discovery of the North Pole added immeasurably to our knowledge of the earth, aided scientific research, and facilitated further polar explorations. On his return the Government made Peary a Rear Admiral, and when he died in 1920 he was buried with high honors in the National Cemetery at Arlington.

In the following text Peary describes how he felt at the moment of his greatest achievement:

"When I knew for certain that we had reached the goal, there was not a thing in the world I wanted but sleep." Robert E. Peary.

"THE NORTH POLE: ITS DISCOVERY"
Robert E. Peary

. . . in a space between the ice blocks of a pressure ridge, I deposited a glass bottle containing a diagonal strip of my flag and records. . . .

If it were possible for a man to arrive at 90 north latitude without being utterly exhausted, body and brain, he would doubtless enjoy a series of unique sensations and reflections. But the attainment of the Pole was the culmination of days and weeks of forced marches, physical discomfort, insufficient sleep and racking anxiety. It was a wise provision of nature that the human consciousness can grasp only such degree of intense feeling as the brain can endure, and the grim guardians of earth's remotest spot will accept no man as guest until he has been tried and tested by the severest ordeal.

Perhaps it ought not to be so, but when I knew for certain that we had reached the goal, there was not a thing in the world I wanted but sleep. But after I had a few hours of it, there succeeded a condition of mental exaltation which made further rest impossible. For more than a score of years that point on the earth's surface had been the object of my every effort. To its attainment my whole being, physical, mental, and moral, had been dedicated. Many times my own life and the lives of those with me had been risked. My own material and forces and those of my friends had been devoted to this object. This journey was my eighth into the Arctic wilderness. In that wilderness I had spent nearly twelve years out of twenty-three between my thirtieth and fifty-third year, and the intervening time spent in civilized communities during that period had been mainly occupied with preparations for

215

returning to the wilderness. The determination to reach the Pole had become so much a part of my being that, strange as it may seem, I long ago ceased to think of myself save as an instrument for the attainment of that end. To the layman this may seem strange, but an inventor can understand it, or an artist, or anyone who has devoted himself for years . . . to the service of an idea. . . .†

FIFTY YEARS OF FLYING

The exhibition label on the original plane installed in the National Museum in Washington reads as follows:

THE ORIGINAL WRIGHT BROTHERS' AEROPLANE

THE WORLD'S FIRST
POWER-DRIVEN HEAVIER-THAN-AIR MACHINE IN WHICH MAN
MADE FREE, CONTROLLED, AND SUSTAINED FLIGHT
INVENTED AND BUILT BY WILBUR AND ORVILLE WRIGHT
FLOWN BY THEM AT KITTY HAWK, NORTH CAROLINA
DECEMBER 17, 1903
BY ORIGINAL SCIENTIFIC RESEARCH THE WRIGHT BROTHERS
DISCOVERED THE PRINCIPLES OF HUMAN FLIGHT
AS INVENTORS, BUILDERS, AND FLYERS
THEY FURTHER DEVELOPED THE AEROPLANE, TAUGHT MAN TO
FLY, AND OPENED THE ERA OF AVIATION

"HOW WE MADE THE FIRST FLIGHT"
Orville Wright
Article in Flying, *December, 1913*

During the night of December 16, 1903, a strong cold wind blew from the north. When we arose on the morning of the 17th, the puddles of water, which had been standing about camp since the recent rains, were covered with ice. The wind had a velocity of 22 to 27 miles an hour. We thought it would die down before long, but when 10 o'clock arrived, and the wind was as brisk as ever, we decided that we had better get the machine out. . . .

Wilbur, having used his turn in the unsuccessful attempt on the 14th, the right to the first trial now belonged to me. Wilbur ran at the side, holding the wing to balance it on the track. The machine, facing a 27-mile wind, started very slowly. Wilbur was able to stay with it till it lifted from the track after a forty foot run.

The course of the flight up and down was exceedingly erratic. The control of the front rudder was difficult. As a result the machine would rise suddenly to about ten feet, and then as suddenly dart for the ground. A sudden dart when a little over 120 feet from the point at which it rose into the air, ended the flight. This flight lasted only 12 seconds, but it was nevertheless the first in the history of the world in which a machine carrying a man had raised itself by its own power into the air in full flight, has sailed forward without reduction of speed, and had finally landed at a point as high as that from which it started.

Wilbur started the fourth and last flight at just 12 o'clock. The first few hundred feet were up and down as before, but by the time three hundred feet had been covered, the machine was under much better control. The course for the next four or five hundred feet had but little undulation. However, when out about eight hundred feet the machine began pitching again, and, in one of its darts downward, struck the ground. The distance over the ground was measured and found to be 852 feet; the time of the flight 59 seconds.†

"Wilbur ran at the side, holding the wing to balance it on the track."
First flight at Kitty Hawk, North Carolina, December 17, 1903.

EARLY HISTORY OF THE AIRPLANE
Orville and Wilbur Wright

The first flights with the power machine were made on December 17, 1903. Only five persons besides ourselves were present. . . . Although a general invitation had been extended to the people living within five or six miles, not many were willing to face the rigors of a cold December wind in order to see, as they no doubt thought, another flying machine not fly. The first flight lasted only 12 seconds, a flight very modest compared with that of birds, but it was, nevertheless, the first in the history of the world in which a machine carrying a man had raised itself by its own power into the air in free flight, had sailed forward on a level course without reduction of speed, and had finally landed without being wrecked. The second and third flights were a little longer, and the fourth lasted 59 seconds, covering a distance of 852 feet over the ground against a 20-mile wind. . . .

In order to show the general reader the way in which the machine operates, let us fancy ourselves ready for the start. The machine is placed upon a single-rail track facing the wind, and is securely fastened with a cable. The engine is put in motion, and the propellers in the rear whir. You take your seat at the center of the machine beside the operator. He slips the cable, and you shoot forward. An assistant who has been holding the machine in balance on the rail starts forward with you, but before you have gone fifty feet the speed is too great for him, and he lets go. Before reaching the end of the track the operator moves the front rudder, and the machine lifts from the rail like a kite supported by the pressure of the air underneath it. The ground under you is at first a perfect blur, but as you rise the objects become clearer. At a height of 100 feet you feel hardly any motion at all, except for the wind which strikes your face. If you did not take the precaution to fasten your hat before starting, you have probably lost it by this time. The operator moves a lever: the right wing rises, and the machine swings about to the left. You make a very short turn, yet you do not feel the sensation of being thrown from your seat, so often experienced in automobile and railway travel. You find yourself facing toward the point from which you started. The objects on the ground now seem to be moving at much higher speed, though you perceive no change in the pressure of the wind on your face. You know then that you are travelling with the wind. When you near the starting point the operator stops the motor while still high in the air. The machine coasts down at an oblique angle to the ground, and after sliding 50 or 100 feet, comes to rest. Although the machine often lands when travelling at a speed of a mile a minute, you feel no shock whatever, and cannot, in fact, tell the exact moment at which it first touched the ground. The motor close beside you kept up an almost deafening roar during the whole flight, yet in your excitement you did not notice it till it stopped!

Our experiments have been conducted entirely at our own expense. In the beginning we had no thought of recovering what we were expending, which was not great,* and was limited to what we could afford in recreation. Later, when a successful flight had been made with a motor, we gave up the business in which we were engaged, to devote our entire time and capital to the development of a machine for practical use. . . .†

AVIATION IN THE TWENTIES

In its early days aviation was generally regarded as an exciting stunt. A handful of daredevil pilots barnstormed around the country, appearing at local fairs and meetings and, for a fee of five or ten dollars, gave rides to adventurous passengers.

Among these men was Charles A. Lindbergh. Stunt-flying, wing-walking, parachuting into the fields of startled farmers and, later, becoming a licensed air-mail pilot, Lindbergh learned his profession the hard way. Then, in 1927, in his small monoplane, the Spirit of St. Louis, he flew solo across the Atlantic to Paris. It was this spectacular flight that captured the imagination of the public and lifted aviation, once and for all, out of the realm of novelty and supplied the impetus that was needed to make man's final conquest of the air a universal fact.

In the following excerpt Lindbergh describes the early days of flying. He and a fellow pilot, Leon Klink, were barnstorming through the South in an old war-time Canuck: "It was a trip of many stops, for the fuel-tank held only 23 gallons—enough to fly for two and a half hours. If we left a half hour reserve for locating a field . . . our plane had a range of 150 miles in still air."

BARNSTORMING

"The Spirit of St. Louis," 1953

Charles A. Lindbergh

. . . . At Brooks Field, San Antonio, our load-carrying troubles began. We'd filled both our cans and all our tanks with gasoline, and started our engine soon after sunrise. I never had a plane stick to the ground so long. Our Canuck must have run across a half-mile of sod before the wheels broke free. Fortunately, the field was both large and smooth. . . .

The Canuck labored upward slowly . . . Within fifteen minutes we were several hundred feet high, and making about 50 miles an hour against a quartering westerly wind. . . . An hour after leaving Brooks Field, our engine at full power, we were skimming mesquite and cactus in a country that had changed from plains to eroded, stony hills. Finally I had to nose down into a ravine, and signal Klink to heave his gas can overboard to keep us from running out of altitude completely. How he hated to give up the fuel we'd worked so hard

* Orville told Fred C. Kelly, Wright biographer, that out-of-pocket expenses were under $1,000.

to lift! I had to shout and motion twice before he'd let it go. After that, we struggled up and over the hills in front of us. . . .

There were no good fields around Camp Wood, Texas, so being low on fuel, we landed in the town square. In spite of its poles, wires, and rows of stores, it was the largest open area we could find that was smooth enough to land on. People came running from all directions as we taxied to a corner. Horses were hitched to posts; stores were locked; school was let out. A crowd surrounded the Canuck in no time at all. What was wrong? Why were we there? Where were we going? Where had we come from? What were the wings made of? Was there anything they could do to help? . . .

The next morning (the wind had shifted), buildings blocked our take-off from the square. There was a possibility that I could use one of the adjoining streets as a runway. I looked over the street carefully, walking up and down its center. There was a depression a few hundred feet from the point where I'd have to start; but my wheels should be clear before I reached it, if I took off alone and with a light fuel load. After that I'd have to brush my wing tips through some tree branches that overhung the road, but they were little more than twigs. Then, there'd be open miles of air in which to climb. But to get off before the depression in the road I'd have to pass between two telegraph poles, about fifty feet from my starting point, and only two or three feet farther apart than the span of the upper wings.

. . . After all, one drove a car regularly between objects with only a few inches clearance. Why shouldn't one do it with an airplane? I could mark the exact center of the street between the poles, and imagine that I was in an automobile. We pushed our Canuck into position, and warmed up the engine.

I thought I was rolling precisely along the center of the street, but I failed by three inches to clear the right-hand telephone pole. I jerked the throttle shut, but it was too late. The pole held my wing, while the plane's momentum carried the fuselage around and poked its nose right through the board wall of the hardware store. The propeller was shattered, of course, and the engine stopped at once. But pots and pans kept on crashing down inside the store for several seconds.

That did bring people running. The hardware dealer told us that he and his son thought an earthquake was taking place. But instead of being angry, he appeared quite pleased. When we tried to pay for the damage we'd done, he refused to take a cent. It had been an interesting experience, he said, and the advertising value was worth much more than the cost of the few boards needed for repairs.

To my surprise I could find nothing broken on our Canuck aside from the propeller and wing tip. We wired Houston for a new prop and a can of dope to be expressed to Camp Wood C.O.D. With the help of the crowd, we pushed our plane back into the square.

Three days later, we were ready to start again. The wind blew in the right direction that morning, and we took off with two of our wing tanks full. The Canuck flew as well as ever, except that it carried a little extra left rudder. By leaving the throttle wide open and following the valleys, we were able to hold an average altitude of several hundred feet.

A half hour before sunset, we began looking for a place to come down for the night. There wasn't a town within sight; but beside the railroad ahead of us we saw a section house and three old boxcars which, we learned later, were dignified by the name of Maxon, Texas. A quarter-mile to the west lay a long, sloping, irregularly-shaped area of relatively smooth ground. It contained scattered clumps of cactus, but there was room for our wheels and wings to pass between them. There we landed, with an east wind.

The section boss and most of the Mexicans from the boxcars rushed over to meet us. They helped tie our plane down, and the "boss" invited us to stay at his house.

"Sure, there's an extra bed, an' ye'll be welcome company," he said. "I'm livin' here all alone—except fur the Mexicans. Don't see many people to talk to. It's thirty-two miles to the nearest store. Good thing ye stopped today, though; I'm goin' off fur a week t'morrow."†

Erickson

Lindbergh's *Spirit of St. Louis*

LINDBERGH TELLS OF HIS FLIGHT TO PARIS

"We," 1927

Charles A. Lindbergh

On May 21, 1927, Charles A. Lindbergh completed the first nonstop airplane flight between the continents of North America and Europe, traveling alone in his small airplane, the Spirit *of St. Louis. The elapsed time was 33½ hours.*

Soon after landing, Lindbergh agreed to take part in publishing a book about the flight. He was under the impression it would be an account taken from interviews, written and signed by somebody else, and that he would simply authenticate the facts and add a foreword. Instead he was handed a ghost-written manuscript, written in the first person. He refused to attach his name, but publication had already been announced and he felt obligated to see the project through. He sat down and in three weeks wrote the book himself, in longhand. It was brought out under the title of We, *and the excerpt that follows is from this, the author's first account of his historic flight:*

As the fog cleared, I dropped down closer to the water, sometimes flying within ten feet of the waves and seldom higher than two hundred. There is a cushion of air close to the ground or water through which a plane flies with less effort than when at a higher altitude, and for hours at a time I took advantage of this factor.

220

Also, it was less difficult to determine the wind drift near the water. During the entire flight the wind was strong enough to produce white caps on the waves. When one of these formed, the foam would be blown off, showing the wind's direction and approximate velocity. This foam remained on the water long enough for me to obtain a general idea of my drift.

During the day I saw a number of porpoises and a few birds but no ships, although I understand that two different boats reported me passing over.

The first indication of my approach to the European coast was a small fishing boat which I first noticed a few miles ahead and slightly to the south of my course. There were several of these fishing boats grouped within a few miles of each other.

Charles A. Lindbergh, 1927.

I flew over the first boat without seeing any signs of life. As I circled over the second, however, a man's face appeared, looking out of the cabin window.

I have carried on short conversations with people on the ground by flying low with throttled engine, shouting a question, and receiving the answer by some signal. When I saw this fisherman, I decided to try to get him to point towards land. I had no sooner made the decision than the futility of the effort became apparent. In all likelihood he could not speak English, and even if he could, he would undoubtedly be far too astounded to answer. However, I circled again and closing the throttle as the plane passed within a few feet of the boat, I shouted "Which way is Ireland?" Of course the attempt was useless, and I continued on my course. . . .

I first saw the lights of Paris a little before 10 P.M., or 5 P.M., New York time, and a few minutes later I was circling the Eiffel Tower at an altitude of about four thousand feet.

The lights of Le Bourget were plainly visible, but appeared to be very close to Paris. I had understood that the field was farther from the city; so I continued out to the northeast into the country for four or five miles to make sure that there was not another field farther out which might be Le Bourget. Then I returned and spiraled down closer to the lights. Presently I could make out long lines of hangars, and the roads appeared to be jammed with cars.

I flew low over the field once, then circled around into the wind and landed.

After the plane stopped rolling I turned it around and started to taxi back to the lights. The entire field ahead, however, was covered with thousands of people all running toward my ship. When the first few arrived, I attempted to get them to hold the rest of the crowd back, but apparently no one could understand or would have been able to conform to my request if he had.

I cut the switch to keep the propeller from killing someone, and attempted to organize an impromptu guard for the plane. The impossibility of any immediate organization became apparent, and when parts of the ship began to crack from the pressure of the multitude, I decided to climb out of the cockpit in order to draw the crowd away.

Speaking was impossible; no words could be heard in the uproar, and nobody apparently cared to hear any. I started to climb out of the cockpit, but as soon as one foot appeared through the door, I was dragged the rest of the way without assistance on my part.

For nearly half an hour I was unable to touch the ground, during which time I was ardently carried around in what seemed to be a very small area, and in every position it is possible to be in. Everyone had the best of intentions, but no one seemed to know just what they were.

The French military flyers very resourcefully took the situation in hand. A number of them mingled with the crowd; then, at a given signal, they placed my helmet on an American correspondent and cried: "Here is Lindbergh." That helmet on an American was sufficient evidence. The correspondent immediately became the center of attraction, and while he was being taken protestingly to the Reception Committee via a rather devious route, I managed to get inside one of the hangars.

Meanwhile a second group of soldiers and police had surrounded the plane and soon placed it out of danger in another hangar. The French ability to handle an unusual situation with speed and capability was remarkably demonstrated that night at Le Bourget.

Ambassador Herrick extended me an invitation to remain at his Embassy while I was in Paris, which I gladly accepted. But grateful as I was at the time, it did not take me long to realize that a kind Providence had placed me in Ambassador Herrick's hands. The ensuing days found me in situations that I had certainly never expected to be in and in which I relied on Ambassador Herrick's sympathetic aid.

These situations were brought about by the whole-hearted welcome to me—an American —that touched me beyond any point that any words can express. . . .†

222

...assenger plane over New York.

COMMERCIAL AVIATION*

Edward V. Rickenbacker

Top Ace, U.S. Air Force, World War I,
Chairman of the Board, Eastern Air Lines, Inc.

Commercial aviation, as we know it today, had its beginnings in the mid-twenties, more than two decades after the birth of powered flight. Between the first success of the Wright Brothers at Kitty Hawk in 1903 and the non-stop span of the Atlantic by Charles A. Lindbergh in 1927, aviation was pretty much in the hands of the military.

Though the Country floated on a wave of prosperity after World War I, the handful of barnstorming airmen demonstrating the wonders of the flying machine at state and county fairs eked out only a meager living. A few other optimistic ex-war flyers went broke trying to establish scheduled service between various groups of cities. They failed for the simple reasons: there was no such thing as a dependable airplane, and the public still had no confidence in flying.

Colonel Lindbergh's feat was the ray of light that pierced those black clouds of disbelief. But even before that heroic and historic flight, there were a few men of vision who foresaw that the airplane would some day come into its own as a vital part of our transportation system.

Passage of the Kelly Act in 1925 fostered the granting of air mail contracts to private carriers and in effect stimulated aircraft manufacture by creating the need for a specific type of plane to do a specific job. Aviation pioneers responded by organizing the small companies that formed the nucleus of our modern air transport network. Such outfits blazed the commercial air trails using small but sturdy Mailwings, Travel-Airs and Stearmans to fulfill their mail contracts.

* Original article.

Within a few years these men branched into air passenger and air express service, capturing the imagination of the public with the introduction of larger planes like the tri-motor Ford and Fokker, the Curtis Condor and Kingbird, and the still heavier Boeing and Douglas aircraft.

Progress received a severe setback, however, in February, 1934, when all of the private airmail contracts were cancelled by the Post Office Department, and the service was turned over to the U. S. Army. While the airlines staggered from the loss of the mail revenue, a dozen courageous but inexperienced Army pilots perished in their attempts to carry on this specialized flying. It was a terrible price to pay but out of this dark chapter came a national realization of the importance of commercial aviation. After a few months, new improved contracts were drawn up with the airlines, new air patterns were worked out and the foundations for the present system were established. Little by little the individual operators joined forces with, or were taken over by, large holding companies until most of the small outfits were welded into one vast air network.

The Civil Aeronautics Act, passed in 1938, set up guiding bodies to assure the continual development of air commerce, and to protect the public safety. New routes multiplied, faster and larger equipment was introduced, including the world-famous DC-3 which became the "backbone of the air transportation industry." The airline theme of superior service made many new friends. And yet the industry as a whole continued to lose money because of high operation costs, too many flying "frills" and most important, lack of confidence of the traveling public.

Prototype of the first American jet transport plane

The advent of World War II presented the airlines with an opportunity to prove their importance to the national defense picture. They gladly contributed most of their equipment and personnel to the armed forces. This meant a wholesale curtailment of their own services, but these services did business as never before. From the wartime flying boom evolved new, larger, faster and more dependable aircraft, experienced operating and maintenance personnel, and a vast market for potential passengers.

With the introduction of mighty four-engine airliners, improved services and increased safety finally "sold" the public on flying as a conventional mode of travel. The past few years have seen more and more airlines use less and less red ink.

Since the mid-century mark, attention has been focused on the use of jet and turbo-prop engines in commercial aircraft.

Within the next ten years, the airlines in this country will be flying jet passenger planes over long-haul routes, turbo-prop aircraft on intermediate trips and huge helicopters between cities 300 miles apart and less. Then will come the era of atomic fuel, fantastic speeds, and developments that are as far beyond our imaginations as the visualization of today's aircraft would have been for people at the turn of the century.

"THE FATHER OF MODERN ROCKETRY": ROBERT H. GODDARD (1882–1945)

Rockets and guided missiles are becoming increasingly important both as weapons of war and as scientific instruments of exploration into outer space.

In the thirteenth century, Marco Polo told how the Chinese used rockets as displays during celebrations. In war, rockets have long been used as weapons and flares. Sir William Congreve, 1772–1828, was a pioneer in this field and "the rocket's red glare" mentioned in our Star Spangled Banner was undoubtedly a Congreve rocket used on H.M.S. Surprise *to bombard Fort McHenry.*

Modern rocketry began with the pioneering work of Robert H. Goddard, who carried on his experiments from 1909 until his death in 1945. In the following selections Harry F. Guggenheim summarizes Dr. Goddard's position as the "father of modern rocketry"; Dr. Goddard describes two of his early experiments; and a local newspaper carries an account of one of them:

HARRY F. GUGGENHEIM'S FOREWORD TO "ROCKET DEVELOPMENT" (1948) BY ROBERT H. GODDARD

When Robert H. Goddard first began his monumental work on the development of rockets, about 1909, there was no real technical information anywhere on the subject. In the thirty-five years that followed, he brought a new science and a new branch of engineering into being, launched a new industry, and probably changed the course of human history. . . .

There is evidence that the German rocket engineers followed Dr. Goddard's work very closely from the time of publication of his first Smithsonian report in 1919 until his death. They were familiar with his patents, all his published material, and any additional data which they were able to obtain by correspondence directly or through engineers of other nationalities. . . .

. . . the much discussed German V-2 rockets, though larger, were almost identical versions of some of Dr. Goddard's missiles tested in flight. Rockets of the V-2 type were within our grasp in this country long before the Germans used them.

All of the Goddard experiments and patents were made available to our Government before Pearl Harbor by the Daniel and Florence Guggenheim Foundation. . . .

Dr. Goddard was the undisputed father of modern rocketry, and in some respects current efforts in liquid-fuel rocket development may still lag behind his accomplishments.†

FIRST FLIGHT OF A LIQUID-PROPELLANT ROCKET
*From the Diary of Dr. Robert H. Goddard**

March 17, 1926

The first flight with a rocket using liquid-propellants was made yesterday at Aunt Effie's farm in Auburn.

The day was clear and comparatively quiet. The anemometer on the Physics lab. was turning leisurely when Mr. Sachs and I left in the morning, and was turning as leisurely when we returned at 5:30 P.M.

Even though the release was pulled, the rocket did not rise at first, but the flame came out, and there was a steady roar. After a number of seconds it rose, slowly until it cleared the frame, and then at express train speed, curving over to the left, and striking the ice and snow, still going at a rapid rate.

It looked almost magical as it rose, without any appreciably greater noise or flame, as if it said "I've been here long enough; I think I'll be going somewhere else, if you don't mind." . . .

The sky was clear, for the most part, with large shadowy white clouds, but late in the afternoon there was a large pink cloud in the west, over which the sun shone.

One of the surprising things was the absence of smoke, the lack of very loud roar, and the smallness of the flame.

This first flight of a liquid-propellant rocket is of very considerable significance, inasmuch as it demonstrated the possibility of using liquid propellants to secure actual flight, thereby making possible a rocket which could be simple in construction, and of small weight compared with the weight of the propellant.

* Permission to quote from Dr. Goddard's diary and to use the photograph of the first flight was granted by Mrs. Robert H. Goddard.

Test of the first liquid-propellant rocket, Auburn, Massachusetts, March 16, 1926. Dr. Goddard stands by the launching platform.

NEWSPAPER ACCOUNT FROM THE *WORCESTER EVENING POST*

TERRIFIC EXPLOSION AS PROF. GODDARD
OF CLARK SHOOTS HIS "MOON ROCKET"

WOMAN THOUGHT ROCKET
WAS WRECKED AIRPLANE

AMBULANCE RUSHED TO AUBURN TO CARE FOR "VICTIMS OF CRASH," FIND CLARK PROFESSOR AND ASSISTANTS MAKING EXPERIMENTS WITH ROCKET—PLANE FROM LOCAL AIRPORT ALSO MADE SEARCH FROM AIR FOR REPORTED "VICTIMS"

Worcester, Mass. Wednesday, July 17, 1929. A terrific detonation which shook houses and sent a police ambulance scouring the Auburn-Quinsigamond Village section and an airplane into the air from the Worcester Airport in search of a "cracked" plane this afternoon, was traced to experiments of Dr. Robert H. Goddard of Clark University and his "moon rocket" on the Ward Farm in Auburn, just over the Worcester line. . . .

TEST OF JULY 17, 1929
Described by Dr. Goddard

"Report on the Development of Liquid-propelled Rocket,"
August, 1929

In the present rocket the total weight was reduced to 32 lbs., and the same camera, barometer, and thermometer were installed as in the test of July 8, 1929. . . . Fourteen lbs. of gasoline were placed in the gasoline tank . . . and 11 lbs. of liquid oxygen were placed in the liquid oxygen tank following which 5 cups of liquid oxygen were placed in the pressure-generating tank. . . .

Those taking part, and the duty of each, was as follows: Dr. Roope was well in the rear of the shelter with his theodolite and stop watch, Mrs. Goddard stood just outside the right end of the shelter, holding the Ciné-Kodak camera in her hands. Beside her was Mr. Kisk, who was asked to watch the cord to the cotter pin, to make certain that it was pulled off. I came next, and to my left was Mr. Sachs, who operated the pressure-generating tank. . . . At the extreme left end of the shelter, Mr. Mansur was stationed, and asked to watch the behavior of the rocket as closely as possible.

The test was carried out at 2 P.M. . . . Thirty seconds after the alcohol stove was lighted, the igniter was fired, and the next three controls were operated. Mr. Sachs then gave the rocket 125 lbs. pressure. As before, I waited until the rocket had risen three inches, as indicated by the aluminum vanes on the rocket rising up to the white marks, 3″ long, on the vertical ⅜″ pipe guides. I then pulled the two releasing cords in succession. The noise did not appear to change, and I kept pulling the ¼″ rope, thinking that the rocket had not been released, until I heard someone shout "Look out!" When I looked out of the right end of the shelter I saw the rocket just before it hit the ground. . . .

According to Dr. Roope . . . the rocket started to lift at 13 seconds, started to rise at 14½ seconds, reached the top of its flight at 17 seconds, and hit the ground at 18½ seconds. . . . The rocket went rather straight until it was 20 feet above the 60-foot tower, then it turned over to the right, and moved along a straight line inclined about 20° to the horizontal for a distance of 43 feet, rising at the same time 10 feet higher, and reaching 42 feet horizontally from the center of the tower. Then it turned again and moved in a nearly straight line downward about 45° from the horizontal, a distance of 158 feet, striking the ground 129 feet from a point directly under the highest point of the flight, and 171 feet from the center of the tower. The average velocity was about 55 ft/sec. . . .

The camera was scorched, but still operated. The spectacle lens was intact and the barometer continued to read accurately, although the glass covering the dial was broken. The thermometer was broken, however, evidently owing to its being heated higher than it could register. . . .

PUBLIC NOTICE OF THE TEST

Owing to the flight being the highest so far attained, and the flame using an excess of gasoline producing a loud noise and a bright white flare, neighbors sent in calls for ambulances, thinking that an airplane had caught fire and crashed. Unknown to me, two police ambulances searched through Auburn for "victims," and an airplane was sent from the Grafton airport for the same purpose.

We should have been packed up and back to the laboratory before they could have found us, had it not been for the lever device on the top of the cap for the gasoline tank, to open as a vent in an emergency. This could not be found, and as it represented considerable work we stayed and hunted for it.

We were nearly packed up when over the hill from the direction of the farmhouse I saw about a dozen automobiles, raising a great cloud of dust, the first two being ambulances. I asked the two officers if they could not keep the thing quiet. For answer, one of them said, "Do you see these two men coming?" I answered, "Yes, why?" "They are two reporters, one for the *Post* and one for the *Gazette*," was his reply. I tried to arrange to keep it quiet with the two city editors, but by that time extras were coming out.

I planned to make no statement whatever, but when I learned that all the reports featured solely a rocket to the moon exploding in midair, I issued a short statement, as follows: "The test this afternoon was one of a long series of experiments with rockets using entirely new propellants. There was no attempt to reach the moon, or anything of such a spectacular nature. The rocket is normally noisy, possibly enough to attract considerable attention. The test was thoroughly satisfactory; nothing exploded in the air, and there was no damage except incident to landing." . . .

There were many curious press comments regarding the nature of the flight. All agreed that the rocket travelled with a loud roar, heard, it was said, for a radius of two miles. Some mentioned a loud droning noise, like that of an airplane propeller, before it started. Of course the burning is irregular until the pressure has risen considerably. Much of the vegetation about the tower was charred by previous tests, and this condition caused comment. The rocks directly under the nozzle excited interest. They were piled on pipes, on a frame suspended from the two ⅜" pipe guides, to keep the latter as straight as possible, by the tension produced in this way. The rocks were much blackened due to smoky gasoline flames and were largely disintegrated, owing to the prolonged heat in tests in which the rocket did not rise out of the tower.

The tower and shelter were measured and photographed by reporters, who also carefully examined the place where the rocket landed.

Mrs. Goddard secured a moving picture of the rocket from the start until it was about 10 feet above the top of the tower, but was unable to follow it further. The flame appeared to be about 20 feet long, and about 3 feet across at the widest place. Moving pictures were also taken of the group around the rocket after it landed. Unfortunately, the film was not long enough to show the group drinking the health of the rocket, in ginger ale.†

Opposite: Launching of a modern rocket

ELECTRONICS—TODAY AND TOMORROW*

Brig. General David Sarnoff
Chairman of the Board, Radio Corporation of America

Any Profile of America and the lives of its people would be incomplete without mention of scientific research and the many manifestations of its effect on the pattern of modern existence. The homes we live in, the cars, the planes, the trains we ride in are all products of exhaustive investigation and experimentation. Our social, political, and economic institutions are altered by the new ideas, new products, new services, and renewed vitality in business that are created by the discovery of new scientific facts. In no industry is this fact more evident than in electronics, for diligent research is the constructive and creative force upon which the electronics industry has been built.

Electronics had its beginning in 1897 when Sir Joseph John Thomson discovered the electron and demonstrated its true character as the smallest particle of the electrical structure of the atom. The tiny electron, aided by research, has vastly changed the profile of many phases of American life and a great new industry has been created in a relatively short period of time.

As the situation stands today, all modern methods of electric communication depend on the electron. That means telephone, telegraph, facsimile, teletype, broadcasting, and, of course, television. It also includes phonograph recording and reproduction, tape recording and reproduction, and talking movies.

And what about atomic energy and the hydrogen bomb? Without the electron, they would not exist. Neither the power of the atom bomb nor the hydrogen bomb could be controlled and released were it not for electronic devices.

The new field for electronics that may reach a reasonable stage of commercial maturity within the next decade seem to me to promise the following:

First, there is color television. This service began to develop as a commercial reality after the Federal Communications Commission approved signal standards in December 1953. Production of color receivers for the public started in April 1954.

Transistors are next in importance. They will bring into existence, among other things, the wide use of personal radios, including the vest-pocket radio no larger than a memorandum book, and ultimately, a radio possibly no larger than a pocket watch. These miniature receivers will require only the power supplied by a tiny battery, easily replaced and as inexpensive as a flashlight battery.

Industrial television and electronic equipment for manufacturing plants is another great field of operation for the electron. Industrial television means the use of television in factories, so that management can see what is going on along the production line and "keep an eye" on other activities. There are places where man cannot go with safety, and there a television camera can be installed; for example, in factories where deadly fumes would endanger life, near furnaces, and in mines. It can serve also in stores and other places where the public comes en masse. It is my belief that within the next decade, industrial television will be a bigger business than entertainment television is today.

The next item concerns electronic household products. You have heard some reference to the development of an air-conditioning unit that will be noiseless and will not use moving parts. It is still in the research stage, but we are hopeful that we will be able to get the answers to it before many years. If we can make an electronic air conditioner, we can make an electronic washing machine, an electronic refrigerator, and many other kinds of household appliances.

Then there is the broad field of microwave radio relays. When a television picture comes

* Original article.

Work on an electronic data processing machine.

from any other city, even from across the country, it is carried by microwave relays built by the American Telephone and Telegraph Company and installed every thirty miles or so.

Electronics is growing more essential to transportation. There was a time when electronic devices were added to airplanes. Today—especially in military aviation—the plane is likely to be designed around electronic devices. Certainly, airplanes will not use glass vacuum tubes if a transistor is available that is rugged, draws little power, and has a perpetual life.

Electronic computers and their uncanny ability to memorize and quickly produce vast stores of information are leading to what might well be called "the second industrial revolution," created by electronics.

In the first industrial revolution, which has been under way for about one hundred years, machines have replaced manual labor to a large extent. Now in the electronic industrial revolution, or the Age of Automation, machines will in many cases do the work now performed by human brains. In offices, industries and in scientific laboratories these machines will make it possible to put a lot of information in one side of the instrument and get the answers, possibly in a split second, from the other side.

231

This concept of replacing the drudgery of routine and repetitive mental tasks by electronic instruments is likely to have far reaching effects, economically and socially.

The electron is sure to play a vital role in the field of medicine and medical research. Foremost among electronic tools already in use is the electron microscope. Human cells, blood corpuscles, tissues and nerve fibers, tremendously magnified up to 350,000 diameters, can now be photographed and studied as never before.

Other electronic developments that will render great service to the field of medicine are the Sanguinometer—a device in which the television camera has been turned into the eye of a simple and ingenious computer to count microscopic particles such as blood cells, bacterial cultures, or grains of photographic emulsion—and the vibrating plate viscometer, a new instrument that has been used in studies of human blood clotting.

The development of atomic energy for use in peace as well as in war will have a close relationship to electronic developments. It is too long and complex a story to discuss briefly, but that field may one day prove larger for electronics than any other field I have mentioned.

I hold to the conviction that if we intelligently accept the challenges that spring from our opportunities, the wonders we have witnessed in the past fifty years will be dwarfed. Indeed, the advances of the next half century will make those of our generation pale into insignificance. Our great hope for continued advance stems from the fact that the sum total of our knowledge of science and nature is but a drop in the ocean of knowledge that spreads to the far distant shores of the future.

All of us have a right to take special pride in the fact that America, supremely the land of liberty, is also supremely the land of science. Freedom is the oxygen without which science cannot breathe. At their best, at their most creative, science and engineering are attributes of liberty—noble expressions of man's God-given right to investigate and explore the universe without fear of social or political or religious reprisals.

Without freedom there can be no genuine research, which is the uninhibited pursuit of truth no matter where it may lead. In the final analysis science is a search for the truth about the natural laws governing the universe.

Always and everywhere freedom and science flourish best in the same climate, each fortifying the other. They draw their vitamins for healthy growth from the same political soil.

True, there have been periods in history that saw advances in science despite the absence of democracy. But its most magnificent flowering, in the last century, has taken place in countries where liberty prevailed, especially in the United States. Surely this is no accident. Scientific progress rests, in the final analysis, on freedom of research—on the right of man to follow truth wherever it may lead, without fear and without inhibitions.

That is why there have been no major scientific discoveries and inventions in totalitarian countries. The best they can do is to buy or steal, then adapt, the products of freedom. Behind the Iron Curtain, truth has been outlawed. It leads a secret and stunted existence in the underground of men's minds. But science cannot prosper under such conditions, for it needs the invigorating air and sunshine of liberty.

Science alone cannot guarantee security for civilization. Yet the problems facing man cannot be solved without science. Indeed, today man faces a thrilling opportunity as well as a great threat. The potentialities of science enable him to look bravely at the stars and to seek a finer destiny. He needs most the faith and the spiritual guidance that would lead him to apply his new knowledge to peaceful pursuits. For the hope of peace that is lasting and a world that is free lies within the soul, the heart, and the mind of man.

Opposite: Television studio control room.

Andreas Feininger, courtesy "Life"

The 4200-foot steel suspension bridge, Golden Gate, San Francisco

American Enterprise

The American system of free enterprise has played a tremendous part in making the United States the strongest and wealthiest nation in the world. It encourages competition *in all fields, maintaining the constant incentive to improve products;* mass production, *which lowers costs and makes products available to the greatest number of people;* research, *instigated and financed by industry itself, which creates new products, opens new markets, and sustains our high rate of employment.*

Under this dynamic system America continues to gain wealth because it continues to produce wealth through scientific and industrial advances that create the modern tools necessary for more efficient production. And, finally, under our system of free enterprise, it is possible for every American to be a capitalist by investing his savings in almost any company of his choice, through the medium of public securities markets.

In the following section are sketches of four of America's outstanding industries, with quotations from their founders telling of the early days in which the companies were formed; and statistics tracing their growth up to the present:

234

ANDREW CARNEGIE: PIONEER IN STEEL

"The nation that makes the cheapest steel has the other nations at its feet so far as manufacturing in most of its branches is concerned. The cheapest steel means the cheapest ships, the cheapest machinery, the cheapest thousand and one articles of which steel is the base. We are on the eve of a development of the manufacturing powers of the republic such as the world has never seen."

ANDREW CARNEGIE, 1901

COMPARATIVE INTERNATIONAL STATISTICS, 1953

Source: *Iron Age*, December, 1953

Production: Thousand Net Tons (Estimated)

United States	111,855	Russia	41,900
United Kingdom	19,700	Czechoslovakia	4,130
West Germany	17,080	Poland	3,660
France	11,030	East Germany	2,300
Japan	7,600	Hungary	1,630
Belgium	4,870	Romania	770
Canada	4,117	Total Nations of Soviet Axis	54,390
Italy	3,800		
Saar	2,970		
Luxembourg	2,950		
Australia	2,230		
Sweden	1,890		
Other Free Nations	10,150		
Total Free Nations	200,242		

CARNEGIE TELLS HOW HE STARTED

Andrew Carnegie (1835–1919), steel pioneer and public benefactor, emigrated from Scotland at the age of 13. His first job was as a bobbin boy in a cotton factory where he earned a dollar a week. He studied telegraphy and secured a job as an operator for the Pennsylvania Railroad; progressed to divisional superintendent, acquired an interest in the Woodruff Sleeping Car Company, and saved enough to invest in Pennsylvania oil land.

In the following excerpts, testifying before the House Committee (Stanley Committee) on Investigation of the United States Steel Corporation, 1912, Carnegie tells how he started in the iron and steel industries:

In 1862 I organized the Keystone Bridge Works. I found an engineer on the Pennsylvania Railroad, of which I was superintendent at Pittsburgh, who had built a cast-iron bridge. I was satisfied that the day of wooden bridges on railroads was passing, and I organized a company of two bridge builders and a bridge engineer, and five or six of us started the Keystone Bridge Works. I borrowed $1,500 from the Third National Bank of Pittsburgh to pay my share. That was my first start.

In 1863 we built another mill in Pittsburgh, and 1864 I was one of the organizers of the Superior rail mill and furnaces at Pittsburgh.

In 1867 we united two mills in Pittsburgh in which I had an interest . . . and in 1866 I started a locomotive works at Pittsburgh. . . .

. . . I have not told you where we began in steel. I have given you only the beginning of the iron business. Steel was a different problem. I had been a superintendent of the Pennsylvania Railroad. I saw iron rails taken out of the track every six weeks at a point on the Pennsylvania Railroad, as the traffic became heavier. The iron rails could not stand the strain. I went to Europe every summer, and I watched the Bessemer process for steel. Britain was then the pioneer country in making steel. We made none.

. . . I knew Mr. Bessemer, and visited him in England. . . . I was satisfied that the steel process was a success in Britain. I returned and told my partners that iron was to be dethroned and steel would be king; but they were afraid to join me in building a steel works. I got other friends, outside of my partners and we organized the Edgar Thomson Steel Works. . . . We were building the works, and the panic of 1873 struck us and we suspended work for a time; and so many of my friends needed the money that they begged me to repay them. I did so, and bought out five or six of them. That is what gave me my leading interest in the steel business.

If I remember right, I think we each put in about $20,000 only; but I had to buy so many of them out during the panic that I became the controlling one. That is how we began in the steel business. †

FORMATION OF THE UNITED STATES STEEL CORPORATION, 1901

Toward the close of the nineteenth century, Carnegie wished to retire and devote his life to public benefaction. He made several abortive attempts to sell his steel properties, and in 1901 he sold them to J. P. Morgan and Company for $420,000,000. Morgan and Company also financed the purchase of a number of other steel companies which were combined with the Carnegie Company to form the United States Steel Corporation, with an authorized capitalization of $1,400,000,000.

BEGINNING OF THE STEEL INDUSTRY
"THE EMPIRE OF BUSINESS" 1901

Andrew Carnegie

To write of the manufacture of steel in the United States during the last century is indeed to begin at the beginning. . . . As late as 1810 there were produced in the whole country only 917 tons of steel. . . . Even in 1831 the production of steel was only 1,600 tons, an amount which was said then to equal the whole amount imported, so that the market for steel was divided equally with the foreigner seventy years ago. . . .

. . . The struggle with foreign steel became severe until the invader was finally driven from the field. At first European makers could "dump their surplus" upon the market and force American makers to accept for their entire output the extreme low rates which had only to be taken by the invader for a small part of his. The party in control of a profitable home market can most successfully invade the foreign markets. In recent years it is the American manufacturer who is "dumping his surplus" in foreign territory. First conquer your home market and the foreign market will probably be added to you is the rule with manufacturers in international trade. . . .

It was not till 1864, when the last century was almost two-thirds gone, that the revolution in steel manufacture came to us, and the Iron Age began to give way to the new King Steel, for our first Bessemer steel was made in that notable year, and steel hitherto costing from six to seven cents per pound for ordinary grades has since sold at less than one cent per pound, while steel billets by the hundred thousand tons have sold at "three pounds of steel for two cents." . . .

Various contributory causes have made steel billets at $15 a ton possible, among which automatic machinery ranks first, and in this the American excels; continuous processes come second. . . . One essential for cheap production is magnitude. Concerns making one thousand tons of steel per day have little chance against one making ten. We see this law in all departments of industry. It evolves the twenty-thousand-ton steamship and the fifty-ton railroad car. Improved engines and the use of electricity as a motor, the new loading and unloading machinery, are all contributory causes to the cheapening of steel.

There is one element of cost, however, which every student of sociology will rejoice to know has not been cheapened, and that is human labor. It has risen and the tendency is to higher earnings per man. In one of the largest steel works last year (1900) the average wages per man, including all the paid-by-the-day labourers, boys, and mechanics, exceeded $4 per day* for 311 days. Fewer men being required the labour cost per ton is less, and contrary to the opinion often expressed, these men are of higher quality than ever as men. It is a mistake to suppose that men are becoming mere machines; the workman of former days would be unable to take charge of the complicated machinery of today or to meet the demands made by present methods upon his brain and alertness. . . .

. . . The age of iron, which passed away during the last century, was succeeded by the age of Bessemer steel, which enjoyed a reign of only thirty-six years, beginning, as it did, in 1864, and is now in turn passing away to be succeeded by the age of Siemens open-hearth steel. . . .

It is scarcely within the bounds of belief that any cheaper or better process of making steel remains to be discovered, or that improvements upon present methods can possibly be such as to greatly reduce the cost and enable steel to be made without loss at less than 3 pounds for 2 cents. The twentieth century, with all its wonders yet to be revealed, will probably end with the manufacture of steel substantially as it is now, by the open-hearth. There does not seem room for much improvement. . . .

The last few years have witnessed the export of steel from our country to other lands. The republic has not only supplied its own wants but is competing to supply the wants of the world, not only in steel but in the thousand and one articles of which steel is the chief component part. The cheapness with which steel is made is multiplying its uses to such an extent that estimates made of the possible wants of the world in the future can only be the merest guesses. One illustration out of many that could be given is that three years ago there was not a ton of steel used for railway freight cars in this country; today a thousand tons of steel per day are used for that purpose alone; indeed, so rapidly is the use of steel extending that it is difficult to see how the world's demands can be filled. . . .

The republic's progress and commanding position as a steel-producer are told in a few words: In 1873, only twenty-seven years ago, the United States produced 198,796 tons of steel, and Great Britain, her chief competitor, 653,500 tons, more than three times as much. Twenty-six years later, in 1899, the republic made more than twice as much as the monarchy, the figures being 10,639,857 and 5,000,000 tons respectively, an eight-fold increase for Great Britain and a fifty-three-fold for the republic, and it made almost 40 per cent of all the steel made in the world, which was 27,000,000 tons. Industrial history has nothing to show comparable to this.†

* 1953 average pay: $2.25 per hour

Bessemer process, introduced in the 1850's,
the first modern method of producing steel.

Open-hearth process, introduced in the 1870's, today produces 90 per cent of all steel made in the United States.

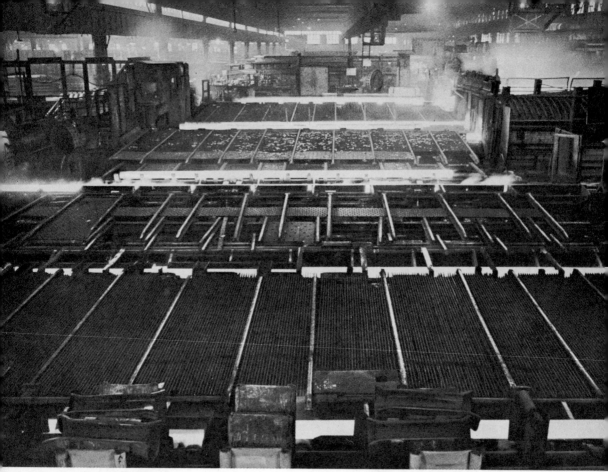

Andreas Feininger, courtesy "Life"

Seamless steel pipes made on a modern mill

STEEL IN THE TWENTIETH CENTURY*

Benjamin F. Fairless
Chairman of the Board, United States Steel Corporation

If history teaches us anything, it teaches us that in any generation we should never think that man has reached the ultimate horizon of achievement. The horizon recedes continually as we advance toward it.

This is well illustrated in the progress made by the steel industry of the United States during this century. Although many of the essential principles of steel-making remain virtually the same as in 1900, steel itself has changed so much that it hardly resembles the product of 50-odd years ago. Our way of life today, with streamlined trains, mass-produced automobiles, aircraft and numerous home appliances simply could not exist with the steels of 1900.

The explanation lies in the discoveries made by the research scientist and the improvements designed by the engineering technologist. The former has exposed many of the secrets of steel and by so doing has developed many new varieties of steel to meet the exacting requirements of today. The latter has designed the equipment needed to manufacture the new steels.

Steels have been developed that can withstand the elevated temperatures and corrosive conditions encountered in various industries. Stainless steel is a noteworthy example, its

* Original article.

use for hygienic and sanitary purposes in hospitals, kitchens and homes being well known.

Indeed, there has been great progress throughout the entire steel industry—in mining iron ore, in transporting it, in the furnaces and in the rolling and finishing mills. All these improvements—in both metallurgy and technology—have enabled the steel industry to provide this nation with the least expensive and most versatile metal known to man, and in ever increasing quantity.

Production has increased from 11,410,000 tons in 1900 to 111,610,000 tons in 1953. In the same period, annual steel production per capita increased from 300 pounds to 1400 pounds. The United States alone can produce more than twice as much steel as the countries behind the Iron Curtain.

. . . The living standards of the wage earner in the American steel industry have kept pace with the general rise in living standards throughout the nation. In 1900, he received approximately 21 cents an hour, and worked 66 hours a week; in 1953 his average wage $2.27 an hour, and he worked an average of 39.4 hours a week.

In other ways, the life of the steel wage earner has been improved. So great an advance has been made in accident prevention that the steel industry is one of the safest industries in which to work. Pensions, life insurance, sickness and accident benefits also add to his security and well-being.

This nation today has reached a standard of living so fabulous that our grandfathers could not have imagined it even in their wildest dreams. Let no one tell us that we have reached the end of the Golden Age; for this, in truth, is only the beginning. In my opinion we stand on the doorstep of the greatest era of progress this nation has ever seen.

GROWTH OF THE OIL INDUSTRY, 1859–1954

The existence of petroleum, or "rock oil," had been known for centuries. In the mid-nineteenth century people were distilling kerosene from "rock oil" and using it as a fuel for lamps, and in the United States there were more than fifty primitive oil refineries.

It was a theory advanced by the owners of the Seneca Oil Company in 1857 that started the modern oil industry. Oil seepages gave them the clue that oil, like water, could be found by drilling. They hired "Colonel" Edwin L. Drake, a retired railroad conductor, to test their theory by drilling a well near Titusville, Pennsylvania. Drake started drilling in the early summer of 1859, and in August of that year he struck oil at 69½ feet. Like the gold rush of '49, the oil rush was on—men poured into Titusville and soon a forest of wooden derricks had sprung up in the area.

Before long the market for crude oil was flooded and the price of petroleum dropped from twenty dollars a barrel in 1859 to ten cents a barrel in 1861. Obviously the future of oil lay not in merely producing it, but in developing a refining industry and a market. Into this picture, in 1863, came John D. Rockefeller, who was to exert a tremendous influence not only in the oil industry, but on the whole trend of business. Following the biographical sketch, Mr. Rockefeller tells of the early days of the Standard Oil Company.

JOHN D. ROCKEFELLER (1839–1937)

John D. Rockefeller, financier and philanthropist, accumulated probably the largest single fortune in America, and at the time of his death had given to various charities and endowments a total of $530,853,632.

Rockefeller was born in Richford, New York; attended public school in Ohio, and started work as an assistant bookkeeper in a commission house. When Drake was drilling his well, Rockefeller was twenty years old and was establishing himself as a dealer in farm produce in Cleveland, Ohio. In 1863, convinced of the great future of oil, Rockefeller, his partner in the produce business, Maurice B. Clark, and a young Englishman, Samuel Andrews, began

The first oil well in the world—Drake's well, drilled in 1859.

operating an oil refinery in Cleveland. In 1865, Rockefeller bought Clark's share of the refinery and formed the oil firm of Rockefeller and Andrews. By 1870, joined by other partners, they were operating the largest refinery in Cleveland and that year formed the Standard Oil Company, incorporated in Ohio and capitalized at $1,000,000. By the end of the '70's, the Standard Oil Company controlled about 75 per cent of the oil refining capacity in the country. As the company expanded, Rockefeller succeeded in controlling the means of oil transportation through agreements with the railroads and by building his own trunk pipelines. Other companies, either unable to compete on such a scale or seeking the advantages of joining with Standard, sold out for cash or for stock in the Company. In the following selection Rockefeller tells of the early days of the Standard Oil Company:

EARLY DEVELOPMENT OF THE STANDARD OIL COMPANY
"RANDOM REMINISCENCES OF MEN AND EVENTS," 1909
John D. Rockefeller

For years the Standard Oil Company has developed step by step, and I am convinced that it has done well its work of supplying to the people the products from petroleum at prices which have decreased as the efficiency of the business has been built up. It gradually extended its services first to the large centres, and then to towns, and now to the smallest places, going to the homes of its customers, delivering the oil to suit the convenience of the actual users. . . .

This plan of selling our products direct to the consumer and the exceptionally rapid growth of the business bred a certain antagonism which I suppose could not have been avoided, but this same idea of dealing with the consumer directly has been followed by others and in many lines of trade, without creating, so far as I recall, any serious opposition.

242

This is a very interesting and important point, and I have often wondered if the criticism which centred upon us did not come from the fact that we were among the first, if not the first, to work out the problems of direct selling to the user on a broad scale. This was done in a fair spirit and with due consideration for every one's rights. We did not ruthlessly go after the trade of our competitors and attempt to ruin it by cutting prices or instituting a spy system. We had set ourselves the task of building up as rapidly and as broadly as possible the volume of consumption. Let me try to explain just what happened.

To get the advantage of the facilities we had in manufacture, we sought the utmost market in all lands—we needed volume. To do this we had to create selling methods far in advance of what then existed; we had to dispose of two, or three, or four gallons of oil where one had been sold before, and we could not rely upon the usual trade channels then existing to accomplish this. It was never our purpose to interfere with a dealer who adequately cultivated his field of operations, but when we saw a new opportunity or a new place for extending the sale by further and effective facilities, we made it our business to provide them. In this way we opened many new lines in which others have shared. . . .

Every week in the year for many, many years, this concern has brought into this country more than a million dollars gold, all from the products produced by American labour. I am proud of the record, and believe most Americans will be when they understand some things better. These achievements, the development of this great foreign trade, the owning of ships to carry the oil in bulk by the most economical methods, the sending out of men to fight for the world's markets, have cost huge sums of money, and the vast capital

"A forest of derricks sprang up."   View of Signal Hill, California.

Andreas Feininger

employed could not be raised nor controlled except by such an organization as the Standard is to-day.

To give a true picture of the early conditions, one must realize that the oil industry was considered a most hazardous undertaking, not altogether unlike the speculative mining undertakings we hear so much of to-day. . . .

None of us ever dreamed of the magnitude of what proved to be the later expansion. We did our day's work as we met it, looking forward to what we could see in the distance and keeping well up to our opportunities, but laying our foundations firmly. . . .

It is a common thing to hear people say that this company has crushed out its competitors. Only the uninformed could make such an assertion. It has and always has had, and always will have, hundreds of active competitors; it has lived only because it has managed its affairs well and economically and with great vigour. To speak of competition for a minute: Consider not only the able people who compete in refining oil, but all the competition in the various trades which make and sell by-products—a great variety of different businesses. And perhaps of even more importance is the competition in foreign lands. The Standard is always fighting to sell the American product against the oil produced from the great fields of Russia, which struggles for the trade of Europe, and the Burma oil, which largely affects the market in India. In all these various countries we are met with tariffs which are raised against us, local prejudices, and strange customs. In many countries we had to teach the people—the Chinese, for example—to burn oil by making lamps for them; we packed the oil to be carried by camels or on the backs of runners in the most remote portions of the world; we adapted the trade to the needs of strange folk. Every time we succeeded in a foreign land, it meant dollars brought to this country, and every time we failed, it was a loss to our nation and its workmen. . . .

The Standard has not now, and never did have a royal road to supremacy, nor is its success due to any one man, but to the multitude of able men who are working together. . . .

. . . If there is any better function of business management than giving profitable work to employees year after year, in good times and bad, I don't know what it is.

. . . A labourer is worthy of his hire, no less, but no more, and in the long run he must contribute an equivalent for what he is paid. If he does not do this . . . you at once throw out the balance of things. You can't hold up conditions artificially, and you can't change the underlying laws of trade.†

FORMATION AND GROWTH OF STANDARD OIL (NEW JERSEY)

The Standard organization grew with mushroom rapidity until it became a complex of companies in virtually all branches of the oil business. Nine men who owned stock in these companies coordinated the management of them by pooling their holdings in a trust agreement. In 1892 the state of Ohio enjoined the original Ohio corporation from recognizing the transfer of its stock to the Trust, and it thus became necessary to find a new form of management. The Trust was dissolved, and stock in the various companies transferred to the Standard Oil Company which had been incorporated in New Jersey. Nineteen years later, in a suit under the Sherman Anti-Trust law, the New Jersey company was required to divest itself of all stock in thirty-three subsidiaries. The date of the Supreme Court decision in that suit— 1911—may be said to mark the beginning of the modern history of the company. The decision left Jersey Standard with several refineries on the East Coast and with some foreign business, but with little crude oil production or domestic marketing facilities, and the future did not appear too bright. The company, however, set about building a better balanced enterprise and entered into new oil ventures both in the United States and abroad.

Oil transport.   Worker on a Mississippi towboat.

Standard Oil Co. (N.J.)

Standard Oil Co. (N.J.)

Oil refinery at Baton Rouge, Louisiana

Today Standard Oil (*New Jersey*) is the largest of the many hundreds of companies that comprise the American oil industry. It operates as a holding company, conducts no operations directly, but is the parent of a group of affiliates, some wholly and some partly owned, which operate in almost all countries of the free world. The following statistics trace the growth of Standard Oil (*New Jersey*):

GROWTH OF STANDARD OIL (NEW JERSEY) AND AFFILIATES

Year	Number of shareowners	Total assets	Crude oil production (barrels per day)	Refining runs (barrels per day)
1912	5,832	$ 369,265.000	13,000	101,000
1920	8,744	1,102,313,000	112,000	232,000
1930	111,952	1,770,993,803	278,000	495,000
1940	136,355	2,071,537,919	640,000	789,000
1950	222,064	4,187,994,173	1,444,000	1,605,000

HENRY FORD PUTS THE NATION ON WHEELS, 1903

"I will build a motor car for the great multitude. It will be large enough for the family but small enough for the individual to run and care for. It will be constructed of the best materials, by the best men to be hired, after the simplest designs that modern engineering can devise. But it will be so low in price that no man making a good salary will be unable to own one—and enjoy with his family the blessing of hours of pleasure in God's great open spaces."

HENRY FORD, 1909

TOURING CAR PRICE AND PRODUCTION 1909–1917

Year	Price	Production
1909–10	$950	18,664 cars
1910–11	780	34,528 "
1911–12	690	78,440 "
1912–13	600	168,220 "
1913–14	550	248,307 "
1914–15	490	308,213 "
1915–16	440	533,921 "
1916–17	360	785,432 "

HENRY FORD (1863–1947)

Henry Ford was born on a farm near Dearborn, Michigan, and attended public school in Greenfield. At the age of sixteen he started work as a machinist's apprentice at $2.50 a week. In 1887 he moved to Detroit, where he became chief engineer of the Detroit Automobile Company. After building several successful automobiles he organized and became president of the Ford Motor Company, 1903, developing it into the largest motor car company in the world. In the text that follows, Ford tells how he did it:

"MY LIFE AND WORK," 1922
Henry Ford

Power and machinery, money and goods, are useful only as they set us free to live. They are but means to an end. For instance, I do not consider the machines which bear my name simply as machines. If that was all there was to it I would do something else. I take them as concrete evidence of the working out of a theory of business which I hope is something more than a theory of business—a theory that looks toward making this world a better place in which to live. The fact that the commercial success of the Ford Motor Company has been most unusual is important only because it serves to demonstrate, in a way which no one can fail to understand, that the theory to date is right. . . .

. . . Most of the present acute troubles of the world arise out of taking on new ideas without first carefully investigating to discover if they are good ideas. An idea is not necessarily good because it is old, or necessarily bad because it is new, but if an old idea works, then the weight of the evidence is all in its favour. . . . Almost any one can think up an idea. The thing that counts is developing it into a practical product.

I am now most interested in fully demonstrating that the ideas we have put into practice are capable of the largest application—that they have nothing peculiarly to do with motor cars or tractors but form something in the nature of a universal code. I am quite certain that it is the natural code and I want to demonstrate it so thoroughly that it will be accepted, not as a new idea, but as a natural code. . . .

... In a little dark shop on a side street an old man had labored for years making axe handles. Out of seasoned hickory he fashioned them, with the help of a draw shave, a chisel, and a supply of sandpaper. Carefully was each handle weighed and balanced. No two of them were alike. The curve must exactly fit the hand and must conform to the grain of the wood. From dawn until dark the old man labored. His average product was eight handles a week, for which he received a dollar and a half each. And often some of these were unsaleable—because the balance was not true.

Today you can buy a better axe handle, made by machinery, for a few cents. And you need not worry about the balance. They are all alike—and every one is perfect. Modern methods applied in a big way have not only brought the cost of axe handles down to a fraction of their former cost—but they have immensely improved the product.

Making "to order" instead of making in volume, is, I suppose, a habit, a tradition, that has descended from the old handicraft days. Ask a hundred people how they want a particular article made. About eighty will not know; they will leave it to you. Fifteen will think that they must say something, while five will really have preferences and reasons. The ninety-five, made up of those who do not know and admit it and the fifteen who do not know but do not admit it, constitute the real market for any produce. ... The majority will consider quality and buy the biggest dollar's worth of quality. If, therefore, you discover what will give this 95 per cent of the people the best all-round service and then arrange to manufacture at the very highest quality and sell at the very lowest price, you will be meeting a demand which is so large that it may be called universal. ...

All of this seems self-evident to me. It is the logical basis of any business that wants to serve 95 per cent of the community. It is the logical way in which the community can serve itself. I cannot comprehend why all business does not go on this basis. All that has to be done in order to adopt it is to overcome the habit of grabbing at the nearest dollar as though it were the only dollar in the world. ... The only further step required is to throw overboard the idea of pricing on what the traffic will bear and instead go to the common-sense basis of pricing on what it costs to manufacture and then reducing the cost of manufacture. ...

My associates were not convinced that it was possible to restrict our cars to a single model. The automobile trade was following the old bicycle trade, in which every manu-facturer thought it necessary to bring out a new model each year and made it so unlike all previous models that those who had bought the former models would want to get rid of the old and buy the new. That was supposed to be good business. It is the same idea that women submit to in their clothing and hats. That is not service—it seeks only to provide something new, not something better. It is extraordinary how firmly rooted is the notion that business—continuous selling—depends not on satisfying the customer once and for all, but on first getting his money for one article and then persuading him he ought to buy a new and different one. The plan which I then had in the back of my head but to which we were not then sufficiently advanced to give expression, was that, when a model was settled upon, then every improvement on that model should be interchangeable with the old models, so that a car should never get out of date. It is my ambition to have every piece of machinery, or other non-consumable product that I turn out, so strong and so well made that no one ought ever to have to buy a second one. A good machine of any kind ought to last as long as a good watch.

BIRTH OF THE ASSEMBLY LINE

A Ford car contains about five thousand parts—that is counting screws, nuts, and all. Some of the parts are fairly bulky and others are almost the size of watch parts. In our first assembling we simply started to put a car together at a spot on the floor and work-

Henry Ford.

men brought to it the parts as they were needed in exactly the same way that one builds a house. When we started to make parts it was natural to create a single department of the factory to make that part, but usually one workman performed all of the operations necessary on a small part. The rapid press of production made it necessary to devise plans of production that would avoid having the workers falling over one another. The undirected worker spends more of his time walking about for materials and tools than he does in working; he gets small pay because pedestrianism is not a highly paid line.

The first step forward in assembly came when we began taking the work to the men instead of the men to the work. We now have two general principles in all operations— that a man shall never have to take more than one step, if possibly it can be avoided, and that no man need ever stoop over.

The principles of assembly are these:

(1) Place the tools and the men in the sequence of the operation so that each component part shall travel the least possible distance while in the process of finishing.

(2) Use work slides or some other form of carrier so that when a workman completes his operation, he drops the part always in the same place—which place must always be the most convenient place to his hand—and if possible have gravity carry the part to the next workman for his operation.

(3) Use sliding assembly lines by which the parts to be assembled are delivered at convenient distances.

The net result of the application of these principles is the reduction of the necessity for thought on the part of the worker and the reduction of his movements to a minimum. He does as nearly as possible only one thing with only one movement. . . .

Along about April 1, 1913, we first tried the experiment of an assembly line. We tried it on assembling the fly-wheel magneto. We try anything in a little way first—we will rip out anything once we discover a better way, but we have to know absolutely that the new way is going to be better than the old before we do anything drastic.

I believe that this was the first moving line ever installed. The idea came in a general way from the overhead trolley that the Chicago packers use in dressing beef. We had previously assembled the fly-wheel magneto in the usual method. With one workman doing a complete job he could turn out from thirty-five to forty pieces in a nine-hour day, or about twenty minutes to an assembly. What he did alone was then spread into twenty-nine operations; that cut down the assembly line to thirteen minutes, ten seconds. Then we raised the height of the line eight inches—this was in 1914—and cut the time to seven minutes. Further experimenting with the speed that the work should move at cut the time down to five minutes. In short, the result is this: by the aid of scientific study one man is now able to do somewhat more than four did only a comparatively few years ago. That line established the efficiency of the method and we now use it everywhere. The assembling of the motor, formerly done by one man, is now divided into eight-four operations—those men do the work that three times their number formerly did. . . .

It must not be imagined, however, that all this worked out as quickly as it sounds. The speed of the moving work had to be carefully tried out; in the fly-wheel magneto we first had a speed of sixty inches per minute. That was too fast. Then we tried eighteen inches per minute. That was too slow. Finally we settled on forty-four inches per minute. The idea is that a man must not be hurried in his work—he must have every second necessary but not a single unnessary second. We have worked out speeds for each assembly, for the success of the chassis assembly caused us gradually to overhaul our entire method of manufacturing and to put all assembling in mechanically driven lines. The chassis assembling line, for instance, goes at a pace of six feet per minute. In the chassis assembling are

Ford Motor Company

forty-five separate operations or stations. The first men fasten four mud-guard brackets to the chassis frame; the motor arrives on the tenth operation and so on in detail. Some men do only one or two small operations, others do more. The man who places a part does not fasten it—the part may not be fully in place until after several operations later. The man who puts in a bolt does not put on the nut; the man who puts on the nut does not tighten it. On operation number thirty-four the budding motor gets its gasoline; it has previously received lubrication; on operation number forty-four the radiator is filled with water, and on operation number forty-five the car drives out onto John R. Street.

It was the application of these same methods to the making of the Ford car that at the very start lowered the price and heightened the quality. We just developed an idea. The nucleus of a business may be an idea. That is, an inventor or a thoughtful workman works out a new and better way to serve some established human need; the idea commends itself and people want to avail themselves of it. In this way a single individual may prove, through his idea or discovery, the nucleus of a business. But the creation of the body and bulk of that business is shared by everyone who has anything to do with it. No manufacturer can say: "I built this business"—if he has required the help of thousands of men in building it. It is a joint production. Everyone employed in it has contributed something to it. By working and producing they make it possible for the purchasing work to

Ford Motor Company. River Rouge plant, Dearborn, Michigan

Fairchild Aerial Surveys

...he nation on wheels. Clover-leaf highway, Long Island, New York.

keep coming to that business for the type of service it provides, and thus they help establish a custom, a trade, a habit which supplies them with a livelihood. That is the way our company grew.†

GROWTH OF THE FORD MOTOR COMPANY

Year	Passenger Car Production (U.S.)	Average Employees (U.S.)	Manufacturing and Assembly Plants
1903	1,700	125	1
1910	32,053	3,190	3
1920	419,517	63,568	34
1930	1,158,677	154,720	46
1940	705,966	122,586	47
1950	1,556,688	144,715	45
1953	1,546,518	185,020	41

THE STORY OF AN AMERICAN ENTERPRISE: THE DU PONT COMPANY* (FOUNDED 1802)

It was the turmoil of the French Revolution that caused the du Pont family to emigrate to America in 1800. During the Revolution, Pierre Samuel du Pont, who had been raised to the nobility for his efforts in effecting the Paris Peace Treaty of 1783, was imprisoned and only escaped the guillotine when political prisoners were released after the execution of Robespierre.

Eleuthère Irénée du Pont, Pierre's son, was a chemist who had studied under the great French scientist, Antoine Laurent Lavoisier. It was in apprenticeship to him that Irénée learned the methods of making black powder that were later to found the Du Pont industry in the United States. When Robespierre announced that France no longer needed scientists, Lavoisier was among those beheaded.

In emigrating to America it was the original intention of the elder du Pont to set up a colony to which Frenchmen like himself could come and start life anew. The United States, he said, was a place where "liberty, safety and independence really exist." But the funds necessary for his venture, though subscribed to by such prominent Frenchmen as La Fayette, Beaumarchais, and Rousseau, failed to materialize fully and, in 1800, the du Ponts found themselves in America in the position of so many immigrants who brought with them nothing but their hopes, plans, and individual skills.

While Irénée was out hunting one day, an incident occurred that led to the formation of the Du Pont Company. In firing his gun, Irénée was shocked to discover that the powder was of such poor quality that as often as not it failed to discharge at all.

To settlers, gunpowder was essential. Ammunition was needed to procure food and skins and to ward off hostile Indians. Explosives were needed to clear the land and build roads. Here, Irénée decided, was a basic need on which a business could be founded, and one he was technically equipped to fulfill. He discussed the situation with his father, who in turn consulted the president, Thomas Jefferson, as to the attitude of the government. Domestic powder being unreliable, foreign powder scarce, and import prices exorbitant, Jefferson was heartily in favor of setting up powder plants in the United States.

In 1801 Irénée du Pont, who had been to France to secure backing, returned, bringing with him technical and financial help and a document with the formidable title of "Articles of Incorporation for the Establishment of the Manufacture of Military and Sporting Powder." It stipulated that the capital of the company should be $36,000 in eighteen shares of $2,000 each; that Irénée du Pont was to direct the enterprise for $1,800 a year and one-third of the profits or losses. A site was bought for $6,740 on the Brandywine Creek near Wilmington, Delaware, and in 1804 the first Du Pont powder went on sale. Thomas Jefferson gave du Pont his first order—refining saltpeter. The following correspondence highlights some of the early struggles of the founders of Du Pont:

E. I. DU PONT TO HIS FATHER, PIERRE SAMUEL DU PONT

June 12, 1803

Ever since the spring I have had more than 40 men at work. I have to arrange their jobs, direct and supervise them and be with them all the time; and in a strange country where one scarcely understands the language and where work is so difficult, my duties are truly appalling. I do my best . . . but I often wonder how and when I will reach the end of all that is still to be done. It is the more difficult because I have never had so many vexations, anxieties and physical and mental sufferings as I have had this year.

* This story was written from information obtained from the Du Pont Company. Permission to use the letters was granted by the late Pierre S. du Pont.

E. I. DU PONT TO HIS FATHER

August 8, 1803

[About three weeks ago] I wrote to the President [Jefferson] to ask his interest, and work for the mills. The result was a letter from the Minister of War giving us the refining of the saltpetre now in possession of the Government; the making over of damaged powder; and the furnishing of new powder when the Government shall need it. There is nothing more we could wish; nor could we start under better auspices. I hope at last that my work and your confidence will not be wasted.

THOMAS JEFFERSON TO E. I. DU PONT

November 23, 1804

Dear Sir:

It is with real pleasure I inform you that it is concluded to be for the public interest to apply to your establishment for whatever can be had from that for the use either of the naval or military department. The present is for your private information; you will know it officially by applications from those departments whenever their wants may call for them. Accept my friendly salutations and assurances of esteem and respect.

THOS. JEFFERSON

E. I. DU PONT TO HIS FATHER

July 26, 1808

. . . being unknown here and having no influence we get but a very small part of the government work. The Ministers prefer to give it to their friends and acquaintances against the well known wish of the President [Jefferson] and certainly against the interests of the public—since the others do not make it [powder] nearly as well as we do.

E. I. DU PONT TO HIS FATHER

January 28, 1809

This country is now ready for manufacturing; with the industry and activity natural to Americans they will soon make for themselves whatever they most need; if we do not begin others will. . . . In four years I have made 600,000 lbs. of powder that would have come from England if I had not made it.

PIERRE SAMUEL DU PONT TO E. I. DU PONT

July 10, 1812

I am perfectly convinced that every personal advantage we experience is a motive and an obligation for us to do our duty to our fellow men. Those who are courageous are made to defend others; and those who have wisdom, to enlighten them.

All capacity is a trust. To labor for one's self—is that a merit? For one's family—is that a trial? . . . To work for one's Country is the beginning of improvement and dignity; that is like the Beaver, the Bee and the Ant. To work for humanity, for our fellow beings—that is the duty of Heroes, of true philosophers—of Angels.

E. I. DU PONT TO HIS FATHER

August 8, 1814

. . . my salary of $1800 does not nearly suffice for the education of my children, the support of my family, and the various expenses I have had to bear. . . .

CHANGES IN THE DU PONT COMPANY

For the first hundred years the Du Pont Company was largely a family concern devoted to the production of explosives. In the beginning of the twentieth century the Company underwent a complete change. Their scattered holdings were unified, company after company dissolved, and their properties vested in the Du Pont Company by outright purchase. Research facilities were augmented and Du Pont entered the field of industrial chemistry. In 1903 the precedent of keeping the Company in the hands of the family was broken when an Executive Committee was formed from the ranks. Bonuses of Du Pont stock were awarded for conspicuous services, and thousands of employees became shareowners. Today the Du Pont Company is the largest over-all producer in the chemical industry in America. The extraordinary development of the Company can be seen in the following statistics:

GROWTH OF THE DU PONT COMPANY, 1804–1954

Year	Employees	Plants	Products	Shareowners
1804	18	1	1	6
1825	140	1	1	6
1850	200	1	1	6
1875	260	2	2	6
1900	2,500	6	6	6
1925	14,000	38	800	13,000
1950	73,500	80	1,200	110,000
1954	90,000	72	1,250	146,000

Chemical research, Wilmington, Delaware

William M. Rittase

Nylon parachutes—one of the earliest uses of this first man-made fiber.

"It is more important to carry on research than it is to pay dividends," was the statement made by Lammot du Pont in 1933, during the depression, when he refused to have the research budget pared down.

The extraordinary success of the Du Pont research programs has been one of the miracles of modern industry. Within fifty years they transformed the company from an organization of six plants turning out six products to its present status, with seventy-two plants turning out 1,250 products and product lines. From their research laboratories have come such things as Nylon, Orlon, and "Dacron" in the fiber fields; "Duco" finishes; neoprene synthetic rubber; moisture-proof cellophane; agricultural chemicals; "Lucite" acrylic resin; dyes, pigments, flame retardants, water repellents, synthetic detergents; "Nitramon" safe blasting agents; and "Mylar" polyester film. Perhaps this story can best be illustrated through an example of one of their many research projects:

257

In 1927, under its new long-range program of fundamental research, Du Pont engaged Dr. Wallace H. Carothers to head one of its projects. Thirty-one years old, fresh from teaching at Harvard University, Dr. Carothers was placed in charge of a team of well-trained organic chemists, and together these men set out on a program of fundamental research directed toward a better understanding of polymerization. At first the information they turned up was largely of academic value, but after two years something happened that was destined to revolutionize the textile industry. A strange long fiber was drawn from a molten polymer. The more this phenomenon was examined and tested the more potentialities it appeared to have. Other chemists and chemical engineers joined Carothers' original group and for the next several years, countless experiments were carried out. Finally, on October 27, 1938, about ten years after the fundamental research had been begun, the first truly man-made synthetic fiber was introduced to the world under the name "Nylon." The over-all cost to Du Pont, from basic research to commercial production of nylon, was $27,000,000.

SUMMARY: BENEFITS OF FREE ENTERPRISE

William James, in *Memories and Studies*, said: "The world is only beginning to see that the wealth of a nation consists more than anything else in the number of superior men it harbors. In the practical realm it has always recognized this, and knows that no price is too high to pay for a great statesman or great captain of industry. . . .

"From the bare economic point of view the importance of geniuses is only beginning to be appreciated. . . . One main care of every country in the future ought to be to find out who its first-rate thinkers are and to help them. . . . Where quality is the thing sought after, the thing of supreme quality is cheap, whatever the price one has to pay for it."

Today America's great industries, under our system of free enterprise, are doing much to achieve this goal. Through grants to universities and colleges, private enterprise gives training to the nation's youth. Jobs requiring skill are open to young men and women as soon as they graduate, as are research facilities on a scale unknown to any previous age. In this way America is able to go forward in the highly competitive industrial and scientific world in which we live.

Through brief sketches of four of America's industries, this section has attempted to show examples of the story of the evolution of American free enterprise. It is a tremendous story and one that is only beginning to be understood.

Philanthropy

Organized charity in America was first dispensed through religious institutions. Later, fraternal orders were formed and members of these orders have continued to support and maintain numerous charitable activities. During the latter part of the nineteenth century accumulation of large fortunes by individuals led to the formation of great philanthropic organizations which have brought tremendous benefits not only to the nation but to the world. Among the best known are the Carnegie and Rockefeller Foundations whose range of activities are so vast it would be impossible to describe them in this volume. Instead, in the following section Mr. Carnegie and Mr. Rockefeller relate some of their principles of philanthropy on which these organizations were built:

ANDREW CARNEGIE (1835–1919)

Andrew Carnegie was 66 years old at the time of his retirement. In 1889 he set down his principles of philanthropy in an eighty-two page essay entitled "The Gospel of Wealth" and actually spent the last eighteen years of his life putting it into practice. The benefactions given in his lifetime totalled about $350,000,000.

PARTIAL LIST OF ANDREW CARNEGIE'S PUBLIC GIFTS AND BEQUESTS

Free Public Library Buildings	$ 43,068,838
Colleges, Universities and Schools	15,043,477
Carnegie Corporation of New York	135,336,867
Carnegie Institution of Washington	22,000,000
Carnegie Foundation for the Advancement of Teaching	15,000,000

"THE GOSPEL OF WEALTH," 1889
Andrew Carnegie

In bestowing charity, the main consideration should be to help those who will help themselves; to provide part of the means by which those who desire to improve may do so; to give those who desire to rise the aids by which they may rise; to assist, but rarely or never to do all. Neither the individual nor the race is improved by almsgiving. . . .

This, then, is held to be the duty of the man of wealth: First, to set an example of modest, unostentatious living, shunning display or extravagance; to provide moderately for the legitimate wants of those dependent upon him; and, after doing so, to consider all surplus revenues which come to him simply as trust funds, which he is called upon to administer, and strictly bound as a matter of duty to administer in the manner which, in his judgment, is best calculated to produce the most beneficial results for the community—the man of wealth thus becoming the mere trustee and agent for his poorer brethren, bringing to their service his superior wisdom, experience, and ability to administer, doing for them better than they would or could do for themselves. . . .

It is not the privilege, however, of millionaires alone to work for or aid measures which are certain to benefit the community. Everyone who has but a small surplus above his moderate wants may share this privilege with his richer brothers, and those without surplus can give at least a part of their time, which is usually as important as funds, and often more so.

CARNEGIE GIVES 2,811 LIBRARIES

The result of my own study of the question, What is the best gift which can be given to a community? is that a free library occupies the first place, provided the community will accept and maintain it as a public institution, as much a part of the city property as its public schools, and, indeed, an adjunct to these. It is, no doubt, possible that my own personal experience may have led me to value a free library beyond all other forms of beneficence. When I was a working-boy in Pittsburgh, Colonel Anderson of Allegheny . . . opened his little library of four hundred books to boys. Every Saturday afternoon he was in attendance at his house to exchange books. No one but he who has felt it can ever know the intense longing with which the arrival of Saturday was awaited, that a new book might be had. . . . I resolved, if ever wealth came to me, that it should be used to establish free libraries, that other poor boys might receive opportunities similar to those for which we were indebted to that noble man.†

THE CARNEGIE CORPORATION OF NEW YORK
FIRST LETTER OF GIFT*

New York, *November 10, 1911*

To the Trustees of
  Carnegie Corporation of New York.

GENTLEMEN: I hereby assign and transfer twenty-five millions of dollars in first mortgage, fifty-year bonds of the United States Steel Corporation, the principal of which is to be held and the interest and income thereof applied for the purposes of the Corporation, as stated in its charter, viz., "to promote the advancement and diffusion of knowledge and understanding among the people of the United States by aiding technical schools, institutions of higher learning, libraries, scientific reserch, hero funds, useful publications, and by such other agencies and means as shall from time to time be found appropriate therefor."

My desire is that the work which I hav been carrying on, or similar beneficial work, shall continue during this and future generations.

Conditions upon the erth inevitably change; hence, no wise man will bind Trustees forever to certain paths, causes or institutions. I disclaim any intention of doing so. On the contrary, I giv my Trustees full authority to change policy or causes hitherto aided, from time to time, when this, in their opinion, has become necessary or desirable. They shall best conform to my wishes by using their own judgment.

I direct that out of this fund each Trustee receive five thousand dollars per year for his servises.

My chief happiness as I write these lines lies in the thot that even after I pass away the welth that came to me to administer as a sacred trust for the good of my fellow men is to continue to benefit humanity for generations untold, under your devoted and sympathetic guidance and that of your successors, who can not fail to be able and good men.

My dear, dear friends, I thank you one and all. God bless you.

Ever your devoted

ANDREW CARNEGIE

JOHN D. ROCKEFELLER (1839–1937)

When John D. Rockefeller retired in 1894, he devoted the remaining years of his life to philanthropy, using the same organizing genius in the bestowal of his wealth as he had in the acquiring of it. Following the list of some of his gifts is a selection in which he explains his principles of philanthropy.

PRINCIPAL TRUSTS CREATED BY JOHN D. ROCKEFELLER

1901	The Rockefeller Institute for Medical Research	$ 60,673,409.45
1903	General Education Board	129,209,167.10
1913	The Rockefeller Foundation	182,851,480.90
1918	Laura Spelman Rockefeller Memorial	73,985,313.77
	Total	$446,719,371.22

* When this letter of gift was written, Mr. Carnegie was interested in a movement to simplify spelling.

Opposite: John D. Rockefeller. Painting by John Singer Sargent (February, 1917).

'THE DIFFICULT ART OF GIVING'

John D. Rockefeller

"RANDOM REMINISCENCES OF MEN AND EVENTS," 1909

The best philanthropy, the help that does the most good and the least harm, the help that nourishes civilization at its very root, that most widely disseminates health, righteousness, and happiness, is not what is usually called charity. It is, in my judgment, the investment of effort or time or money . . . to expand and develop the resources at hand, and to give opportunity for progress and healthful labour where it did not exist before. No mere money-giving is comparable to this in its lasting and beneficial results. . . .

If the people can be educated to help themselves, we strike at the root of many of the evils of the world. . . . The only thing which is of lasting benefit to a man is that which he does for himself. Money which comes to him without effort on his part is seldom a benefit and often a curse. . . . It is only in the exceptional case that the receiver is really benefited. But, if we can help people to help themselves, then there is a permanent blessing conferred.

. . . It is my belief that the principal cause for the economic differences between people is their difference in personality, and that it is only as we can assist in the wider distribution of those qualities which go to make up a strong personality that we can assist in the wider distribution of wealth. Under normal conditions the man who is strong in body, in mind, in character, and in will need never suffer want. But these qualities can never be developed in a man unless by his own efforts, and the most that any other can do for him is, as I have said, to help him to help himself.

Some Underlying Principles

. . . I may perhaps be pardoned if I set down here some of the fundamental principles which have been at the bottom of all my own plans. . . .

My own conversion to the feeling that an organized plan was an absolute necessity came about in this way.

About the year 1890 I was still following the haphazard fashion of giving here and there as appeals presented themselves. I investigated as I could, and worked myself almost to a nervous break-down in groping my way, without sufficient guide or chart, through this ever-widening field of philanthropic endeavour. There was then forced upon me the necessity to organize and plan this department of our daily tasks on as distinct lines of progress as we did our business affairs; and I will try to describe the underlying principles we arrived at, and have since followed out, and hope still greatly to extend.

. . . If you were to go into our office, and ask our committee on benevolence or our committee on investment in what they consider civilization to consist, they would say that they have found in their study that the most convenient analysis of the elements which go to make up civilization runs about as follows:

1st. Progress in the means of subsistence, that is to say, progress in abundance and variety of food-supply, clothing, shelter, sanitation, public health, commerce, manufacture, the growth of public wealth, etc.

2nd. Progress in government and law, that is to say, in the enactment of laws securing justice and equity to every man, consistent with the largest individual liberty, and the due and orderly enforcement of the same upon all.

3rd. Progress in literature and language.

4th. Progress in science and philosophy.

5th. Progress in art and refinement.

6th. Progress in morality and religion.

. . . We have not been satisfied with giving to causes which have appealed to us. We have felt that the mere fact that this or the other cause makes its appeal is no reason why we should give to it any more than to a thousand other causes, perhaps more worthy, which do not happen to have come under our eye. The mere fact of a personal appeal creates no claim which did not exist before, and no preference over other causes more worthy which may not have made their appeal. . . . This department has studied the field of human progress, and sought to contribute to each of those elements which we believe tend most to promote it. Where it has not found organizations ready to its hand for such purpose, the members of the committee have sought to create them. We are still working on new, and, I hope, expanding lines, which make large demands on one's intelligence and study. . . .

If a combination to do business is effective in saving waste and in getting better results, why is not combination far more important in philanthropic work? . . .

Fortunately my children have been as earnest as I, and much more diligent, in carefully and intelligently carrying out the work already begun, and agree with me that at least the same energy and thought should be expended in the proper and effective use of money when acquired as was exerted in the earning of it. . . .

It is easy to do harm in giving money. To give to institutions which should be supported by others is not the best philanthropy. Such giving only serves to dry up the natural springs of charity.

It is highly important that every charitable institution shall have at all times the largest possible number of current contributors. This means that the institution shall constantly be making its appeals; but, if these constant appeals are to be successful, the institution is forced to do excellent work and meet real and manifest needs. Moreover, the interest of many people affords the best assurance of wise economy and unselfish management as well as of continued support.

We frequently make our gifts conditional on the giving of others, not because we wish to force people to do their duty, but because we wish in this way to root the institution in the affections of as many people as possible, who, as contributors, become personally concerned, and thereafter may be counted on to give to the institution their watchful interest and cooperation. Conditional gifts are often criticized, and sometimes, it may be, by people who have not thought the matter out fully. . . .

Surely it is wise to be careful not to duplicate effort and not to inaugurate new charities in fields already covered, but rather to strengthen and perfect those already at work. There is a great deal of rivalry and a vast amount of duplication, and one of the most difficult things in giving is to ascertain when the field is fully covered. Many people simply consider whether the institution to which they are giving is thoughtfully and well managed, without stopping to discover whether the field is not already occupied by others; and for this reason one ought not to investigate a single institution by itself, but always in its relation to all similar institutions in the territory. . . .

The giver who works out these problems for himself will, no doubt, find many critics. So many people see the pressing needs of everyday life that possibly they fail to realize those which are, if less obvious, of an even larger significance—for instance, the great claims of higher education. Ignorance is the source of a large part of the poverty and a vast amount of the crime in the world—hence the need of education. If we assist the highest forms of education—in whatever field—we secure the widest influence in enlarging the boundaries of human knowledge; for all the new facts discovered or set in motion become the universal heritage. I think we cannot overestimate the importance of this matter. The mere fact that most of the great achievements in science, medicine, art, and literature are the flower of the higher education is sufficient. Some great writer will one day show how these things have ministered to the wants of all the people, educated and uneducated, high and low, rich and poor, and made life more what we all wish it to be.

The best philanthropy is constantly in search of the finalities—a search for cause, an attempt to cure evils at their source.†

SEVEN

War

> "There never was a war that was
>   not inward; I must
> fight till I have conquered in myself what
>   causes war...."
>
> **MARIANNE MOORE**

War

From the beginning America's military forces have been under civil authority. During the Revolutionary War they were under the control of the Continental Congress; and when the Constitution was ratified, this authority was vested in the President and the Congress, as stated in the following Articles from the Constitution:

ARTICLE I

Section 8. The Congress shall have the power . . .
To declare war . . .
To raise and support armies . . .
To provide and maintain a navy;
To make rules for the government and regulation of the land and naval forces;

ARTICLE II

Section 2. The President shall be the Commander-in-Chief of the Army and Navy of the United States. . . .

Below are statistics concerning our principal wars. The rest of the section contains Presidential war messages to Congress; material relative to the Civil War; an excerpt from President Truman's announcement of the atomic bomb; and from an address by General MacArthur:

Principal Wars and Their Estimated Cost	Battle Deaths
Revolutionary War, 1775–1783 $370,000,000	4,044[a]
War of 1812, 1812–1815 $112,912,543	1,877[a]
Mexican War, 1846–1848 $97,705,860	1,721[a]
Civil War, 1861–1865 $6,006,232,513	110,070[a] (Union) 74,524[a] (Confederate)
Spanish-American War, 1898 $444,599,343	700[a]
World War I, 1917–1918 $20,737,493,826	50,510[b]
World War II, 1941–1945	293,986[b]
Korean War, 1950–	25,604[b]

Sources: [a]War Department. [b]Department of Defense. Estimated costs from George Frederick Ashworth in *Dictionary of American History*, vol. 5, edited by James Truslow Adams (Charles Scribner's Sons).

THE REVOLUTIONARY WAR, 1775–1783

"DECLARATION OF THE CAUSES AND NECESSITY OF TAKING UP ARMS," JULY 6, 1775

If it was possible for men, who exercise their reason to believe, that the divine Author of our existence intended a part of the human race to hold an absolute property in, and an unbounded power over others, marked out by his infinite goodness and wisdom, as the objects of a legal domination never rightfully resistible, however severe and oppressive, the inhabitants of these colonies might at least require from the parliament of Great-Britain some evidence, that this dreadful authority over them, has been granted to that body. But a reverence for our great Creator, principles of humanity, and the dictates of common sense, must convince all those who reflect upon the subject, that government was instituted to promote the welfare of mankind, and ought to be administered for the attainment of that end. The legislature of Great-Britain, however, stimulated by an inordinate passion for a power not only unjustifiable, but which they know to be peculiarly reprobated by the very constitution of that kingdom, and desperate of success in any mode of contest, where regard should be had to truth, law, or right, have at length, deserting those, attempted to effect their cruel and impolitic purpose of enslaving these colonies by violence, and have thereby rendered it necessary for us to close with their last appeal from reason to arms.—Yet, however blinded that assembly may be, by their intemperate rage for unlimited domination, so to slight justice and the opinion of mankind, we esteem ourselves bound by obligations of respect to the rest of the world, to make known the justice of our cause.

Our forefathers, inhabitants of the island of Great-Britain, left their native land, to seek on these shores a residence for civil and religious freedom. At the expense of their blood, at the hazard of their fortunes, without the least charge to the country from which they removed, by unceasing labour, and an unconquerable spirit, they effected settlements in the distant and inhospitable wilds of America, then filled with numerous and warlike nations of barbarians.—Societies or governments, vested with perfect legislatures, were formed under charters from the crown, and an harmonious intercourse was established between the colonies and the kingdom from which they derived their origin. The mutual benefits of this union became in a short time so extraordinary, as to excite astonishment. It is universally confessed, that the amazing increase of the wealth, strength, and navigation of the realm, arose from this source; and the minister, who so wisely and successfully directed the measures of Great-Britain in the late war, publicly declared, that these colonies enabled her to triumph over her enemies.—Towards the conclusion of that war, it pleased our sovereign to make a change in his counsels.—From that fatal moment, the affairs of the British empire began to fall into confusion, and gradually sliding from the summit of glorious prosperity, to which they had been advanced by the virtues and abilities of one man, are at length distracted by the convulsions, that now shake it to its deepest foundations. . . .

. . . They have undertaken to give and grant our money without our consent, though we have ever exercised an exclusive right to dispose of our own property; statutes have been passed for extending the jurisdiction of courts of admiralty, and vice-admiralty beyond their ancient limits; for depriving us of the accustomed and inestimable privilege of trial by jury, in cases affecting both life and property; for suspending the legislature of one of the colonies; for interdicting all commerce to the capital of another; and for altering fundamentally the form of government established by charter, and secured by acts of its own legislature solemnly confirmed by the crown; for exempting the "murderers" of colonists from legal trial, and in effect, from punishment; for erecting in a neighbouring province, acquired by the joint arms of Great-Britain and America, a despotism dangerous to our very existence; and for quartering soldiers upon the colonists in time of profound peace. It has also been resolved in parliament, that colonists charged with committing certain offences, shall be transported to England to be tried.

But why should we enumerate our injuries in detail? . . . We saw the misery to which such depotism would reduce us. We for ten years incessantly and ineffectually besieged the throne as supplicants; we reasoned, we remonstrated with parliament, in the most mild and decent language. But administration sensible that we should regard these oppressive measures as freemen ought to do, sent over fleets and armies to enforce them. . . .

Fruitless were all the entreaties, arguments, and eloquence of an illustrious band of the most distinguished peers, and commoners, who nobly and strenuously asserted the justice of our cause, to stay, or even to mitigate the heedless fury with which these accumulated and unexampled outrages were hurried on. . . .

. . . General Gage, who in the course of the last year had taken possession of the town of Boston, in the province of Massachusetts-Bay . . . on the 19th day of April, sent out from that place a large detachment of his army, who made an unprovoked assault on the inhabitants of the said province, at the town of Lexington, as appears by the affidavits of a great number of persons, some of whom were officers and soldiers of that detachment, murdered eight of the inhabitants, and wounded many others. From thence the troops proceeded in warlike array to the town of Concord, where they set upon another party of the inhabitants of the same province, killing several and wounding more, until compelled to retreat by the country people suddenly assembled to repel this cruel aggression. Hostilities, thus commenced by the British troops, have been since prosecuted by them without regard to faith or reputation. . . .

The General, further emulating his ministerial masters, by a proclamation bearing date on the 12th day of June, after venting the grossest falsehoods and calumnies against the good people of these colonies, proceeds to "declare them all, either by name or description, to be rebels and traitors, to supersede the course of the common law, and instead thereof to publish and order the use and exercise of the law martial."—His troops have butchered our countrymen, have wantonly burnt Charlestown, besides a considerable number of houses in other places; our ships and vessels are seized; the necessary supplies of provisions are intercepted, and he is exerting his utmost power to spread destruction and devastation around him.

. . . In brief, a part of these colonies now feel, and all of them are sure of feeling, as far as the vengeance of administration can inflict them, the complicated calamities of fire, sword, and famine. We are reduced to the alternative of chusing an unconditional submission to the tyranny of irritated ministers, or resistance by force.—The latter is our choice.—We have counted the cost of this contest, and find nothing so dreadful as voluntary slavery.—Honour, justice, and humanity, forbid us tamely to surrender that freedom which we received from our gallant ancestors, and which our innocent posterity have a right to receive from us. We cannot endure the infamy and guilt of resigning succeeding generations to that wretchedness which inevitably awaits them, if we basely entail hereditary bondage upon them.

Our cause is just. Our union is perfect. Our internal resources are great, and, if necessary, foreign assistance is undoubtedly attainable. . . . With hearts fortified with these animating reflections, we most solemnly, before God and the world, declare, that, exerting the utmost energy of those powers, which our beneficent Creator hath graciously bestowed upon us, the arms we have been compelled by our enemies to assume, we will, in defiance of every hazard, with unabating firmness and perseverance, employ for the preservation of our liberties; being with one mind resolved to die freemen rather than to live slaves. . . .

Bunker Hill, the first pitched battle of the Revolutionary
War, June 17, 1775. Painting by John Trumbull (detail).

In our own native land, in defence of the freedom that is our birth-right, and which
we ever enjoyed till the late violation of it—for the protection of our property, acquired
solely by the honest industry of our fore-fathers and ourselves, against violence actually
offered, we have taken up arms. We shall lay them down when hostilities shall cease on
the part of the aggressors, and all danger of their being renewed shall be removed, and
not before.

With an humble confidence in the mercies of the supreme and impartial Judge and Ruler
of the Universe, we most devoutly implore his divine goodness to protect us happily
through this great conflict, to dispose our adversaries to reconciliation on reasonable
terms, and thereby to relieve the empire from the calamities of civil war. . . .†

By order of Congress
JOHN HANCOCK
President

269

THE WAR OF 1812, 1812–1815

PRESIDENT MADISON'S WAR MESSAGE TO CONGRESS, JUNE 1, 1812

To the Senate and House of Representatives of the United States:

I communicate to Congress certain documents, being a continuation of those heretofore laid before them on the subject of our affairs with Great Britain. . . .

British cruisers have been in the continued practice of violating the American flag on the great highway of nations, and of seizing and carrying off persons sailing under it, not in the exercise of a belligerent right founded on the law of nations against an enemy, but of a municipal prerogative over British subjects. British jurisdiction is thus extended to neutral vessels in a situation where no laws can operate but the law of nations and the laws of the country to which the vessels belong, and a self-redress is assumed which, if British subjects were wrongfully detained and alone concerned, is that substitution of force for a resort to the responsible sovereign which falls within the definition of war. . . .

The practice, hence, is so far from affecting British subjects alone that, under the pretext of searching for these, thousands of American citizens, under the safeguard of public law and of their national flag, have been torn from their country and from everything dear to them; have been dragged on board ships of war of a foreign nation and exposed, under the severities of their discipline, to be exiled to the most distant and deadly climes, to risk their lives in the battles of their oppressors, and to be the melancholy instruments of taking away those of their own brethren.

Against this crying enormity, which Great Britain would be so prompt to avenge if committed against herself, the United States have in vain exhausted remonstrances and expostulations. . . .

British cruisers have been in the practice also of violating the rights and the peace of our coasts. They hover over and harass our entering and departing commerce. To the most insulting pretensions they have added the most lawless proceedings in our very harbors, and have wantonly spilt American blood within the sanctuary of our territorial jurisdiction. . . .

Under pretended blockades . . . our commerce has been plundered in every sea, the great staples of our country have been cut off from their legitimate markets, and a destructive blow aimed at our agricultural and maritime interests. . . . And to render the outrage the more signal these mock blockades have been reiterated and enforced in the face of official communications from the British Government declaring as the true definition of a legal blockade "that particular ports must be actually invested and previous warning given to vessels bound to them not to enter."

Not content with these occasional expedients for laying waste our neutral trade, the cabinet of Britain resorted at length to the sweeping system of blockades, under the name of orders in council, which has been molded and managed as might best suit its political views, its commercial jealousies, or the avidity of British cruisers. . . .

It has become, indeed, sufficiently certain that the commerce of the United States is to be sacrificed, not as interfering with the belligerent rights of Great Britain; not as supplying the wants of her enemies, which she herself supplies; but as interfering with the monopoly which she covets for her own commerce and navigation. She carries on a war against the lawful commerce of a friend that she may the better carry on a commerce with an enemy—a commerce polluted by the forgeries and perjuries which are for the most part the only passports by which it can succeed. . . .

In reviewing the conduct of Great Britain toward the United States our attention is necessarily drawn to the warfare just renewed by the savages on one of our extensive

The *Constitution* ("Old Ironsides"), America's famous 44-gun frigate, destroys the *Java* off the coast of Brazil, December 28, in the war of 1812.

frontiers—a warfare which is known to spare neither age nor sex and to be distinguished by features peculiarly shocking to humanity. It is difficult to account for the activity and combinations which have for some time been developing themselves among tribes in constant intercourse with British traders and garrisons without connecting their hostility with that influence and without recollecting the authenticated examples of such interpositions heretofore furnished by the officers and agents of that Government.

Such is the spectacle of injuries and indignities which have been heaped on our country, and such the crisis which its unexampled forbearance and conciliatory efforts have not been able to avert. . . .

We behold, in fine, on the side of Great Britain a state of war against the United States, and on the side of the United States a state of peace toward Great Britain.

Whether the United States shall continue passive under these progressive usurpations and these accumulating wrongs, or, opposing force to force in defense of their national rights . . . is a solemn question which the Constitution wisely confides to the legislative department of the Government. In recommending it to their early deliberations I am happy in the assurance that the decision will be worthy the enlightened and patriotic councils of a virtuous, a free, and a powerful nation. . . .†

JAMES MADISON

271

Mexican War. The storming of Monterrey, 1846. Lithograph by Kelloggs and Thayer.

THE MEXICAN WAR, 1846–1848

PRESIDENT JAMES K. POLK'S WAR MESSAGE

May 11, 1846

To the Senate and House of Representatives:

The existing state of the relations between the United States and Mexico renders it proper that I should bring the subject to the consideration of Congress. . . .

In my message at the commencement of the present session I informed you that upon the earnest appeal both of the Congress and convention of Texas I had ordered an efficient military force to take a position "between the Nueces and the Del Norte." This had become necessary to meet a threatened invasion of Texas by the Mexican forces, for which extensive military preparations had been made. The invasion was threatened solely because Texas had determined, in accordance with a solemn resolution of the Congress of the United States, to annex herself to our Union, and under these circumstances it was plainly our duty to extend our protection over her citizens and soil.

This force was concentrated at Corpus Christi, and remained there until after I had received such information from Mexico as rendered it probable, if not certain, that the Mexican Government would refuse to receive our envoy.

Meantime Texas, by the final action of our Congress, had become an integral part of our Union. The Congress of Texas, by its act of December 19, 1836, had declared the Rio del Norte to be the boundary of that Republic. Its jurisdiction had been extended and exercised beyond the Nueces. The country between that river and the Del Norte had been represented in the Congress and in the convention of Texas, had thus taken part in the act of annexation itself, and is now included within one of our Congressional districts. Our own Congress had, moreover, with great unanimity, by the act approved December 31, 1845, recognized the country beyond the Nueces as a part of our territory by including it within our own revenue system, and a revenue officer to reside within that district has been appointed by and with the advice and consent of the Senate. It became, therefore, of urgent necessity to provide for the defense of that portion of our country. Accordingly, on the 13th of January last instructions were issued to the general in command of these troops to occupy the left bank of the Del Norte. This river, which is the southwestern boundary of the State of Texas, is an exposed frontier. From this quarter invasion was threatened; upon it and in its immediate vicinity, in the judgment of high military experience, are the proper stations for the protecting forces of the Government. In addition to this important consideration, several others occurred to induce this movement. Among these are the facilities afforded by the ports at Brazos Santiago and the mouth of the Del Norte for the reception of supplies by sea, the stronger and more healthful military positions, the convenience for obtaining a ready and a more abundant supply of provisions, water, fuel, and forage, and the advantages which are afforded by the Del Norte in forwarding supplies to such posts as may be established in the interior and upon the Indian frontier.

The movement of the troops to the Del Norte was made by the commanding general under positive instructions to abstain from all aggressive acts toward Mexico or Mexican citizens and to regard the relations between that Republic and the United States as peaceful unless she should declare war or commit acts of hostility indicative of a state of war. He was specially directed to protect private property and respect personal rights. . . .

The Mexican forces at Matamoras assumed a belligerent attitude, and on the 12th of April General Ampudia, then in command, notified General Taylor to break up his camp within twenty-four hours and to retire beyond the Nueces River, and in the event of his failure to comply with these demands announced that arms, and arms alone, must decide

273

the question. But no open act of hostility was committed until the 24th of April. On that day General Arista, who had succeeded to the command of the Mexican forces, communicated to General Taylor that "he considered hostilities commenced and should prosecute them." A party of dragoons of 63 men and officers were on the same day dispatched from the American camp up the Rio del Norte, on its left bank, to ascertain whether the Mexican troops had crossed or were preparing to cross the river, "became engaged with a large body of these troops, and after a short affair, in which some 16 were killed and wounded, appear to have been surrounded and compelled to surrender."

The grievous wrongs perpetrated by Mexico upon our citizens throughout a long period of years remain unredressed, and solemn treaties pledging her public faith for this redress have been disregarded. A government either unable or unwilling to enforce the execution of such treaties fails to perform one of its plainest duties.

Our commerce with Mexico has been almost annihilated. It was formerly highly beneficial to both nations, but our merchants have been deterred from prosecuting it by the system of outrage and extortion which the Mexican authorities have pursued against them, whilst their appeals through their own Government for indemnity have been made in vain. Our forbearance has gone to such an extreme as to be mistaken in its character. Had we acted with vigor in repelling the insults and redressing the injuries inflicted by Mexico at the commencement, we should doubtless have escaped all the difficulties in which we are now involved. . . .

The cup of forbearance has been exhausted even before the recent information from the frontier of the Del Norte. But now, after reiterated menaces, Mexico has passed the boundary of the United States, has invaded our territory and shed American blood upon the American soil. She has proclaimed that hostilities have commenced, and that the two nations are now at war.

As war exists, and, notwithstanding all our efforts to avoid it, exists by the act of Mexico herself, we are called upon by every consideration of duty and patriotism to vindicate with decision the honor, the rights, and the interests of our country. . . .

In further vindication of our rights and defense of our territory, I invoke the prompt action of Congress to recognize the existence of the war, and to place at the disposition of the Executive the means of prosecuting the war with vigor, and thus hastening the restoration of peace. . . .†

JAMES K. POLK

THE CIVIL WAR, 1861–1865

PRESIDENT LINCOLN'S MESSAGE TO CONGRESS RECOGNIZING A STATE OF CIVIL WAR, APRIL 15, 1861

Whereas the laws of the United States have been for some time past and are now opposed and the execution thereof obstructed in the States of South Carolina, Georgia, Alabama, Florida, Mississippi, Louisiana, and Texas by combinations too powerful to be suppressed by the ordinary course of judicial proceedings or by the powers vested in the marshals by law:

Now, therefore, I, Abraham Lincoln, President of the United States, in virtue of the power in me vested by the Constitution and the laws, have thought fit to call forth, and hereby do call forth, the militia of the several States of the Union to the aggregate number of 75,000, in order to suppress said combinations and to cause the laws to be duly executed.

The details for this object will be immediately communicated to the State authorities through the War Department.

I appeal to all loyal citizens to favor, facilitate, and aid this effort to maintain the honor, the integrity, and the existence of our National Union and the perpetuity of popular government and to redress wrongs already long enough endured.

I deem it proper to say that the first service assigned to the forces hereby called forth will probably be to repossess the forts, places, and property which have been seized from the Union; and in every event the utmost care will be observed, consistently with the objects aforesaid, to avoid any devastation, any destruction of or interference with property, or any disturbance of peaceful citizens in any part of the country.

And I hereby command the persons composing the combinations aforesaid to disperse and retire peaceably to their respective abodes within twenty days from this date.

Deeming that the present condition of public affairs presents an extraordinary occasion, I do hereby, in virtue of the power in me vested by the Constitution, convene both Houses of Congress. Senators and Representatives are therefore summoned to assemble at their respective chambers at 12 o'clock noon on Thursday, the 4th day of July next, then and there to consider and determine such measures as, in their wisdom, the public safety and interest may seem to demand.

In witness whereof I have hereunto set my hand and caused the seal of the United States to be affixed.

ABRAHAM LINCOLN

Profound social and economic differences between the industrial North and agricultural South brought on the Civil War. Reconciliation having failed, Southern States claimed a Constitutional right to secede from the Union, a right denied by the Northern States. South Carolina, first to secede, demanded withdrawal of Federal troops from the garrison at Fort Sumter, announcing that any Union attempts to send reinforcements would be met by force of arms. On April 12, when Union men and supplies arrived at Sumter, Confederate soldiers fired on them and the war began.

Although preservation of the Union was the fundamental issue, to many it was overshadowed by the issue of slavery. Northern abolitionists brought great pressure on the President to declare emancipation the goal of the Union. Both views are represented in the following exchange in which, in his widely circulated New York Tribune, *editor Horace Greeley writes an open letter to the President, and Mr. Lincoln replies:*

"THE PRAYER OF TWENTY MILLIONS"
Horace Greeley, August 19, 1862

To ABRAHAM LINCOLN, president of the United States:

DEAR SIR: I do not intrude to tell you—for you must know already—that a great proportion of those who triumphed in your election, and of all who desire the unqualified suppression of the Rebellion now desolating our country, are sorely disappointed and deeply pained by the policy you seem to be pursuing with regard to the slaves of the Rebels. I write only to set succinctly and unmistakably before you what we require, what we think we have a right to expect, and of what we complain.

I. We require of you, as the first servant of the Republic, charged especially and preeminently with this duty, that you EXECUTE THE LAWS. Most emphatically we do demand that such laws as have been recently enacted, which therefore may fairly be presumed to embody the present will and to be dictated by the present needs of the Republic, and which, after due consideration have received your personal sanction, shall by you be carried into full effort, and that you publicly and decisively, instruct your subordinates that such laws exist, that they are binding to all functionaries and citizens, and that they are to be obeyed to the letter.

II. We think you are strangely and disastrously remiss in the discharge of your official and imperative duty with regard to the emancipation provisions of the new Confiscation Act. Those provisions were designed to fight Slavery with Liberty. They prescribe that men loyal to the Union, and willing to shed their blood in her behalf, shall no longer be held, with the Nation's consent, in bondage to persistent, malignant traitors, who for twenty years have been plotting and for sixteen months have been fighting to divide and destroy our country. Why these traitors should be treated with tenderness by you, to the prejudice of the dearest rights of loyal men, we cannot conceive.

III. We think you are unduly influenced by the counsels, the representations, the menaces, of certain fossil politicians hailing from the Border Slave States . . . we ask you to consider that Slavery is everywhere the inciting cause and sustaining base of treason: the most slaveholding sections of Maryland and Delaware being this day, though under the Union flag, in full sympathy with the Rebellion, while the Free-Labor portions of Tennessee and of Texas, though writhing under the bloody heel of Treason, are unconquerably loyal to the Union. . . . It seems to us the most obvious truth, that whatever strengthens or fortifies Slavery in the Border States strengthens also Treason, and drives home the wedge intended to divide the Union. Had you from the first refused to recognize in those States, as here, any other than unconditional loyalty—that which stands for the Union, whatever may become of Slavery—those States would have been, and would be, far more helpful and less troublesome to the defenders of the Union than they have been, or now are.

IV. We think timid counsels in such crisis calculated to prove perilous, and probably disastrous. It is the duty of a Government so wantonly, wickedly assailed by Rebellion as ours has been to oppose force to force in a defiant, dauntless spirit. It cannot afford to temporize with traitors nor with semi-traitors. It must not bribe them to behave themselves, nor make them fair promises in the hope of disarming their causeless hostility. Representing a brave and high-spirited people, it can afford to forfeit anything else better than its own self-respect, or their admiring confidence. For our Government even to seek, after war has been made on it, to dispel the affected apprehensions of armed traitors that their cherished privileges may be assailed by it, is to invite insult and encourage hopes of its own downfall. The rush to arms of Ohio, Indiana, Illinois, is the true answer at once to the Rebel raids of John Morgan and the traitorous sophistries of Beriah Magoffin.

V. We complain that the Union cause has suffered, and is now suffering immensely, from mistaken deference to Rebel Slavery. Had you, Sir, in your Inaugural Address, unmistakably given notice that, in case the Rebellion already commenced were persisted in, and your efforts to preserve the Union and enforce the laws should be resisted by armed force, you would recognize no loyal person as rightfully held in Slavery by a traitor, we believe the Rebellion would therein have received a staggering if not fatal blow. . . .

VI . . . And finally, we complain that you, Mr. President, elected as a Republican, knowing well what an abomination Slavery is, and how emphatically it is the core and essence of this atrocious Rebellion, seem never to interfere with these atrocities, and never give a direction to your Military subordinates, which does not appear to have been conceived in the interest of Slavery rather than of Freedom.

. . . VIII. On the face of this wide earth, Mr. President, there is not one disinterested, determined, intelligent champion of the Union cause who does not feel that all attempts to put down the Rebellion and at the same time uphold its inciting cause are preposterous and futile—that the Rebellion, if crushed out tomorrow, would be renewed within a year if Slavery were left in full vigor—that Army officers who remain to this day devoted to Slavery can at best be but half-way loyal to the Union—and that every hour of deference

276

to Slavery is an hour of added and deepened peril to the Union. I appeal to the testimony of your Embassadors in Europe. It is freely at your service, not at mine. Ask them to tell you candidly whether the seeming subserviency of your policy to the slaveholding, slavery-upholding interest, is not the perplexity, the despair of statesmen of all parties, and be admonished by the general answer.

IX. I close as began with the statement that what an immense majority of the Loyal Millions of your countrymen require of you is a frank, declared, unqualified, ungrudging execution of the laws of the land, more especially of the Confiscation Act. That Act gives freedom to the slaves of Rebels coming within our lines, or whom those lines may at any time inclose—we ask you to render it due obedience by publicly requiring all your subordinates to recognize and obey it. The Rebels are everywhere using the late anti-negro riots in the North, as they have long used your officers' treatment of negroes in the South, to convince the slaves that they have nothing to hope from a Union success—that we mean in that case to sell them into a bitter bondage to defray the cost of war. Let them impress this as a truth on the great mass of their ignorant and credulous bondsmen, and the Union will never be restored—never. We cannot conquer Ten Millions of People united in solid phalanx against us, powerfully sided by the Northern sympathizers and European allies. We must have scouts, guides, spies, cooks, teamsters, diggers and choppers from the Blacks of the South, whether we allow them to fight for us or not, or we shall be baffled and repelled. As one of the millions who would gladly have avoided this struggle at any sacrifice but that of Principle and Honor, but who now feel that the triumph of the Union is indispensable not only to the existence of our country but to the well-being of mankind, I entreat you to render a hearty and unequivocal obedience to the law of the land.†

Yours,
HORACE GREELEY

New York, August 19, 1862

LINCOLN'S REPLY TO GREELEY, 1862

If there be those who would not save the Union unless they could at the same time save slavery, I do not agree with them. If there be those who would not save the Union unless they could at the same time destroy slavery I do not agree with them. My paramount object in this struggle is to save the Union, and is not either to save or destroy slavery. If I could save the Union without freeing any slave, I would do it; if I could do it by freeing all the slaves, I would do it; and if I could do it by freeing some and leaving others alone, I would also do that. . . . I have here stated my purpose according to my view of official duty, and I intend no modification of my oft-expressed personal wish that all men, everywhere, could be free.†

GETTYSBURG, DECISIVE BATTLE OF THE CIVIL WAR, JULY 1–3, 1863

Southern and Northern Eyewitness Accounts of Pickett's Charge

COLONEL JOSEPH C. MAYO, THIRD VIRGINIA REGIMENT,
DESCRIBES PICKETT'S CHARGE

. . . Where the Third and the greater part of the Seventh lay there was a depression in the ridge, exposing them to the full fury of the tempest of shot and shell which soon came raining down upon them. A faint conception of its indescribable horror may be gathered from a few incidents of which I retain to this day a shuddering recollection. At the sound of the signal guns I went to the centre of the regiment in front of the flag, and sat down upon a pile of blankets resembling a coil of rope; but the intolerable heat of the sun quickly drove me back to the shelter of the apple tree, under which men and officers of both regiments were crowded together thick as herring in a barrel, where I managed to squeeze in between Colonel Patton and Colonel Collcote.

The first shot or two flew harmlessly over our heads; but soon they began to get the range, and then came—well, what General Gibbon, on the other side, called "pandemonium." First there was an explosion in the top of our friendly tree, sending a shower of limbs upon us. In a second there was another, followed by a piercing shriek, which caused Patton to spring up and run to see what was the matter. Two killed outright and three frightfully wounded, he said on his return. Immediately after a like cry came from another apple tree close by in the midst of the Third. . . . Then, for more than an hour it went on. Nearly every minute the cry of mortal agony was heard above the roar and rumble of the guns. In his modest book, *Four Years a Soldier*, one who was left for dead under that apple tree describes it in these feeling words: "Turn you where you would, there were to be seen at almost every moment of time guns, swords, haversacks, human flesh and bones flying and dangling in the air or bouncing above the earth, which now trembled beneath us as shaken by an earthquake. Over us, in front of us, behind us, in our midst and through our ranks, poured solid shot and bursting shell dealing out death on every hand; yet the men stood bravely at their post in an open field with a blistering July sun beating upon their unprotected heads." Doubtless there would have been some consolation to know, as we afterwards learned, that our blue-coated friends over the way were in the same, if not in a worse predicament. General Gibbon who with Hancock's Corps held the position we were about to storm says of the execution done by our batteries that it exceeded anything he had dreamed of in artillery warfare; and I believe it is now an admitted historical fact that from the time that the "nimble gunner with limstock the devilish cannon touched," that awful din at Gettysburg was the most fearful sound that ever pealed from the "red throat of roaring war."

. . . as the terrific duel was drawing to a close, General Pickett came riding briskly down the rear of the line, calling to the men to get up and prepare to advance, and "Remember Old Virginia." Our dear old Third, it was a heart-rending sight which greeted me as I moved along your decimated ranks!—while quickly, and without a word of command, the men fell into their places; especially to see our color-bearer, Murden, as fine a type of true soldiership as ever stepped beneath the folds of the spotless stars and bars, now lying there stark and stiff, a hideous hole sheer through his stalwart body, and his right hand closed in a death grip around the staff of that beautiful new flag which to-day for the first and last time had braved the battle and the breeze. The devoted little column moved to the assault, with Garnett, and Kemper in front, and Armistead behind in close supporting distance. Soon after clearing our batteries it was found necessary to change direction to the left. While conducting the movement, which was made in perfect order under a galling flank fire from the Round Top, General Pickett, for the second time, cautioned me to be sure and keep the proper interval with General Garnett; Armistead was expected to catch up and extend the line on the left. Then we swept onward again, straight for the Golgotha of Seminary Ridge, half a mile distant, across the open plain. As we neared the Emmitsburg road, along which, behind piles of rails, the enemy's strong line of skirmishers was posted, General Kemper called to me to give attention to matters on the left, while he went to see what troops those were coming up behind us. Glancing after him, I caught a glimpse of a small body of men, compact and solid as a wedge, moving swiftly to the left oblique, as if aiming to uncover Garnett's Brigade. They were Armistead's people, and as Kemper cantered down their front on his mettlesome sorrel they greeted him with a rousing cheer, which I know made his gallant heart leap for joy. . . .

278

... as we were getting into shape again, several things were impressed on my memory. First, the amusement it seemed to afford Orderly Waddy Forward, who might, if he pleased, have stayed behind with the horses, to see me duck my head as a ball whizzed within an ace of my nose; next, to see Captain Lewis, of Company C, looking as lazy and lackadaisical, and, if possible, more tired and bored than usual, carrying his sword point foremost over his shoulder, and addressing his company in that invariable plaintive tone, half command, half entreaty, "Don't crowd, boys; don't crowd." "Pretty hot, Captain," I said in passing. "It's redicklous, Colonel; perfectly redicklous"—which, in his vocabulary, meant as bad as bad could be; then Captain Tom Hodges directing my attention to a splendid looking Federal officer, magnificently mounted, straining his horse at full speed along the crest of the hill a hundred yards in our front, and both of us calling to the skirmishers, "Don't shoot him! don't shoot him!" and, lastly, the impetuous Kemper, as rising in his stirrups and pointing to the left with his sword, he shouted, "There are the guns, boys, go for them." It was an injudicious order; but they obeyed with a will, and mingled with Garnett's people pushed rapidly up the heights.†

COLONEL THOMAS RAFFERTY, UNITED STATES VOLUNTEER,
DESCRIBES PICKETT'S CHARGE

On the third day Lee put forth his last effort, incited thereto by his apparent success of the two previous days, and threw forward Pickett's Division in that memorable charge, in the vain hope of breaking through our centre. When that splendid division of Virginia troops formed behind the cover of the Emmitsburg road and advanced to the attack, there was presented a spectacle which might well elicit admiration of their generous foes. . . .

From our position on Cemetery Ridge to the Emmitsburg road, a distance of full half a mile, there was a clear, unobstructed field, without a single vantage point or cover behind which the troops might find temporary shelter, and as the head of that magnificent column rose into view it was at once opened upon by eighty guns of our artillery. The mark was a fair one. He was a poor artillerist who could not hit it. They did hit it; nearly every shot told. But unchecked and almost unfaltering that grand body of men moved on, with the shells tearing great lanes through them, until within the range of our rifles, when a perfect storm of leaden hail was poured upon them; but still

> "In one dark torrent broad and strong
> The advancing onset rolled along,"

seemingly regardless of the certain death which awaited them. No Tennyson has risen to sing paeans of the memory of that heroic band whom I am proud to-day to hail as comrades, for they too were Americans. . . .

On, on they came, that heroic band of noble but misguided men, closing up their diminishing ranks, and literally melting under that fierce fire as the rising sun dissipates the morning mists. But still they halt not, falter not; and now our first line is reached—is broken and forced back and their colors are planted amongst the batteries of our second line. But there that impetuous wave has struck the rock. They have met men as brave as themselves, and they are hurled back, in broken fragments, and the wave is dissipated into spray, hundreds of them now throwing down their arms, while the remainder in broken and detached fragments endeavor to find their way back to their own lines. And so great was the admiration for their bravery entertained by our troops that they were permitted to do so almost unharmed. I myself heard our men call out, "Boys, don't shoot! It is a pity to kill such brave fellows." That charge was made by 15,000 men, and I believe it is stated that there was only one field officer who escaped unharmed, and that was the heroic Pickett himself.

While recognizing to the fullest extent the heroism and bravery of our own men, I am constrained to admit that the magnificent position we occupied contributed very largely to the repulse of that charge.

LINCOLN'S GETTYSBURG ADDRESS, 1863

During the dedication ceremonies at Gettysburg, Edward Everett, the principal speaker, delivered a tremendously long oration. Immediately following this, President Lincoln rose to speak. Lincoln's Gettysburg Address, which took two minutes, is considered one of the finest speeches ever made in the English language. The next day Everett wrote a letter to the President, to which Lincoln replied. This correspondence follows the Gettysburg Address:

Fourscore and seven years ago our fathers brought forth on this continent a new nation, conceived in liberty and dedicated to the proposition that all men are created equal. Now we are engaged in a great civil war, testing whether that nation, or any nation so conceived and so dedicated, can long endure. We are met on a great battlefield of that war. We have come to dedicate a portion of that field as a final resting place for those who here gave their lives that that nation might live. It is altogether fitting and proper that we should do this. But, in a larger sense, we cannot dedicate—we cannot consecrate—we cannot hallow—this ground. The brave men, living and dead, who struggled here have consecrated it far above our poor power to add or detract. The world will little note nor long remember what we say here, but it can never forget what they did here. It is for us, the living, rather to be dedicated here to the unfinished work which they who fought here have thus far so nobly advanced. It is rather for us to be here dedicated to the great task remaining before us—that from these honored dead we take increased devotion to that cause for which they gave the last full measure of devotion; that we here highly resolve that these dead shall not have died in vain; that this nation, under God, shall have a new birth of freedom; and that government of the people, by the people, and for the people, shall not perish from the earth.

EDWARD EVERETT'S LETTER TO LINCOLN

Washington, 20 Nov. 1863

My dear Sir:
Permit me also to express my great admiration of the thoughts expressed by you, with such eloquent simplicity & appropriateness, at the consecration of the Cemetery. I should be glad, if I could flatter myself, that I came as near to the central idea of the occasion in two hours, as you did in two minutes. . . .†

LINCOLN'S REPLY TO EVERETT'S LETTER

Executive Mansion
Washington, Nov. 20, 1863

My dear Sir:
Your kind note of to-day is received. In our respective parts yesterday, you could not have been excused to make a short address, nor I a long one. I am pleased to know that, in your judgment, the little I did say was not entirely a failure. . . .†

Your Obt. Servt.
A. LINCOLN

ettysburg.

END OF THE CIVIL WAR, APRIL 26, 1865

After four years of bloody fighting the closing scenes of the Civil War took place near Richmond, Virginia. General Ulysses S. Grant, commander in chief of the Union Army, had surrounded the badly beaten, outnumbered, and starving Confederate forces under their commander in chief, Robert E. Lee. In a communiqué, April 8, Grant demanded Lee's surrender, and on April 9 the two generals met at the McLean home in the village of Appomattox Court-House to discuss terms. There Grant, magnanimous in victory, Lee, gallant in defeat, signed the Articles of Capitulation. With the surrender of General Johnston's forces, April 26, hostilities ceased.

In the selections that follow General Grant describes this meeting; General Lee writes Jefferson Davis, President of the Confederacy, announcing surrender of the Army of Northern Virginia; and President Lincoln "binds up the nation's wounds."

281

LEE'S SURRENDER AT APPOMATTOX

told by Ulysses S. Grant, April 9, 1865

. . . We greeted each other, and after shaking hands took our seats. I had my staff with me, a good portion of whom were in the room during the whole of the interview.

What General Lee's feelings were I do not know. As he was a man of much dignity, with an impassible face, it was impossible to say whether he felt inwardly glad that the end had finally come, or felt sad over the result, and was too manly to show it. Whatever his feelings, they were entirely concealed from my observation; but my own feelings, which had been quite jubilant on the receipt of his letter, were sad and depressed. I felt like anything rather than rejoicing at the downfall of a foe who had fought so long and valiantly, and had suffered so much for a cause, though that cause was, I believe, one of the worst for which a people ever fought, and one for which there was the least excuse. I do not question, however, the sincerity of the great mass of those who were opposed to us.

General Lee was dressed in a full uniform which was entirely new, and was wearing a sword of considerable value, very likely the sword which had been presented by the State of Virginia; at all events, it was an entirely different sword from the one that would ordinarily be worn in the field. In my rough traveling suit, the uniform of a private with the straps of a lieutenant-general, I must have contrasted very strangely with a man so handsomely dressed, six feet high and of faultless form. But this was not a matter that I thought of until afterwards.

We soon fell into a conversation about old army times. He remarked that he remembered me very well in the old army; and I told him that as a matter of course I remembered him perfectly, but from the difference in our ages, I had thought it very likely that I had not attracted his attention sufficiently to be remembered by him after such a long interval. Our conversation grew so pleasant that I almost forgot the object of our meeting. After the conversation had run on in this style for some time, General Lee called my attention to the object of our meeting, and said that he had asked for this interview for the purpose of getting from me the terms I proposed to give his army. I said that I meant merely that his army should lay down their arms, not to take them up again during the continuance of the war, unless duly and properly exchanged. He said that he had so understood my letter.

Then we gradually fell off again into conversation about matters foreign to the subject which had brought us together. This continued for some little time, when General Lee again interrupted the course of the conversation by suggesting that the terms I proposed to give his army ought to be written out. I called to General Parker, secretary on my staff, for writing materials, and commenced writing out the following terms. . . .

"(April 9.) . . . In accordance with the substance of my letter to you of the 8th inst., I propose to receive the surrender of the Army of N. Va. on the following terms, to wit: Rolls of all the officers and men to be made in duplicate. One copy to be given to an officer designated by me, the other to be retained by such officer or officers as you may designate. The officers to give their individual paroles not to take up arms against the Government of the United States until properly exchanged, and each company or regimental commander sign a like parole for the men of their commands. The arms, artillery and public property to be parked and stacked, and turned over to the officer appointed by me to receive them. This will not embrace the sidearms of the officers, nor their private horses or baggage. This done, each officer and man will be allowed to return to their homes, not to be dis-

Appomattox Courthouse, where Lee met Grant to sign the terms of surrender

· APPOMATTOX ·
HERE ON SUNDAY APRIL 9, 1865.
AFTER FOUR YEARS OF HEROIC STRUGGLE
IN DEFENSE OF PRINCIPLES BELIEVED FUNDAMENTAL
TO THE EXISTENCE OF OUR GOVERNMENT
LEE SURRENDERED 9,000 MEN THE REMNANT
OF AN ARMY STILL UNCONQUERED IN SPIRIT
TO 118,000 MEN UNDER GRANT.

Ulysses S. Grant, Commander in Chief of the Union Army

turbed by the United States authority so long as they observe their paroles and the laws in force where they may reside. . . ."

When I put my pen to the paper I did not know the first word that I should make use of in writing the terms. I only knew what was in my mind, and I wished to express it clearly, so that there could be no mistaking it. As I wrote on, the thought occurred to me that the officers had their own private horses and effects, which were important to them, but of no value to us; also that it would be an unnecessary humiliation to call upon them to deliver their sidearms.

No conversation, not one word, passed between General Lee and myself, either about private property, side arms or kindred subjects. He appeared to have no objections to the terms first proposed; or if he had a point to make against them he wished to wait until they were in writing to make it. When he read over that part of the terms about side arms, horses and private property of the officers, he remarked, with some feeling, I thought, that this would have a happy effect upon his army. . . .

I then said to him that I thought this would be about the last battle of the war—I sincerely hoped so; and I said further I took it that most of the men in the ranks were small farmers. The whole country had been so raided by the two armies that it was doubtful whether they would be able to put in a crop to carry themselves and their families through the next winter without the aid of the horses they were then riding. The United States did not want them and I would, therefore, instruct the officers I left behind to receive the paroles of his troops to let every man of the Confederate army who claimed to own a horse or mule take the animal to his home. Lee remarked again that this would have a happy effect.

bert E. Lee, Commander in Chief of the Confederate Army.

Brady

He then sat down and wrote out the following letter:

"(April 9.) . . . I received your letter of this date containing the terms of the surrender of the Army of Northern Virginia as proposed by you. As they are substantially the same as those expressed in your letter of the 8th inst., they are accepted. I will proceed to designate the proper officers to carry the stipulations into effect. . . ."

General Lee, after all was completed and before taking his leave, remarked that his army was in a very bad condition for want of food, and that they were without forage; that his men had been living for some days on parched corn exclusively, and that he would have to ask me for rations and forage. I told him "certainly," and asked for how many men he wanted rations. His answer was "about twenty-five thousand": and I authorized him to send his own commissary and quartermaster to Appomattox Station.

When news of the surrender first reached our lines our men commenced firing a salute of a hundred guns in honor of the victory. I at once sent word, however, to have it stopped. The Confederates were now our prisoners, and we did not want to exult over their downfall. . . .†

LEE'S LETTER TO JEFFERSON DAVIS, APRIL 12, 1865

NEAR APPOMATTOX COURT-HOUSE, VA. APRIL 12, 1865

Mr. PRESIDENT: It is with pain that I announce to Your Excellency the surrender of the Army of Northern Virginia. . . .

Learning the condition of affairs on the lines, where I had gone under the expectation of meeting General Grant to learn definitely the terms he proposed in a communication received from him on the 8th, in the event of the surrender of the army, I requested a suspension of hostilities until these terms could be arranged. In the interview which occurred with General Grant in compliance with my request, terms having been agreed on, I surrendered that portion of the Army of Northern Virginia which was on the field, with its arms, artillery, and wagon trains, the officers and the men to be paroled, retaining their side-arms and private effects. I deemed this course the best under all the circumstances by which we were surrounded. On the morning of the 9th, according to the reports of the ordnance officers, there were 7,892 organized infantry with arms, with an average of seventy-five rounds of ammunition per man. The artillery, though reduced to sixty-three pieces, with ninety-three rounds of ammunition, was sufficient. These comprised all the supplies of ordnance that could be relied on in the State of Virginia. I have no accurate report of the cavalry, but believe it did not exceed 2,100 effective men. The enemy were more than five times our numbers. If we could have forced our way one day longer it would have been at a great sacrifice of life, and at its end I did not see how a surrender could have been avoided. We had no subsistence for man or horse, and it could not be gathered in the country. The supplies ordered to Pamplin's Station from Lynchburg could not reach us, and the men, deprived of food and sleep for many days, were worn out and exhausted.†

With great respect, your obedient servant,

R. E. LEE
General

His Excellency JEFFERSON DAVIS

ABRAHAM LINCOLN'S SECOND INAUGURAL ADDRESS, 1865

. . . On the occasion corresponding to this four years ago, all thoughts were anxiously directed to an impending civil war. All dreaded it—all sought to avert it. While the inaugural address was being delivered from this place, devoted altogether to saving the Union without war, insurgent agents were in the city seeking to destroy it without war—seeking to dissolve the Union, and divide effects, by negotiation. Both parties deprecated war; but

Abraham Lincoln.

one of them would make war rather than let the nation survive; and the other would accept war rather than let it perish. And the war came. . . .

Neither party expected for the war the magnitude or the duration which it has already attained. Neither anticipated that the cause of the conflict might cease with, or even before, the conflict itself should cease. Each looked for an easier triumph, and a result less fundamental and astounding. Both read the same Bible, and pray to the same God; and each invokes His aid against the other. It may seem strange that any men should dare to ask a just God's assistance in wringing their bread from the sweat of other men's faces; but let us judge not, that we be not judged. The prayers of both could not be answered. That of neither has been answered fully. . . .

With malice toward none, with charity for all, with firmness in the right, as God gives us to see the right, let us strive on to finish the work we are in, to bind up the nation's wounds, to care for him who shall have borne the battle, and for his widow, and his orphan—to do all which may achieve and cherish a just and lasting peace among ourselves and with all nations.†

THE SPANISH-AMERICAN WAR, 1898

PRESIDENT WILLIAM McKINLEY'S WAR MESSAGE, 1898

To the Congress of the United States:

. . . it becomes my duty to now address your body with regard to the grave crisis that has arisen in the relations of the United States to Spain by reason of the warfare that for more than three years has raged in the neighboring island of Cuba. . . .

The present revolution is but the successor of other similar insurrections which have occurred in Cuba against the dominion of Spain, extending over a period of nearly half a century, each of which during its progress has subjected the United States to great effort and expense in enforcing its neutrality laws, caused enormous losses to American trade and commerce, caused irritation, annoyance, and disturbance among our citizens, and, by the exercise of cruel, barbarous, and uncivilized practices of warfare, shocked the sensibilities and offended the humane sympathies of our people. . . .

Our trade has suffered, the capital invested by our citizens in Cuba has been largely lost, and the temper and forbearance of our people have been so sorely tried as to beget a perilous unrest among our own citizens, which has inevitably found its expression from time to time in the National Legislature, so that issues wholly external to our own body politic engross attention and stand in the way of that close devotion to domestic advancement that becomes a self-contained commonwealth whose primal maxim has been the avoidance of all foreign entanglements. All this must needs awaken, and has, indeed, aroused, the utmost concern on the part of this Government, as well during my predecessor's term as in my own.

In April, 1896, the evils from which our country suffered through the Cuban war became so onerous that my predecessor made an effort to bring about a peace through the mediation of this Government in any way that might tend to an honorable adjustment of the contest between Spain and her revolted colony, on the basis of some effective scheme of self-government for Cuba under the flag and sovereignty of Spain. It failed through the refusal of the Spanish government then in power to consider any form of mediation or, indeed, any plan of settlement which did not begin with the actual submission of the insurgents to the mother country, and then only on such terms as Spain herself might see fit to grant. The war continued unabated. The resistance of the insurgents was in no wise diminished. . . .

The war in Cuba is of such a nature that, short of subjugation or extermination, a final military victory for either side seems impracticable. The alternative lies in the physical exhaustion of the one or the other party, or perhaps of both—a condition which in effect ended the ten years' war by the truce of Zanjon. The prospect of such a protraction and conclusion of the present strife is a contingency hardly to be contemplated with equanimity by the civilized world, and least of all by the United States, affected and injured as we are, deeply and intimately, by its very existence. . . .

The forcible intervention of the United States as a neutral to stop the war, according to the large dictates of humanity and following many historical precedents where neighboring states have interfered to check the hopeless sacrifices of life by internecine conflicts beyond their borders, is justifiable on rational grounds. It involves, however, hostile constraint upon both parties to the contest, as well to enforce a truce as to guide the eventual settlement.

The grounds for such intervention may be briefly summarized as follows:

First. In the cause of humanity and to put an end to the barbarities, bloodshed, starvation, and horrible miseries now existing there, and which the parties to the conflict are either unable or unwilling to stop or mitigate. It is no answer to say this is all in another country, belonging to another nation, and is therefore none of our business. It is specially our duty, for it is right at our door.

Second. We owe it to our citizens in Cuba to afford them that protection and indemnity for life and property which no government there can or will afford, and to that end to terminate the conditions that deprive them of legal protection.

Third. The right to intervene may be justified by the very serious injury to the commerce, trade, and business of our people and by the wanton destruction of property and devastation of the island.

Fourth, and which is of the utmost importance. The present condition of affairs in Cuba is a constant menace to our peace and entails upon this Government an enormous expense. With such a conflict waged for years in an island so near us and with which our people have such trade and business relations; when the lives and liberty of our citizens are in constant danger and their property destroyed and themselves ruined; where our trading vessels are liable to seizure and are seized at our very door by war ships of a foreign nation; the expeditions of filibustering that we are powerless to prevent altogether, and the irritation questions and entanglements thus arising—all these and others that I need not mention, with the resulting strained relations, are a constant menace to our peace and compel us to keep on a semi war footing with a nation with which we are at peace.

These elements of danger and disorder already pointed out have been strikingly illustrated by a tragic event which has deeply and justly moved the American people. I have already transmitted to Congress the report of the naval court of inquiry on the destruction of the battleship *Maine* in the harbor of Havana during the night of the 15th of February. The destruction of that noble vessel has filled the national heart with inexpressible horror. Two hundred and fifty-eight brave sailors and marines and two officers of our Navy, reposing in the fancied security of a friendly harbor, have been hurled to death, grief and want brought to their homes and sorrow to the nation.

The naval court of inquiry, which, it is needless to say, commands the unqualified confidence of the Government, was unanimous in its conclusion that the destruction of the *Maine* was caused by an exterior explosion—that of a submarine mine. It did not assume to place the responsibility. That remains to be fixed.

In any event, the destruction of the *Maine*, by whatever exterior cause, is a patent and impressive proof of a state of things in Cuba that is intolerable. That condition is thus shown to be such that the Spanish Government can not assure safety and security to a vessel of the American Navy in the harbor of Havana on a mission of peace, and rightfully there. . . .

289

Ewing Galloway

The sinking of the *Maine* in Havana harbor started the Spanish-American War

The long trial has proved that the object for which Spain has waged the war can not be attained. The fire of insurrection may flame or may smolder with varying seasons, but it has not been and it is plain that it can not be extinguished by present methods. The only hope or relief and repose from a condition which can no longer be endured is the enforced pacification of Cuba. In the name of humanity, in the name of civilization, in behalf of endangered American interests which give us the right and the duty to speak and to act, the war in Cuba must stop.

In view of these facts and of these considerations I ask the Congress to authorize and empower the President to take measures to secure a full and final termination of hostilities between the Government of Spain and the people of Cuba, and to secure in the island the establishment of a stable government, capable of maintaining order and observing its international obligations, insuring peace and tranquillity and the security of its citizens as well as our own, and to use the military and naval forces of the United States as may be necessary for these purposes.

And in the interest of humanity and to aid in preserving the lives of the starving people of the island I recommend that the distribution of food and supplies be continued and that an appropriation be made out of the public Treasury to supplement the charity of our citizens.

The issue is now with the Congress. It is a solemn responsibility. I have exhausted every effort to relieve the intolerable condition of affairs which is at our doors. Prepared to execute every obligation imposed upon me by the Constitution and the law, I await your action.†

WILLIAM McKINLEY

WORLD WAR I, 1917–1918

PRESIDENT WILSON'S WAR MESSSAGE TO CONGRESS, APRIL 2, 1917

Gentlemen of the Congress: I have called the Congress into extraordinary session because there are serious, very serious choices of policy to be made, which it was neither right nor constitutionally permissible that I should assume the responsibility of making.

On the third of February last I officially laid before you the extraordinary announcement of the Imperial German Government that on and after the first day of February it was its purpose to put aside all restraints of law or of humanity and use its submarines to sink every vessel that sought to approach either the ports of Great Britain and Ireland or the western coasts of Europe or any of the ports controlled by the enemies of Germany within the Mediterranean. That had seemed to be the object of the German submarine warfare earlier in the war, but since April of last year the Imperial Government had somewhat restrained the commanders of its undersea craft in conformity with its promise then given to us that passenger boats should not be sunk and that due warning would be given to all other vessels which its submarines might seek to destroy, when no resistance was offered or escape attempted, and care taken that their crews were given at least a fair chance to save their lives in their open boats. The precautions taken were meager and haphazard enough, as was proved in distressing instance after instance in the progress of the cruel and unmanly business, but a certain degree of restraint was observed. The new policy has swept every restriction aside. Vessels of every kind, whatever their flag, their character, their cargo, their destination, their errand, have been ruthlessly sent to the bottom without warning and without thought of help or mercy for those on board, the vessels of friendly neutrals along with those of belligerents. Even hospital ships and ships carrying relief to the sorely bereaved and stricken people of Belgium, though the latter were provided with safe conduct through the proscribed areas by the German Government itself and were distinguished by unmistakable marks of identity, have been sunk with the same reckless lack of compassion or of principle. . . .

I am not now thinking of the loss of property involved, immense and serious as that is, but only of the wanton and wholesale destruction of the lives of non-combatants, men, women, and children, engaged in pursuits which have always, even in the darkest periods of modern history, been deemed innocent and legitimate. Property can be paid for; the lives of peaceful and innocent people cannot be. The present German submarine warfare against commerce is a warfare against mankind.

It is a war against all nations. American ships have been sunk, American lives taken, in ways which it has stirred us very deeply to learn of, but the ships and people of other neutral and friendly nations have been sunk and overwhelmed in the waters in the same way. There has been no discrimination. The challenge is to all mankind. Each nation must decide for itself how it will meet it. The choice we make for ourselves must be made with a moderation of counsel and a temperateness of judgment befitting our character and our motives as a nation. We must put excited feeling away. Our motive will not be revenge or the victorious assertion of the physical might of the nation, but only the vindication of right, of human right, of which we are only a single champion. . . .

With a profound sense of the solemn and even tragical character of the step I am taking and of the grave responsibilities which it involves, but in unhesitating obedience to what I deem my constitutional duty, I advise that the Congress declare the recent course of the Imperial German Government to be in fact nothing less than war against the Government and people of the United States; that it formally accept the status of belligerent which has thus been thrust upon it; and that it take immediate steps not only to put the country in a more thorough state of defense, but also to exert all its power and employ all its resources to bring the Government of the German Empire to terms and end the war. . . .

I shall take the liberty of suggesting, through the several executive departments of the Government, for the consideration of your committees, measures for the accomplishment of the several objects I have mentioned. I hope that it will be your pleasure to deal with them as having been framed after very careful thought by the branch of the Government upon whom the responsibility of conducting the war and safeguarding the nation will most directly fall. . . .

Neutrality is no longer feasible or desirable where the peace of the world is involved and the freedom of its people, and the menace to that peace and freedom lies in the existence of autocratic governments, backed by organized force which is controlled wholly by their will, not by the will of their people. We have seen the last of neutrality in such circumstances. We are at the beginning of an age in which it will be insisted that the same standards of conduct and of responsibility for wrong done shall be observed among nations and their governments that are observed among the individual citizens of civilized States.

We have no quarrel with the German people. We have no feelings towards them but one of sympathy and friendship. It was not upon their impulse that their government acted in entering this war. It was not with their previous knowledge or approval. It was a war determined upon as wars used to be determined upon in the old, unhappy days when peoples were nowhere consulted by their rulers and wars were provoked and waged in the interest of dynasties or of little groups of ambitious men who were accustomed to use their fellow-men as pawns and tools. Self-governed nations do not fill their neighbor states with spies or set the course of intrigue to bring about some critical posture of affairs which will give them an opportunity to strike and make conquest. Such designs can be successfully worked out only under cover and where no one has the right to ask questions. Cunningly contrived plans of deception or aggression, carried, it may be, from generation to generation, can be worked out and kept from the light only within the privacy of courts or behind the carefully guarded confidences of a narrow and privileged class. They are happily impossible where public opinion commands and insists upon full information concerning all the nation's affairs. . . .

We are accepting this challenge of hostile purpose because we know that in such a government, following such methods, we can never have a friend; and that in the presence of its organized power, always lying in wait to accomplish we know not what purpose, there can be no assured security for the democratic governments of the world. We are now about to accept the gauge of battle with this natural foe to liberty and shall, if necessary, spend the whole force of the nation to check and nullify its pretensions and its power. We are glad, now that we see the facts with no veil of pretense about them, to fight thus for the ultimate peace of the world and for the liberation of its peoples, the German peoples included; for the rights of nations, great and small, and the privilege of men everywhere to choose their way of life and of obedience. The world must be made safe for democracy. Its peace must be planted upon the tested foundations of political liberty. We have no selfish ends to serve. We desire no conquest, no domination. We seek no indemnities for ourselves, no material compensation for the sacrifices we shall freely make. We are but one of the champions of the rights of mankind. We shall be satisfied when those rights have been made as secure as the faith and the freedom of nations can make them.

Just because we fight without rancor and without selfish object, seeking nothing for ourselves but what we shall wish to share with all free peoples, we shall, I feel confident, conduct our operations as belligerents without passion and ourselves observe with proud punctilio the principles of right and of fair play we profess to be fighting for. . . .

It is a distressing and oppressive duty, Gentlemen of the Congress, which I have per-

World War I. Meuse-Argonne offensive, 1918.

formed in thus addressing you. There are, it may be, many months of fiery trial and sacrifice ahead of us. It is a fearful thing to lead this great peaceful people into war, into the most terrible and disastrous of all wars, civilization itself seeming to be in the balance. But the right is more precious than peace, and we shall fight for the things which we have always carried nearest our hearts—for democracy, for the right of those who submit to authority to have a voice in their own governments, for the rights and liberties of small nations, for a universal dominion of right by such a concert of free peoples as shall bring peace and safety to all nations and make the world itself at last free. To such a task we can dedicate our lives and our fortunes, everything that we are and everything that we have, with the pride of those who know that the day has come when America is privileged to spend her blood and her might for the principles that gave her birth and happiness and the peace which she has treasured. God helping her, she can do no other.†

Ewing Galloway

World War II. Japanese attack on Pearl Harbor, December 7, 1941

WORLD WAR II, 1941–1945

PRESIDENT ROOSEVELT'S WAR MESSAGE TO CONGRESS, DECEMBER 8, 1941

MR. VICE-PRESIDENT, MR. SPEAKER, MEMBERS OF THE SENATE AND THE HOUSE OF REPRESENTATIVES:

Yesterday, December 7, 1941—a date that will live in infamy—the United States of America was suddenly and deliberately attacked by naval and air forces of the empire of Japan.

The United States was at peace with that nation, and, at the solicitation of Japan, was still in conversation with its government and its Emperor looking toward the maintenance of peace in the Pacific.

Indeed, one hour after Japanese air squadrons had commenced bombing in the American island of Oahu the Japanese Ambassador to the United States and his colleague delivered to our Secretary of State a formal reply to a recent American message. And, while this reply stated that it seemed useless to continue the existing diplomatic negotiations, it contained no threat or hint of war or armed attack.

It will be recorded that the distance of Hawaii from Japan makes it obvious that the attack was deliberately planned many days or even weeks ago. During the intervening time the Japanese Government has deliberately sought to deceive the United States by false statements and expressions of hope for continued peace.

The attack yesterday on the Hawaiian Islands has caused severe damage to American naval and military forces. I regret to tell you that very many American lives have been lost. In addition, American ships have been reported torpedoed on the high seas between San Francisco and Honolulu.

Yesterday the Japanese Government also launched an attack against Malaya.

Last night the Japanese forces attacked Hong Kong.

Last night Japanese forces attacked Guam.

Last night Japanese forces attacked the Philippine Islands.

Last night the Japanese attacked Wake Island.

Japan has therefore undertaken a surprise offensive extending throughout the Pacific area. The facts of yesterday and today speak for themselves. The people of the United States have already formed their opinions and well understand the implications to the very life and safety of our nation.

As Commander in Chief of the Army and Navy I have directed that all measures be taken for our defense, that always will our whole nation remember the character of the onslaught against us.

No matter how long it may take us to overcome the premeditated invasion, the American people, in their righteous might, will win through to absolute victory.

European front: D-Day landing of allied forces, Omaha Beach, June 6, 1944.

I.N.P.

Formation of B-24 "Liberator" bombers over Europe, March 22, 1945.

I believe that I interpret the will of the Congress and of the people when I assert that we will not only defend ourselves to the uttermost but will make it very certain that this form of treachery shall never again endanger us.

Hostilities exist. There is no blinking at the fact that our people, our territory and our interests are in grave danger.

With confidence in our armed forces, with the unbounding determination of our people, we will gain the inevitable triumph. So help us God.

I ask that the Congress declare that since the unprovoked and dastardly attack by Japan on Sunday, December 7, 1941, a state of war has existed between the United States and the Japanese Empire.

December 8, 1941

PRESIDENT TRUMAN'S REPORT ON THE ATOMIC BOMB, MONDAY, AUGUST 6, 1945

Sixteen hours ago an American airplane dropped one bomb on Hiroshima, an important Japanese army base. That bomb had more power than 20,000 tons of TNT. It had more than 2,000 times the blast power of the British "Grand Slam," which is the largest bomb ever yet used in the history of warfare.

The Japanese began the war from the air at Pearl Harbor. They have been repaid manyfold. And the end is not yet. With this bomb we have now added a new and revolutionary

296

increase in destruction to supplement the growing power of our armed forces. In their present form these bombs are now in production and even more powerful forms are in development.

It is an atomic bomb. It is a harnessing of the basic power of the universe. The force from which the sun draws its power has been loosed against those who brought war to the Far East.

The atomic bomb.

Before 1939, it was the accepted belief of scientists that it was theoretically possible to release atomic energy. But no one knew any practical method of doing it.

By 1942, however, we knew that the Germans were working feverishly to find a way to add atomic energy to the other engines of war with which they hoped to enslave the world. But they failed. . . .

Beginning in 1940, before Pearl Harbor, scientific knowledge useful in war was pooled between the United States and Great Britain, and many priceless helps to our victories have come from that arrangement. Under the general policy the research on the atomic bomb was begun. With American and British scientists working together we entered the race of discovery against the Germans.

The United States had available the large number of scientists of distinction in the many needed areas of knowledge. It had the tremendous industrial and financial resources necessary for the project and they could be devoted to it without undue impairment of other vital war work.

In the United States the laboratory work and the production plants, on which a substantial start had already been made, would be out of reach of enemy bombing, while at that time Britain was exposed to constant air attack and was still threatened with the possibility of invasion.

For these reasons Prime Minister Churchill and President Roosevelt agreed that it was wise to carry on the project here. . . .

We have spent $2,000,000,000 on the greatest scientific gamble in history and won.

But the greatest marvel is not the size of the enterprise, its secrecy or its cost, but the achievement of scientific brains in putting together infinitely complex pieces of knowledge held by many men in different fields of science into a workable plan. And hardly less marvelous has been the capacity of industry to design, and of labor to operate, the machines and methods to do things never done before so that the brain child of many minds came forth in physical shape and performed as it was supposed to do.

Both science and industry worked under the direction of the United States Army, which achieved a unique success in managing so diverse a problem in the advancement of knowledge in an amazingly short time.

It is doubtful if such another combination could be got together in the world. What has been done is the greatest achievement of organized science in history. It was done under high pressure and without failure. . . .

The fact that we can release atomic energy ushers in a new era in man's understanding of nature's forces. . . .†

THE KOREAN WAR, 1950–

PRESIDENT TRUMAN'S WAR MESSAGE TO CONGRESS, JULY 19, 1950

To the Congress of the United States:

I am reporting to the Congress on the situation which has been created in Korea, and on the actions which this Nation has taken, as a member of the United Nations, to meet this situation. . . .

At 4 o'clock in the morning, Sunday, June 25, Korean time, armed forces from north of the thirty-eighth parallel invaded the Republic of Korea.

The Republic of Korea was established as an independent nation in August 1948, after a free election held under the auspices of the United Nations. This election which was originally intended to cover all of Korea, was held only in the part of the Korean peninsula south of the thirty-eighth parallel, because the Soviet Government, which occupied the peninsula north of that parallel, refused to allow the election to be held in the area under its control.

The hard facts of the present situation require relentless determination and firm action. The course of the fighting thus far in Korea shows that we can expect no easy solution to the conflict there. We are confronted in Korea with well-supplied, well-led forces which have been long trained for aggressive action. We and the other members of the United Nations who have joined in the effort to restore peace in Korea must expect a hard and costly military operation.

We must also prepare ourselves better to fulfill our responsibilities toward the preservation of international peace and security against possible further aggression. In this effort we will not flinch in the face of danger or difficulty.

The free world has made it clear, through the United Nations, that lawless aggression will be met with force. This is the significance of Korea—and it is a significance whose importance cannot be over-estimated.

I shall not attempt to predict the course of events. But I am sure that those who have it in their power to unleash or withhold acts of armed aggression must realize that new recourse to aggression in the world today might well strain to the breaking point the fabric of world peace.

The United States can be proud of the part it has played in the United Nations action in this crisis. We can be proud of the unhesitating support of the American people for the resolute actions taken to halt the aggression in Korea and to support the cause of world peace.

The Congress of the United States, by its strong, bipartisan support of the steps we are taking and by repeated actions in support of international cooperation, has contributed most vitally to the cause of peace. The expressions of support which have been forthcoming from the leaders of both political parties for the actions of our Government and of the United Nations in dealing with the present crisis, have buttressed the firm morale of the entire free world in the face of this challenge.

The American people, together with other free peoples, seek a new era in world affairs. We seek a world where all men may live in peace and freedom, with steadily improving living conditions, under governments of their own free choice.

For ourselves, we seek no territory or domination over others. We are determined to maintain our democratic institutions so that Americans now and in the future can enjoy personal liberty, economic opportunity, and political equality. We are concerned with advancing our prosperity and our well-being as a Nation, but we know that our future is inseparably joined with the future of other free peoples.

We will follow the course we have chosen with courage and with faith, because we carry in our hearts the flame of freedom. We are fighting for liberty and for peace—and with God's blessing we shall succeed.†

GENERAL MACARTHUR'S ADDRESS TO CONGRESS, APRIL 19, 1951

I know war as few other men now living know it, and nothing to me—nothing to me—is more revolting. I have long advocated its complete abolition, as its very destructiveness on both friend and foe has rendered it useless as a means of settling international disputes.

Indeed, on the second of September, 1945, just following the surrender of the Japanese nation on the battleship "Missouri," I formally cautioned as follows:

"Men since the beginning of time have sought peace. Various methods through the ages have been attempted to devise an international process to prevent or settle disputes

Korean War. Landing at Inchon, September 15, 1950.

between nations. From the very start workable methods were found in so far as individual citizens were concerned, but the mechanics of an instrumentality of larger international scope have never been successful. Military alliances, balances of power, leagues of nations, all in turn failed, leaving the only path to be by way of the crucible of war. The utter destructiveness of war now blocks out this alternative. We have had our last chance. If we will not devise some greater and more equitable system, Armageddon will be at our door. The problem basically is theological and involves a spiritual recrudescence and improvement of human character that will synchronize with our almost matchless advances in science, art, literature, and all material and cultural developments of the past 2,000 years. It must be of the spirit if we are to save the flesh.''

But once war is forced upon us, there is no other alternative than to apply every available means to bring it to a swift end. War's very object is victory, not prolonged indecision.

In war there can be no substitute for victory.†

A soldier comes home.

College of William and Mary, Williamsburg, Virginia,
founded 1693, second oldest college in the United States.

EIGHT

Education

"Nothing in education is so astonishing as the amount of ignorance it accumulates in the form of inert facts."

HENRY ADAMS

Education

Our great hope for the future—our great safeguard against danger—is to be found in the general and thorough education of our people.

JAMES A. GARFIELD

In no country in the world are there as many educational opportunities for as many people as in the United States. Education is, of course, compulsory for everybody from the ages of six to sixteen, with slight age and attendance variations in individual states. But Americans look on education not merely as a preparation for life, but as a continuing process. Evidence of this is borne out by the tremendous enrollment in higher educational institutions (professional schools, colleges, universities), vocational schools, extension courses, and, above all, in the numerous adult education courses.

STATISTICS 1949–1950
Source: U. S. Office of Education

Number of Schools and Higher Educational Institutions

Public elementary schools	128,225
Public secondary schools	24,542
Private elementary schools	10,375
Private secondary schools	3,331
Public higher educational institutions	641
Private higher educational institutions	1,210

Enrollment in Schools and Higher Educational Institutions

Public elementary schools	18,818,254
Public secondary schools	5,658,404
Private elementary schools	2,451,430
Private secondary schools	602,484
Higher educational institutions	2,296,592

Average annual salaries of teachers, supervisors, and principals in public, elementary, and secondary schools:	$2,846

Among educators there is little unanimity of opinion concerning methods of education in America. New systems are continually evolving to meet what appear to be changing needs (junior colleges being a recent example). Today in the universities there has been a decline in classical and humanistic studies and a sharp increase in professional or specialized training. Many of the professional schools function within established universities, others function independently. Among professional schools are such outstanding examples as the Harvard School of Business, Harvard School of Law, Colorado School of Mines, John Hopkins School of Medicine, Cornell College of Agriculture, Columbia School of Architecture, and the California and Massachusetts Institutes of Technology.

The selections that follow show some of the early educational laws and plans, descriptions of classes, lessons from the quaint McGuffey Readers, and opinions of well-known educators:

Elementary Education

MASSACHUSETTS SCHOOL LAW, 1647

It being one chief project of the old deluder, Satan to keep men from the knowledge of the Scriptures, as in former times by keeping them in an unknown tongue, so in these latter times by persuading from the use of tongues, so at least the true sense & meaning of the original might be clouded by false glosses of saint seeming deceivers, that learning may not be buried in the grave of our fathers in the church and commonwealth, the Lord assisting our endeavors,—

It is therefore ordered, that every township in this jurisdiction, after the Lord hath increased them in number to 50 householders; shall then forthwith appoint one within their town to teach all such children as shall resort to him to write & read, whose wages shall be paid either by the parents or masters of such children, or by the inhabitants in general, by way of supply, as the major part of those that order the prudentials the town shall appoint; provided, Those that send their children be not oppressed by paying much more than they can have them taught for in other towns; & it is further ordered that where any town shall increase to the number of 100 families or householders, they shall set up a grammar school, the master thereof being able to instruct youth so far as they shall be fitted for the university, provided, that if any town neglect the performance hereof above one year, that every such town shall pay 5 pounds to the next school till they shall perform this order.

HORACE MANN ON THE MASSACHUSETTS SCHOOL LAW, 1846

It is common to say that the act of 1647 laid the foundation of our present system of free schools; but the truth is, it not only laid the foundation of the present system, but, in some particulars, it laid a far broader foundation than has since been built upon, and reared a far higher superstructure than has since been sustained. Modern times have witnessed great improvements in the methods of instruction, and in the motives of discipline; but, in some respects, the ancient foundation has been narrowed, and the ancient superstructure lowered. The term "grammar school," in the old laws, always meant a school where the ancient languages were taught, and where youth could be "fitted for the university." . . . But the term "grammar school" has wholly lost its original meaning . . . The contrast between our ancestors and ourselves in this respect is most humiliating. Their meanness in wealth was more than compensated by their grandeur of soul.

. . . The Pilgrim Fathers conceived the magnificent idea, not only of a universal, but of a free education, for the whole people. . . . Two divine ideas filled their great hearts,— their duty to God and to posterity. For the one, they built the church; for the other, they opened the school. . . .

It is impossible for us adequately to conceive the boldness of the measure which aimed at universal education through the establishment of free schools. As a fact, it had no precedent in the world's history; and, as a theory, it could have been refuted and silenced by a more formidable array of argument and experience than was ever marshalled against any other institution of human origin. But time has ratified its soundness. Two centuries of successful operation now proclaim it to be as wise as it was courageous, and as beneficent as it was disinterested. Every community in the civilized world awards it the meed of praise; and states at home, and nations abroad, in the order of their intelligence, are copying the bright example. What we call the enlightened nations of Christendom are approaching, by slow degrees, to the moral elevation which our ancestors reached at a

"The Country School." Painting by Winslow Homer.

single bound; and the tardy convictions of the one have been assimilating, through a period of two centuries, to the intuitions of the other.

The establishment of free schools was one of those grand mental and moral experiments whose effects could not be developed and made manifest in a single generation.†

ERA OF THE LITTLE RED SCHOOLHOUSE
THE McGUFFEY READERS

In the era of the little red schoolhouse in America, generations of children were brought up on McGuffey Readers. William Holmes McGuffey (1800–1873), educator and professor of moral philosophy at the University of Virginia, compiled his Eclectic Readers from 1836 to 1857. They contained lessons in articulation, inflection, accent and emphasis, the voice, gesture, and reading verse and prose, as well as grammar, punctuation, and spelling. The preface to the Fifth Reader says: "The Reading Lessons have been very carefully selected. It has been the great object of the compiler to present the best specimens of style, to insure interest in the subjects, to impart valuable information, and, especially, to exert a decided and healthy moral and religious influence." The influence of these little books can hardly be exaggerated. They were constantly revised and republished and had an estimated total sale of 122,000,000 copies.

HAMLIN GARLAND WRITES OF THE McGUFFEY READERS
"A Son of the Middle Border," 1917

Our readers were almost the only counterchecks to the current of vulgarity and baseness which ran through the talk of the older boys, and I wish to acknowledge my deep obligation to Professor McGuffey, whoever he may have been, for the dignity and literary grace of his selections. From the pages of his readers I learned to know and love the poems of Scott, Byron, Southey, Wordsworth and a long line of the English masters. I got my first taste of Shakespeare from the selected scenes which I read in these books.

With terror as well as delight I rose to read *Lochiel's Warning*, *The Battle of Waterloo* or *The Roman Captive*. Marco Bozzaris and William Tell were alike glorious to me. I soon knew not only my own reader, the fourth, but all the selections in the fifth and sixth as well. I could follow almost word for word the recitations of the older pupils and at such times I forgot my squat little body and my mop of hair, and became imaginatively a page in the train of Ivanhoe, or a bowman in the army of Richard the Lion Heart battling the Saracen in the Holy Land.

With a high ideal of the way in which these grand selections should be read, I was scared almost voiceless when it came my turn to read them before the class. "STRIKE FOR YOUR ALTARS AND YOUR FIRES. STRIKE FOR THE GREEN GRAVES OF YOUR SIRES—GOD AND YOUR NATIVE LAND," always reduced me to a trembling breathlessness. The sight of the emphatic print was a call to the best that was in me and yet I could not meet the test. Excess of desire to do it just right often brought a ludicrous gasp and I often fell back into my seat in disgrace, the titter of the girls adding to my pain.

Then there was the famous passage, "Did ye not hear it?" and the careless answer, "No, it was but the wind or the car rattling o'er the stony street."—I knew exactly how those opposing emotions should be expressed but to do it after I rose to my feet was

A little red school house, built 1750.

impossible. Burton was even more terrified than I. Stricken blind as well as dumb, he usually ended by helplessly staring at the words which, I conceive, had suddenly become a blur to him.

No matter, we were taught to feel the force of these poems and to reverence the genius that produced them, and that was worth while. Falstaff and Prince Hal, Henry and his wooing of Kate, Wolsey and his downfall, Shylock and his pound of flesh all became a part of our thinking and helped us to measure the large figures of our own literature, for Whittier, Bryant and Longfellow also had a place in these volumes. . . .†

LESSONS FROM McGUFFEY'S NEW FIFTH READER

LESSON LXVIII

1. REV′EL-RY; *n.* noisy feasting and gayety
1. CHIV′AL-RY; *n.* knighthood; a body of knights or brave men.
1. VO-LUPT′U-OUS; *adj.* exciting animal pleasure.

4. SQUAD′RON; *n.* a body of troops.
5. AR′DENNES; *n.* (pro. Ar′dens), a forest near Waterloo.
6. MAR′SHAL-ING; *n.* arranging in order.
6: BLENT; *v.* mixed; united.

BATTLE OF WATERLOO*

In reading the following extract, much variety of expression is required. The description of the ball should be read in a lively, animated manner; that of the distant alarm in low, hurried tones, as if intently listening and deeply anxious; the haste of preparation and departure requires life; and the third and last two stanzas should be read in a mournful and plaintive style.

1. There was a sound of revelry by night,
   And Belgium's ‡capital had gathered then
   Her beauty and her chivalry, and bright
   The lamps shone o'er fair women and brave men.
   A thousand hearts beat happily; and when
   Music arose with its voluptuous swell,
   Soft eyes looked love to eyes which spake again,
   And all went merry as′ a marriage-bell;
   But hush‵! hark‵!—a deep sound strikes like a rising knell!

2. Did ye not hear it?—No‵; 't was but the wind,
   Or the car rattling o'er the stony street;
   On with the *dance*‵! let joy be ‡unconfined;

---

* This battle was fought on June 18th, 1815, between the French army on one side, commanded by Napoleon Bonaparte, and the English army and allies on the other side, commanded by the Duke of Wellington. At the commencement of the battle, some of the officers were at a ball at Brussels, a short distance from Waterloo, and being notified of the approaching contest by a cannonade, left the ballroom for the field of battle. This was the last of Napoleon's battles. He was here completely overthrown.

‡ Words marked thus should be spelled and defined in addition to those whose definitions are given.
Words marked ‵ and ′ should be given rising inflection.

No sleep till morn, when youth and pleasure meet
To chase the ‡glowing hours with flying feet—
But, hark`!—that heavy sound breaks in once more,
As if the clouds its echo would repeat`,
And *nearer*`, *clearer*`, *deadlier*` than before!
Arm`! *arm*`! it is—it is the *cannon's*` opening roar!

3. Ah! then and there was ‡hurrying to and fro`,
   And gathering tears, and ‡tremblings of distress,
   And cheeks all pale`, which, but an hour ago
   Blushed at the praise of their own ‡loveliness`;
   And there were sudden partings, such as press
   The life from out young hearts, and choking sighs
   Which ne'er might be repeated—who could guess
   If ever more should meet those ‡mutual eyes,
Since upon night so sweet such awful morn could rise.

4. And there was ‡mounting in hot haste`; the steed`,
   The ‡mustering squadron`, and the ‡clattering car′
   Went pouring forward with ‡impetuous speed,
   And swiftly forming in the ranks of war;
   And the deep thunder, peal on peal afar,
   And near, the beat of the alarming drum
   Roused up the soldier ere the morning star;
   While ‡thronged the ‡citizens with terror dumb,
Or whispering with white lips—"The *foe*`! They *come*`! They *come*`!"

5. And Ardennes waves above them her green leaves,
   Dewy with nature's tear-drops, as they pass,
   ‡Grieving, if aught ‡inanimate e'er grieves,
   Over the ‡unreturning brave!—alas!
   Ere evening to be trodden like the grass,
   Which, *now*, *beneath* them, but *above*, *shall grow*,
   In its next verdure, when this fiery mass
   Of living valor, rolling on the foe,
And burning with high hope, shall ‡molder, cold and low.

6. Last noon beheld them full of lusty life.
   Last eve in beauty's circle proudly gay,
   The midnight brought the signal-sound of ‡strife,
   The morn, the marshaling in arms—the day,
   Battle's magnificently stern array!
   The thunder clouds close o'er it, which when rent,
   The earth is covered thick with other clay,
   Which her own clay shall cover, heaped and ‡pent,
Rider and horse—friend, foe—in one red burial blent.

EXERCISES.—When, where, and between what parties and commanders was the battle of Waterloo fought? What is described in the first few lines? What place is meant by the capital of Belgium? What were the officers doing when the sound of the distant battle was heard?

What instances of absolute emphasis in the second stanza? What, of relative emphasis in the fifth stanza? How should the last line of the fourth stanza be read?

LESSON XCV

2. AD-VENT'UR-ERS; *n.* those who attempt difficult enterprises.
2. SUM'MA-RY; *adj.* short; brief.
2. OUT'RAGE; *n.* violence.

3. SIG'NAL-IZ-ED; *v.* made remarkable.
3. DE-TACH'MENT; *n.* a party sent off from the main body.

SPEECH OF LOGAN, CHIEF OF THE MINGOES

REMARK.—Let every pupil notice, as each one reads, when the final consonant of any word is joined to the vowel of the next word.

ARTICULATE distinctly. Do not say *who lof* for "whole of"; *an dindeed*, for "and indeed"; *eminen torators*, for "eminent orators"; *talen tsin*, for "talents in"; *celebraty din pea san dwar*, for "celebrated in peace and war."

1. I MAY ‡challenge the whole of the orations of Demosthenes and Cicero, and indeed, of any more eminent orators, if Europe or the world, has furnished more eminent, to produce a single passage superior to the speech of Logan, a Mingo chief, delivered to Lord Dunmore, when governor of Virginia. As a ‡testimony of Indian talents in this line, I beg leave to introduce it, by first stating the ‡incidents necessary for understanding it.

2. In the spring of the year 1774, a robbery was committed by some Indians, upon certain land adventurers on the Ohio river. The whites in that quarter, according to their custom, undertook to punish this outrage in a summary way. Captain Michael Cresap and one Daniel Greathouse, leading on these parties, surprised, at different times, traveling and hunting parties of the Indians, who had their women and children with them, and murdered many. Among these, were ‡unfortunately the family of Logan, a chief celebrated in peace and war, and long ‡distinguished as the friend of the whites.

3. This unworthy return provoked his ‡vengeance. He accordingly signalized himself in the war which ensued. In the autumn of the same year, a ‡decisive battle was fought at the mouth of the Great Kanawha, between the collected forces of the Shawnees, the Mingoes, and the Delawares, and a detachment of the Virginia militia. The Indians were defeated, and sued for peace. Logan, however, ‡disdained to be seen among the ‡suppliants; but, lest the ‡sincerity of a treaty, from which so distinguished a chief absented himself, should be distrusted, he sent, by a messenger, the following speech to be delivered to Lord Dunmore.

4. "I appeal to any white man to say, if ever he entered Logan's cabin hungry, and he gave him not meat; if ever he came cold and naked, and he clothed him not. During the course of the last long and bloody war, Logan remained idle in his cabin, an ‡advocate for peace. Such was my love for the whites, that my countrymen pointed as they passed, and said, 'Logan is the friend of the white men.' I had even thought to live with you, but for the injuries of one man.

5. "Colonel Cresap, last spring, in cold blood, and ‡unprovoked, murdered all the ‡relatives of Logan, not sparing even my women and children. There runs not a drop of my blood in the veins of any living creature. This called on me for revenge. I have sought it. I have killed many. I have fully ‡glutted my ‡vengeance. For my country, I rejoice at the

310

Reading class for second graders. Photographed in Vermont.

beams of peace: but do not ‡harbor a thought that mine is the joy of fear. Logan never felt fear. He will not turn on his heel to save his life. Who is there to mourn for Logan? Not one."

Exercises.—Who was Demosthenes? Cicero? Who undertook to punish the Indians? Whose family were killed? Where was a decisive battle fought? Where does the Kanawha rise? Why did not Logan appear among the suppliants?

In the sentence, "Logan never felt fear," which is the subject? Which the attribute? See Pinneo's Analytical Grammar.

AN IMMIGRANT FAMILY GOES TO SCHOOL

"THE PROMISED LAND," 1912

Mary Antin

The public school has done its best for us foreigners, and for the country, when it made us into good Americans. I am glad it is mine to tell how the miracle was wrought in one case. You should be glad to hear it, you born Americans; for it is the story of the growth of your country. . . . And you will be glad to hear it, my comrades in adoption; for it is a rehearsal of your own experience. . . .

In America . . . everything was free, as we had heard in Russia. Light was free; the streets were as bright as a synagogue on a holy day. Music was free. . . .

Education was free. That subject my father had written about repeatedly, as comprising his chief hope for us children, the essence of American opportunity, the treasure that no thief could touch, not even misfortune or poverty. . . . No application made, no questions asked, no examinations, rulings, exclusions; no machinations, no fees. The doors stood open for every one of us. . . .

Father himself conducted us to school. He would not have delegated that mission to the President of the United States. He had awaited the day with impatience equal to mine, and the visions he saw as he hurried us over the sun-flecked pavements transcended all my dreams . . . he had left home in search of bread for his hungry family, but he went blessing the necessity that drove him to America. The boasted freedom of the New World meant to him far more than the right to reside, travel, and work wherever he pleased; it meant the freedom to speak his thoughts, to throw off the shackles of superstition, to test his own fate, unhindered by political or religious tyranny. He was only a young man when he landed—thirty-two; and most of his life he had been held in leading-strings. . . .

So it was with a heart full of longing and hope that my father led us to school on that first day. He took long strides in his eagerness, the rest of us running and hopping to keep up.

At last the four of us stood around the teacher's desk; and my father, in his impossible English, gave us over in her charge, with some broken words of his hopes for us that his swelling heart could no longer contain. I venture to say that Miss Nixon was struck by something uncommon in the group we made, something outside of Semitic features and the abashed manner of the alien. . . . This foreigner, who brought his children to school as if it were an act of consecration, who regarded the teacher of the primer class with reverence, who spoke of visions, like a man inspired, in a common schoolroom, was not like other aliens, who brought their children in dull obedience to the law; was not like the native fathers, who brought their unmanageable boys, glad to be relieved of their care. I think Miss Nixon guessed what my father's best English could not convey. I think she divined that by the simple act of delivering our school certificates to her he took possession of America.†

A typical modern high school. Photographed in New Jersey.

Higher Education

Thomas Jefferson held that the welfare of the republic depended on the enlightenment of all its citizens. He achieved one of his most cherished ambitions when he founded the University of Virginia in 1819, designing the original buildings and becoming its first rector. In the letter which follows Jefferson outlines his plans for a state university:

JEFFERSON'S LETTER TO PETER CARR, 1817

In the first place, we must ascertain with precision the object of the institution, by taking a survey of the general field of science, and marking out the portion we mean to occupy at first, and the ultimate extension of our views beyond that, should we be enabled to render it, in the end, as comprehensive as we would wish.

1. ELEMENTARY SCHOOLS

It is highly interesting to our country, and it is the duty of its functionaries, to provide that every citizen in it should receive an education proportioned to the condition and pursuits of his life. The mass of our citizens may be divided into two classes—the laboring and

313

the learned. The laboring will need the first grade of education to qualify them for their pursuits and duties; the learned will need it as a foundation for further acquirements. . . .

2. General Schools

At the discharging of the pupils from the elementary schools, the two classes separate—those destined for labor will engage in the business of agriculture, or enter into apprenticeships to such handicraft art as may be their choice; their companions, destined to the pursuits of science, will proceed to the college, which will consist, 1st, of General Schools; and 2d, of Professional Schools. The General Schools will constitute the second grade of education.

The learned class may still be subdivided into two sections; 1, Those who are destined for learned professions, as a means of livelihood; and 2, The wealthy, who, possessing independent fortunes, may aspire to share in conducting the affairs of the nation, or to live with usefulness and respect in the private ranks of life. Both of these sections will require instruction in all the higher branches of science; the wealthy to qualify them for either public or private life; the professional section will need those branches, especially, which are the basis of their future profession, and a general knowledge, of the others, as auxiliary to that, and necessary to their standing and associating with the scientific class. All the branches, then, of useful science, ought to be taught in the general schools, to a competent extent, in the first instance. These sciences may be arranged into three departments, not rigorously scientific, indeed, but sufficiently so for our purposes. These are I, Language; II, Mathematics; III, Philosophy. . . .

3. Professional Schools

At the close of this course the students separate; the wealthy retiring, with sufficient stock of knowledge, to improve themselves to any degree to which their views may lead them, and the professional section to the professional schools, constituting the third grade of education, and teaching the particular sciences which the individuals of this section mean to pursue, with more minuteness and detail than was within the scope of the general schools for the second grade of instruction. In these professional schools each science is to be taught in the highest degree it has yet attained. They are to be the

1st *Department*, the fine arts, to wit: Civil Architecture, Gardening, Painting, Sculpture, and the theory of Music; the

2d *Department*, Architecture, Military and Naval; Projectiles, Rural Economy, (comprehending Agriculture, Horticulture and Veterinary,) Technical Philosophy, the practice of Medicine, Materia Medica, Pharmacy and Surgery. In the

3d *Department*, Theology and Ecclesiastical History; Law, Municipal and Foreign.

To these professional schools will come those who separated at the close of their first elementary course, to wit:

The lawyer to the school of law.

The ecclesiastic to that of theology and ecclesiastical history.

The physician to those of the practice of medicine, materia medica, pharmacy and surgery.

The military man to that of military and naval architecture and projectiles.

The agricultor to that of rural economy.

The gentleman, the architect, the pleasure gardener, painter and musician to the school of fine arts.

314

And to that of technical philosophy will come the mariner, carpenter, ship-wright, plough-wright, wheel-wright, mill-wright, pump maker, clock maker, machinist, optician, metallurgist, founder, cutler, druggist, brewer, vintner, distiller, dyer, painter, bleacher, soap maker, tanner, powder maker, salt maker, glass maker, to learn as much as shall be necessary to pursue their art understandingly, of the sciences of geometry, mechanics, statics, hydrostatics, hydraulics, hydrodynamics, navigation, astronomy, geography, optics, pneumatics, acoustics, physics, chemistry, natural history, botany, mineralogy and pharmacy.

The school of technical philosophy will differ essentially in its functions from the other professional schools. The others are instituted to ramify and dilate the particular sciences taught in the schools of the second grade on a general scale only. The technical school is to abridge those which were taught there too much *in extenso* for the limited wants of the artificer or practical man. These artificers must be grouped together, according to the particular branch of science in which they need elementary and practical instruction; and a special lecture or lectures must be prepared for each group—and these lectures should be given in the evening, so as not to interrupt the labors of the day. The school, particularly, should be maintained wholly at the public expense, on the same principles with that of the ward schools. Through the whole of the collegiate course, at the hours of recreation on certain days, all the students should be taught the manual exercise, military evolutions and manoeuvres; should be under a standing organization as a military corps, and with proper officers to train and command them. . . .†

THE MORRILL ACT, 1862

Under this Land Grant Act some 13,000,000 acres have been given to the states for the establishment of colleges.

An Act donating Public Lands to the several States and Territories which may provide Colleges for the Benefit of Agriculture and the Mechanic Arts

Be it enacted by the Senate and House of Representatives of the United States of America in Congress assembled, That there be granted to the several States, for the purposes hereinafter mentioned, an amount of public land, to be apportioned to each State a quantity equal to thirty thousand acres for each senator and representative in Congress to which the States are respectively entitled by the apportionment under the census of eighteen hundred and sixty: Provided, That no mineral lands shall be selected or purchased under the provisions of this act.

SEC. 2. And be it further enacted, That the land aforesaid, after being surveyed, shall be apportioned to the several States in sections or subdivisions of sections, not less than one quarter of a section . . . . and the Secretary of the Interior is hereby directed to issue to each of the States in which there is not the quantity of public lands subject to sale at private entry at one dollar and twenty-five cents per acre, to which said State may be entitled under the provisions of this act, land scrip to the amount in acres for the deficiency of its distributive share: said scrip to be sold by said States and the proceeds thereof applied to the uses and purposes prescribed in this act, and for no other use or purpose whatsoever. . . .

SEC. 4. And be it further enacted, That all moneys derived from the sale of the lands aforesaid by the States to which the lands are apportioned, and from the sale of land scrip hereinbefore provided for, shall be invested in stocks of the United States, or of the States, or some other safe stocks, yielding not less than five per centum upon the par value of said stocks; and that the moneys so invested shall constitute a perpetual fund, the capital of which shall remain forever undiminished, (except so far as may be provided in section fifth of this act,) and the interest of which shall be inviolably appropriated, by each State which may take and claim the benefit of this act, to the endowment, support, and maintenance of at least one college where the leading object shall be, without excluding other scientific and classical studies, and including military tactics, to teach such branches of learning as are related to agriculture and mechanic arts, in such manner as the legislatures of the States may respectively prescribe, in order to promote the liberal and practical education of the industrial classes in the several pursuits and professions in life. . . .†

RULES AND PRECEPTS OF HARVARD UNIVERSITY, 1642
AND
ENTRANCE REQUIREMENTS OF HARVARD COLLEGE, 1952

RULES AND PRECEPTS, 1642

The following is an excerpt from an anonymous letter dated September 25, 1642.

Rules and precepts that are observed in the college.

1. When any scholar is able to understand Tully, or such like classical Latin author extempore, and make and speak true Latin in verse and prose, And decline perfectly the paradigms of nouns and verbs in the Greek tongue: Let him then and not before be capable of admission into the college.

2. Let every student be plainly instructed, and earnestly pressed to consider well, the main end of his life and studies is, to know God and Jesus Christ which is eternal life, John 17, 3. and therefore to lay Christ in the bottom, as the only foundation of all sound knowledge and learning. And seeing the Lord only giveth wisdom, let every one seriously set himself by prayer in secret to seek it of him Prov. 2, 3. . . .

5. That they studiously redeem the time; observe the general hours appointed for all the students, and the special hours for their own classes: and then diligently attend the lectures without any disturbance by word or gesture. And if in any thing they doubt, they shall inquire as of their fellows, so, (in case of non satisfaction) modestly of their tutors.

6. None shall under any pretense whatsoever, frequent the company and society of such men as lead an unfit, and desolate life. Nor shall any without his tutor's leave, or (in his absence) the call of parents or guardians, go abroad to other towns.

7. Every scholar shall be present in his tutor's chamber at the seventh hour in the morning, immediately after the sound of the bell, at his opening the Scripture and prayer, so also at the fifth hour at night, and then give account of his own private reading, as aforesaid in particular the third, and constantly attend lectures in the hall at the hours appointed. But if any (without necessary impediment) shall absent himself from prayer or lectures, he shall be liable to admonition, if he offend above once a week.

8. If any scholar shall be found to transgress any of the laws of God, or the school, after twice admonition, he shall be liable, if not adultus, to correction, if adultus, his name shall be given up to the overseers of the college, that he may be admonished at the public monthly act. . . .†

Above: Harvard University, Cambridge, Massachusetts. View across the Charles River. *Right:* Commencement procession.

ENTRANCE REQUIREMENTS, 1952

"Official Register of Harvard University," Vol. XLIX

There are three basic requirements for admission to Harvard College:

1.) A secondary school diploma.

2.) The school's recommendation that the candidate is morally and academically fitted for Harvard.

3.) A satisfactory record in a single-day set of examinations given by the College Entrance Examination Board.

The function of Harvard College is liberal education, not technical or vocational training. Our society requires good technical schools of all sorts and a steady supply of competent technicians, but it also needs colleges which have as their clear primary purpose that broad education for civilized living and responsible citizenship which we call liberal. This has been Harvard's task for more than three centuries. . . .

Harvard therefore is not the place for a student who is interested *only* in preparing as fast as possible for business or a specialized occupation such as agriculture, journalism, or accounting. It is a college for those who feel the need for a broad development of their powers, for a greater understanding of their world, and for an enriched cultural life. In other words, Harvard exists for the student who wants to become a truly educated man in the old-fashioned sense of the word. . . .

This does not mean, however, that a Harvard education has no relevance to earning a living. . . . But discovering career goals and developing competence along special lines are secondary to the main purpose of a Harvard education. In the Harvard plan, specialized professional training comes after college, in the graduate schools.

STUDENTS

The college has a normal enrollment of about 4,200 students. . . . A recent government survey shows that eighty per cent of all American college students attend colleges in their own state. At Harvard there are students from every state and territory . . . and from forty-eight foreign countries.

UNIVERSITY COLLEGE

The distinction between Harvard College and Harvard University is not always clear. . . . Harvard College . . . is concerned only with the liberal education of undergraduates. It is the original, historic Harvard. In the last century and a half, however, various professional schools have been added and Harvard has become a great university in the full sense of the word. . . .

Harvard University thus consists of the College plus nine professional schools which offer professional training at the graduate level. . . . All the graduate schools are part of one closely knit university, but each is administratively separate and has its own endowment, faculty, curriculum, and admissions and administrative officers. Admission to Harvard College does not constitute admission to one of the graduate schools.

Ordinarily there are special values and handicaps in the small college and values and handicaps of a different sort in the large university. The small college can provide a close relationship between teacher and student. All of its energies and resources are concentrated on the undergraduate. . . . The special advantages of the large university are distinction in the faculty, richness of course offerings, extensive library and laboratory facilities. . . .

Research and teaching, college and university, march together, each contributing to the other. This is what is meant by the phrase "University College." . . .†

THE REVOLUTION IN HIGHER EDUCATION

"MEMOIRS OF A SUPERFLUOUS MAN," 1942

Albert Jay Nock

My life has afforded me few diversions more engaging than that of watching the progress of our educational revolution. . . . The revolution began with a drastic purge, a thorough guillotining of the classical curriculum, wherever found. . . . The elective system came in as a substitute, proposing instruction *in omni re scibili* as its final consummation. During a visit to Germany, the president of Harvard, Mr. Eliot, had taken note that the elective system was working well in German universities, and he saw no reason why it should not work as well in an undergraduate college like Harvard, so he introduced it there. The country promptly carried his logic to its full length. If the thing was good for the university, good for the college, why not for the secondary school, why not for the primary school? Why not try a tentative dab at its being good for the kindergarten?—surely in a free democracy the free exercise of self-expression and the development of an untrammelled personality can hardly begin too young.

So the old regime's notion that education is in its nature selective . . . was swept away and replaced by the popular notion that everybody should go to school, college, university, and should have every facility afforded for studying anything that any one might choose. Our institutions grew to enormous size; the country's student-population exceeded anything ever known. Gifts, grants, subsidies, endowments, brought an incredible flow of money; and our system at once began to take on the aspect of a huge bargain-counter or a modern drug-store. The results, however, were increasingly unsatisfactory, so much so that in forty years the revolution has not been able to consolidate its gains. After its preliminary clean sweep of the old regime, the succeeding period has been one of incessant and unsuccessful tinkering with the mechanics of the new. At the present time it seems that about all the possibilities of further tinkering have been exhausted, and that nobody can think of anything more to do. . . .

In fairness it must be said that the revolution was not altogether without reasons. The earlier discipline was as a rule administered poorly and, which is worse, undiscriminately. . . . Too often a routine of elementary Greek and Latin was forced on ineducable children; too often those who forced it even on the educable were themselves ineducable. . . . So between the ineducable pupil on the one hand and the ineducable gerund-grinder, as Carlyle calls him, on the other, the system, speaking generally, did fail; it failed, as many a good system has failed, through getting into bad hands. . . .

. . . I have never been able to find any one who would tell me what the net social value of a compulsory universal literacy actually comes to when the balance of advantage and disadvantage is drawn, or wherein that value consists. . . . Universal literacy helps business by extending the reach of advertising and increasing its force; and also in other ways. Beyond that I see nothing on the credit side. On the debit side, it enables scoundrels to beset, dishevel and debauch such intelligence as is in the power of the vast majority of mankind to exercise. . . . the evidence of it is daily spread wide before us on all sides. More than this, it makes many articulate who should not be so, and otherwise would not be so. It enables mediocrity to run rampant, to the detriment of both intelligence and taste. In a word, it puts into a people's hands an instrument which very few can use, but which everyone supposes himself fully able to use; and the mischief thus wrought is very great.

One might assume that as the level of literacy rose, the level of general intelligence would rise with it. . . . This, roughly, was Mr. Jefferson's idea, and indeed it has always been at the root of our system of free public instruction for everyone. It has, however, somehow failed to work out according to expectation. The level of literacy has been pushed up very nearly to the practicable limit, but the level of general intelligence seems not to have risen appreciably. . . . The reason for this is plain enough; there is nothing recondite about it. . . . very few literate persons are able to read, very few indeed. This can be proven by observation and experiment of the simplest kind. I do not mean that the great majority are unable to read intelligently; I mean they are unable to read at all—unable, that is, to carry away from a piece of printed matter anything like a correct idea of its content. They are more or less adept at passing printed matter through their minds, after a fashion, especially such matter as is addressed to mere sensation, (and knowledge of this is nine-tenths of a propagandist's equipment), but this is not reading. Reading implies a use of the reflective faculty, and very few have that faculty developed much beyond the anthropoid stage, let alone possessing it at a stage of development which makes reading practicable. . . .

The ex-president of one of our colleges tells me that for a dozen years he carried on experiments in the value of literacy. . . . Selecting a paragraph of very simple but non-sensational prose, he asked his students, taking them one by one, to read it carefully; then to read it carefully again; then to read it aloud to him; then to write down the gist of it in their own words. Hardly any one could do it; hardly any one was able to bring anything like an adequate power of reflective thought to bear upon the substance of a simple paragraph. In other words, they could not read.†

Annapolis, Maryland. Graduates of the United States Naval Academy, established 1845, receiving the congratulations of President Franklin D. Roosevelt

Louis Tager

Vest Point, New York. Cadets at the United States
Military Academy, founded by Act of Congress, 1802.

The Educators Speak

"SOME FRUITS OF SOLITUDE"

William Penn (1644–1718)

EDUCATION

4. We are in Pain to make them Scholars, but not Men! To talk rather than to know, which is true Canting. . . .

6. We press their Memory too soon, and puzzle, strain, and load them with Words and Rules; to know Grammar and Rhetorick, and a strange Tongue or two, that it is ten to one may never be useful to them; Leaving their natural Genius to Mechanical and Physical, or natural Knowledge uncultivated and neglected; which would be of exceeding Use and Pleasure to them through the whole Course of their Life. . . .

9. It were Happy if we studied Nature more in natural Things; and acted according to Nature; whose rules are few, plain and most reasonable. . . .

11. The Creation would not be longer a Riddle to us: The Heavens, Earth, and Waters, with their respective, various and numerous Inhabitants: Their Productions, Natures, Seasons, Sympathies and Antipathies; Their Use, Benefit and Pleasure, would be better understood by us. . . .

12. And it would go a great way to caution and direct People in their Use of the World, that they were better studied and known in the Creation of it. . . .†

321

ERRORS OF EDUCATION

"THOUGHTS, SELECTED FROM THE WRITINGS OF HORACE MANN," 1846

The unpardonable error of education has been, that it has not begun with simple truths, with elementary ideas, and risen by gradations to combined results. It has begun with teaching systems, rules, schemes, complex doctrines, which years of analysis would scarcely serve to unfold. All is administered in a mass. The learner, not being able to comprehend, has endeavored to remember, and has thus been put off with a fact, in lieu of a principle explanatory of an entire class of facts. In this way we pass our errors and our truths over to our successors done up in the same bundle, they to others, to be perpetual sources of error, alienation, and discord.†

INAUGURAL ADDRESS, AS PRESIDENT OF HARVARD UNIVERSITY, 1869
Charles W. Eliot

The endless controversies whether language, philosophy, mathematics, or science supplies the best mental training, whether general education should be chiefly literary or chiefly scientific, have no practical lesson for us to-day. This University recognizes no real antagonism between literature and science, and consents to no such narrow alternatives as mathemathics or classics, science or metaphysics. We would have them all, and at their best. To observe keenly, to reason soundly, and to imagine vividly are operations as essential as that of clear and forcible expression; and to develop one of these faculties, it is not necessary to repress and dwarf the others. . . .

The best result of the discussion which has raged so long about the relative educational value of the main branches of learning is the conviction that there is room for them all in a sound scheme, provided that right methods of teaching be employed. . . . The actual problem to be solved is not what to teach, but how to teach. . . . With good methods, we may confidently hope to give young men of twenty to twenty-five an accurate general knowledge of all the main subjects of human interest, besides a minute and thorough knowledge of the one subject which each may select as his principal occupation in life. To think this impossible is to despair of mankind; for unless a general acquaintance with many branches of knowledge, good so far as it goes, be attainable by great numbers of men, there can be no such thing as an intelligent public opinion; and in the modern world the intelligence of public opinion is the one indispensable condition of social progress. . . .†

"SCHOOL AND SOCIETY," 1899
John Dewey

While training for the profession of learning is regarded as the type of culture, or a liberal education, the training of a mechanic, a musician, a lawyer, a doctor, a farmer, a merchant, or a railroad manager is regarded as purely technical and professional. The result is that which we see about us everywhere—the division into "cultured" people and "workers," the separation of theory and practice. . . . While our educational leaders are talking of culture, the development of personality, etc., as the end and aim of education, the great majority of those who pass under the tuition of the school regard it only as a narrowly practical tool with which to get bread and butter enough to eke out a restricted life. If we were to conceive our educational end and aim in a less exclusive way, if we were to introduce into education processes the activities which appeal to those whose dominant interest is to do and to make, we should find the hold of the school upon its members to be more vital, more prolonged, containing more of culture.

But why should I make this labored presentation? The obvious fact is that our social life has undergone a thorough and radical change. If our education is to have any meaning for life, it must pass through an equally complete transformation. . . . The introduction of active occupations, of nature-study, of elementary science, of art, of history; the relegation of the merely symbolic and formal to a secondary position; the change in the moral school atmosphere, in the relation of pupils and teachers—of discipline; the introduction of more active, expressive, and self-directing factors—all these are not mere accidents, they are necessities of the larger social evolution. It remains but to organize all these factors, to appreciate them in their fulness of meaning, and to put the ideas and ideals involved into complete, uncompromising possession of our school system. To do this means to make each one of our schools an embryonic community life, active with types of occupations that reflect the life of the larger society and permeated throughout with the spirit of art, history, and science. . . .

The child can carry over what he learns in the home and utilize it in the school; and the things learned in the school he applies at home. These are the two great things in breaking down isolation, in getting connection—to have the child come to school with all the experience he has got outside the school, and to leave it with something to be immediately used in his everyday life. . . .†

"THE HIGHER LEARNING IN AMERICA," 1936
Robert Hutchins

GENERAL EDUCATION

If we are educators we must have a subject matter, and a rational, defensible one. If that subject matter is education, we cannot alter it to suit the whims of parents, students, or the public. . . .

. . . It is a good principle of educational administration that a college or university should do nothing that another agency can do as well. This is a good principle because a college or university has a vast and complicated job if it does what only it can do. In general education, therefore, we may wisely leave experience to life and set about our job of intellectual training.

If there are permanent studies which every person who wishes to call himself educated should master; if those studies constitute our intellectual inheritance, then those studies should be the center of a general education. They cannot be ignored because they are difficult, or unpleasant, or because they are almost totally missing from our curriculum today. The child-centered school may be attractive to the child, and no doubt is useful as a place in which the little ones may release their inhibitions and hence behave better at home. But educators cannot permit the students to dictate the course of study unless they are prepared to confess that they are nothing but chaperons, supervising an aimless, trial-and-error process which is chiefly valuable because it keeps young people from doing something worse. The free elective system as Mr. Eliot introduced it at Harvard and as Progressive Education adapted it to lower age levels amounted to a denial that there was content to education. Since there was no content to education, we might as well let students follow their own bent. They would at least be interested and pleased and would be as well educated as if they had pursued a prescribed course of study. This overlooks the fact that the aim of education is to connect man with man, to connect the present with the past, and to advance the thinking of the race. If this is the aim of education, it cannot be left to the sporadic, spontaneous interests of children or even of undergraduates. . . .

A typical state university building. Photographed in the Midwest.

THE FUNCTION OF A UNIVERSITY

Turning professional schools into vocational schools degrades the universities and does not elevate the professions. I should also contend that it cannot accomplish the only purpose it can have, namely, the preparation of the student for the practice of his life work. It is, in short, bad for the student as well as for the universities and the professions.

My contention is that the tricks of the trade cannot be learned in a university, and that if they can be they should not be. They cannot be learned in a university because they get out of date and new tricks take their place, because the teachers get out of date and cannot keep up with current tricks, and because tricks can be learned only in the actual situation in which they can be employed. . . .

Left: Mount Holyoke College, South Hadley Massachusetts, chartered 1836. (Reading room in the library. One of the earliest institutions of higher education for women, founded by Mary Lyon, Mount Holyoke Seminary was rechartered in 1893 as Mount Holyoke College and has continued to be one of the nation's outstanding women's colleges.

All that can be learned in a university is the general principles, the fundamental propositions, the theory of any discipline. The practices of the profession change so rapidly that an attempt to inculcate them may merely succeed in teaching the student habits that will be a disservice to him when he graduates. . . .

The subject matter of a learned profession is intellectual. Though the rules of the trade may be learned in the practice, and indeed can only be learned there, the intellectual content of the profession can generally be mastered only in a university; at least a university should be the ideal place for such study. To the extent to which the attention of the student is directed to vocational interests and away from the intellectual content of the discipline the university fails to do the only thing it might do and attempts something in which it is bound to fail. . . .†

Eliot Elisofon

SUMMARY

In the final analysis the success of a nation's educational system must be measured by the kind of citizens it produces. In America educational opportunities are great. What use we make of them constantly shapes the nation's history. This is the test that faces each generation in carrying out the high ideal of American democracy with its belief in the dignity of the individual and in his capacity for self-government.

This section has attempted to illustrate how deeply aware of this were our forefathers when they strove to make education available to all. The opinions of modern educators, though differing sharply as to methods, shows no less concern as they strive to meet the needs of our times.

"Toilers of the Sea," by Albert Pinkham Ryder.

NINE

The

American Expression

"Works of art are of an infinite loneliness and with nothing to be so little reached as with criticism. Only love can grasp and hold and fairly judge them."

RAINER MARIA RILKE

The American Expression

Works of living writers have been omitted from the following selections of poetry and prose. Generally speaking, passage of time is necessary to sift a permanent work of art from what is currently popular. For this reason, and because of the obvious limitations of space, it has seemed wisest to present, chronologically, excerpts from works that have already survived the test of time.

"TO MY DEAR AND LOVING HUSBAND"
Anne Bradstreet (1612–1672)

If ever two were one, then surely we.
If ever man were loved by wife, then thee.
If ever wife was happy in a man,
Compare with me, ye women, if you can.
I prize thy love more than whole Mines of gold,
Or all the riches that the East doth hold
My love is such that rivers cannot quench,
Nor aught but love from thee give recompense.
Thy love is such I can no way repay;
The heavens reward thee manifold I pray.
Then while we live, in love let's so persever,
That when we live no more, we may live ever.

"MEDITATIONS DIVINE AND MORALL"—A MANUSCRIPT LEFT BY ANNE BRADSTREET TO HER CHILDREN

Youth is the time of getting, middle age of improving, and old age of spending; a negligent youth is usually attended by an ignorant middle age, and both by an empty old age. He that hath nothing to feed on by vanity and lyes must needs lye down on a Bed of sorrow.

A ship that beares much saile, and little or no ballast, is easily overset; and that man whose head hath great abilities, and his heart little or no grace, is in danger of foundering.

Fire hath its force abated by water, not by winde; and anger must be alayed by cold words, and not by blustering threates.

A sharp appetite and a thorough concoction is a signe of a healthful body; so a quick reception and a deliberate cogitation, argues a sound mind.

There is no object that we see; no action that we doe; no good that we enjoy; no evill that we feele or fear, but we may make some spirituall advantage of all.†

"RIP VAN WINKLE"
Washington Irving (1783–1859)

Times grew worse and worse with Rip Van Winkle as years of matrimony rolled on; a tart temper never mellows with age, and a sharp tongue is the only edged tool that grows keener with constant use. For a long while he used to console himself, when driven from home, by frequenting a kind of perpetual club of the sages, philosophers, and other idle personages of the village, which held its sessions on a bench before a small inn, designated by a rubicund portrait of His Majesty George the Third. Here they used to sit in the shade through a long, lazy summer's day, talking listlessly over village gossip, or telling endless, sleepy stories about nothing. . . .

From even this stronghold the unlucky Rip was at length routed by his termagant wife, who would suddenly break in upon the tranquility of the assemblage, and call the members all to nought; nor was that august personage, Nicholas Vedder himself, sacred from the daring tongue of this terrible virago, who charged him outright with encouraging her husband in habits of idleness.

Poor Rip was at last reduced almost to despair; and his only alternative, to escape from the labor of the farm and the clamor of his wife, was to take a gun in hand, and stroll away into the woods. . . .

In a long ramble of the kind, on a fine autumnal day, Rip had unconsciously scrambled to one of the highest parts of the Kaatskill Mountains. He was after his favorite sport of squirrel-shooting, and the still solitudes had echoed and re-echoed with the reports of his gun. Panting and fatigued, he threw himself, late in the afternoon, on a green knoll, covered with mountain herbage, that crowned the brow of a precipice. From an opening between the trees he could overlook all the lower country for many a mile of rich woodland. He saw at a distance the lordly Hudson, far, far below him, moving on its silent but majestic course, with the reflection of a purple cloud or the sail of a lagging bark here and there sleeping on its glassy bosom, and at last losing itself in the blue highlands.

On the other side he looked down into a deep mountain glen, wild, lonely, and shagged, the bottom filled with fragments from the impending cliffs, and scarcely lighted by the reflected rays of the setting sun. For some time Rip lay musing on this scene; evening was gradually advancing; the mountains began to throw their long blue shadows over the valleys; he saw that it would be dark long before he could reach the village; and he heaved a heavy sigh when he thought of encountering the terrors of Dame Van Winkle.

As he was about to descend, he heard a voice from a distance hallooing: "Rip Van Winkle! Rip Van Winkle!" He looked around, but could see nothing but a crow winging its solitary flight across the mountain. He thought his fancy must have deceived him, and turned again to descend, when he heard the same cry ring through the still, evening air, "Rip Van Winkle! Rip Van Winkle!"—at the same time Wolf bristled up his back, and giving a low growl, skulked to his master's side, looking fearfully down into the glen. Rip now felt a vague apprehension stealing over him; he looked anxiously in the same direction, and perceived a strange figure slowly toiling up the rocks, and bending under the weight of something he carried on his back. He was surprised to see any human being in this lonely and unfrequented place, but supposing it to be someone of the neighborhood in need of his assistance, he hastened down to yield it.

On nearer approach, he was still more surprised at the singularity of the stranger's appearance. He was a short, square-built old fellow, with thick bushy hair, and a grizzled beard. His dress was of the antique Dutch fashion—a cloth jerkin strapped round the waist— several pairs of breeches, the outer one of ample volume, decorated with rows of buttons down the sides, and bunches at the knees. He bore on his shoulders a stout keg, that seemed full of liquor, and made signs for Rip to approach and assist him with the load. Through rather shy and distrustful of this new acquaintance, Rip complied with his usual alacrity; and mutually relieving each other, they clambered up a narrow gully, apparently the dry bed of a mountain torrent. As they ascended, Rip every now and then heard long rolling peals, like distant thunder, that seemed to issue out of a deep ravine, or rather cleft between lofty rocks, toward which their rugged path conducted. He paused for an instant, but supposing it to be the muttering of one of those transient thundershowers which often take place in the mountain heights, he proceeded. Passing through the ravine they came to a hollow, like a small amphitheatre, surrounded by perpendicular precipices, over the brinks of which impending trees shot their branches, so that you only caught glimpses of the azure sky, and the bright evening cloud. During the whole time Rip and his companion had labored on in silence; for though the former marvelled greatly what could be the object of carrying a keg of liquor up this wild mountain, yet there was something strange and incomprehensible about the unknown, that inspired awe, and checked familiarity.

On entering the amphitheatre, new objects of wonder presented themselves. On a level spot in the center was a company of odd-looking personages playing at ninepins. They were dressed in quaint outlandish fashion; some wore short doublets, others jerkins, with long knives in their belts, and most of them had enormous breeches, of similar style with that of the guide's. Their visages, too, were peculiar; one had a large head, broad face, and small piggish eyes; the face of another seemed to consist entirely of nose, and was surmounted by a white sugar-loaf hat, set off with a little red cock's tail. They all had beards, of various shapes and colors. There was one who seemed to be the commander. He was a stout old gentleman, with a weather-beaten countenance; he wore a laced doublet, broad belt and hanger, high-crowned hat and feather, red stockings, and high-heeled shoes with roses on them. The whole group reminded Rip of the figures in an old Flemish painting, in the parlor of Dominie Van Shaick, the village parson, and which had been brought over from Holland at the time of the settlement.

What seemed particularly odd to Rip was, that though these folks were evidently amusing themselves, yet they maintained the gravest faces, the most mysterious silence, and were, withal, the most melancholy party of pleasure he had ever witnessed. Nothing interrupted the stillness of the scene but the noise of the balls, which, whenever they were rolled, echoed along the mountains like rumbling peals of thunder.

As Rip and his companion approached them they suddenly desisted from their play, and stared at him with such fixed statue-like gaze, and such strange, uncouth, lack-lustre countenances, that his heart turned within him, and his knees smote together. His companion now emptied the contents of the keg into large flagons, and made signs to him to wait upon the company. He obeyed with fear and trembling; they quaffed the liquor in profound silence, and then returned to their game.

By degrees, Rip's awe and apprehension subsided. He even ventured, when no eye was fixed upon him, to taste the beverage, which he found had much of the flavor of excellent Hollands. He was naturally a thirsty soul, and was soon tempted to repeat the draught. One taste provoked another; and he reiterated his visits to the flagon so often, that at length his senses were overpowered, his eyes swam in his head, his head gradually declined, and he fell into a deep sleep.†

"THE HOUSE OF THE SEVEN GABLES"
Nathaniel Hawthorne (1804–1864)

Phoebe Pyncheon slept, on the night of her arrival, in a chamber that looked down on the garden of the old house. It fronted towards the east, so that at a very seasonable hour a glow of crimson light came flooding through the window, and bathed the dingy ceiling and paper-hanging in its own hue. There were curtains to Phoebe's bed; a dark, antique canopy and ponderous festoons, of a stuff which had been rich, and even magnificent, in its time; but which now brooded over the girl like a cloud, making a night in that one corner, while elsewhere it was beginning to be day. The morning light, however, soon stole into the aperture at the foot of the bed, betwixt those faded curtains. Finding the new guest there,—with a bloom on her cheeks like the morning's own, and a gentle stir of departing slumber in her limbs, as when an early breeze moves the foliage,—the dawn kissed her brow. It was the caress which a dewy maiden—such as the Dawn is, immortally—gives to her sleeping sister, partly from the impulse of irresistible fondness, and partly as a pretty hint that it is time now to unclose her eyes.

At the touch of those lips of light, Phoebe quietly awoke, and, for a moment, did not recognize where she was, nor how those heavy curtains chanced to be festooned around her. Nothing, indeed, was absolutely plain to her, except that it was now early morning, and that, whatever might happen next, it was proper, first of all, to get up and say her prayers. She was the more inclined to devotion, from the grim aspect of the chamber and its furniture, especially the tall stiff chairs; one of which stood close by her bedside, and looked as if some old-fashioned personage had been sitting there all night, and had vanished only just in season to escape discovery.

When Phoebe was quite dressed, she peeped out of the window, and saw a rose-bush in the garden. Being a very tall one, and of luxurious growth, it had been propped up against the side of the house, and was literally covered with a rare and very beautiful species of white rose. . . . Hastening down the creaking and carpetless staircase, she found her way into the garden, gathered some of the most perfect of the roses, and brought them to her chamber.

Little Phoebe was one of those persons who possess, as their exclusive patrimony, the gift of practical arrangement. It is a kind of natural magic that enables these favoured ones to bring out the hidden capabilities of things around them; and particularly to give a look of comfort and habitableness to any place which, for however brief a period, may happen to be their home. A wild hut of underbrush, tossed together by wayfarers through the primitive forest, would acquire the home aspect by one night's lodging of such a woman, and would retain it long after her quiet figure had disappeared into the surrounding shade. No less a portion of such homely witchcraft was requisite, to reclaim, as it were, Phoebe's waste, cheerless, and dusky chamber, which had been untenanted so long—except by spiders, and mice, and rats, and ghosts—that it was all overgrown with the desolation which watches to obliterate every trace of man's happier hours. What was precisely Phoebe's process, we find it impossible to say. She appeared to have no preliminary design, but gave a touch here and another there; brought some articles of furniture to light, and dragged others into the shadow; looped up or let down a window-curtain; and, in the course of half an hour, had fully succeeded in throwing a kindly and hospitable smile over the apartment.†

"ICHABOD"

John Greenleaf Whittier (1807–1892)

So FALLEN! so lost! the light withdrawn
 Which once he wore!
The glory from his gray hairs gone
 Forevermore!

Revile him not.—The Tempter hath
 A snare for all;
And pitying tears, not scorn and wrath,
 Befit his fall!

O, dumb be passion's stormy rage,
 When he who might
Have lighted up and led his age,
 Falls back in night.

Scorn! would the angels laugh, to mark
    A bright soul driven,
Fiend-goaded, down the endless dark,
    From hope and heaven!

Let not the land once proud of him
    Insult him now,
Nor brand with deeper shame his dim,
    Dishonored brow.

But let its humbled sons, instead,
    From sea to lake,
A long lament, as for the dead,
    In sadness make.

Of all we loved and honored, naught
    Save power remains:
A fallen angel's pride of thought,
    Still strong in chains.

All else is gone; from those great eyes
    The soul has fled:
When faith is lost, when honor dies,
    The man is dead!

Then, pay the reverence of old days
    To his dead fame;
Walk backward, with averted gaze,
    And hide the shame!

"EVANGELINE"
Henry Wadsworth Longfellow (1807–1882)

A TALE OF ACADIE

This is the forest primeval. The murmuring pines and the hemlocks,
Bearded with moss, and in garments green, indistinct in the twilight,
Stand like Druids of old, with voices sad and prophetic,
Stand like harpers hoar, with beards that rest on their bosoms.
Loud from its rocky caverns, the deep-voiced neighboring ocean
Speaks, and in accents disconsolate answers the wail of the forest.

This is the forest primeval; but where are the hearts that beneath it
Leaped like the roe, when she hears in the woodland the voice of the huntsman?
Where is the thatch-roofed village, the home of Acadian farmers,—
Men whose lives glided on like rivers that water the woodlands,
Darkened by shadows of earth, but reflecting an image of heaven?
Waste are those pleasant farms, and the farmers forever departed!
Scattered like dust and leaves, when the mighty blasts of October
Seize them, and whirl them aloft, and sprinkle them far o'er Grand-Pre.

Ye who believe in affection that hopes, and endures, and is patient,
Ye who believe in the beauty and strength of woman's devotion,
List to the mournful tradition still sung by the pines of the forest;
List to a Tale of Love in Acadie, home of the happy.†

"ISRAFEL"

Edgar Allan Poe (1808–1849)

And the angel Israfel, whose heart-strings are a lute,
and who has the sweetest voice of all God's creatures.

KORAN

In Heaven a spirit doth dwell
   'Whose heart-strings are a lute';
None sing so wildly well
As the angel Israfel,
And the giddy stars (so legends tell),
Ceasing their hymns, attend the spell
   Of his voice, all mute.

Tottering above
   In her highest noon,
   The enamoured moon
Blushes with love,
   While, to listen, the red levin
   (With the rapid Pleiades, even,
   Which were seven,)
   Pauses in Heaven.

And they say (the starry choir
   And the other listening things)
That Israfeli's fire
Is owing to that lyre
   By which he sits and sings—
The trembling living wire
   Of those unusual strings.

But the skies that angel trod,
   Where deep thoughts are a duty,
Where Love's a grown-up God,
   Where the Houri glances are
Imbued with all the beauty
   Which we worship in a star.

Therefore, thou are not wrong,
   Israfeli, who despisest
An unimpassioned song;
To thee the laurels belong,
   Best bard, because the wisest!
Merrily live, and long!

The ecstasies above
With thy burning measures suit—
Thy grief, thy joy, thy hate, thy love,
With the fervour of thy lute—
Well may the stars be mute!

Yes, Heaven is thine; but this
Is a world of sweets and sours,
Our flowers are merely—flowers,
And the shadows of thy perfect bliss
Is the sunshine of ours.

If I could dwell
Where Israfel
Hath dwelt, and he where I,
He might not sing so wildly well
A mortal melody,
While a bolder note than this might swell
From my lyre within the sky.

"SELF-RELIANCE," 1841
Ralph Waldo Emerson (1803–1882)

. . . There is a time in every man's education when he arrives at the conviction that envy is ignorance; that imitation is suicide; that he must take himself for better or for worse as his portion; that though the wide universe is full of good, no kernel of nourishing corn can come to him but through his toil bestowed on that plot of ground which is given to him to till. The power which resides in him is new in nature, and none but he knows what that is which he can do, nor does he know until he has tried. Not for nothing one face, one character, one fact, makes such impression on him, and another none. It is not without preestablished harmony, this sculpture in the memory. The eye was placed where one ray should fall, that it might testify of that particular ray. Bravely let him speak the utmost syllable of his confession. We but half express ourselves, and are ashamed of that divine idea which each of us represents. It may be safely trusted as proportionate and of good issues, so it be faithfully imparted, but God will not have his work made manifest by cowards. It needs a divine man to exhibit anything divine. A man is relieved and gay when he has put his heart into his work and done his best; but what he has said or done otherwise shall give him no peace. It is a deliverance which does not deliver. In the attempt his genius deserts him; no muse befriends; no invention, no hope. . . .

Whoso would be a man, must be a nonconformist. He who would gather immortal palms must not be hindered by the name of goodness, but must explore if it be goodness. Nothing is at last sacred but the integrity of our own mind. Absolve you to yourself, and you shall have the suffrage of the world. I remember an answer which when quite young I was prompted to make to a valued adviser who was wont to importune me with the dear old doctrines of the church. On my saying, What have I to do with the sacredness of traditions, if I live wholly from within? my friend suggested,—"But these impulses may be from below, not from above." I replied, "They do not seem to me to be such; but if I am the devil's child, I will live then from the devil." No law can be sacred to me but that of my nature. Good and bad are but names very readily transferable to that or this; the only right is what is after my constitution; the only wrong what is against it. A man is to carry himself in the presence of all opposition as if every thing were titular and ephemeral but

Mount Wilson Observatory

"Imbued with all the beauty
Which we worship in a star."—Edgar Allan Poe

335

he. I am ashamed to think how easily we capitulate to badges and names, to large societies and dead institutions. Every decent and well-spoken individual affects and sways me more than is right. I ought to go upright and vital, and speak the rude truth in all ways. . . .

What I must do is all that concerns me, not what the people think. This rule, equally arduous in actual and in intellectual life, may serve for the whole distinction between greatness and meanness. It is the harder because you will always find those who think they know what is your duty better than you know it. It is easy in the world to live after the world's opinion; it is easy in solitude to live after your own; but the great man is he who in the midst of the crowd keeps with perfect sweetness the independence of solitude. . . .†

"WALDEN"

Henry David Thoreau (1817–1862)

The mass of men lead lives of quiet desperation. What is called resignation is confirmed desperation. From the desperate city you go into the desperate country, and have to console yourself with the bravery of minks and muskrats. A stereotyped but unconscious despair is concealed even under what are called the games and amusements of mankind. There is no play in them, for this comes after work. But it is a characteristic of wisdom not to do desperate things.

When we consider what, to use the words of the catechism, is the chief end of man, and what are the true necessaries and means of life, it appears as if men had deliberately chosen the common mode of living because they preferred it to any other. Yet they honestly think there is no choice left. But alert and healthy natures remember that the sun rose clear. It is never too late to give up our prejudices. No way of thinking or doing, however ancient, can be trusted without proof. What everybody echoes or in silence passes by as true today may turn out to be falsehood tomorrow, mere smoke of opinion, which some had trusted for a cloud that would sprinkle fertilizing rain on their fields. What old people say you cannot do, you try and find that you can. Old deeds for old people, and new deeds for new. Old people did not know enough once, perchance, to fetch fresh fuel to keep the fire a-going; new people put a little dry wood under a pot, and are whirled around the globe with the speed of birds, in a way to kill old people, as the phrase is. Age is no better, hardly so well, qualified for an instructor as youth, for it has not profited so much as it has lost. One may almost doubt if the wisest man has learned anything of absolute value by living. Practically, the old have no very important advice to give the young, their own experience has been so partial, and their lives have been such miserable failures, for private reasons, as they must believe; and it may be that they have some faith left which belies that experience, and they are only less young than they were. . . .

I went to the woods because I wished to live deliberately, to front only the essential facts of life, and see if I could not learn what it had to teach, and not, when I came to die, discover that I had not lived. I did not wish to live what was not life, living is so dear; nor did I wish to practise resignation, unless it was quite necessary. I wanted to live deep and suck out all the marrow of life, to live so sturdily and Spartanlike as to put to rout all that was not life, to cut a broad swath and shave close, to drive life into a corner, and reduce it to its lowest terms, and if it proved to be mean, why then to get the whole and genuine meanness of it, and publish its meanness to the world; or if it were sublime, to know it by experience, and be able to give a true account of it in my next excursion. For most men, it appears to me, are in a strange uncertainty about it, whether it is of the devil or of God, and have *somewhat hastily* concluded that it is the chief end of man here to "glorify God and enjoy him forever." . . .

Aaron Siskind

I left the woods for as good a reason as I went there. Perhaps it seemed to me that I had several more lives to live, and could not spare any more time for that one. It is remarkable how easily and insensibly we fall into a particular route, and make a beaten track for ourselves. I had not lived there a week before my feet wore a path from my door to the pond-side; and though it is five or six years since I trod it, it is still quite distinct. It is true, I fear, that others may have fallen into it, and so helped to keep it open. The surface of the earth is soft and impressible by the feet of men; and so with the paths which the mind travels. How worn and dusty, then, must be the highways of the world, how deep the ruts of tradition and conformity!†

"WHEN LILACS LAST IN THE DOORYARD BLOOM'D"
Walt Whitman (1819–1892)

When lilacs last in the dooryard bloom'd,
And the great star early droop'd in the western sky in the night,
I mourn'd, and yet shall mourn with ever-returning spring.

Ever-returning spring, trinity sure to me you bring,
Lilac blooming perennial and drooping star in the west,
And thought of him I love.

· · · · · ·

Come lovely and soothing death,
Undulate round the world, serenely arriving, arriving,
In the day, in the night, to all, to each,
Sooner or later delicate death.

Prais'd be the fathomless universe,
For life and joy, and for objects and knowledge curious,
And for love, sweet love—but praise! praise! praise!
For the sure-enwinding arms of cool-enfolding death.

Dark mother always gliding near with soft feet,
Have none chanted for thee a chant of fullest welcome?
Then I chant it for thee, I glorify thee above all,
I bring thee a song that when thou must indeed come, come unfalteringly.

Approach, strong deliveress,
When it is so, when thou hast taken them I joyously sing the dead,
Lost in the loving floating ocean of thee,
Loved in the flood of thy bliss, O death.

From me to thee glad serenades,
Dances for thee I propose saluting thee, adornments and feastings for thee,
And the sights of the open landscape and the high-spread sky are fitting,
And life and the fields, and the huge and thoughtful night.

The night in silence under many a star,
The ocean shore and the husky whispering wave whose voice I know,
And the soul turning to thee O vast and well-veil'd death,
And the body gratefully nestling close to thee.

Over the tree-tops I float thee a song,
Over the rising and sinking waves, over the myriad fields and the prairies wide,
Over the dense-pack'd cities all and the teeming wharves and ways,
I float this carol with joy, with joy to thee O death. . . .†

"MOBY DICK"
Herman Melville (1819–1891)

It was a cloudy, sultry afternoon; the seamen were lazily lounging about the decks, or vacantly gazing over into the lead-colored waters. Queequeg and I were mildly employed weaving what is called a sword-mat, for an additional lashing to our boat. So still and subdued and yet somehow preluding was all the scene, and such an incantation of revelry lurked in the air, that each silent sailor seemed resolved into his own invisible self.

I was the attendant or page of Queequeg, while busy at the mat. As I kept passing and repassing the filling or woof of marline between the long yarns of the warp, using my own hand for the shuttle, and as Queequeg, standing sideways, ever and anon slid his heavy oaken sword between the threads, and idly looking off upon the water, carelessly and unthinkingly drove home every yarn: I say so strange a dreaminess did there then reign all over the ship and all over the sea, only broken by the intermitting dull sound of the sword, that it seemed as if this were the Loom of Time, and I myself were a shuttle mechanically weaving and weaving away at the Fates. There lay the fixed threads of the warp subject to but one single, ever returning, unchanging vibration, and that vibration merely enough to admit of the crosswise interblending of other threads with its own. This warp seemed necessity; and here, thought I, with my own hand I ply my own shuttle and weave my own destiny into these unalterable threads. Meantime, Queequeg's impulsive, indifferent sword, sometimes hitting the woof slantingly, or crookedly, or strongly, or weakly, as the case might be; and by this difference in the concluding blow producing a corresponding contrast in the final aspect of the completed fabric; this savage's sword, thought I, which thus finally shapes and fashions both warp and woof; this easy, indifferent sword must be chance —aye, chance, free will, and necessity—no wise incompatible—all interweavingly working together. The straight warp of necessity, not to be swerved from its ultimate course—its every alternating vibration, indeed, only tending to that; free will still free to ply her shuttle between given threads; and chance, though restrained in its play within the right lines of necessity, and sideways in its motions directed by free will, though thus prescribed to by both, chance by turns rules either, and has the last featuring blow at events.

Thus we were weaving and weaving away when I started at a sound so strange, long drawn, and musically wild and unearthly, that the ball of free will dropped from my hand, and I stood gazing up at the clouds whence that voice dropped like a wing. High aloft in the cross-trees was that mad Gay-Header, Tashtego. His body was reaching eagerly forward, his hand stretched out like a wand, and at brief sudden intervals he continued his cries. To be sure the same sound was that very moment perhaps being heard all over the seas, from hundreds of whalemen's look-outs perched as high in the air; but from few of those lungs could that accustomed old cry have derived such a marvellous cadence as from Tashtego the Indian's.

As he stood hovering over you half suspended in air, so wildly and eagerly peering towards the horizon, you would have thought him some prophet or seer beholding the shadows of Fate, and by those wild cries announcing their coming.

"There she blows! there! there! there! she blows! she blows!"

"Where-away?"

"On the lee-beam, about two miles off! a school of them!"†

EMILY DICKINSON (1830–1886)

"THIS IS MY LETTER TO THE WORLD"

This is my letter to the world,
    That never wrote to me,—
The simple news that Nature told,
    With tender majesty.

Her message is committed
    To hands I cannot see;
For love of her, sweet countrymen,
    Judge tenderly of me!

"I TASTE A LIQUOR NEVER BREWED"

I taste a liquor never brewed,
From tankards scooped in pearl;
Not all the vats upon the Rhine
Yield such an alcohol!

Inebriate of air am I,
And debauchee of dew,
Reeling, through endless summer days,
From inns of molten blue.

When landlords turn the drunken bee
Out of the foxglove's door,
When butterflies renounce their drams,
I shall but drink the more!

Till seraphs swing their snowy hats,
And saints to windows run,
To see the little tippler
Leaning against the sun!

"PAIN HAS AN ELEMENT"

Pain has an element of blank;
It cannot recollect
When it began, or if there were
A day when it was not.

It has no future but itself,
Its infinite realms contain
Its past, enlightened to perceive
New periods of pain.

"BEAUTY IS NOT CAUSED,—IT IS"

Beauty is not caused,—it is;
Chase it and it ceases,
Chase it and it abides,
Overtake the creases

In the meadow when the wind
Run his fingers thro' it?
Deity will see to it
That you never do it.

"WHO HAS NOT FOUND THE HEAVEN BELOW"

Who has not found the heaven below
    Will fail of it above.
God's residence is next to mine,
    His furniture is love.

"AND THIS OF ALL MY HOPES"

And this of all my hopes—
This is the silent end.
Bountiful colored my morning rose,
Early and sere its end.

Never bud from a stem
Stepped with so gay a foot,
Never a worm so confident
Bored at so brave a root.

"TOM SAWYER"

Mark Twain (1835–1910)

"WHITEWASHING"

Tom appeared on the side-walk with a bucket of whitewash and a long-handled brush. He surveyed the fence, and the gladness went out of nature, and a deep melancholy settled down upon his spirit. Thirty yards of broad fence nine feet high! It seemed to him that life was hollow, and existence but a burden. Sighing he dipped his brush and passed it along the topmost plank; repeated the operation; did it again; compared the insignificant whitewashed streak with the far-reaching continent of unwhitewashed fence, and sat down on a tree-box discouraged. Jim came skipping out at the gate with a tin pail, and singing "Buffalo Gals." Bringing water from the town pump had always been hateful work in Tom's eyes before, but now it did not strike him so. He remembered that there was company at the pump. White, mulatto, and negro boys and girls were always there waiting their turns,

341

resting, trading playthings, quarrelling, fighting, skylarking. And he remembered that although the pump was only a hundred and fifty yards off, Jim never got back with a bucket of water in under an hour; and even then somebody generally had to go after him. Tom said:

"Say, Jim; I'll fetch the water if you'll whitewash some."

Jim shook his head, and said:

"Can't, Ma'rs Tom. Ole missis she tole me I got to go an' git dis water an' not stop foolin' 'roun' wid anybody. She say she spec' Ma'rs Tom gwyne to ax me to whitewash, an' so she tole me go 'long an' 'tend to my own business—she 'lowed *she'd* 'tend to de whitewashin'."

"Oh, never you mind what she said, Jim. That's the way she always talks. Gimme the bucket—I won't be gone only a minute. She won't ever know."

"Oh, I dasn't, Ma'rs Tom. Ole missis she'd take an' tar de head off'n me. 'Deed she would."

"*She!* she never licks anybody—whack 'em over the head with her thimble, and who cares for that, I'd like to know? She talks awful, but talk don't hurt—anyways, it don't if she don't cry. Jim, I'll give you a marble. I'll give you a white alley!"

Jim began to waver.

"White alley, Jim; and it's a bully too."

"My; dat's a mighty gay marvel, I tell you. But, Ma'rs Tom, I's powerful 'fraid ole missis."

But Jim was only human—this attraction was too much for him. He put down his pail, took the white alley. In another minute he was flying down the street with his pail and a tingling rear, Tom was whitewashing with vigour, and Aunt Polly was retiring from the field with a slipper in her hand and triumph in her eye.

But Tom's energy did not last. He began to think of the fun he had planned for this day, and his sorrows multiplied. Soon the free boys would come tripping along on all sorts of delicious expeditions, and they would make a world of fun of him for having to work— the very thought of it burnt him like fire. He got out his worldly wealth and examined it— bits of toys, marbles, and trash; enough to buy an exchange of work maybe, but not enough to buy so much as half-an-hour of pure freedom. So he returned his straitened means to his pocket, and gave up the idea of trying to buy the boys. At this dark and hopeless moment an inspiration burst upon him. Nothing less than a great, magnificent inspiration. He took up his brush and went tranquilly to work. Ben Rogers hove in sight presently; the very boy of all boys whose ridicule he had been dreading. Ben's gait was the hop, skip, and jump—proof enough that his heart was light and his anticipations high. He was eating an apple, and giving a long, melodious whoop at intervals, followed by a deep-toned ding dong dong, dong dong dong, for he was personating a steamboat. As he drew near he slackened speed, took the middle of the street; leaned far over to starboard, and rounded-to ponderously, and with laborious pomp and circumstance, for he was personating the *Big Missouri*, and considered himself to be drawing nine feet of water. He was boat, and captain, and engine-bells combined, so he had to imagine himself standing on his own hurricane-deck giving the orders and executing them.

"Stop her, sir! Ling-a-ling." The headway ran almost out, and he drew up slowly toward the side-walk. "Ship up to back! Ling-a-ling!" His arms straightened and stiffened down his sides. "Set her back on the stabboard! Ling-a-ling! Chow! ch-chow-wow-chow!" his right hand meantime describing stately circles, for it was representing a forty-foot wheel. "Let her go back on the labboard! Ling-a-lin-lin! Chow-ch-chow-chow!" The left hand began to describe circles.

"Stop the stabboard! Ling-a-ling-ling! Stop the labboard! Come ahead on the stabboard! Stop her! Let your outside turn over slow! Ling-a-ling-ling! Chow-ow-ow! Get out that head-line! Lively, now! Come—out with your spring-line—what're you about there?

342

Take a turn round that stump with the bight of it! Stand by that stage now—let her go! Done with the engines, sir! Ling-a-ling-ling!"

"*Sh't! s'sht! sht!*" (Trying the gauge-cocks.)

Tom went on whitewashing—paid no attention to the steamer. Ben stared a moment, and then said:

"Hi-yi! You're up a stump, ain't you!"

No answer. Tom surveyed his last touch with the eye of an artist; then he gave his brush another gentle sweep, and surveyed the result as before. Ben ranged up alongside of him. Tom's mouth watered for the apple, but he stuck to his work. Ben said:

"Hello, old chap! you got to work, hey?"

"Why, it's you Ben! I warn't noticing."

"Say, I'm going in a-swimming, I am. Don't you wish you could? But of course you'd druther work, wouldn't you? 'Course you would!"

Tom contemplated the boy a bit, and said:

"What do you call work?"

"Why, ain't that work?"

Tom resumed his whitewashing, and answered carelessly:

"Well, maybe it is, and maybe it ain't. All I know is, it suits Tom Sawyer."

"Oh, come now, you don't mean to let on that you like it?"

The brush continued to move.

"Like it? Well, I don't see why I oughtn't to like it. Does a boy get a chance to white-wash a fence every day?"

That put the thing in a new light. Ben stopped nibbling his apple. Tom swept his brush daintily back and forth—stepped back to note the effect—added a touch here and there—criticized the effect again. Ben watching every move, and getting more and more interested, more and more absorbed. Presently he said:

"Say, Tom, let me whitewash a little."

Tom considered; was about to consent; but he altered his mind; "No, no; I reckon it wouldn't hardly do, Ben. You see, Aunt Polly's awful particular about this fence—right here on the street, you know—but if it was the back fence I wouldn't mind, and she wouldn't. Yes, she's awful particular about this fence; it's got to be done very careful; I reckon there ain't one boy in a thousand, maybe two thousand, that can do it the way it's got to be done."

"No—is that so? Oh, come now; lemme just try, only just a little. I'd let you, if you was me, Tom."

"Ben, I'd like to, honest Injun; but Aunt Polly—well, Jim wanted to do it, but she wouldn't let him. Sid wanted to do it, but she wouldn't let Sid. Now, don't you see how I am fixed? If you was to tackle this fence, and anything was to happen to it—"

"Oh, shucks; I'll be just as careful. Now lemme try. Say—I'll give you the core of my apple."

"Well, here. No, Ben; now don't; I'm afeard—"

"I'll give you all of it!"

Tom give up the brush with reluctance in his face, but alacrity in his heart. And while the late steamer *Big Missouri* worked and sweated in the sun, the retired artist sat on a barrel in the shade close by, dangled his legs, munched his apple, and planned the slaughter of more innocents. There was no lack of material; boys happened along every little while; they came to jeer, but remained to whitewash. By the time Ben fagged out, Tom had traded the next change to Billy Fisher for a kite in good repair; and when he played out, Johnny Miller bought in for a dead rat and a string to swing it with; and so on, and so on, hour after hour. And when the middle of the afternoon came, from being a poor poverty-stricken boy in the morning, Tom was literally rolling in wealth. He had, besides the things I have mentioned, twelve marbles, part of a jew's harp, a piece of blue bottle-glass to look through, a spool-cannon, a key that wouldn't unlock anything, a fragment of chalk, a glass stopper of a decanter, a tin soldier, a couple of tadpoles, six fire-crackers, a kitten with only one eye, a brass door-knob, a dog-collar—but no dog—the handle of a knife, four pieces of orange-peel, and a dilapidated old window-sash. He had had a nice, good, idle time all the while—plenty of company—and the fence had three coats of whitewash on it! If he hadn't run out of whitewash, he would have bankrupted every boy in the village.

Tom said to himself that it was not such a hollow world after all. He had discovered a great law of human action, without knowing it, namely, that, in order to make a man or a boy covet a thing, it is only necessary to make the thing difficult to attain. If he had been a great and wise philosopher, like the writer of this book, he would now have comprehended that work consists of whatever a body is obliged to do, and that play consists of whatever a body is not obliged to do. And this would help him to understand why constructing artificial flowers, or performing on a treadmill, is work, whilst rolling nine-pins or climbing Mont Blanc is only amusement. There are wealthy gentlemen in England who drive four-horse passenger-coaches twenty or thirty miles on a daily line, in the summer, because the privilege costs them considerable money; but if they were offered wages for the service, that would turn it into work, and then they would resign.†

Opposite: "He had had a nice, good, idle time."—Mark Twai

"THE VARIETIES OF RELIGIOUS EXPERIENCE"
William James (1842–1910)

If we were to ask the question: "What is human life's chief concern?" one of the answers we should receive would be: "It is happiness." How to gain, how to keep, how to recover happiness, is in fact for most men at all times the secret motive of all they do, and of all they are willing to endure. The hedonistic school in ethics deduces the moral life wholly from the experiences of happiness and unhappiness which different kinds of conduct bring; and, even more in the religious life than in the moral life, happiness and unhappiness seem to be the poles round which the interest revolves. . . .

With such relations between religion and happiness, it is perhaps not surprising that men come to regard the happiness which a religious belief affords as a proof of its truth. If a creed makes a man feel happy, he almost inevitably adopts it. Such a belief ought to be true; therefore it is true—such, rightly or wrongly, is one of the "immediate inferences" of the religious logic used by ordinary men. . . .

In many persons, happiness is congenital and irreclaimable. "Cosmic emotion" inevitably takes in them the form of enthusiasm and freedom. I speak not only of those who are animally happy. I mean those who, when unhappiness is offered or proposed to them, positively refuse to feel it, as if it were something mean and wrong. We find such persons in every age, passionately flinging themselves upon their sense of the goodness of life, in spite of the hardships of their own condition, and in spite of the sinister theologies into which they may be born. From the outset their religion is one of union with the divine. . .

If, then, we give the name of healthy-mindedness to the tendency which looks on all things and sees that they are good, we find that we must distinguish between a more involuntary and a more voluntary or systematic way of being healthy-minded. In its involuntary variety, healthy-mindedness is a way of feeling happy about things immediately. In its systematical variety, it is an abstract way of conceiving things as good. Every abstract way of conceiving things selects some one aspect of them as their essence for the time being, and disregards the other aspects. Systematic healthy-mindedness, conceiving good

344

Hannibal, Missouri.

as the essential and universal aspect of being, deliberately excludes evil from its field of vision; and although, when thus nakedly stated, this might seem a difficult feat to perform for one who is intellectually sincere with himself and honest about facts, a little reflection shows that the situation is too complex to lie open to so simple a criticism. . . .

. . . . Much of what we call evil is due entirely to the way men take the phenomenon. It can so often be converted into a bracing and tonic good by a simple change of the sufferer's inner attitude from one of fear to one of fight; its sting so often departs and turns into a relish when, after vainly seeking to shun it, we agree to face about and bear it cheerfully, that a man is simply bound in honor, with reference to many of the facts that seem at first to disconcert his peace, to adopt this way of escape. Refuse to admit their badness; despise their power; ignore their presence; turn your attention the other way; and so far as you yourself are concerned at any rate, though the facts may still exist, their evil character exists no longer. Since you make them evil or good by your own thoughts about them, it is the ruling of your thoughts which proves to be your principal concern.

The deliberate adoption of an optimistic turn of mind thus makes its entrance into philosophy. And once in, it is hard to trace its lawful bounds. Not only does the human instinct for happiness, bent on self-protection by ignoring, keep working in its favor, but higher inner ideals have weighty words to say. The attitude of unhappiness is not only painful, it is mean and ugly. What can be more base and unworthy than the pining, puling, mumping mood, no matter by what outward ills it may have been engendered? What is more injurious to others? What less helpful as a way out of the difficulty? It but fastens and perpetuates the trouble which occasioned it, and increases the total evil of the situation. At all costs, then, we ought to reduce the sway of that mood; we ought to scout it in ourselves and others, and never show it tolerance. But it is impossible to carry on this discipline in the subjective sphere without zealously emphasizing the brighter and minimizing the darker aspects of the objective sphere of things at the same time. And thus our resolution not to indulge in mise.y, beginning at a comparatively small point within ourselves, may not stop until it has brought the entire frame of reality under a systematic conception optimistic enough to be congenial with its needs. . . .

The systematic cultivation of healthy-mindedness as a religious attitude is therefore consonant with important currents in human nature, and is anything but absurd. In fact, we all do cultivate it more or less, even when our professed theology should in consistency forbid it. We divert our attention from disease and death as much as we can; and the slaughter-houses and indecencies without end on which our life is founded are huddled out of sight and never mentioned, so that the world we recognize officially in literature and in society is a poetic fiction far handsomer and cleaner and better than the world that really is.

The advance of liberalism, so-called, in Christianity, during the past fifty years, may fairly be called a victory of healthy-mindedness within the church over the morbidness with which the old hell-fire theology was more harmoniously related. We have now whole congregations whose preachers, far from magnifying our consciousness of sin, seem devoted rather to making little of it. They ignore, or even deny, eternal punishment, and insist on the dignity rather than on the depravity of men. They look at the continual preoccupation of the old-fashioned Christian with the salvation of his soul as something sickly and reprehensible rather than admirable; and a sanguine and "muscular" attitude, which to our forefathers would have seemed purely heathen, has become in their eyes an ideal element of Christian character. I am not asking whether or not they are right, I am only pointing out the change.†

Opposite: "Healthy-mindedness is a way of feeling happy about things immediately."—William James

Lisa Larsen, courtesy "Life"

"THE AMERICAN"
Henry James (1843–1916)

On a brilliant day in May, of the year 1868, a gentleman was reclining at his ease on the great circular divan which at that period occupied the centre of the Salon Carre, in the Museum of the Louvre. This commodious ottoman has since been removed, to the extreme regret of all weak-kneed lovers of the fine arts; but our visitor had taken serene possession of its softest spot, and with his head thrown back and his legs outstretched, was staring at Murillo's beautiful moon-borne Madonna in deep enjoyment of his posture. He had removed his hat and flung down beside him a little red guide-book and an opera-glass. . . . He had looked out all the pictures to which an asterisk was affixed in those formidable pages of fine print in his Baedeker; his attention had been strained and his eyes dazzled; he had sat down with an aesthetic headache. . . . Raphael and Titian and Rubens were a new kind of arithmetic, and they made him for the first time in his life wonder at his vagueness.

An observer with anything of an eye for local types would have had no difficulty in referring this candid connoisseur to the scene of his origin, and indeed such an observer might have made an ironic point of the almost ideal completeness with which he filled out the mould of race. The gentleman on the divan was the superlative American; to which affirmation of character he was partly helped by the general easy magnificence of his manhood. He appeared to possess that kind of health and strength which, when found in perfection, are the most impressive—the physical tone which the owner does nothing to "keep up." If he was a muscular Christian it was quite without doctrine. If it was necessary to walk to a remote spot he walked, but he had never known himself to "exercise." He had no theory with regard to cold bathing or the use of Indian clubs; he was neither an oarsman, a rifleman nor a fencer—he had never had time for these amusements—and he was quite unaware that the saddle is recommended for certain forms of indigestion. He was by inclination a temperate man; but he had supped the night before his visit to the Louvre at the Cafe Anglais—some one had told him it was an experience not to be omitted—and he had slept none the less the sleep of the just. His usual attitude and carriage had a liberal looseness, but when, under a special inspiration, he straightened himself he looked a grenadier on parade. He had never tasted tobacco. He had been assured—such things are said—that cigars are excellent for the health, and he was quite capable of believing it; but he would no more have thought of "taking" one than of taking a dose of medicine. His complexion was brown and the arch of his nose bold and well-marked. His eye was of a clear, cold grey, and save for the abundant droop of his moustache he spoke, as to cheek and chin, of the joy of the matutinal steel. He had the flat jaw and the firm, dry neck which are frequent in the American type; but the betrayal of native conditions is a matter of expression even more than of feature, and it was in this respect that our traveller's countenance was supremely eloquent. The observer we have been supposing might, however, perfectly have measured its expressiveness and yet have been at a loss for names and terms to fit it. It had that paucity of detail which is yet not emptiness, that blankness which is not simplicity, that look of being committed to nothing in particular, of standing in a posture of general hospitality to the chances of life, of being very much at one's own disposal, characteristic of American faces of the clear strain. It was the eye, in this case, that chiefly told the story; an eye in which the unacquainted and the expert were singularly blended. It was full of contradictory suggestions; and though it was by no means the glowing orb of a hero of romance, you could find in it almost anything you looked for. Frigid and yet friendly, frank yet cautious, shrewd yet credulous, positive yet sceptical, confident yet shy, extremely intelligent and extremely good-humoured, there was something vaguely defiant in its concessions and something profoundly reassuring in its reserve.

The wide yet partly folded wings of this gentleman's moustache, with the two premature wrinkles in the cheek above it, and the fashion of his garments, in which an exposed shirt-front and a blue satin necktie of too light a shade played perhaps an obtrusive part, completed the elements of his identity.†

"THE AGE OF INNOCENCE"
Edith Wharton (1862–1937)

On a January evening of the early seventies, Christine Nilsson was singing in Faust at the Academy of Music in New York.

Though there was already talk of the erection, in remote metropolitan distances "above the Forties," of a new Opera House which should compete in costliness and splendour with those of the great European capitals, the world of fashion was still content to re-assemble every winter in the shabby red and gold boxes of the sociable old Academy. Conservatives cherished it for being small and inconvenient, and thus keeping out the "new people" whom New York was beginning to dread and yet be drawn to; and the sentimental clung to it for its historic associations, and the musical for its excellent acoustics, always so problematic a quality in halls built for the hearing of music.

It was Madame Nilsson's first appearance that winter, and what the daily press had already learned to describe as "an exceptionally brilliant audience" had gathered to hear her, transported through the slippery snow streets in private broughams, in the spacious family landau, or in the humbler but more convenient "Brown *coupé*." To come to the Opera in a Brown *coupé* was almost as honourable a way of arriving as in one's own car-riage; and departure by the same means had the immense advantage of enabling one (with a playful allusion to democratic principles) to scramble into the first Brown conveyance in the line, instead of waiting till the cold-and-gin congested nose of one's own coachman gleamed under the portico of the Academy. It was one of the great livery-stableman's most masterly intuitions to have discovered that Americans want to get away from amuse-ment even more quickly than they want to get to it.

When Newland Archer opened the door at the back of the club box the curtain had just gone up on the garden scene. There was no reason why the young man should not have come earlier, for he had dined at seven, alone with his mother and sister, and had lingered afterward over a cigar in the Gothic library with glazed black-walnut bookcases and finial-topped chairs which was the only room in the house where Mrs. Archer allowed smoking. But, in the first place, New York was a metropolis, and perfectly aware that in metrop-olises it was "not the thing" to arrive early at the opera; and what was or was not "the thing" played a part as important in Newland Archer's New York as the inscrutable totem terrors that had ruled the destinies of his forefathers thousands of years ago.

The second reason for his delay was a personal one. He had dawdled over his cigar be-cause he was at heart a dilettante, and thinking over a pleasure to come often gave him a subtler satisfaction than its realization. This was especially the case when the pleasure was a delicate one, as his pleasures mostly were; and on this occasion the moment he looked forward to was so rare and exquisite in quality that—well, if he had timed his arrival in accord with the prima donna's stage-manager he could not have entered the Academy at a more significant moment than just as she was singing: "He loves me—he loves me not—*he loves me!*" and sprinkling the falling daisy petals with notes as clear as dew.

She sang, of course, "M'ama!" and not "he loves me," since an unalterable and un-unquestioned law of the musical world required that the German text of French operas sung by Swedish artists should be translated into Italian for the clearer understanding of English-speaking audiences. This seemed as natural to Newland Archer as all the other conventions on which his life was moulded: such as the duty of using two silver-backed brushes with his monogram in blue enamel to part his hair, and of never appearing in society without a flower (preferably a gardenia) in his buttonhole.

"*M'ama . . . non m'ama . . .*" the prima donna sang, and "*M'ama!*", with a final burst of love triumphant, as she pressed the dishevelled daisy to her lips and lifted her large eyes to the sophisticated countenance of the little brown Faust–Capoul, who was vainly trying, in a tight purple velvet doublet and plumed cap, to look as pure and true as his artless victim.

Newland Archer, leaning against the wall at the back of the club box, turned his eyes from the stage and scanned the opposite side of the house. Directly facing him was the box of old Mrs. Manson Mingott, whose monstrous obesity had long since made it impossible for her to attend the Opera, but who was always represented on fashionable nights by some of the younger members of the family. On this occasion, the front of the box was filled by her daughter-in-law, Mrs. Lovell Mingott, and her niece, Mrs. Welland; and slightly withdrawn behind these brocaded matrons sat a young girl in white with eyes ecstatically fixed on the stage-lovers. As Madame Nilsson's "*M'ama!*" thrilled out above the silent house (the boxes always stopped talking during the Daisy Song) a warm pink mounted to the girl's cheek, mantled her brow to the roots of her fair braids, and suffused the young slope of her breast to the line where it met a modest tulle tucker fastened with a single gardenia. She dropped her eyes to the immense bouquet of lilies-of-the-valley on her knee, and Newland Archer saw her white-gloved finger-tips touch the flowers softly. He drew a breath of satisfied vanity and his eyes returned to the stage.

No expense had been spared on the setting, which was acknowledged to be very beautiful even by people who shared his acquaintance with the Opera Houses of Paris and Vienna. The foreground, to the footlights, was covered with emerald green cloth. In the middle distance symmetrical mounds of woolly green moss bounded by croquet hoops formed the base of shrubs shaped like orange-trees but studded with large pink and red roses. Gigantic pansies, considerably larger than the roses, and closely resembling the floral penwipers made by female parishioners for fashionable clergymen, sprang from the moss beneath the rose-trees; and here and there a daisy grafted on a rose-branch flowered with a luxuriance prophetic of Mr. Luther Burbank's far-off prodigies.

In the centre of this enchanted garden Madame Nilsson, in white cashmere slashed with pale blue satin, a reticule dangling from a side of her muslin chemisette, listened with downcast eyes to M. Capoul's impassioned wooing, and affected a guileless incomprehension of his designs whenever, by word or glance, he persuasively indicated the ground floor window of the neat brick villa projecting obliquely from the right wing.

"The darling!" thought Newland Archer, his glance flitting back to the young girl with the lilies-of-the-valley. "She doesn't even guess what it's all about." And he contemplated her absorbed young face with a thrill of possessorship in which pride in his own masculine initiation was mingled with a tender reverence for her abysmal purity. "We'll read Faust together . . . by the Italian lakes . . . " he thought, somewhat hazily confusing the scene of his projected honey-moon with the masterpieces of literature which it would be his manly privilege to reveal to his bride. It was only that afternoon that May Welland had let him guess that she "cared" (New York's consecrated phrase of maiden avowal), and already his imagination, leaping ahead of the engagement ring, the betrothal kiss and the march from Lohengrin, pictured her at his side in some scene of old European history.

He did not in the least wish the future Mrs. Newland Archer to be a simpleton. He meant her (thanks to his enlightening companionship) to develop a social tact and readiness of wit enabling her to hold her own with the most popular married women of the "younger set," in which it was the recognized custom to attract masculine homage while playfully discouraging it. If he had probed to the bottom of his vanity (as he sometimes nearly did) he would have found there the wish that his wife should be as worldly-wise and as eager to please as the married lady whose charms had held his fancy through two mildly agitated years; without, of course, any hint of the frailty which had so nearly marred that unhappy being's life, and had disarranged his own plans for a whole winter.

How this miracle of fire and ice was to be created, and to sustain itself in a harsh world, he had never taken the time to think out; but he was content to hold his view without analysing it, since he knew it was that of all the carefully-brushed, white-waistcoated, buttonhole-flowered gentlemen who succeeded each other in the club box, exchanged friendly greetings with him, and turned their opera-glasses critically on the circle of ladies who were the product of the system. In matters intellectual and artistic Newland Archer felt himself distinctly the superior of these chosen specimens of old New York gentility; he had probably read more, thought more, and even seen a good deal more of the world, than any other man of the number. Singly they betrayed their inferiority; but grouped together they represented "New York," and the habit of masculine solidarity made him accept their doctrine on all issues called moral. He instinctively felt that in this respect it would be troublesome—and also rather bad form—to strike out for himself.†

"BARREN GROUND"
Ellen Glasgow (1874–1945)

After he had gone, she lay there still shivering beneath the blankets, with her eyes on the low white ceiling, where the firelight made shimmering patterns. Outside, the wind grew louder. She heard it now at a distance, howling like a pack of wolves in the meadow. She heard it whistling round the eaves of the house and whining at the sills of the doors. All night the gusts shook the roof and the chimneys, and all night she lay there staring up at the wavering shadows of the flames.

And the youth that she had never had, the youth that might have been hers and was not, came back, in delusive mockery, to torment her. It was as if the sardonic powers of life assumed, before they vanished for ever, all the enchanting shapes of her dreams. She remembered the past, not as she had found it, but as she had once imagined that it might be. She saw Jason, not as she had seen him yesterday or last year, but as he was when she had first loved him. Though she tried to think of him as broken, ruined, and repellent, through some perversity of recollection, he returned to her in the radiance of that old summer. He returned to her young, ardent, with the glow of happiness in his eyes and the smile of his youth, that smile of mystery and pathos, on his lips. In that hour of memory the work of thirty years was nothing. Time was nothing. Reality was nothing. Success, achievement, victory over fate, all these things were nothing beside that imperishable illusion. Love was the only thing that made life desirable, and love was irrevocably lost to her.

Toward morning she fell asleep, and when she awoke at dawn the wind had lulled and a crystal light was flooding the room. Within herself also the storm was over. Life had washed over her while she slept, and she was caught again in the tide of material things. Rising from the couch she bathed and dressed and went out of doors into the clear flame of the sunrise.

Around her the earth smelt of dawn. After the stormy night the day was breaking, crisp, fair, windless, with the frost of a mirage on the distant horizon. The trees were bare overhead. Bronze, yellow, crimson and wine-colour, the wet leaves strewed the flagged walk and the grass. Against the eastern sky the boughs of the harp-shaped pine were emblazoned in gold.

Turning slowly, she moved down the walk to the gate, where, far up the road, she could see the white fire of the life-everlasting. The storm and the hag-ridden dreams of the night were over, and the land which she had forgotten was waiting to take her back to its heart. Endurance, Fortitude. The spirit of the land was flowing into her, and her own spirit,

strengthened and refreshed, was flowing out again toward life. This was the permanent self, she knew. This was what remained to her after the years had taken their bloom. She would find happiness again. Not the happiness for which she had once longed, but the serenity of mind which is above the conflict of frustrated desires. Old regrets might awaken again, but as the years went on, they would come rarely and they would grow weaker. "Put your heart in the land," old Matthew had said to her. "The land is the only thing that will stay by you." Yes, the land would stay by her. Her eyes wandered from far horizon to horizon. Again she felt the quickening of that sympathy which was deeper than all other emotions of her heart, which love had overcome only for an hour and life had been power-less to conquer in the end,—the living communion with the earth under her feet. While the soil endured, while the seasons bloomed and dropped, while the ancient, beneficent ritual of sowing and reaping moved in the fields, she knew that she could never despair of contentment.

Strange, how her courage had revived with the sun! She saw now, as she had seen in the night, that life is never what one dreamed, that it is seldom what one desired; yet for the vital spirit and the eager mind, the future will always hold the search for buried treasure and the possibilities of high adventure. Though in a measure destiny had defeated her, for it had given her none of the gifts she had asked of it, still her failure was one of those defeats, she realized, which are victories. At middle age, she faced the future without romantic glamour, but she faced it with integrity of vision. The best of life, she told herself with clear-eyed wisdom, was ahead of her. She saw other autumns like this one, hazy, bountiful in harvests, mellowing through the blue sheen of air into the red afterglow of winter; she saw the coral-tinted buds of the spring opening into the profusion of summer; and she saw the rim of the harvest moon shining orange-yellow through the boughs of the harp-shaped pine. Though she remembered the time when loveliness was like a sword in her heart, she knew now that where beauty exists the understanding soul can never remain desolate.†

"AH, WILDERNESS!"

Eugene O'Neill (1888–1954)

from Act IV, Scene III

MILLER. (*quietly but firmly now*) You better leave Richard and me alone for a while, Essie.

MRS. MILLER. (*turns to stare at him apprehensively*) Well—all right. I'll go sit on the piazza. Call me if you want me. (*Then a bit pleadingly*) But you'll remember all I've said, Nat, won't you? (*MILLER nods reassuringly. She disappears through the front parlor. RICHARD, keenly conscious of himself as the about-to-be-sentenced criminal by this time, looks guilty and a bit defiant, searches his father's expressionless face with uneasy side glances, and steels himself for what is coming.*)

MILLER. (*casually, indicating MRS. MILLER'S rocker*) Sit down, Richard. (*RICHARD slumps awkwardly into the chair and sits in a self-conscious, unnatural position. MILLER sizes him up keenly—then suddenly smiles and asks with quiet mockery*) Well, how are the vine leaves in your hair this evening?

RICHARD. (*totally unprepared for this approach—shamefacedly mutters*) I don't know, Pa.

MILLER. Turned out to be poison ivy, didn't they? (*Then kindly*) But you needn't look so alarmed. I'm not going to read you any temperance lecture. That'd bore me more than

Opposite: "But listen here, Richard, it's about time you and I had a serious talk . . ." George M. Cohan in Eugene O'Neill's *Ah, Wilderness!*

it would you. And, in spite of your damn foolishness last night, I'm still giving you credit for having brains. So I'm pretty sure anything I could say to you you've already said to yourself.

RICHARD. (*his head down—humbly*) I know I was a darned fool.

MILLER. (*thinking it well to rub in this aspect—disgustedly*) You sure were—not only a fool but a downright, stupid, disgusting fool! (*RICHARD squirms, his head still lower*) It was bad enough for you to let me and Arthur see you, but to appear like that before your mother and Mildred—! And I wonder if Muriel would think you were so fine if she ever saw you as you looked and acted then. I think she'd give you your walking papers for keeps. And you couldn't blame her. No nice girl wants to give her love to a stupid drunk!

RICHARD. (*writhing*) I know, Pa.

MILLER. (*after a pause—quietly*) All right. Then that settles—the booze end of it. (*He sizes RICHARD up searchingly—then suddenly speaks sharply*) But there is another thing, that's more serious . . . . (*After a quick, furtive glance at RICHARD, he nerves himself for the ordeal and begins with a shamefaced, self-conscious solemnity*) Listen here, Richard, it's about time you and I had a serious talk about—hmm—certain matters pertaining to— and now that the subject's come up of its own accord, it's a good time—I mean, there's no use in procrastinating further—so, here goes. (*But it doesn't go smoothly and as he goes on he becomes more and more guiltily embarrassed and self-conscious and his expressions more stilted. RICHARD sedulously avoids even glancing at him, his own embarrassment made tenfold more painful by his father's*) Richard, you have now come to the age when—Well, you're a fully developed man, in a way, and it's only natural for you to have certain desires of the flesh, to put it that way— I mean, pertaining to the opposite sex—certain natural feelings and temptations—that'll want to be gratified—and you'll want to gratify them. Hmm—well, human society being organized as it is, there's only one outlet for—unless you're a scoundrel and go around ruining decent girls—which you're not, of course. Well, there are a certain class of women—always have been and always will be as long as human nature is what it is— It's wrong, maybe, but what can you do about it? I mean, girls like that one you—girls there's something doing with—and lots of 'em are pretty, and it's human nature if you— But that doesn't mean to ever get mixed up with them seriously! You just have what you want and pay 'em and forget it. I know that sounds hard and un-feeling, but we're talking facts and— But don't think I'm encouraging you to— If you can stay away from 'em, all the better—but if—why—hmm— Here's what I'm driving at, Richard. They're apt to be whited sepulchres—I mean, your whole life might be ruined if—so, darn it, you've got to know how to— I mean, there are ways and means— (*Suddenly he can go no farther and winds up helplessly*) But, hell, I suppose you boys talk all this over among yourselves and you know more about it than I do. I'll admit I'm no authority. I never had anything to do with such women, and it'll be a hell of a lot better for you if you never do!

RICHARD. (*without looking at him*) I'm never going to, Pa. (*Then shocked indignation coming into his voice*) I don't see how you could think I could—now—when you know I love Muriel and am going to marry her. I'd die before I'd—— !

MILLER. (*immensely relieved—enthusiastically*) That's the talk! By God, I'm proud of you when you talk like that! (*Then hastily*) And now that's all of that. There's nothing more to say and we'll forget it, eh?

RICHARD. (*after a pause*) How are you going to punish me, Pa?

MILLER. I *was* sort of forgetting that, wasn't I? Well, I'd thought of telling you you couldn't go to Yale—

RICHARD. (*eagerly*) Don't I have to go? Gee, that's great! Muriel thought you'd want me to. I was telling her I'd rather you gave me a job on the paper because then she and I could get married sooner. (*Then with a boyish grin*) Gee, Pa, you picked a lemon. That isn't any punishment. You'll have to do something besides that.

354

MILLER. (*grimly—but only half concealing an answering grin*) Then you'll go to Yale and you'll stay there till you graduate, that's the answer to that! Muriel's got good sense and you haven't (*RICHARD accepts this philosophically*) And now we're finished, you better call your mother. (*RICHARD opens the screen door and calls "Ma," and a moment later she comes in. She glances quickly from son to husband and immediately knows that all is well and tactfully refrains from all questions.*)

MRS. MILLER. My, it's a beautiful night. The moon's way down low—almost setting. (*She sits in her chair and sighs contentedly. RICHARD remains standing by the door, staring out at the moon, his face pale in the moonlight.*)

MILLER. (*with a nod at RICHARD, winking at his wife*) Yes I don't believe I've hardly ever seen such a beautiful night—with such a wonderful moon. Have you, Richard?

RICHARD. (*turning to them—enthusiastically*) No! It was wonderful—down at the beach— (*He stops abruptly, smiling shyly.*)

MILLER. (*watching his son—after a pause—quietly*) I can only remember a few nights that were as beautiful as this—and they were long ago, when your mother and I were young and planning to get married.

RICHARD. (*stares at him wonderingly for a moment, then quickly from his father to his mother and back again, strangely, as if he'd never seen them before—then he looks almost disgusted and swallows as if an acrid taste had come into his mouth—but then suddenly his face is transfigured by a smile of shy understanding and sympathy. He speaks shyly*) Yes, I'll bet those must have been wonderful nights, too. You sort of forget the moon was the same way back then—and everything.

MILLER. (*huskily*) You're all right, Richard. (*He gets up and blows his nose.*)

MRS. MILLER. (*fondly*) You're a good boy, Richard. (*RICHARD looks dreadfully shy and embarrassed at this. His father comes to his rescue.*)

MILLER. Better get to bed early tonight, Son, hadn't you?

RICHARD. I couldn't sleep. Can't I go out on the piazza and sit until the moon sets?

MILLER. All right. Then you better say good night now. I don't know about your mother, but I'm going to bed right away. I'm dead tired.

MRS. MILLER. So am I.

RICHARD. (*goes to her and kisses her*) Good night, Ma.

MRS. MILLER. Good night. Don't you stay up till all hours now.

RICHARD. (*comes to his father and stands awkwardly before him*) Good night, Pa.

MILLER. (*puts his arm around him and gives him a hug*) Good night, Richard.†

"CHAMPION"

Ring Lardner (1885-1933)

A HERO

Midge picked up the stack of letters and postcards and glanced them over. From the pile he sorted out three letters and laid them on the table. The rest he tossed into the wastebasket. Then he picked up the three and sat for a few moments holding them, while his eyes gazed off into space. At length he looked again at the three unopened letters in his hand; then he put one in his pocket and tossed the other two at the basket. They missed their target and fell on the floor.

"Hell!" said Midge, and stooping over picked them up.

He opened the one postmarked Milwaukee and read:

Dear Husband:

I have wrote to you so many times and got no anser and I don't know if you ever got

355

them, so I am writing again in the hopes you will get this letter and anser. I don't like to bother you with my trubles and I would not only for the baby and I am not asking you should write to me but only send a little money and I am not asking for myself but the baby has not been well a day sence last Aug. and the dr. told me she can't live much longer unless I give her better food and thats impossible the way things are. Lou has not been working for a year and what I make dont hardley pay for the rent. I am not asking for you to give me any money, but only you should send what I loaned when convenient and I think it amts. to about $36.00. Please try and send that amount and it will help me, but if you can't send the whole amt. try and send me something.

Your Wife,

EMMA

Midge tore the letter into a hundred pieces and scattered them over the floor.

"Money, money, money!" he said. "They must think I'm made o' money. I s'pose the old woman's after it, too."

He opened his mother's letter:

dear Michael Connie wonted me to rite and say you must beet the dutchman and he is sur you will and wonted me to say we wont you to rite and tell us about it, but I guess you havent no time to rite or we herd from you long beffore this but I wish you would rite jest a line or 2 boy becaus it wuld be better for Connie then a barl of medisin. It wuld help me to keep things going if you send me money now and then when you can spair it but if you cant send no money try and fine time to rite a letter onely a few lines and it will please Connie. Jest think boy he hasent got out of bed in over 3 yrs. Connie says good luck.

Your Mother,

ELLEN F. KELLY

"I thought so," said Midge. "They're all alike."

The third letter was from New York. It read:

Hon:—This is the last letter you will get from me before your champ, but I will send you a telegram Saturday, but I can't say as much in a telegram as I am writeing this to let you know I am thinking of you and praying for good luck.

Lick him good hon and don't wait no longer than you have to and don't forget to wire me as soon as its over. Give him that little old left of yours on the nose hon and don't be afraid of spoiling his good looks because he couldn't be no homlier than he is. But don't let him spoil my baby's pretty face. You won't will you hon.

Well hon I would give anything to be there and see it, but I guess you love Haley better than me or you wouldn't let him keep me away. But when your champ hon we can do as we please and tell Haley to go to the devil.

Well hon I will send you a telegram Saturday and I almost forgot to tell you I will need some more money, a couple hundred say and you will have to wire it to me as soon as you get this. You will won't you hon.

I will send you a telegram Saturday and remember hon I am pulling for you.

Well good-bye sweetheart and good luck.

GRACE

"They're all alike," said Midge. "Money, money, money."†

"SPOON RIVER ANTHOLOGY"

Edgar Lee Masters (1869–1950)

LUCINDA MATLOCK

I went to the dance at Chandlerville,
And played snap-out at Winchester.
One time we changed partners,
Driving home in the moonlight of middle June,
And then I found Davis.
We were married and lived together for seventy years,
Enjoying, working, raising the twelve children,
Eight of whom we lost
Ere I had reached the age of sixty.
I spun, I wove, I kept the house, I nursed the sick,
I made the garden, and for holiday
Rambled over the fields where sang the larks,
And by Spoon River gathering many a shell,
And many a flower and medicinal weed—
Shouting to the wooded hills, singing to the green valleys.
At ninety-six I had lived enough, that is all,
And passed to a sweet repose.
What is this I hear of sorrow and weariness,
Anger, discontent and drooping hopes?
Degenerate sons and daughters,
Life is too strong for you—
It takes life to love Life.

"JOHN BROWN'S BODY"

Stephen Vincent Benét (1898–1943)

Invocation

American muse, whose strong and diverse heart
So many men have tried to understand
But only made it smaller with their art,
Because you are as various as your land,

As mountainous-deep, as flowered with blue rivers,
Thirsty with deserts, buried under snows,
As native as the shape of Navajo quivers,
And native, too, as the sea-voyaged rose.

Swift runner, never captured or subdued,
Seven-branched elk beside the mountain stream,
That half a hundred hunters have pursued
But never matched their bullets with the dream,

357

Where the great huntsmen failed, I set my sorry
And mortal snare for your immortal quarry.

You are the buffalo-ghost, the broncho-ghost
With dollar-silver in your saddle-horn,
The cowboys riding in from Painted Post,
The Indian arrow in the Indian corn,

And you are the clipped velvet of the lawns
Where Shropshire grows from Massachusetts sods,
The grey Maine rocks—and the war-painted dawns
That break above the Garden of the Gods.

The prairie-schooners crawling toward the ore
And the cheap car, parked by the station-door.

Where the skyscrapers lift their foggy plumes
Of stranded smoke out of a stony mouth
You are that high stone and its arrogant fumes,
And you are ruined gardens in the South

And bleak New England farms, so winter-white
Even their roofs look lonely, and the deep
The middle grainland where the wind of night
Is like all blind earth sighing in her sleep.

A friend, an enemy, a sacred hag
With two tied oceans in her medicine-bag

They tried to fit you with an English song
And clip your speech into the English tale.
But, even from the first, the words went wrong,
The catbird pecked away the nightingale.

The homesick men begot high-cheekboned things
Whose wit was whittled with a different sound
And Thames and all the rivers of the kings
Ran into Mississippi and were drowned.

They planted England with a stubborn trust.
But the cleft dust was never English dust.

Stepchild of every exile from content
And all the disavouched, hard-bitten pack
Shipped overseas to steal a continent
With neither shirts nor honor to their back.

Pimping grandee and rump-faced regicide,
Apple-cheeked younkers from a windmill-square,
Puritans stubborn as the nails of Pride,
Rakes from Versailles and thieves from County Clare,

The black-robed priests who broke their hearts in vain
To make you God and France or God and Spain.

These were your lovers in your buckskin-youth,
And each one married with a dream so proud
He never knew it could not be the truth
And that he coupled with a girl of cloud.

And now to see you is more difficult yet
Except as an immensity of wheel
Made up of wheels, oiled with inhuman sweat
And glittering with the heat of ladled steel.

All these you are, and each is partly you,
And none is false, and none is wholly true.

So how to see you as you really are,
So how to suck the pure, distillate, stored
Essence of essence from the hidden star
And make it pierce like a riposting sword.

For, as we hunt you down, you must escape
And we pursue a shadow of our own
That can be caught in a magician's cape
But has the flatness of a painted stone.

Never the running stag, the gull at wing,
The pure elixir, the American thing.†

Architecture

Architecture is worth great attention. As we double our number every twenty years we must double our houses. . . . It is, then, among the most important of arts; and it is desirable to introduce taste into an art which shows so much.

THOMAS JEFFERSON, 1788

In the following section are examples of American architecture in the eighteenth, nineteenth, and twentieth centuries, with excerpts from the writings of two outstanding pioneers in modern architecture: Louis Sullivan and Frank Lloyd Wright.

"AUTOBIOGRAPHY OF AN IDEA"
Louis Henry Sullivan (1856–1924)

. . . his conviction was this: That the architectural art to be of contemporary immediate value must be *plastic;* all senseless conventional rigidity must be taken out of it; it must intelligently serve—it must not supress. In this wise the forms under his hand would grow naturally out of the needs and express them frankly and freshly. This meant in his courageous mind that he would put to the test a formula he had evolved through long contemplation of living things, namely that *form follows function*, which would mean, in practice, that architecture might become a living art, if this formula were but adhered to.†

"AMERICAN ARCHITECTURE," 1953
Frank Lloyd Wright

Organic architecture is a new idea of what constitutes a building. It introduces wholly new values into building. An entirely new ethic—and esthetic—comes into life when the building is so conceived as intrinsic, as the result of the nature of materials, tools, situations, and the human beings it shelters. Wherever it is honestly built, you may see a new countenance, the countenance of truth emerging.

Architecture is primarily interior of the thing, not on it. It is not a dead aspect of style but style itself, bearing ever fresh form, like all living things in nature.

Only when art is indigenous, the work of a particular time, according to the nature and character of the people of that time, is it for all time. Our American civilization is only a way of life. Our culture would consist of means of making that way of life beautiful. Either we die without a culture of our own or we live by moving forward into a more beautiful concordant life than we now have.

Organic or truly American architecture emerged from the confusion of the sudden awakening of architecture as a new idea 60 years ago. The strength of the philosophy of a free, intrinsic or organic architecture is that it loves and cherishes these infinitely individual, human traditions of the great Tradition.

Because of our increased techniques, organic architecture could easily afford all nations new means of realization, on their own soil, along lines of character and development already peculiar to themselves. Whatever is really modern in architecture should, in this new view of reality, intensify the individualities of all nations, not strip them of the charm of their innate distinctions.

The "International Style" is nothing but the old architecture of the box with its face lifted.

Any box is more a coffin for the human spirit than an inspiration. The box dominates, constricts, and constrains the individual into something made fit only for collectivism. Its champions now declare dictatorially that the old box is *it*. This is their great gift to the world—their "style."

It is being more accidental than creative to mistake a disciplined sterility for austerity, mistake the plainness of bones or a barn door for simplicity (knowing nothing of real simplicity—the innate grace and significance of a wild flower). This is the mistake their promoters seem to make.

In their dubious champions, there is no sense of the depth called the third dimension. They operate on only two. Among these puppets of promotion, façades again become of uppermost importance. These façades all add up to the same thing—a cliché for tyros,

Opposite: Monticello, home of Thomas Jefferson, near Charlottesville, Virginia.

Eliot Elisofon

Monticello, illustrated on the previous page, was designed by Jefferson about 1767. It was built of stone, brick, and timber prepared on the estate. Actual construction was done by hired workers and his slaves. Jefferson moved into Monticello with his bride in 1772 and lived there over half a century.

Left: Louis Sullivan's famous Guaranty Trust Building, 1894–1895, in Buffalo, New York. Sullivan broke from the revival of classicism in his era and pioneered in designing steel-framed buildings that did not attempt to hide the structural skeletons.

Below: "Falling Water," Bear Run, Pennsylvania, designed by Frank Lloyd Wright, 1937.

teachers, and sycophants who crook the little finger and talk esthetics. Or by duped educators grasping something easy to teach, and approved as a foreign cult.

Sterilization is again mistaken for refinement. Provincial apostles of refinement name it "Classic," stupidly comparing it to frozen Greek classicism as though the ancient sterilization were a huge virtue. But the cause of great architecture, the great truth of building beautiful buildings beautifully according to the nature of architecture, is travestied by this superficial mimicry, that always seems to follow in the wake of great ideas.

The classic or camouflaged old post-and-lintel box is still practiced in the glassed-in cage or the glass-walled dwelling, both approved by these publicists and this latest procession of callow-professionals, now baptized "International." But this latest form of glassification is no true revolt, no actual dissidence.

Old Man Box merely looks different when glassified, that's all. The more the box is glassed, the more it becomes evident as a box. No new ideas whatever are involved as might easily be demonstrated by intelligent reference to the origin of their drawing-board façades. The old sham front has had its face lifted; the only change is merely one of outward appearance. It is a change of face, not of heart.

There are fresh ideas to be brought to life, if you learn to labor for them and are willing to work for them and wait. You must tire, as I do, of seeing these original forms merely renamed. All we have received from "internationalism," aside from the dropped coping, is merely: "Make the walls all glass, boys."

If as a nation we are to have our own richly humane culture, we must work for it. Unless we waken soon to the nature of the nation we designed, we will see no more of the creative architecture of creative architects.

Our "plan factories" and the factory-produced young architect emerging from college (now hanging by his eye-brows from sky-hooks or playing "jack-in-the-box" on bare sticks) seem to have found in this hangover—this negation—just what he needed to make the long labor of becoming an architect less long and arduous. Such architects are appearing only to disappear as our culture appears.

This servile recourse to a machine-made style parallels the malevolent rise of mediocrity now flooding what should be high places. The world we share in is not smaller than it used to be because of airships, atom bombs, and electrification. The world is larger now because more comprehensive, though less apprehended by us. As human beings, our view, both personal and national, comprises so much we never dreamed of before and do not seem to understand now. What merely existed for us before mechanization set in and "International Style" appeared as an expedient is a menace—a growing problem for our culture to solve.

These new facilities do not mean one world, but as many as there are civilizations! Too many? Perhaps. If so, it will be because we are not yet ready with our own?

If international co-operation is ever to come true, the need for solidarity of the independent nation and the individual grows immensely in importance. With the easy intercommunication we have already achieved, the strength of our native spirit is now more necessary than ever not only for the freedom of ourselves but the welfare of the entire world of worlds. †

Journalism: The Small-Town Newspaper

Americans are probably the most profusely "informed" people in the world. News is flashed to them hourly over radio and television, daily in the country's 2,009 daily newspapers, and in an endless stream of magazines. Freedom of the press is jealously guarded, and is expressed in the wide range of opinions exhibited in all these mediums. One way of illustrating this is to show it in action, through the editorials of an outstanding newspaperman:

Newsstands thrive on keeping Americans "profusely 'informed.' "

WILLIAM ALLEN WHITE (1868–1945)

William Allen White was born and spent most of his life in Kansas. One of the most respected newspapermen in the nation, he was often urged to run for public office, but chose to remain in his home town, running his own paper, feeling it was in this way that he could be most useful. The story of William Allen White is best seen through his own editorials, three of which follow:

"ENTIRELY PERSONAL"

From the first issue of the Emporia Gazette *under Mr. White's ownership, 1895*

To the gentle reader who may, through the coming years during which we are spared to one another, follow the course of this paper, a word of personal address from the new editor of *The Gazette* is due. In the first place, the new editor hopes to live here until he is the old editor, until some of the visions which rise before him as he dreams shall have come true. He hopes always to sign "from Emporia" after his name, when he is abroad, and he trusts that he may so endear himself to the people that they will be as proud of the first words of the signature as he is of the last words. He expects to perform all the kind offices of the country editor in this community for a generation to come. It is likely that he will write the wedding notices of the boys and girls in the schools; that he will announce the birth of the children who will some day honor Emporia, and that he will say the final words over those of middle age who read these lines. His relations with the people of this town and country are to be close and personal. He hopes that they may be kindly and just. The new editor of *The Gazette* is a young man now, full of high purposes and high ideals. But he needs the close touch of older hands. His endeavor will be to make a paper for the best people of the city. But to do that he must have their help. They must counsel with him, be his friends, often show him what their sentiment is. On them rests the responsibility somewhat. The "other fellows" will be around. They will give advice. They will attempt to show what the public sentiment is. They will try to work their schemes, which might dishonor the town. If the best people stay away from the editor's office, if they neglect to stand by the editor, they must not blame him for mistakes. An editor is not all wise. He judges only by what he sees and hears. Public sentiment is the only sentiment that prevails. Good sentiment, so long as it does not assert itself, so long as it is a silent majority, is only private sentiment. If the good, honest, upright, God-fearing, law-abiding people of any community desire to be reflected to the world, they must see that their private opinion is public opinion. . . .

It is a plain business proposition. The new editor of *The Gazette* desires to make a clean, honest local paper. He is a Republican and will support Republican nominees first, last, and all the time. There will be no bolting, no sulking, no "holier than thou" business about his politics—but politics is so little. Not one man in ten cares for politics more than two weeks in a year. In this paper, while the politics will be straight, it will not be obtrusive. It will be confined to the editorial page—where the gentle reader may venture at his peril. The main thing is to have this paper represent the average thought of the best people of Emporia and Lyon county in all their varied interests. The editor will do his best. He has no axes to grind. He is not running the paper for a political pull. If he could get an office he wouldn't have it. He is in the newspaper business as he would be in the drygoods business—to make an honest living and to leave an honest name behind. If the good people care for a fair, honest home paper, that will stand for the best that is in the town—here it is.

In the meantime, I shall hustle advertising, job work and subscriptions, and write editorials and "telegraph" twelve hours a day in spite of my ideals. The path of glory is barred hog tight for the man who does not labor while he waits †

"TO AN ANXIOUS FRIEND"*

July 27, 1922

You tell me that law is above freedom of utterance. And I reply that you can have no wise laws nor free enforcement of wise laws unless there is free expression of the wisdom of the people—and, alas, their folly with it. But if there is freedom, folly will die of its own poison, and the wisdom will survive. That is the history of the race. It is the proof of man's kinship with God. You say that freedom of utterance is not for time of stress, and I reply with the sad truth that only in time of stress is freedom of utterance in danger. No one questions it in calm days, because it is not needed. And the reverse is true also; only when free utterance is suppressed is it needed, and when it is needed, it is most vital to justice. Peace is good. But if you are interested in peace through force and without free discussion—that is to say, free utterance decently and in order—your interest in justice is slight. And peace without justice is tyranny, no matter how you may sugar-coat it with expediency. This state to-day is in more danger from suppression than from violence, because, in the end, suppression leads to violence. Violence, indeed, is the child of suppression. Whoever pleads for justice helps to keep the peace; and whoever tramples upon the plea for justice temperately made in the name of peace only outrages peace and kills something fine in the heart of man which God put there when we got our manhood. When that is killed, brute meets brute on each side of the line.

So, dear friend, put fear out of your heart. This nation will survive, this state will prosper, the orderly business of life will go forward if only men can speak in whatever way given

* Pulitzer Prize winning editorial.

them to utter what their hearts hold—by voice, by posted card, by letter or by press. Reason never has failed men. Only force and repression have made the wrecks in the world.

"FIFTY YEARS OF IT"

From the Emporia Gazette, *May 31, 1935*

This must be written in the first person singular for it is a personal story:

Sheer luck put me into the newspaper business. Fifty years ago June 1, 1885, I walked into the office of the El Dorado *Democrat* to take a job as printer's devil. Fifty years ago last week I was a student at the College of Emporia, living with John Morgan at the corner of Fifth and Congress, and I wrote three letters to El Dorado, my home town. One to George Tolle, who ran a grocery store there; one to Cass Friedburg, who ran a dry-goods store, and one to T. P. Fulton, asking each of them for a job. My mother was keeping boarders in El Dorado sending me to the College of Emporia, and after a year of it I didn't think it fitting and proper for a 17-year-old boy to let his mother keep boarders for him to go to college. Hence the letters. Hence the sheer luck that fated me. George Tolle and Cass Friedburg knew my desultory ways and rejected my job suggestion. T. P. Fulton knew my father and took a chance. So 50 years ago this week the El Dorado *Democrat*, a 4-page paper, on the third page fourth column, printed this item:

"Will A. White will take a position on the *Democrat* June 1st."

June 1st I walked into the office of the Butler County *Democrat*, took off my coat and vest, rolled up my sleeves and began the dirty work of a printer's devil. It was a little office. The boss was a printer. There was a foreman, one printer and the foreman's son, an apprentice. I did everything around the shop. I swept out, set type, helped to make up the forms, fed the big press and the job press, rustled up locals, clipped reprint for editorials when the boss was fishing, collected and knocked down the money which he owed me, when he was out of town. During the last two or three months I worked there in the winter of 1886, while the boss was away in Washington, I wrote a little editorial and got up the local copy for the paper. Ewing Herbert and I met in that printing office as boys and began a life-long friendship. When I came to Emporia again to re-enter the College of Emporia, after nine months' absence, I got a job setting type at piece work on the Emporia *News* on afternoons and Saturdays. A job known as a "sub." I made 85 cents the first afternoon and sometimes as little as 65 cents and once as much as $1.25. But work was irregular, and when J. M. McCown, editing the Emporia *Democrat* in the spring of 1886, offered me $3 a week for afternoons and Saturdays, I grabbed it. That May, 49 years ago, when Ewing Herbert, with whom I roomed in Emporia, left town, I got his job as reporter on the Emporia *News* and never went back to work in a printing office again.

But when I bought *The Gazette*, exactly 10 years later, June 1, 1895, I could do everything in that little 1-room office on Sixth Avenue that I asked anyone else to do. I could set type, put the paper to press, feed the press, kick the jobber, set the meager advertising that was used in those days, keep the books, solicit the advertising, take charge of the circulation, deliver the paper, solicit subscribers and run the bank account, such as it was. All these things I had learned in 10 years working in El Dorado, Lawrence, Topeka, Kansas City. I was 17 years old when I first picked up a printer's stick, 27 years old when I bought *The Gazette*.

Today, after 50 years in the business, I go into the back room of *The Gazette* office and instead of being familiar with every process and being able to do every mechanical thing necessary to print *The Gazette*, I can do practically nothing, though my hands retain their one-time printer's skill. But nothing in *The Gazette* office is done today as it was done 40 years ago. The type is set by machinery, the forms are not locked up as they were. Instead of being printed from type on sheets fed into a press, *The Gazette* is not printed from type, but from tubular, stereotyped plates from a continuous roll of paper. Four processes to which I am almost a stranger, now follow the copy from the printer to the reader.

Of the 25 men now engaged in the mechanical end of producing *The Gazette*, only three or four are old-fashioned, all-around printers who could set the type, make up the forms, put the paper to press, feed it and fold it in the old-fashioned way. So times have changed in 50 years.

Another thing, in the little paper where I learned what I know in my trade all the machinery that T. P. Fulton owned could have been bought for $750. When I bought *The Gazette* the material of the plant was estimated at $1,500—a high price. In those days any industrious young man who could save or talk a banker into lending $700 or $800 could go to Kansas City with that cash and come home with an outfit and start a newspaper. Ten times that amount would be needed today—and more, to pay for the machinery it takes to print *The Gazette*. Opportunity for youth is thus restricted by the machine age by the rise and dominance of capital in the world. And yet I am satisfied it is a much better world than it was 50 years ago. Justice abounds here in this town and country more abundantly than when I worked 12 hours a day and sometimes 14 as a cub printer in the office of the El Dorado *Democrat* for $1.50 a week and had to steal part of it to get it. When I came to Emporia as a proprietor I could hire a fairly good printer for $1 a day, and the day was 11 hours and often more without overtime. I didn't work hard enough to hurt me and I would do it over if I had to—and gladly even now. It has been a gorgeous adventure—life in these 50 years— happy, gay and free. Much anxiety, a little pain, many hours of sorrow, but through it all the self respect that makes for tolerance and understanding, for joy and for some semblance at least of usefulness; the net of which is happiness.

Fifty years ago Emporia was a little town, somewhere between five and ten thousand— the embryo of all that it is now. We have grown old together and the town has been good to me, charitable beyond my deserts, and I have tried to be loyal to the town. I have made many mistakes for which I am sincerely sorry. But I couldn't help it. I was that kind of a fool and have tried to profit by my mistakes, and I hope I have profited. Fifty years teach a man something. Anyway there they are, and here am I. And if I could have the health I have, the dear ones near me and if above and through all I could cherish in my heart the experience of my follies, I wouldn't mind another 50 years. As it is I fear life much more keenly than death. But I am ready to take greedily whichever comes.—W. A. W.†

Motion Picture and the Dance

MOTION PICTURES

Moving pictures in the United States are both an art form and a giant industry. Following the editor's historical outline of the beginnings of the industry are quotations from two pioneers who have done much to enhance the art of film-making in America:

EARLY DAYS

The moving picture was developed out of a long series of photographic experiments and inventions carried on in France, England, and America. It is generally agreed that the commercial development of films began when Thomas Edison patented the Kinetoscope in

1887. Celluloid-coated film invented by George Eastman and used by Edison in 1889 brought the peep show into being. The popularity of these shows was instantaneous.

Robert Paul in England and the Lumière brothers in France were working with combinations of Edison's Kinetoscope and the magic-lantern to project the peep show onto a screen so that it could be seen by audiences instead of being limited to a single viewer. Various devices came out of these efforts. In America, Thomas Armant's Vitascope finally became the property of the Edison Company and, with this machine, moving pictures were presented to the public in a variety house in 1896. Admission to early films was a nickel and the theaters in which they were shown became known as nickelodeons.

The first real attempt to tell a story by moving pictures came in 1903 with the showing of "The Great Train Robbery." For the next decade, story pictures continued to be shown in concert halls, variety houses, and nickelodeons. Film studios were erected, stock companies formed, stars were born, and one-reel melodramas and slapstick comedies drew capacity audiences. The motion picture industry grew with tremendous rapidity, but the best pictures began to come out of Europe.

In 1908 the first great American director, David Wark Griffith, entered the field. Stage actor, playwright, he started directing against his will when he was induced to make "The Adventures of Dolly" in 1908. Griffith was the first person to organize the scenario-manuscript. He recognized that films had potentialities quite different from those of plays and, through the use of new technical devices such as close-ups, fade-ins, and spectacular action shots, he brought new meaning to the making of films. When, in 1913, Italy sent over "Quo Vadis," the forerunner of all spectacular films since, David W. Griffith was ready. His answer to this Italian epic was "The Birth of a Nation."

Seymour Stern, in an article in *International Photographer*, April, 1935, says:

The picture with which significant cinematic history begins is David Wark Griffith's *The Birth of a Nation*. Aside from its signal artistic merit, the world-wide waves of purely external commotion which the picture stirred up form a teeming chapter in the annals of the Cinema. . . . With it the cinema became at one stroke a self-respecting art, and its first masterpiece was acclaimed by the critics. . . .

"D. W. GRIFFITH, AMERICAN FILM MASTER"
Iris Barry

Quoting "Billy" Bitzer, Griffith's cameraman, Miss Barry begins:

"*The Birth of a Nation* changed David Wark Griffith's personality entirely. Where heretofore he was wont to refer in starting on a new picture to 'grinding out another sausage' and go at it lightly his attitude in beginning on this one was all eagerness. He acted like here we have something worth while. . . . Personally I did not share the enthusiasm. . . ." [Miss Barry continues] However, cameraman and director were perfectly *en rapport;* Bitzer could tell by the look of the back of Griffith's head or a wiggling of his foot whether any given scene had gone well or not. The company was particularly well rehearsed, everyone flung himself into this new, unbelievably long and ambitious picture. Before it was over the money began to run out: Members of the cast and Bitzer chipped in. Griffith called for new and unheard of effects, he even wanted closeups of the flying feet of the mounts of the riding clansmen. Bitzer, down on the ground, did his best as the Klan advanced upon him in a cloud of dust, horses as well as riders half-blinded by flapping sheets. One side of the camera was kicked in, but Bitzer came through. The film was finished; it was cut; a special musical score had been composed for it; it was 12 reels long. . . . The film opened in New York at the Liberty Theatre at $2 a ticket. The most important single film ever made was thus given to the public. The response was overwhelming: people had not realized that they *could* be

368

The Birth of a Nation—"the picture with which significant cinematic history begins."—Seymour Stern

so moved by what, after all, is only a succession of photographs passed across a screen. All depends, they found, upon what is the order and manner of that passing. *The Birth of a Nation*, which had cost about $100,000 to make, grossed $18,000,000 in the next few years. Even more important, it established the motion picture once and for all as the most popular and persuasive of entertainments and compelled the acceptance of the film as art.†

GRIFFITH TELLS OF INNOVATIONS IN THE MOTION PICTURE ART

From the Cincinnati Tribune, *April 15, 1917*

David Wark Griffith, the producer of *The Birth of a Nation*, was recently telling about the sensation he caused in the old Biograph Studios in 14th Street, New York, when he invented the "close-up." " 'That will never do at all,' objected the studio manager. 'The actors look as if they were swimming. You can't have them float on, without legs or feet.' Nevertheless, I persisted and finally had my way, although I was still told that audiences kicked disapproval with their feet whenever the 'close-ups' were shown. Today the 'close-up' is essential to every motion picture, for the near view of the actors' lineaments conveys intimate thought and emotion that can never be conveyed in the crowded scene.

"I borrowed the 'cut-back' from Charles Dickens. Novelists think nothing of leaving one set of characters in the midst of affairs and going back to deal with earlier events, in which another set of characters is involved. I elaborated the 'cut-back' to the 'story within a story,' and to the so-called parallel action. I found that a picture could carry not merely

369

two, but even three or four simultaneous threads of action, all without in the least confusing the spectator.

"At one point in my latest drama four actions are represented simultaneously by the device of switching scenes every few moments. Each action heightens the effects of the other—a technique that so far as I am aware is absolutely novel in the story-telling art."

WALT DISNEY AND HIS ANIMATED WORLD

Cartoons, like fairy tales, are as old as the human race. The comic strip, forerunner of the animated cartoon, first found its place in America when the San Francisco Examiner *published James Swinnerton's "Little Bears and Tigers" in 1892. Thus the funnies had already become a part of the American scene when the movie industry began and it was only natural that the comic strip should be transplanted to the animated cartoon. Felix the Cat was among the first to achieve popularity in the new medium.*

Unquestionably, the chief exponent of animated cartoons has been Walt Disney. Born in Chicago in 1901, Disney was the youngest of five children. His Irish-Canadian father and German-American mother were constantly on the move and Disney never finished his high-school education. Too young to enlist in World War I, he joined the Red Cross as an ambulance driver. When the war was over, having made up his mind to become a cartoonist, he attended the Chicago Academy of Art. Answering an ad in the paper for a job with an advertising slide company, Disney had his first opportunity to experiment directly with the medium of the animated cartoon. His first effort, the Laugh-o'-grams, *were produced in 1920 and were along conventional lines.*

In 1923 he left the established field and moved to Hollywood to work on his own. The Disney Studio, according to reports, was started with a capital of $280—forty of his own and the rest contributed by his brother, Roy.

One of his earliest characters, Oswald the Rabbit, was taken from him by the producer who, following a common practice, bought the right of ownership and, when Disney was no longer under contract to him, had other artists and other studios carry on the adventures of this successful character. Disney, deprived of his rabbit, sought another figure to animate. He came up with a mouse.

Mickey Mouse made his debut in October, 1928, in "Steamboat Willie."

SPEAKING OF HIS WORK, WALT DISNEY SAYS:

Every good play or picture has a lesson to teach, a moral to apply. That's been true of fables since Aesop and of plays since Shakespeare. That's why writers have always insisted the stage—and now the screen—is truly and effectively a moral force.

What's the sense of making a picture unless you've got something important to say? The trick is to say it without preaching. Say it in terms of entertainment. . . .

Some people are still fooled by the sound and the meaning of the words "fable," "fairy tale," "legend," and "folk tale." These stories, the ones that have survived, are apt to be packed solid with the wisdom of the ages. Properly screened, they can be as powerful as any force on earth to form opinion and judgment and tolerance and neighborliness. So can original fables with the same ingredients. . . .

Every normal person, I have found, reacts to the beauty of honest human drama, of color and music and imaginative transports properly presented.

The difficult art of making cartoons calls for the combined talents of a vast number of craftsmen. It is through countless conferences that they work out the details of music, sound effects,

Gone with the Wind represents another of the great achievements of the film industry. Based on Margaret Mitchell's novel of the same name, this epic of the South in the 1860's was released in 1939. It has won virtually every award ever presented for film artistry.

Walt Disney's "Mickey Mouse."
Above: sketch for *Fantasia.*

story ideas, choreography and synchronization. The excerpt that follows is taken from an actual conference on one of Walt Disney's outstanding feature-length films:

STORY CONFERENCE ON "FANTASIA"

WALT

At first, ripples coming up. I like an indefinite effect here. (Suggests that tambourines be added to music.)

I say these are the backgrounds, and we have to find the action.

I think the fish peeking around should be in the beginning. Then, when you go through the grotto, there should be a regular festival—a ballet of fish—all to that slow Arabian music. All the undergrowth has a slow, wavy rhythm to the slow beats.

You've seen travelogues where they take you into a harem. As you go through the courtyard, veiled ladies peek through the windows and duck back. If the cameraman wants to get a picture, they run away. Two girls peek out and see a stranger and giggle and get back to cover. These fish are beautiful, lazy things—very feminine and sexy—even going further than with the sketches. There is a natural hootchy-kootchy motion to a goldfish that can be made use of here.

J

We come to one fish unexpectedly, and it gives a quick turn.

WALT

Then when we come into the grotto—there is a ballet, using the bubble dance idea. They are all doing a certain routine, letting out a lot of bubbles as they come together. We can finish with a lot of bubbles, and follow them up to—the thistles.

As it is now, you lead up to nothing. A mysterious atmosphere and the little fish peeking around should be the beginning—then the bubble dance ballet.

372

R

Would you like the idea of having the fish, as you say, in the early part, and then have a different thing in the grotto—maybe fairy sprites or water sprites?

WALT

We have these cute little goldfish to use. There are fairy sprites at the end.

D

We could have voluptuous ones—tails and spangles—and black ones, too.

R

I have some interesting models.

WALT

White and black goldfish might be very effective in there. The black ones are the ones that fascinate you. They would be effective against any color in the background. Maybe, if you had a ballerina, she could be a gold one in the center.

J

I especially like the sketch with the blue background. Its position is a little more fishy. There is a swell chance for doing something beautiful with these goldfish.†

THE DANCE IN AMERICA*
Agnes de Mille, Dancer, Choreographer

Four influences have shaped dancing as an art form in America—the indigenous American Indian, the African Negro, the Western European folk forms, and the European theatrical or ballet tradition.

Since the basis for all theatrical or art dancing is understandably a people's social expression, it follows that our theatrical styles rest firmly on the English and French country dances imported by early Colonists. With these immigrants came also a taste for ballet spectacle and court dancing. But lacking the means to develop, lacking all schools, theaters, and endowed institutions, creative dancing lay dormant until the end of the 19th century. For two hundred years, our citizens had to be content with simple social dancing, minstrel shows and a very few distinguished foreign visitors.

Our greatest indigenous source of inspiration, the American Indian, is and has been all but insensible. This is a pity but quite explicable: racially and culturally the Indians had nothing in common with their white neighbors except shared hunger and gunpowder—a tenuous relationship on which to build any art expression. But the Indians have been of mighty importance as a point of reference. The pueblo and plains tribes have maintained the necessity and form of their dances for several thousand years. They remind us of what we have entirely lost from our culture—dancing as a serious practice of the men of the community, dancing as magic, dancing as worship, and as a vital function in life beyond the mere requisites of courtship.

The enormous influx of the alien and powerful African aesthetic during the seventeenth

* Original article. This brief history necessarily omits many contemporary artists.

and eighteenth centuries, the Negroes' persistent and persuasive contribution to music and their reliance on rhythm in all work and play has grafted a characteristic rhythm-syncopation on our main dancing forms that has heightened and perverted them forever. It was the subtle African footwork applied to the Irish clog (jigs and reels) that produced buck and wing and tap dancing. It was the African body pulse and frank sexuality that turned the waltz into our current ballroom form. Every ten years or so from the slums, the wharves, the Negro ghettos and impalements comes a new original contribution to our folk vocabulary—the Rag, the Charleston, the Lindy-hop, the Black Bottom, the Jitterbug, the Shag, the Susie Q, the Big Apple. These are as original and as expressive as the gavotte, the minuet or the waltz, but their most unusual aspect is the rapidity with which they develop. The English and French required 250 years to change the Elizabethan volta to the waltz. This exuberant and prolific people produce each decade a new form. No other racial group boils up constantly in such rich spontaneous gesture.

The basic forms, the mother forms on which these influences have played are, of course, the transplanted dances of Europe, most particularly those of England and Ireland. Old English longways and round country dances produced the Southern Mountain running sets and the Southwestern squares. These are almost identical with their prototypes except for two American characteristics: the tempo and the noise. Every race of people that has lived on this continent, anthropologists tell us, has been nervous, restless and explosive in expression. American dances are raced like no dances in Europe. They are frequently stamped and clapped and shouted by the women as well as the men and the dance masters' calls, simple instructions in Europe, are here developed into a humorous lyric comment shouted or whined at unbroken speed not only to cue the performers but to throw caustic and spicy insight into the manners of the community.

Our theater's history has been far less spontaneous. In 1842, the Viennese ballet star, Fanny Elssler, made a tour of the Eastern states and astonished everyone. Indeed she was probably the first great dancing artist ever seen on this continent. She found not even a legend to compete with. Audiences responded with rapture. Although she came with only two assistants and used a scratch group she picked up and rehearsed after arrival, a circumstance the professional mind quails to envisage, the members of Congress went so far as to unhorse her carriage and pull her through the streets of Washington. In 1865, a very young ballerina, Maria Bonfanti, came with her Italian troup to dance in "The Black Crook" at Niblo's Garden and thereafter there were visiting continental performers of varying rotundity and merit. When finally the Metropolitan Opera was formed, something resembling a resident company of trained ballet dancers with a ballet school attached could be organized. Now at last one was. America, however, was a Puritan country and the forming of an opera ballet elicited no very great respect or faith. The results could have been foretold: nothing creative has come from this source, no works, no school, no great performers. The Metropolitan Ballet has always been fourth-rate and in all the years of its existence has produced from within itself neither great dancer nor choreographer. In fact the attitude toward dancing in all musical circles here has been one of unmodified and continuing condescension. Although the popular theater, which one might have hoped would have been more productive, welcomed foreign virtuosi of sorts, it remained for half a century on the minstrel-show or vaudeville level and developed no first-class creative talent.

Nevertheless, in the current century, America has led the world in a true renaissance of dancing. Four American soloists, Isadora Duncan, Ruth St. Denis, Martha Graham, and Doris Humphrey, have successively started revolutions that have influenced all forms of creative dancing and all choreographic endeavor. Although their achievements are independent and vastly different, they do have points in common: they are all women; they broke outright with tradition; they worked alone without theater, school, or patronage behind

Indian dog dance.

Above: Martha Graham. *Below:* Ballet is incorporated into the American theater. Rodgers and Hammerstein's *Oklahoma!* Choreography, Agnes de Mille.

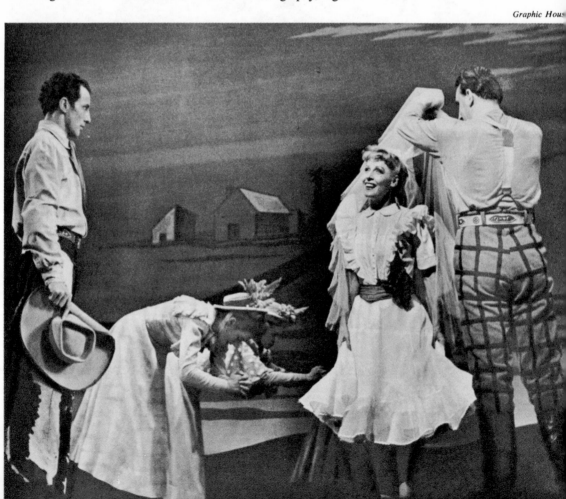

them; they approached dancing not as entertainment but as creative expression; they considered dancing as an independent art in itself and not as a supplementary or complementary adjunct to other theater forms. They were wild-catters in a country of pioneers that valued its women and encouraged pioneers. This made their achievement possible. This perhaps explains why it has been American women and not European that have led the dance.

Duncan was the first and in many ways the most climactic figure. She did not, as is popularly supposed, discover a new type of dance nor yet revive an ancient. Her style has been called Greek simply because she chose to wear Greek tunics and referred always, when speaking, to classic sources. But her idiom was no more Greek than anything else. It was her own personal idiom of expression and for this reason it has proved ephemeral except as an influence. Her achievement was a point of view. She left no vocabulary, no works, no creative school. Her contribution was a clearing away of the accumulated debris of six hundred years of artificiality. Alone she jettisoned the entire code of ballet technique, a fabrication of centuries' effort. She rediscovered the human walk, the run, the easy natural spring and jump, the emotional use of head and arms and hands. She brought the foot once more into contact with the earth. She bared the limbs so that one might see not so much naked body as revealed emotion. She refound spontaneity and individual passion. She was to her art what Luther was to Christianity—a challenging. She questioned. In an art that had been scorned and degraded for generations, she insisted on passion and purpose. She went back to beginnings.

After her and directly in response to her influence came Diaghileff, Pavlova, and Nijinsky and the overwhelming impact of the new Russian Ballet on Western Europe—a transforming experience the like of which our theater had never known before. After her came Dalcroze, the Weisenthal sisters, and the interest in expressive dancing that led to the Middle European rebirth which flowered in Mary Wigman's great school.

In less important matters, Duncan's influence has been vital—the exchange of lights and curtains for painted décor called upon the imagination of the audience and departed thereby from the European tradition of spectacle toward the classic or oriental tradition of symbolism. The exchange of great music for the sugar-water prettiness of Delibes and Tchaikowsky made possible serious and basic themes.

Ruth St. Denis was not perhaps so great an innovator, but her influence has been strong. She brought to our attention the ritual and symbolic dances of the Far East and she reminded us what we had long forgotten: that dancing is the handmaiden of religion. Because of her greater theatricality, her influence was more readily acceptable and her imitators more numerous and flighty. Her work could be easily commercialized, and was on a wholesale scale. Duncan's could not be so successfully. When not sublime, Duncan's style proved to be silly—not to say intolerable—good only for therapy and the releasing of adolescent doubts. St. Denis was seen by more people in this country than any other dancer, possibly excepting Anna Pavlowa. (Duncan was not generally popular except among the intellectuals.) And St. Denis it was who made widely acceptable the brand new notion that dancing was not the function of expensive prostitutes but the work of artists.

Doris Humphrey, whom many critics consider our finest choreographer, was a pupil of St. Denis. Her style, however, derives very little from the early Oriental influences. Her style is lyric rather than dramatic and stresses always form rather than drama. She has experimented in pure dance: that is, nonstorytelling compositions of movement and in works of considerable scope and length. In a sense she can be considered our first symphonist.

But the great lasting contribution to our art has been made unquestionably by Martha Graham. Graham is an unsurpassed performer recalling to many Eleanore Duse at her zenith. It is, however, her creative achievements that are most noteworthy. Firstly, her works must be reckoned among the masterpieces of our time. Beyond this, however, and possibly of more lasting importance is her expansion of dance technique. She has not merely developed traditional exercises; she has invented whole new techniques of leverage, elevation, and bodily dynamics. Graham's discoveries are already fusing with classic ballet and absorbing into the styles of the younger generation. They have got, so to speak, into the blood stream and will undoubtedly influence all dancing for generations hence. It is the most inventive enlarging of dance idiom by any single individual in the history of the western theater.

Her subject matter is serious and challenging, her décor and use of music experimental in the most provocative sense. In fact her influence on all aspects of our theater, though generally unrecognized, has been incalculable. It is interesting to note that she is the first dancer to make creative use of Amerindian styles and sources.

Like St. Denis and Duncan, she is a great teacher. Her pupils number the leading performers and choreographers of the new generation. Her pupils have in turn become teachers and are found in most of the women's colleges training pupils to form a demanding audience and to form intelligent criticism, both requisites to the growth of any art. It is characteristic of the pupils of both Humphrey and Graham that they tend to be creative as few ballet pupils are. Accordingly there is a composing activity now in all fields of the contemporary nonballetic dance never before evinced.

Unlike any other institution is the theater of Katharine Dunham. Dunham is an enchanting performer and a superb craftsman rather than an inventive creative choreographer. But she has brought to our attention the wealth of Negro idiom from all over the United States and the Caribbean Islands, and she has opened the doors of the American concert stage to the members of her race. Serious Negro dancers now have a place to perform where fifteen years ago they had none.

The growth of the ballet here has been less spontaneous. Imported ballet teachers and visiting companies recruited native talent along patterns codified in Europe. Decades passed before native creators emerged and these showed clearly the influence of strong Russian-Parisian training coupled with the styles of their great native predecessors. In the twenties Michael Fokine, of the Imperial Russian and Diaghileff ballets, opened a school in New York and girls and boys could get really first-class technical training for the first time. And they became superb technicians—their strength and virtuosity is an international byword. In the thirties the de Basil Ballet Russe de Monte Carlo began annual tours and schools and companies sprouted everywhere like mushrooms.

There are now several American ballet companies, two first-class ones, as good as anything in Europe, the City Center, developed from the earlier American Ballet Company, and Ballet Theatre. City Center ballet has provided a first-class repertoire and theater for able dancers, a school and a standard of the highest order, all badly needed in a country which has yet to establish any kind of national lyric theater.

Ballet Theatre on the other hand is heterogenous and indigenous. A large group of choreographers are represented, classic and modern, some young ones for the first time. A new type of ballet has been there initiated and matured. In fact nearly every good performing and designing talent has during the last fifteen years passed through Ballet Theatre which boasts, in my opinion, the most stimulating and representative repertoire of any current company.

An interesting development, although a minor one, has been the transforming, during the last ten years, of popular theater dancing into an art form. This is the only country in which major talents work in the musical comedy field. As a result choreography and therefore performance, as well as designing and musical arranging, are on a high level. Lacking any endowed institutions, the serious artists must rely on the popular theater for their living— and in exchange they give in all branches of the dance department polish and fervor that the popular theaters of Europe do not boast. This is becoming increasingly true of motion pictures also. With the development of the 3-D screen, it is to be hoped that the genius of our greatest choreographers will be tempted. Television is still very tentative but it could prove a rich field of discovery and achievement.

The main contribution of America, however, remains—and most gloriously—not so much individual compositions as completely new idoms and vocabularies, new styles and new, or rather old and deeply respected, approaches. That it can now be considered a serious expressive art and that its chief practitioners are women of dignity, probity, intellect, and passion, that these women attract about them as co-workers serious and impassioned men is due largely to four pioneers. The next generation owes them much. They may serve the art with a critical standard and above all with a hope never held by dancers before.

TEN

As

Others See Us

"*O wad some Power the giftie gie us*
To see oursels as ithers see us!
It wad frae mony a blunder free us,
An' foolish notion . . ."

ROBERT BURNS

As Others See Us

To George Bernard Shaw is attributed the aphorism that England and America are two countries separated by the same language. Various opinions on Americans follow:

DR. SAMUEL JOHNSON, 1769

They are a race of convicts and ought to be thankful for any thing we allow them short of hanging.

A REMARKABLE PROPHECY, 1835
"DEMOCRACY IN AMERICA"
Alexis de Tocqueville

There are at the present time two great nations in the world, which started from different points, but seem to tend towards the same end. I allude to the Russians and the Americans. Both of them have grown up unnoticed; and while the attention of mankind was directed elsewhere, they have suddenly placed themselves in the front rank among the nations, and the world learned their existence and their greatness at almost the same time.

All other nations seem to have nearly reached their natural limits, and they have only to maintain their power; but these are still in the act of growth. All the others have stopped, or continue to advance with extreme difficulty; these alone are proceeding with ease and celerity along a path to which no limit can be perceived. The American struggles against the obstacles that nature opposes to him; the adversaries of the Russian are men. The former combats the wilderness and savage life; the latter, civilization with all its arms. The conquests of the American are therefore gained by the plowshare; those of the Russian by the sword. The Anglo-American relies upon personal interest to accomplish his ends and gives free scope to the unguided strength and common sense of the people; the Russian centers all the authority of society in a single arm. The principal instrument of the former is freedom; of the latter, servitude. Their starting-point is different and their courses are not the same; yet each of them seems marked out by the will of Heaven to sway the destinies of half the globe.†

"DOMESTIC MANNERS OF THE AMERICANS," 1832
Mrs. Frances Trollope

In relating all I know of America, I surely must not omit so important a feature as the cooking. . . . I am hardly capable, I fear, of giving a very erudite critique on the subject; general observations, therefore, must suffice. The ordinary mode of living is abundant, but not delicate. They consume an extraordinary quantity of bacon. Ham and beef-steaks appear morning, noon, and night. In eating, they mix things together with the strangest incongruity imaginable. I have seen eggs and oysters eaten together; the sempiternal ham with apple-sauce; beef-steak with stewed peaches; and salt fish with onions. The bread is everywhere excellent, but they rarely enjoy it themselves, as they insist upon eating horrible half-baked hot rolls both morning and evening. . . .

I never saw turbot, salmon, or fresh cod; but the rock and shad are excellent. There is a great want of skill in the composition of sauces; not only with fish but with everything. They use very few made dishes, and I never saw any that would be approved by our savants. They have an excellent wild duck, called the Canvas Back, which, if delicately served, would surpass the black cock; but the game is very inferior to ours; they have no hares, and I never saw a pheasant. . . . Almost every one drinks water at table, and by a strange contradiction, in the country where hard drinking is more prevalent than in any other, there is less wine taken at dinner; ladies rarely exceed one glass, and the majority of females never take any. In fact, the hard drinking, so universally acknowledged, does not take place at jovial dinners, but, to speak in plain English, in solitary dram-drinking. . . .

Their large evening parties are supremely dull; the men sometimes play cards by themselves, but if a lady plays, it must not be for money; no ecarté, no chess; very little music, and that little lamentably bad. Among the blacks I heard some good voices, singing in tune; but I scarcely ever heard a white American, male or female, go through an air without being out of tune before the end of it; nor did I ever meet any trace of science in the singing I hear in society. To eat inconceivable quantities of cake, ice, and pickled oysters—and to show half of their revenue in silks and satins seems to be the chief objects they have in these parties.†

"THE AMERICAN MAN," 1887
Oscar Wilde

One of the prettiest Duchesses enquired the other day of a distinguished traveller whether there was really such a thing as an American man, explaining, as the reason for her question, that, though she knew many fascinating American women, she had never some across any fathers, grandfathers, uncles, brothers, husbands, cousins, or indeed, male relatives of any kind whatsoever.

The exact answer the Duchess received is not worth recording, as it took the depressing form of useful and accurate information; but there can be no doubt that the subject is an extremely interesting one, pointing, as it does, to the curious fact that, as far as society is concerned, the American invasion has been purely female in character. . . no American man has any social existence in London. His women-folk, with their wonderful dresses, and still more wonderful dialogue, shine in our *salons*, and delight our dinner-parties . . . but the poor American man remains permanently in the background, and never rises beyond the level of tourist. . . . With a *naïveté* and a nonchalance that are absolutely charming, he will gravely compare St. James' Palace to the Grand Central depot at Chicago, or Westminster Abbey to the Falls of Niagara. Bulk is his canon of beauty, and size his standard of excellence. To him the greatness of a country consists in the number of square miles that it contains; and he is never tired of telling the waiters at his hotel that the state of Texas is larger than France and Germany put together.

Yet, on the whole, he is happier in London than anywhere else in Europe. Here he can always make a few acquaintances, and, as a rule, can speak the language. Abroad he is terribly at sea. . . . For him Art has no marvel, and Beauty no meaning, and the Past no message. He thinks that civilization began with the introduction of steam, and looks with contempt upon all centuries that had no hot-water apparatuses in their houses. The ruin and decay of Time has no pathos in his eyes. He turns away from Ravenna, because there is rust on her balconies. His one desire is to get the whole of Europe into thorough repair. . . . Finally, having looked at everything, and seen nothing, he returns to his native land.

There he is delightful. For the strange thing about American civilization is, that the women are most charming when they are away from their own country, the men most charming when they are at home.

At home, the American man is the best of companions, as he is the most hospitable of hosts. . . . They know men much better than they know books, and life interests them more than literature. They have no time to study anything but the stock markets, no leisure to read anything but newspapers. . . . Yet, though these cute young speculators may not have culture, in the sense in which we use it, as the knowledge of the best that has been thought and said in the world, they are by no means dull. There is no such thing as a stupid American. . . . Indeed, in America there is no opening for a fool. They expect brains even from a boot-black, and get them. . . .

On the whole, then, the American man at home is a very worthy person. There is just one point in which he is disappointing. American humor is a mere travellers' tale. It has no real existence. Indeed, so far from being humorous, the male American is the most abnormally serious creature who ever existed. . . . He has always been prudent, always practical, and pays a heavy penalty for having committed no mistakes. It is only fair to admit that he can exaggerate; but even his exaggeration has a rational basis. It is not founded on wit or fancy; it does not spring from poetic imagination; it is simply an earnest attempt on the part of language to keep pace with the enormous size of the country. . . .

Yet, though the American man may not be humorous, he is certainly humane. . . . If the English girl ever met him, she would marry him; and if she married him, she would be happy. For, though he may be rough in manner, and deficient in the picturesque insincerity of romance, yet he is invariably kind and thoughtful, and has succeeded in making his own country the Paradise of Women.

This, however, is perhaps the reason why, like Eve, the women are always so anxious to get out of it.†

BUSINESS, 1928

"THROUGH BRITISH EYES"

J. Alfred Spender

. . . In England business is still for the most part an individual occupation in which each man does his best to win bread for his family and leisure for himself. In America it is a movement. "The business of America is business" is a saying attributed to President Coolidge, and as an Englishman looks at it, the entire country seems to be mobilized for the winning of an industrial war. . . . All the newspapers, all the means of publicity and advertisement, even the Government itself seem to be commandeered for and concentrated on an industrial campaign which is broadly conceived as a national effort. . . . Men and women live so much in the future that they seem to have little time either to savor the present or to reflect on the past; they dislike solitude and do everything in common. The Englishman sees an immense gregariousness contrasting with the scattered, individual, private life of his own country; and everybody and everything being carried along on a high tide of confident expectation, which is in still greater contrast with the ebbing spirits of some parts of Europe.

But of course this movement has its casualties, though they may be veiled in the dazzling generalized impression which the traveler brings away with him. The pace is too quick for some and especially for the unacclimatized newcomers. The incessant scrapping of old things and substitution of new, the unceasing search for new labor-saving devices involve a constant displacement which at any given moment and even in times of prosperity mean unemployment and poverty for large numbers. . . . Here the race is to the swift, and for them the constant moving on and the sense of unlimited possibilities, with the attendant risks and chances, are what give spice, savor and color to life. For all these America is uniquely the country of equal opportunity. . . .

It follows that the great men of the United States are the big businessmen, not the politicians. When a committee of American professors and literary men is asked to name the

The American invasion has been purely female in character."—Oscar Wilde

greatest man in the world, it puts Mr. Henry Ford high on the list, but names not a single politician or statesman. It must be said that the businessmen take their position seriously as leading citizens. They play a leading part in all public enterprises of a constructional kind; they give munificently to charity, and endow universities, museums, and art galleries on a scale unknown in any other country. In all this they show an admirable social instinct and make the readiest acknowledgment of the duty which wealth owes to the community. But one thing they will not do, or do very reluctantly, and that is to take an active part in the government and administration of the country.

The onlooker gets the impression, therefore, that far too little of the brains and character of the country is going into its public affairs. . . . Taking the country as a whole, there is no large body of men who can be relied upon to make a career in either Federal, state or municipal politics a steady object of ambition from their youth upwards. For lack of these the bosses and machine politicians who have their ears to the ground (and sometimes their noses in the mud) obtain inordinate power. . . .

Undoubtedly the American scene is puzzling to the stranger who tries to get a consistent picture of the whole. The national virtues are immense but they seldom run through the whole of national life. A breathless futurism in industry goes with a stubborn reluctance to change in politics; the utmost economy in production with an amazing prodigality in consumption. While the manufacturer is making a science of thrift in the workshop, the salesman is all the time discouraging thrift in the household. But the moralist who tries to draw edifying conclusions from either virtues or faults will constantly find himself baffled. He goes to a city which is a by-word for corrupt government and finds there schemes of town planning and public improvements which might be the envy of the best-governed municipality in Europe. Conditions of disorder, which would be thought intolerable in Europe, exist side by side with a prosperous and refined way of life and seem to cause it no inconvenience. The majority of Americans seem to be convinced that if only they stick to business, every thing else will cure itself. . . .†

AN AUSTRIAN VIEWS US WITH ALARM, 1873
Baron von Hubner

From "This Was America," edited by Oscar Handlin

If we, children of old Europe, who cling to the present as the logical natural continuation of the past, who cherish old recollections, traditions, and habits, if we do homage to your success, obtained under institutions which, on all essential points, are contrary to ours, this is a proof of our impartiality. For let us not deceive ourselves, America is the born antagonist of Europe. . . .

All the world admires you. But all the world does not love you. Those among us who judge you from an exclusively European point of view see in you nothing but enemies of the fundamental principles of society. The more they appreciate your work, the more, in fact, they admire, the less they like you. I should add that they fear you. They dread your success as a dangerous example to Europe, and as far as they can they try to stop the spread of your ideas. But they are a minority.

Your friends are more numerous. They see in you the prototype and the last fruits of civilization, and they desire to transform themselves after your example. There is a third class, those who are resigned; their opinion is the widest spread. Although they do not like you, they are willing to submit to you; to submit to your principles, your habits, your institutions. They believe that Europe will become Americanized, fatally, but inevitably.

As for me, I share neither these hopes nor these fears. I maintain that these fears, these

" 'The business of America is business' is a saying attributed to President
Coolidge, and as an Englishman looks at it, the entire country seems to
be mobilized for the winning of an industrial war."—J. Alfred Spender

hopes, this blind faith in imaginary decrees of Providence are founded on an imperfect knowledge of America, and of the fundamental differences between the Old World and the New.

Compared to Europe, your country is as a sheet of white paper. Everything has to be begun; everything is new. . . .

How choose as a model a thing which is incomplete? You are at the growing age; your are not yet fully formed.

What will you be when you have come to maturity? You do not know and no one can predict, for history offers no example of such a genesis. What new race will spring from this mixture of Celts, Germans, and Mongols? We cannot tell, no one can, we only know that a great change will result. . . .†

FOOTBALL AS SEEN BY A FRENCHMAN, 1895
"OUTRE-MER"
Paul Bourget

. . . Even in his diversions the American is too active and too self-willed. Unlike the Latin, who amuses himself by relaxation, he amuses himself by intensity, and this is the case whatever be the nature of his amusements. . . .

Among the distractions of sport, none has been more fashionable for several years past than football. . . .

It is a fearful game, which by itself would suffice to indicate the difference between the Anglo-Saxon and the Latin world—a game of young bull-dogs brought up to bite, to rush upon the quarry; the game of a race made for wild attack, for violent defence, for implacable conquests and desperate struggles. . . . At each extremity of the field is a goal, representing, at the right end, one of the teams, at the left, the other. The entire object is to throw an enormous leather ball, which the champion of one or the other side holds in turn. It is in waiting for this throw that all the excitement of the almost ferocious amusement is concentrated. He who holds the ball is there, bent forward, his companions and his adversaries likewise bent down around him in the attitude of beasts of prey about to spring. All of a sudden he runs to throw the ball, or else with a wildly rapid movement he hands it to another, who rushes off with it. All depends on stopping him.

The roughness with which they seize the bearer of the ball is impossible to imagine without having witnessed it. He is grasped by the middle of the body, by the head, by the legs, by the feet. He rolls over and his assailants with him, and as they fight for the ball and the two sides come to the rescue, it becomes a heap of twenty-two bodies tumbling on top of one another, like an inextricable knot of serpents with human heads. This heap writhes on the ground and tugs at itself. One sees faces, hair, backs, or legs appearing in a monstrous and agitated *mêlée*. Then this murderous knot unravels itself and the ball, thrown by the most agile, bounds away and is again followed with the same fury. It continually happens that, after one of those frenzied entanglements, one of the combatants remains on the field motionless, incapable of rising, so much has he been hit, pressed, crushed, thumped.

A doctor whose duty it is to look after the wounded arrives and examines him. You see those skilled hands shaking a foot, a leg, rubbing the sides, washing a face, sponging the blood which streams from the forehead, the eyes, the nose, the mouth. A compassionate comrade assists in the business and takes the head of the fainting champion on his knee. Sometimes the unlucky player must be carried away. More frequently, however, he recovers his senses, stretches himself, rouses up, and ends by scrambling to his feet. He makes a few steps, leaning on the friendly shoulder, and no sooner is he able to walk than the game begins afresh, and he joins in again with a rage doubled by pain and humiliation. . . .†

Joe Di Paola

"The roughness with which they seize the bearer of the ball is
impossible to imagine without having witnessed it."—Paul Bourget

SPANIARD IN A BARBERSHOP, 1927
Julio Camba
From "This Was America," edited by Oscar Handlin

There is nothing so American as an American barbershop. No, nothing! Not the American
skyscrapers, nor the American saloons, nor American journalism. . . . An American barbershop is much more energetic, much more complicated, much more mechanized, much more
rapid, much more expensive, and much more American than anything else.

One enters and immediately finds himself attacked by two or three prize fighters, who
relieve him of his hat, his coat, vest, collar, and tie. The proceeding is effective enough, if
perhaps too violent.

389

"Why do you manhandle me in this manner?" a stranger is once said to have asked. "It is not necessary. I've no intention of resisting."

The disrobing completed, one is led to a chair that, in a fraction of a second, is converted into a field of operations. Then a man with enormous hands takes the head with one hand, as if he were grasping a peach, and, waving a razor with the other hand, asks:

"What will you have, haircut, facial, massage, manicure, shoeshine, shampoo, quinine. . . .?"

One is completely at his mercy and can deny him nothing. "Yes," you say, "whatever you wish."

The man gives certain orders, which you cannot hear since with a single stroke of the brush he has just covered your eyes and ears with a layer of lather. You feel that someone is working on your hands, and guess it is the manicurist. At the same time a Negro appears to be polishing your boots. Meanwhile, the barber subjects you to a scientific course of torture. . . . You are shaved and the coat of lather gives way to a coat of pomade. The enormous hands massage you. Then your face is covered with a hot towel which scorches the skin. Soon the hot towel is replaced with one soaked in ice-cold water. You cannot see, speak, or breathe. What can be the intention of this man in subjecting you to these alternations of temperature? Is this not a procedure used to kill certain kinds of microbes?

Freed at last of all the towels, you can see the manicurist working on your fingers, you can see the barber and the Negro. All your extremities are in strange hands. Numerous persons work for your comfort, and give you the satisfaction of thinking that you supply a livelihood to so many people. In reality, I have not even enumerated all the persons who serve you. In the corner of the shop there is, for instance, a man whose job it is to brush, polish, and crease your hat. The hat thus receives its own massage; it is, so to speak, your sixth extremity. . . .

At last the torture ends. That is to say, it ends after the bill is paid. You pull out a bundle of bills and distribute them to the crowd. And all that, including the payment, which seems to take the longest, only lasts a quarter of an hour. Everything is effected rapidly and mechanically. Did I not say that the American barbershop is the most American thing in the world!†

HINDU IN AN AUTOMAT, 1943

"INSIDE AMERICA, A POLITICAL SURVEY OF AMERICAN LIFE AND MANNERS"

Chaman Lal

A typical American institution is the Cafeteria system of providing the choicest foods at reasonable prices. It is an excellent method of feeding large numbers of customers. There is no service in a Cafeteria. You help yourself from the moment you enter and eat and drink what you please at a cost of five cents per plate. The customer places himself in queue along with others, picks up a tray, spoons, napkin and a printed ticket like tram tickets. The queue files past specially arranged racks and shelves and grills (in a semi-circle) and everyone helps himself to anything he fancies. Dozens of choicest vegetables, scores of varieties of curds, creams, cheeses, salads, fruits, breads, rice, puddings, pies and all that one can eat are ready to be picked up. One may take three plates or twenty according to his purse. After one has filled up his tray, he reaches the end of the semi-circle, where damsels marvellously quick check up and punch the ticket according to the number of plates.

I wish we could have a public Cafeteria in every town in these days of food scarcity. The system caters for thousands in every town and eliminates waste. I wonder if our government would ever do it, but any businessman can launch the venture. . . .

"You are to be congratulated on your custard pie."

Helen Hokinson depicts a lady in the automat.*

I, however, don't like the automats that serve food at the drop of a coin. Food (I mean lunch and dinner) to be delicious and beneficial must be served by a sweet smiling face. That is my theory, like it or not. Food is too sacred to be served by automats. All who love food know what difference it makes. My experience is whenever my wife prepares and serves a meal I eat twice the usual ration served by servants. While I don't like soulless machines to present me food, I love the American cremation—another miracle of science and hope some day we will be saved the sight of tiresome funeral processions and hours of waiting in the most unhealthy atmosphere of open cremation grounds.

Here is an excellent opportunity for an enterprising capitalist to start Electric Cremation Parlours. By all means employ *Pandits* to recite *mantrams* for the welfare of the departed souls.†

*Reproduced by permission. Copr. 1939 The New Yorker Magazine, Inc.

AMERICAN SUPERFICIALITY, 1925

"THE TRAVEL DIARY OF A PHILOSOPHER"

Hermann Keyserling

There can, however, be no doubt that in America the chasm between external progressiveness and inner perfection is even wider than in Europe. In the process of transplantation the old roots of the Europeans were mutilated and the newly formed have not yet penetrated sufficiently deeply into the ground; also, in the main mass ungrafted plants were transplanted which, in the richer soil, without schooling have even lost in raciness; therefore, it is not surprising that higher civilization corresponds to a lower level of culture. In the old world, too, perfection of institutions means little enough in relation to man. . . . We are more superficial than the Indians, because the spiritual forces among us have been drawn towards the surface where they now function automatically without necessarily drawing the soul into co-operation, whereas, in the case of the Indians, the spiritual forces operate from the depths, and therefore, where they are vital at all, they influence the innermost being. But in the case of the European it still remains noticeable that the external has been derived from within. Take the most pronounced man-of-purpose: if he belongs to an old race, he possesses the humanism of our classics, the idealism of the age of discoveries, the high ethics of the Middle Ages, and, ultimately, classical culture as his living background; this, however, gives him a mental atmosphere and lends a significance to his actions which exists even when it escapes his consciousness completely. Thus, one feels the possibility of profundity through all European superficiality, in every mechanical organization the possibility of animation by the soul. . . . One does not experience this comforting feeling in America. Most of its facts are nothing but facts without living significance and with a background.

This feeling is undoubtedly only justified with reservations: there is no difference of nature, but only of degree, between American and European conditions. No matter how extravagantly the American universities have been equipped, they are wanting in mental atmosphere. The American show buildings are without symbolism, the Americans themselves are superficial to the point of soullessness, because the discrepancy between externals and internals, which also exists among us, is even greater. The Americans are inwardly more crude and more youthful than we are, and externally they have gone further: thus, the disadvantages of this unbalanced equilibrium are more obvious. This would be quite in order, and no word would be wasted on it, if the new world, instead of striving to emulate the old, did not run ahead and were not developing more and more into an example for it. This state of affairs causes anxious thought.†

THE AMERICAN TEMPERAMENT, 1931

G. K. Chesterton

New York Times Magazine, June 28, 1931

I might express it somewhat abruptly by saying that most Americans are born drunk; and really require a little wine or beer to sober them. They have a sort of permanent intoxication from within; a sort of invisible champagne which needs to be weighted and soothed and supplemented by something corresponding to the glass of port with which the English were accustomed to conclude and settle their dinner. Americans do not need drink to inspire them to do anything, though they do sometimes, I think, need a little for the deeper and more delicate purpose of teaching them how to do nothing. †

A CHINESE PHILOSOPHER ON AMERICAN VICES, 1937

"THE IMPORTANCE OF LIVING"

Lin Yutang

The three great American vices seem to be efficiency, punctuality and the desire for achievement and success. They are the things that make the Americans so unhappy and so nervous. They steal from them their inalienable right of loafing and cheat them of many a good, idle and beautiful afternoon. One must start out with a belief that there are no catastrophes in this world, and that besides the noble art of getting things done, there is a nobler art of leaving things undone. On the whole, if one answers letters promptly, the result is about as good or as bad as if he had never answered them at all. After all, nothing happens, and while one may have missed a few good appointments, one may have also avoided a few unpleasant ones. Most of the letters are not worth answering, if you keep them in your drawer for three months; reading them three months afterwards, one might realize how utterly futile and what a waste of time it would have been to answer them all. Writing letters really can become a vice. It turns our writers into fine promotion salesmen and our college professors into good efficient business executives. In this sense, I can understand Thoreau's contempt for the American who always goes to the post office.

Our quarrel is not that efficiency gets things done and very well done, too. I always rely on American water-taps, rather than on those made in China, because American water-taps do not leak. That is a consolation. Against the old contention, however, that we must all be useful, be efficient, become officials and have power, the old reply is that there are always enough fools left in the world who are willing to be useful, be busy and enjoy power, and so somehow the business of life can and will be carried on. The only point is who are the wise, the loafers or the hustlers? Our quarrel with efficiency is not that it gets things done, but that it is a thief of time when it leaves us no leisure to enjoy ourselves and that it frays our nerves in trying to get things done perfectly. An American editor worries his hair gray to see that no typographical mistakes appear on the pages of his magazine. The Chinese editor is wiser than that. He wants to leave his readers the supreme satisfaction of discovering a few typographical mistakes for themselves. More than that, a Chinese magazine can begin printing serial fiction and forget about it half-way. In America it might bring the roof down on the editors, but in China *it doesn't matter*, *simply because it doesn't matter*. American engineers in building bridges calculate so finely and exactly as to make the two ends come together within one-tenth of an inch. But when two Chinese begin to dig a tunnel from both sides of a mountain, both come out on the other side. The Chinese's firm conviction is that it doesn't matter so long as a tunnel is dug through, and if we have two instead of one, why, we have a double track to boot. Provided you are not in a hurry, two tunnels are as good as one, dug somehow, finished somehow and if the train can get through somehow. And the Chinese are extremely punctual, provided you give them plenty of time to do a thing. They always finish a thing on schedule, provided the schedule is long enough. . . .

But above all, the American's inability to loaf comes directly from his desire for doing things and in his placing action above being. We should demand that there be character in our lives as we demand there be character in all great art worthy of the name. Unfortunately, character is not a thing which can be manufactured overnight. Like the quality of mellowness in wine, it is acquired by standing still and by the passage of time. The desire of American old men and women for action, trying in this way to gain their self-respect and the respect of the younger generation, is what makes them look so ridiculous to an Oriental. Too much action in an old man is like a broadcast of jazz music from a megaphone on top of an old cathedral. Is it not sufficient that the old people *are* something? Is it necessary that they must be forever *doing* something? The loss of the capacity for loafing is bad enough in men of middle age, but the same loss in old age is a crime committed against human nature.

Character is always associated with something old and takes time to grow, like the beautiful facial lines of a man in middle age, lines that are the steady imprint of the man's evolving character. It is somewhat difficult to see character in a type of life where every man is throwing away his last year's car and trading it in for the new model. As are the things we make, so are we ourselves. In 1937 every man and woman looks 1937, and in 1938 every man and woman will look 1938. We love old cathedrals, old furniture, old silver, old dictionaries and old prints, but we have entirely forgotten about the beauty of old men. I think an appreciation of that kind of beauty is essential to our life, for beauty, it seems to me, is what is old and mellow and well-smoked.†

ADVERTISING AND THE AMERICAN WOMAN, 1937
"MIDNIGHT ON THE DESERT"

J. B. Priestley

The vitality, courage, and enterprise of American women are famous, needing no words from me. But how they must have to draw on these qualities! It is a bad business being a woman in most places, but in the United States it must be hell. No relaxation. No letting up for a second. Never relieved from the front-line trenches. Never dropping out of the race till Death rings the bell. . . . I had . . . been looking through some popular magazines, those cunning arrangements of advertisement with a little obvious fiction trickling through them. The copy in these advertisements was the literature that told me so much about American women. Most of my American friends laugh at this advertisement copy, as if it had nothing to do with the real America. I cannot believe that. . . . Vast fortunes would not be spent on mere hazy guesswork. It is a knowledge severely tested by results.

These advertisements in the popular magazines tell one far more than the stories and articles they break into such irritating fragments. They showed me very clearly that the ordinary American woman, whose custom they are soliciting, is an unusually competitive being. She has only been freed from most of the drudgery of the European woman in order to lead a still more strenuous life. She has to compete all the time. When she is young she must look prettier than the girls she is with, otherwise the young males will ignore her completely. In my forty-odd years I have never yet been at any social function where all the young men crowded around one girl and left her less dazzling sisters to droop alone, but according to the advertisers this is always liable to happen in America, where the young males have a strange uniformity of taste, and a girl must either dazzle or be ignored. She must get her man. Then, having got him, she must keep him; and if she is not very careful—in various horribly intimate matters—she will not keep him. She has only to slack off for a day or two—and he has gone. If he does not go, and she marries him, then there may be children, and with them a whole host of new and terrible dangers. Mother must know, Mother must see to it, Mother must not grow careless for a moment. Suppose the children are doing well, can she afford to take it easy? No, no. She must serve the right kind of food, surround herself with the right kind of household appointments, go to the right places, read the right books; juggle with kitchen, coquetry, and culture; cultivate her body, cultivate poise, cultivate charm, cultivate personality, cultivate her mind.

American women, it seems, cannot retreat. They must go on and on—you can see the goal gleaming in their eyes—but where exactly it is they are going the rest of us do not know. But if they should occasionally look worried, be intolerant and hard with their slack men folk, we cannot blame them. Not, that is, if the advertisements are true.†

"In America . . . a girl must either dazzle or be ignored . . .
that is, if the advertisements are true."—J. B. Priestley

395

"There was that indefinable American air of happiness and ease."—D. W. Brogan

"THE AMERICAN CHARACTER," 1944

D. W. Brogan

In the late summer of 1936, I arrived in Kansas City [Missouri]. When I tried to buy a ticket for St. Louis at the Union Station, I was interrogated in a friendly, American fashion by the ticket clerk. "You from Europe?" "Yes." "Well, don't go back—it's going to Hell." . . .

I went a day or two later to see a friend of mine who lives in a small town in Illinois We went together to the corner drugstore to get ice cream for supper. It was a scene familiar enough to me and familiar to all movie-goers—the Main Street of a small American town on a Saturday night in late summer. The boys and girls were there in their white summer clothes; there were endless cars. . . . There was over the street and over the town that indefinable American air of happiness and ease, at least for the young. . . .

People called each other by their "given names"; there were friendly inquiries and a few introductions of the visitor. It was a world in which the ominous word "stranger" had been given a friendly flavor. "Howdy, Stranger" is not a hostile greeting, and it was invented in America. Looking at the people, at the boys and girls milling round the drugstores, disappearing in cars that shot off into the warm, welcoming darkness, it was hard to remember the tension of English life, the worse tension of French life. . . . There was an air of confident adaptation to their way of life in the dress, the speech, the manners of the young. This, if a world they had not made, was yet a world that seemed to have been made for them.

In the drugstore there was the usual stock of gadgets, of remedies for all ills. There were soft drinks, no hard liquor; but there was—most impressive sight of all—a book and magazine section. There were the books of the films; there was the book of the year or decade (it was the first year of *Gone with the Wind*). If you wanted to know about dress-making, about cosmetics, about domestic management, about love, about astrology, about business success, about child training, about how to be happy on a small income (the answer being usually a way to make it large), the printed oracles were there. And the spoken oracles, too, for radios blasted the soft summer night and the heat did not empty the movie house.

And it was all American—even the guiding stars. The advertisements, the gadgets, the radio programs, the movies, the patent medicines, the patent solutions to human woes— all were American. . . .

The regional press was already doing a first-class job, a better job than was being done by most English papers, to awaken the people to the truth of the new iron age that we were all living in, to the significance of Manchukuo, to the menace of international war in Spain. Perhaps, the Parent-Teachers' Association had asked for more instruction in civics and in current affairs. Certainly, appeals for charity, for Chinese, or for Spaniards had been or would be answered as soon as made.

But in the warmth and ease of that summer night, the inevitable, the right, the human character of American natural isolation was brought home to me. The road from Jerusalem to Jericho did not pass close to southern Illinois, as it did southern England, and there was no visible good Samaritan in Illinois—or in England—to shame Priest or Levite.†

"THE MIRACLE OF AMERICA," 1940
André Maurois

It is no exaggeration to talk about an American miracle. The growth of the United States has been more rapid than that of any other human community. In a century and a half there has taken shape in North America a nation that is today one of the most powerful on earth and that has become an asylum for the oppressed and afflicted of the entire world. It has created means of production that enable it in time of war to arm not only its own soldiers but those of its allies as well and that will enable it in time of peace, if they are properly employed, to free most of its citizens from want. No doubt much misery and inequality still exist in America; no doubt American institutions remain imperfect; no doubt ambition and corruption play their role here as in every country. But an impartial judge must recognize that from 1787 to 1940 America has given its citizens more peace, stability, and happiness than have the great nations of Europe.

If isolation is losing ground in the United States, imperialism is not gaining. The country as a whole does not want colonial possessions or subject peoples. Certain businessmen would like to see a "dollar diplomacy," but the average American is much more interested in a diplomacy of sentiment. America has always been ready to fight for moral ideals, for the weak against the strong, for liberty against autocracy. Wilson was sincere in saying that the flag of the United States is the flag of humanity. The American's natural tendency is to rush to the aid of a victim. The danger is that some accomplished hypocrite may pass himself off as a victim. A government by public opinion, like that in the United States, cannot pursue a reasonable foreign policy unless public opinion is protected against those who have a selfish interest in perverting it. Freedom of speech is not freedom to lie. The rigid control that is exercised in time of war over the propaganda of foreign nations will be no less necessary in time of peace. Between 1920 and 1940 the American people were in error because they had been misled, and their errors were one of the causes of the present war. But this is an essentially honest nation. It strives to move forward, from error to error, toward what it believes to be right. Tomorrow it will be, if it is well informed, the world's greatest force in the service of justice.†

THE FUTURE, 1940
"THE PILGRIM'S WAY"
John Buchan

The United States is the richest, and, both actually and potentially, the most powerful state on the globe. She has much, I believe, to give to the world; indeed, to her hands is chiefly entrusted the shaping of the future. If democracy in the broadest and truest sense is to survive, it will be mainly because of her guardianship. For, with all her imperfections, she has a clearer view than any other people of the democratic fundamentals. . . .

. . . today she is the chief exponent of a creed which I believe on the whole to be the best in this imperfect world. She is the chief exponent for two reasons. The first is her size; she exhibits its technique in large type, so that he who runs may read. More important, she exhibits it in its most intelligible form, so that its constituents are obvious. Democracy has become with many an unpleasing parrot cry, and . . . it is well to be clear what it means. It is primarily a spiritual testament, from which certain political and economic orders naturally follow. But the essence is the testament; the orders may change while the testament stands. This testament, this ideal of citizenship, she owes to no one teacher. . . . The second is the belief, which is fundamental also in Christianity, of the worth of every human soul—the worth, not the equality. This is partly an honest emotion, and partly a reasoned principle—that something may be made out of anybody, and that there is something likeable about everybody if you look for it—or, in canonical words, that ultimately there is nothing common or unclean.

The democratic testament is one lesson that America has to teach the world. A second is a new reading of nationalism. Some day and somehow the peoples must discover a way to brigade themselves for peace. Now, there are on the globe only two proven large-scale organizations of social units, the United States and the British Empire. The latter is not for export, and could not be duplicated; its strength depends upon a thousand-year-old monarchy and a store of unformulated traditions. But the United States was the conscious work of men's hands, and a task which has once been performed can be performed again. She is the supreme example of a federation in being, a federation which recognizes the rights and individuality of the parts, but accepts the overriding interests of the whole. To achieve this compromise she fought a desperate war. If the world is ever to have prosperity and peace, there must be some kind of federation—I will not say of democracies, but of states which accept the reign of Law. In such a task she seems to me to be the predestined leader. Vigorous as her patriotism is, she has escaped the jealous, barricaded nationalism of the Old World. . . .

. . . But I am not blind to the grave problems which confront her. Democracy, after all, is a negative thing. It provides a fair field for the Good Life, but it is not in itself the Good Life. In these days when lovers of freedom may have to fight for their cause, the hope is that the ideal of the Good Life, in which alone freedom has any meaning, will acquire a stronger potency. It is the task of civilization to raise every citizen above want, but in so doing to permit a free development and avoid the slavery of the beehive and the ant heap. A humane economic policy must not be allowed to diminish the stature of man's

I.N.P.

"The American's natural tendency is to rush
to the aid of a victim."—André Maurois

spirit. It is because I believe that in the American people the two impulses are of equal strength that I see her in the vanguard of that slow upward trend, undulant or spiral, which today is our modest definition of progress. Her major prophet is still Whitman. "Everything comes out of the dirt—everything; everything comes out of the people, everyday people, the people as you find them and leave them; people, people, just people!"

It is only out of the dirt that things grow.†

WINSTON CHURCHILL, 1949

Speech at a dinner in his honor in New York, May 25, 1949

GENTLEMEN—many nations have arrived at the summit of the world but none, before the United States, on this occasion, has chosen that moment of triumph, not for aggrandizement, but for further self-sacrifice—sacrifice for the causes by which the life and strength of mankind is refreshed. The United States has shown itself more worthy of trust and honour than any government of men or associations of nations, that has ever reached pre-eminence by their action on the morrow of the common victory won by all.†

399

CONSTITUTION OF THE UNITED STATES OF AMERICA

PREAMBLE

We, the people of the United States, in order to form a more perfect Union, establish justice, insure domestic tranquillity, provide for the common defence, promote the general welfare, and secure the blessings of liberty to ourselves and our posterity, do ordain and establish this Constitution for the United States of America.

ARTICLE I

Section 1—All legislative powers herein granted shall be vested in a Congress of the United States, which shall consist of a Senate and House of Representatives.

Section 2—1. The House of Representatives shall be composed of members chosen every second year by the people of the several States, and the electors in each State shall have the qualifications requisite for electors of the most numerous branch of the State Legislature.

2. No person shall be a Representative who shall not have attained to the age of twenty-five years and been seven years a citizen of the United States, and who shall not, when elected, be an inhabitant of that State in which he shall be chosen.

3. Representatives and direct taxes shall be apportioned among the several States which may be included within this Union according to their respective numbers, which shall be determined by adding to the whole number of free persons, including those bound to service for a term of years, and excluding Indians not taxed, three-fifths of all other persons. The actual enumeration shall be made within three years after the first meeting of the Congress of the United States, and within every subsequent term of ten years, in such manner as they shall by law direct. The number of Representatives shall not exceed one for every thirty thousand, but each State shall have at least one Representative; and until such enumeration shall be made, the State of New Hampshire shall be entitled to choose 3; Massachusetts, 8; Rhode Island and Providence Plantations, 1; Connecticut, 5; New York, 6; New Jersey, 4; Pennsylvania, 8; Delaware, 1; Maryland, 6; Virginia, 10; North Carolina, 5; South Carolina, 5; and Georgia, 3.

4. When vacancies happen in the representation from any State, the Executive Authority thereof shall issue writs of election to fill such vacancies.

5. The House of Representatives shall choose their Speaker and other officers, and shall have the sole power of impeachment.

Section 3—1. The Senate of the United States shall be composed of two Senators from each State, chosen by the Legislature thereof, for six years; and each Senator shall have one vote.

2. Immediately after they shall be assembled in consequence of the first election, they shall be divided as equally as may be into three classes. The seats of the Senators of the first class shall be vacated at the expiration of the second year, of the second class at the expiration of the fourth year, and of the third class at the expiration of the sixth year, so that one-third may be chosen every second year; and if vacancies happen by resignation or otherwise, during the recess of the Legislature of any State, the Executive thereof may make temporary appointment until the next meeting of the Legislature, which shall then fill such vacancies.

3. No person shall be a Senator who shall not have attained to the age of thirty years, and been nine years a citizen of the United States, and who shall not, when elected, be an inhabitant of that State for which he shall be chosen.

4. The Vice President of the United States shall be President of the Senate, but shall have no vote unless they be equally divided.

5. The Senate shall choose their other officers, and also a President pro tempore, in the absence of the Vice President, or when he shall exercise the office of the President of the United States.

6. The Senate shall have the sole power to try all impeachments. When sitting for that purpose, they shall be on oath or affirmation. When the President of the United States is tried, the Chief Justice shall preside; and no person shall be convicted without the concurrence of two-thirds of the members present.

7. Judgment of cases of impeachment shall not extend further than to removal from office, and disqualification to hold and enjoy any office of honor, trust, or profit under the United States; but the party convicted shall nevertheless be liable and subject to indictment, trial, judgment, and punishment, according to law.

Section 4—1. The times, places and manner of holding elections for Senators and Representatives shall be prescribed in each State by the Legislature thereof; but the Congress may at any time by law make or alter such regulations, except as to places of choosing Senators.

2. The Congress shall assemble at least once in every year, and such meeting shall be on the first Monday in December, unless they shall by law appoint a different day.

Section 5—1. Each House shall be the judge of the elections, returns, and qualifications of its own members, and a majority of each shall constitute a quorum to do business; but a smaller number may adjourn from day to day, and may be authorized to compel the attendance of absent members in such manner and under such penalties as each House may provide.

2. Each House may determine the rules of its proceedings, punish its members for disorderly behavior, and with the concurrence of two-thirds expel a member.

3. Each House shall keep a journal of its proceedings, and from time to time publish the same, excepting such parts as may in their judgment require secrecy; and the yeas and nays of the members of

The Statue of Liberty—gift of the people of France to the people of the United States, symbol of freedom for all peoples.

either House on any question shall, at the desire of one-fifth of those present, be entered on the journal.

4. Neither House, during the session of Congress shall, without the consent of the other, adjourn for more than three days, nor to any other place than that in which the two Houses shall be sitting.

Section 6—1. The Senators and Representatives shall receive a compensation for their services to be ascertained by law, and paid out of the Treasury of the United States. They shall in all cases, except treason, felony, and breach of the peace, be privileged from arrest during their attendance at the session of their respective Houses, and in going to and returning from the same; and for any speech or debate in either House they shall not be questioned in any other place.

2. No Senator or Representative shall, during the time for which he was elected, be appointed to any civil office under the authority of the United States which shall have been created, or the emoluments whereof shall have been increased during such time; and no person holding any office under the United States shall be a member of either House during his continuance in office.

Section 7—1. All bills for raising revenue shall originate in the House of Representatives, but the Senate may propose or concur with amendments, as on other bills.

2. Every bill which shall have passed the House of Representatives and the Senate shall, before it becomes a law, be presented to the President of the United States; if he approve, he shall sign it, but if not, he shall return it, with his objections, to that House in which it shall have originated, who shall enter the objections at large on their journal, and proceed to reconsider it. If after such reconsideration two-thirds of that House shall agree to pass the bill, it shall be sent, together with the objections, to the other House, by which it shall likewise be reconsidered; and if approved by two-thirds of that House it shall become a law. But in all such cases the votes of both Houses shall be determined by yeas and nays, and the names of the persons voting for and against the bill shall be entered on the journal of each House respectively. If any bill shall not be returned by the President within ten days (Sundays excepted) after it shall have been presented to him, the same shall be a law in like manner as if he had signed it, unless the Congress by their adjournment prevent its return; in which case it shall not be a law.

3. Every order, resolution, or vote to which the concurrence of the Senate and House of Representatives may be necessary (except on a question of adjournment) shall be presented to the President of the United States, and before the same shall take effect shall be approved by him, or being disapproved by him, shall be repassed by two-thirds of the Senate and the House of Representatives, according to the rules and limitations prescribed in the case of a bill.

Section 8—1. The Congress shall have power:

To lay and collect taxes, duties, imposts, and excises to pay the debts and provide for the common defense and general welfare of the United States; but all duties, imposts, and excises shall be uniform throughout the United States.

2. To borrow money on the credit of the United States.

3. To regulate commerce with foreign nations, and among the several States and with the Indian tribes.

4. To establish a uniform rule of naturalization and uniform laws on the subject of bankruptcies throughout the United States.

5. To coin money, regulate the value thereof, and of foreign coin, and fix the standard of weights and measures.

6. To provide for the punishment of counterfeiting the securities and current coin of the United States.

7. To establish post-offices and post-roads.

8. To promote the progress of science and useful arts by securing for limited times to authors and inventors the exclusive rights to their respective writings and discoveries.

9. To constitute tribunals inferior to the Supreme Court.

10. To define and punish piracies and felonies committed on the high seas, and offences against the law of nations.

11. To declare war, grant letters of marque and reprisal, and make rules concerning captures on land and water.

12. To raise and support armies, but no appropriation of money to that use shall be for a longer term than two years.

13. To provide and maintain a navy.

14. To make rules for the government and regulation of the land and naval forces.

15. To provide for calling forth the militia to execute the laws of the Union, suppress insurrections, and repel invasions.

16. To provide for organizing, arming, and disciplining the militia, and for governing such part of them as may be employed in the service of the United States, reserving to the States respectively the appointment of the officers, and the authority of training the militia according to the discipline prescribed by Congress.

17. To exercise exclusive legislation in all cases whatsoever over such district (not exceeding ten miles square) as may, by cession of particular States and the acceptance of Congress, become the seat of Government of the United States, and to exercise like authority over all places purchased by the consent of the Legislature of the State in which the same shall be, for the erection of forts, magazines, arsenals, dockyards, and other needful buildings;— And

18. To make all laws which shall be necessary and proper for carrying into execution the foregoing powers and all other powers vested by this Constitution in the Government of the United States, or in any department or officer thereof.

Section 9—1. The migration or importation of such persons as any of the States now existing shall think proper to admit shall not be prohibited by the Congress prior to the year one thousand eight hundred and eight, but a tax or duty may be imposed on such importation, not exceeding ten dollars for each person.

2. The privilege of the writ of habeas corpus shall not be suspended, unless when in cases of rebellion or invasion the public safety may require it.

3. No bill of attainder or ex post facto law shall be passed.

4. No capitation or other direct tax shall be laid, unless in proportion to the census or enumeration hereinbefore directed to be taken.

5. No tax or duty shall be laid on articles exported from any State.

6. No preference shall be given by any regulation of commerce or revenue to the ports of one State over those of another, nor shall vessels bound to or from one State be obliged to enter, clear, or pay duties to another.

7. No money shall be drawn from the Treasury but in consequence of appropriations made by law; and a regular statement and account of the receipts and expenditures of all public money shall be published from time to time.

8. No title of nobility shall be granted by the United States. And no person holding any office of profit or trust under them shall, without the consent of the Congress, accept of any present, emolument, office, or title of any kind whatever from any king, prince, or foreign state.

Section 10—1. No State shall enter into any treaty, alliance, or confederation, grant letters of marque and reprisal, coin money, emit bills of credit, make anything but gold and silver coin a tender in payment of debts, pass any bill of attainder, ex post facto law, or law impairing the obligation of contracts, or grant any title of nobility.

2. No State shall, without the consent of the Congress, lay any impost or duties on imports or exports, except what may be absolutely necessary for executing its inspection laws, and the net produce of all duties and imposts, laid by any State on imports or exports, shall be for the use of the Treasury of the United States; and all such laws shall be subject to the revision and control of the Congress.

3. No State shall, without the consent of Congress, lay any duty of tonnage, keep troops or ships of war in time of peace, enter into agreement or compact with another State, or with a foreign power, or engage in war, unless actually invaded, or in such imminent danger as will not admit of delay.

ARTICLE II

Section 1—1. The Executive power shall be vested in a President of the United States of America. He shall hold his office during the term of four years, and together with the Vice President, chosen for the same term, be elected as follows:

2. Each State shall appoint, in such manner as the Legislature thereof may direct, a number of electors equal to the whole number of Senators and Representatives to which the State may be entitled in the Congress; but no Senator or Representative or person holding an office of trust or profit under the United States shall be appointed an elector.

3. The electors shall meet in their respective States and vote by ballot for two persons, of whom one at least shall not be an inhabitant of the same State with themselves. And they shall make a list of all the persons voted for, and of the number of votes for each, which list they shall sign and certify and transmit, sealed, to the seat of the Government of the United States, directed to the President of the Senate. The President of the Senate shall, in the presence of the Senate and House of Representatives, open all the certificates, and the votes shall then be counted. The person having the greatest number of votes shall be the President, if such number be a majority of the whole number of electors appointed, and if there be more than one who have such a majority, and have an equal number of votes, then the House of Representatives shall immediately choose by ballot one of them for President; and if no person have a majority, then from the five highest on the list the said House shall in like manner choose the President. But in choosing the President, the vote shall be taken by States, the representation from each State having one vote. A quorum, for this purpose, shall consist of a member or members from two-thirds of the States, and a majority of all the States shall be necessary to a choice. In every case, after the choice of the President, the person having the greatest number of votes of the electors shall be the Vice President. But if there should remain two or more who have equal votes, the Senate shall choose from them by ballot the Vice President.

4. The Congress may determine the time of choosing the electors and the day on which they shall give their votes, which day shall be the same throughout the United States.

5. No person except a natural born citizen, or a citizen of the United States at the time of the adoption of the Constitution, shall be eligible to the office of President; neither shall any person be eligible to that office who shall not have attained to the age of thirty-five years and been fourteen years a resident within the United States.

6. In case of the removal of the President from office, or of his death, resignation, or inability to discharge the powers and duties of the said office, the same shall devolve on the Vice President, and the Congress may by law provide for the case of removal, death, resignation, or inability, both of the President and Vice President, declaring what officer shall then act as President, and such officer shall act accordingly until the disability be removed or a President shall be elected.

7. The President shall, at stated times, receive for his services a compensation which shall neither be increased nor diminished during the period for which he shall have been elected, and he shall not receive within that period any other emolument from the United States or any of them.

8. Before he enter on the execution of his office he shall take the following oath or affirmation:

"I do solemnly swear (or affirm) that I will faithfully execute the office of President of the United States, and will, to the best of my ability, preserve, protect, and defend the Constitution of the United States."

Section 2—1. The President shall be Commander in Chief of the Army and Navy of the United States, and of the militia of the several States when called into the actual service of the United States; he may require the opinion, in writing, of the principal officer in each of the executive departments upon any subject relating to the duties of their respective offices, and he shall have power to grant reprieves and pardons for offenses against the United States except in cases of impeachment.

2. He shall have power by and with the advice and consent of the Senate to make treaties, provided

two-thirds of the Senators present concur; and he shall nominate and by and with the advice and consent of the Senate shall appoint ambassadors, other public ministers and consuls, judges of the Supreme Court, and all other officers of the United States whose appointments are not herein otherwise provided for, and which shall be established by law; but the Congress may by law vest the appointment of such inferior officers as they think proper in the President alone, in the courts of law, or in the heads of departments.

3. The President shall have power to fill up all vacancies that may happen during the recess of the Senate by granting commissions, which shall expire at the end of their next session.

Section 3—He shall from time to time give to the Congress information of the state of the Union, and recommend to their consideration such measures as he shall judge necessary and expedient; he may, on extraordinary occasions, convene both Houses, or either of them, and in case of disagreement between them with respect to the time of adjournment, he may adjourn them to such time as he shall think proper; he shall receive ambassadors and other public ministers; he shall take care that the laws be faithfully executed, and shall commission all the officers of the United States.

Section 4—The President, Vice President, and all civil officers of the United States shall be removed from office on impeachment for and conviction of treason, bribery or other high crimes and misdemeanors.

ARTICLE III

Section 1—The judicial power of the United States shall be vested in one Supreme Court, and in such inferior courts as the Congress may from time to time ordain and establish. The judges, both of the Supreme and inferior courts, shall hold their offices during good behavior, and shall at stated times receive for their services a compensation which shall not be diminished during their continuance in office.

Section 2—1. The judicial power shall extend to all cases in law and equity arising under this Constitution, the laws of the United States, and treaties made, or which shall be made, under their authority; to all cases affecting ambassadors, other public ministers and consuls; to all cases of admiralty and maritime jurisdiction; to controversies to which the United States shall be a party; to controversies between two or more States, between a State and citizens of another State, between citizens of different States, between citizens of the same State claiming lands under grants of different States, and between a State, or the citizens thereof, and foreign states, citizens, or subjects.

2. In all cases affecting ambassadors, other public ministers, and consuls, and those in which a State shall be a party, the Supreme Court shall have original jurisdiction. In all the other cases before mentioned the Supreme Court shall have appellate jurisdiction both as to law and fact, with such exceptions and under such regulations as the Congress shall make.

3. The trial of all crimes, except in cases of impeachment, shall be by jury, and such trial shall be held in the State where the said crimes shall have been committed; but when not committed within any State the trial shall be at such place or places as the Congress may by law have directed.

Section 3—1. Treason against the United States shall consist only in levying war against them, or in adhering to their enemies, giving them aid and comfort. No person shall be convicted of treason unless on the testimony of two witnesses to the same overt act, or on confession in open court.

2. The Congress shall have power to declare the punishment of treason, but no attainder of treason shall work corruption of blood or forfeiture except during the life of the person attainted.

ARTICLE IV

Section 1—Ful faith and credit shall be given in each State to the public acts, records, and judicial proceedings of every other State. And the Congress may by general laws prescribe the manner in which such acts, records, and proceedings shall be proved, and the effect thereof.

Section 2—1. The citizens of each State shall be entitled to all privileges and immunities of citizens in the several States.

2. A person charged in any State with treason, felony, or other crime, who shall flee from justice, and be found in another State, shall, on demand of the Executive authority of the State from which he fled, be delivered up, to be removed to the State having jurisdiction of the crime.

3. No person held to service or labor in one State, under the laws thereof, escaping into another shall in consequence of any law or regulation therein, be discharged from such service or labor, but shall be delivered up on claim of the party to whom such service or labor may be due.

Section 3—1. New States may be admitted by the Congress into this Union; but no new State shall be formed or erected within the jurisdiction of any other State, nor any State be formed by the junction of two or more States, or parts of States, without the consent of the Legislature of the States concerned, as well as of the Congress.

2. The Congress shall have power to dispose of and make all needful rules and regulations respecting the territory or other property belonging to the United States; and nothing in this Constitution shall be so construed as to prejudice any claims of the United States, or of any particular State.

Section 4—The United States shall guarantee to every State in this Union a Republican form of government, and shall protect each of them against invasion, and, on application of the Legislature, or of the Executive (when the Legislature cannot be convened) against domestic violence.

ARTICLE V

The Congress, whenever two-thirds of both Houses shall deem it necessary, shall propose amendments to this Constitution, or, on the application of the Legislatures of two-thirds of the several States, shall call a convention for proposing amendments, which in either case, shall be valid to all intents and purposes, as part of this Constitution, when ratified by the Legislatures of three-fourths of the several States, or by conventions in three-fourths thereof, as the one or the other mode of ratification may be proposed by the Congress, provided that no amendment which may be made prior to the year one thousand eight hundred and eight shall in any manner affect the first and fourth clauses in the Ninth Section of the First Article; and that no State, without its consent, shall be deprived of its equal suffrage in the Senate.

ARTICLE VI

1. All debts contracted and engagements entered into before the adoption of this Constitution shall be as valid against the United States under this Constitution as under the Confederation.

2. This Constitution and the laws of the United States which shall be made in pursuance thereof and all treaties made, or which shall be made, under the authority of the United States, shall be the supreme law of the land, and the judges in every State shall be bound thereby, anything in the Constitution or laws of any State to the contrary notwithstanding.

3. The Senators and Representatives before mentioned, and the members of the several State Legislatures, and all executives and judicial officers, both of the United States and of the several States, shall be bound by oath or affirmation to support this Constitution; but no religious test shall ever be required as a qualification to any office or public trust under the United States.

ARTICLE VII

The ratification of the Conventions of nine States shall be sufficient for the establishment of this Constitution between the States so ratifying the same.

Done in convention by the unanimous consent of the States present, the seventeenth day of September, in the year of our Lord one thousand seven hundred and eighty-seven, and of the Independence of the United States of America the twelfth. In witness whereof we have hereunto subscribed our names.

George Washington, President and Deputy from Virginia.

New Hampshire: John Langdon, Nicholas Gilman; Massachusetts: Nathaniel Gorham, Rufus King; Connecticut: Wm. Saml. Johnson, Roger Sherman; New York: Alexander Hamilton; New Jersey: Will. Livingston, David Brearley, Wm. Paterson, Jona. Dayton; Pennsylvania: B. Franklin, Thomas Mifflin, Robt. Morris, Geo. Clymer, Thos. FitzSimons, Jared Ingersoll, James Wilson, Gouv. Morris; Delaware: Geo. Read, Gunning Bedford, Jun., John Dickinson, Richard Bassett, Jacob Broom; Maryland: James McHenry, Dan. Jenifer, of St. Thomas, Dan Carroll; Virginia: John Blair, James Madison, Jr.; North Carolina: Wm. Blount, Rich'd Dobbs Spaight, Hugh Williamson; South Carolina: J. Rutledge, Charles Cotesworth Pinckney, Charles Pinckney, Pierce Butler; Georgia: William Few, Abr. Baldwin.

Attest: William Jackson, Secretary.

AMENDMENTS*

ARTICLE I

Congress shall make no law respecting an establishment of religion, or prohibiting the free exercise thereof; or abridging the freedom of speech or of the press; or the right of the people peaceably to assemble and to petition the Government for a redress of grievances.

ARTICLE II

A well-regulated militia being necessary to the security of a free State, the right of the people to keep and bear arms shall not be infringed.

ARTICLE III

No soldier shall, in time of peace, be quartered in any house without the consent of the owner, nor in time of war but in a manner to be prescribed by law.

ARTICLE IV

The right of the people to be secure in their persons, houses, papers, and effects, against unreasonable searches and seizures, shall not be violated, and no warrants shall issue but upon probable cause, supported by oath or affirmation, and particularly describing the place to be searched, and the persons or things to be seized.

ARTICLE V

No person shall be held to answer for a capital or other infamous crime unless on a presentment or indictment of a Grand Jury, except in cases arising in the land or naval forces, or in the militia, when in actual service, in time of war or public danger; nor shall any person be subject for the same offense to be twice put in jeopardy of life or limb; nor shall be compelled in any criminal case to be a witness against himself, nor be deprived of life, liberty, or property, without due process of law; nor shall private property be taken for public use without just compensation.

ARTICLE VI

In all criminal prosecutions, the accused shall enjoy the right to a speedy and public trial, by an impartial jury of the State and district wherein the crime shall have been committed, which districts shall have been previously ascertained by law, and to be informed of the nature and cause of the accusation; to be confronted with the witnesses against him; to have compulsory process for obtaining witnesses in his favor, and to have the assistance of counsel for his defense.

ARTICLE VII

In suits at common law, where the value in controversy shall exceed twenty dollars, the right of trial by jury shall be preserved, and no fact tried by a jury shall be otherwise re-examined in any court of the United States than according to the rules of the common law.

ARTICLE VIII

Excessive bail shall not be required, nor excessive fines imposed, nor cruel and unusual punishments inflicted.

* The first ten amendments, in effect 1791, constitute the Bill of Rights.

ARTICLE IX

The enumeration in the Constitution of certain rights shall not be construed to deny or disparage others retained by the people.

ARTICLE X

The powers not delegated to the United States by the Constitution, nor prohibited by it to the States, are reserved to the States respectively, or to the people.

ARTICLE XI (1795)

The judicial power of the United States shall not be construed to extend to any suit in law or equity, commenced or prosecuted against one of the United States, by citizens of another State, or by citizens or subjects of any foreign state.

ARTICLE XII (1804)

The Electors shall meet in their respective States, and vote by ballot for President and Vice President, one of whom at least shall not be an inhabitant of the same State with themselves; they shall name in their ballots the person voted for as President, and in distinct ballots the person voted for as Vice President; and they shall make distinct list of all persons voted for as President, and of all persons voted for as Vice President, and of the number of votes for each, which list they shall sign and certify, and transmit, sealed, to the seat of the Government of the United States, directed to the President of the Senate; the President of the Senate shall, in the presence of the Senate and House of Representatives, open all the certificates and the votes shall then be counted; the person having the greatest number of votes for President shall be the President, if such number be a majority of the whole number of Electors appointed; and if no person have such majority, then from the persons having the highest number, not exceeding three, on the list of those voted for as President, the House of Representatives shall choose immediately, by ballot, the President. But in choosing the President, the votes shall be taken by States, the representation from each State having one vote; a quorum for this purpose shall consist of a member or members from two-thirds of the States, and a majority of all the States shall be necessary to a choice. And if the House of Representatives shall not choose a President, whenever the right of choice shall devolve upon them, before the fourth day of March next following, then the Vice President shall act as President, as in the case of the death or other constitutional disability of the President. The person having the greatest number of votes as Vice President shall be the Vice President if such number be a majority of the whole number of Electors appointed, and if no person have a majority, then, from the two highest numbers on the list the Senate shall choose the Vice President; a quorum for the purpose shall consist of two-thirds of the whole number of Senators, and a majority of the whole number shall be necessary to a choice. But no person constitutionally ineligible to the office of President shall be eligible to that of Vice President of the United States.

ARTICLE XIII (1865)

1. Neither slavery nor involuntary servitude, except as a punishment for crime whereof the party shall have been duly convicted, shall exist within the United States, or any place subject to their jurisdiction.

2. Congress shall have power to enforce this article by appropriate legislation.

ARTICLE XIV (1868)

1. All persons born or naturalized in the United States, and subject to the jurisdiction thereof, are citizens of the United States and of the State wherein they reside. No State shall make or enforce any law which shall abridge the privileges or immunities of citizens of the United States, nor shall any State deprive any person of life, liberty, or property without due process of law, nor deny to any person within its jurisdiction the equal protection of the laws.

Apportionment of Representatives in Congress.

2. Representatives shall be apportioned among the several States according to their respective numbers, counting the whole number of persons in each State excluding Indians not taxed. But when the right to Vote at any election for the choice of Electors for President and Vice President of the United States, Representatives in Congress, the executive and judicial officers of a State, or the members of the Legislature thereof, is denied to any of the male inhabitants of such State, being twenty-one years of age, and citizens of the United States, or in any way abridged, except for participation in rebellion, or other crime, the basis of representation therein shall be reduced in the proportion which the number of such male citizens shall bear to the whole number of male citizens twenty-one years of age in such State.

3. No person shall be a Senator or Representative in Congress, or Elector of President and Vice President or hold any office, civil or military, under the United States, or under any State, who, having previously taken an oath, as a member of Congress, or as an officer of the United States, or as a member of any State Legislature or as an executive or judicial officer of any State, to support the Constitution of the United States, shall have engaged in insurrection or rebellion against the same, or given aid and comfort to the enemies thereof. But Congress may, by a vote of two-thirds of each House, remove such disability.

4. The validity of the public debt of the United States, authorized by law, including debts incurred for payment of pensions and bounties for services in suppressing insurrection and rebellion, shall not be questioned. But neither the United States nor any State shall assume or pay any debt or obligation incurred in aid of insurrection or rebellion against the United States, or any claim for the loss or emancipation of any slave; but all such debts, obligations, and claims shall be held illegal and void.

5. The Congress shall have power to enforce by appropriate legislation the provisions of this article.

ARTICLE XV (1870)

1. The right of the citizens of the United States to vote shall not be denied or abridged by the United States or by any State on account of race, color, or previous condition of servitude.

2. The Congress shall have power to enforce the provisions of this article by appropriate legislation.

ARTICLE XVI (1913)

The Congress shall have power to lay and collect taxes on incomes, from whatever sources derived, without apportionment among the several States, and without regard to any census or enumeration.

ARTICLE XVII (1913)

1. The Senate of the United States shall be composed of two Senators from each State, elected by the people thereof, for six years and each Senator shall have one vote. The electors in each State shall have the qualifications requisite for electors of the most numerous branch of the State Legislatures.

2. When vacancies happen in the representation of any State in the Senate, the executive authority of such State shall issue writs of election to fill such vacancies: Provided, That the Legislature of any State may empower the Executive thereof to make temporary appointment until the people fill the vacancies by election as the Legislature may direct.

3. This amendment shall not be so construed as to affect the election or term of any Senator chosen before it becomes valid as part of the Constitution.

ARTICLE XVIII (1919)

1. After one year from the ratification of this article the manufacture, sale, or transportation of intoxicating liquors within, the importation thereof into, or the exportation thereof from the United States and all territory subject to the jurisdiction thereof for beverage purposes is hereby prohibited.

2. The Congress and the several States shall have concurrent power to enforce this article by appropriate legislation.

3. This article shall be inoperative unless it shall have been ratified as an amendment to the Constitution by the Legislatures of the several States, as provided in the Constitution, within seven years from the date of the submission hereof to the States by the Congress.

ARTICLE XIX (1920)

1. The right of citizens of the United States to vote shall not be denied or abridged by the United States or by any State on account of sex.

2. Congress shall have power, by appropriate legislation, to enforce the provisions of this article.

ARTICLE XX (1933)

Section 1. The terms of the President and Vice President shall end at noon on the 20th day of January, and the terms of Senators and Representatives at noon on the 3rd day of January, of the years in which such terms would have ended if this article had not been ratified; and the terms of their successors shall then begin.

Section 2. The Congress shall assemble at least once in every year, and such meeting shall begin at noon on the 3rd day of January, unless they shall by law appoint a different day.

Section 3. If, at the time fixed for the beginning of the term of the President, the President elect shall have died, the Vice President elect shall become President. If a President shall not have been chosen before the time fixed for the beginning of his term, or if the President elect shall have failed to qualify, then the Vice President elect shall act as President until a President shall have qualified; and the Congress may by law provide for the case where-in neither a President elect nor a Vice President elect shall have qualified, declaring who shall then act as President, or the manner in which one who is to act shall be selected, and such person shall act accordingly until a President or Vice President shall have qualified.

Section 4. The Congress may by law provide for the case of the death of any of the persons from whom the House of Representatives may choose a President whenever the right of choice shall have developed upon them, and for the case of the death of any of the persons from whom the Senate may choose a Vice President whenever the right of choice shall have devolved upon them.

Section 5. Sections 1 and 2 shall take effect on the 15th day of October following the ratification of this article [October 1933].

Section 6. This article shall be inoperative unless it shall have been ratified as an amendment to the Constitution by the legislatures of three-fourths of the several States within seven years from the date of its submission.

ARTICLE XXI (1933)

Section 1. The eighteenth article of amendment to the Constitution of the United States is hereby repealed.

Section 2. The transportation or importation into any State, Territory, or Possession of the United States for delivery or use therein of intoxicating liquors, in violation of the laws thereof, is hereby prohibited.

Section 3. This article shall be inoperative unless it shall have been ratified as an amendment to the Constitution by convention in the several States, as provided in the Constitution, within seven years from the date of the submission hereof to the States by the Congress.

ARTICLE XXII (1951)

No person shall be elected to the office of the President more than twice, and no person who has held the office of President, or acted as President, for more than two years of a term to which some other person was elected President shall be elected to the office of the President more than once. But this Article shall not apply to any person holding the office of President when this Article was proposed by the Congress, and shall not prevent any person who may be holding the office of President, or acting as President, during the term within which this Article becomes operative from holding the office of President or acting as President during the remainder of such term.

Index

"Across the Continent," *155*
"Age of Innocence, The," 349–351
agriculture:
  Bromfield, Louis, on, 175–181
  contour farming, *179*
  farm equipment, *180*
  farms, *173, 177, 190*
  Jefferson, Thomas, on, 172
  Washington, George, on, 172, 173–175
  wheat harvesting, *191*
"Ah, Wilderness!" *352,* 353–355
airplanes, *217, 220, 223, 224, 296*
America:
  emigration to, 50–52
  naming of, 30
"American, The," 348–349
"American Character, The," 396–397
"American Man, The," 383–384
anesthesia, 202–203, *204–205*
Annapolis, graduation exercises at, *320*
Anthony, Susan B., 121–123
Antin, Mary, 312
Appomattox Courthouse, *283*
architecture:
  Guaranty Trust Building, *362*
  house by Frank Lloyd Wright, *362*
  Jefferson, Thomas, on, 359
  Monticello, *361*
  Sullivan, Louis Henry, on, 360
  Wright, Frank Lloyd, on, 360, *363*
artists:
  Audubon, John James, *43*
  Bierstadt, Albert, *141*
  Catlin, George, *148*
  Currier and Ives, *147, 155, 162*
  Curry, John Steuart, *117*
  Eakins, Thomas, *204*
  Homer, Winslow, *306*
  Peale, Rembrandt, *57*
  Ranney, William, *139, 145*

artists (*cont.*):
  Remington, Frederic, *163*
  Ryder, Albert Pinkham, *326*
  Sargent, John Singer, *260*
  Trumbull, John, *269*
  Wright, Joseph, *78*
assembly lines, automobile, *250–251*
atom bomb, *297*
  Truman's report on, 296–298
atomic age, Eisenhower's address to U.N., 133–136
Audubon, John James, *43*
automat, 391, *391*
automobile industry, 247–253
aviation, 216–225

barbershops, 389–390
"Barren Ground," 351, 353
Barry, Iris, 368–369
Battle of Lexington, 52–55
Benét, Stephen Vincent, 357–359
Bessemer steel process, *238*
Bierstadt, Albert, *141*
Bill of Rights, 405–406
Birkbeck, Morris, 146
Birth of a Nation, The, 369
Boone, Daniel, *139*
Bourget, Paul, 388
Bradford, William, 39–40
Bradstreet, Anne, 328
bridge, suspension, *234*
Brogan, D. W., 396–397
Bromfield, Louis, 175–181
Brown, John, 113–116, *117*
Bryce, James, 62, 66
Buchan, John, 398–399
buffalo, *148*
buffalo hunt, 146–149
Bunker Hill, *269*
Bunnell, Lafayette Houghton, 158–159

Figures in italics denote illustrations.

cabin, building of, *147*
Cabrillo, Juan Rodriguez, 30–31
cafeteria, 390
California:
  ghost town, *158*
  Gold Rush, 150–152, 154–157
  Golden Gate Bridge, *234*
  missions, *49, 86*
  sequoias, *170*
  Yosemite Valley, 158–159, *160–161*
Camba, Julio, 389–390
Capitol:
  Charleston, West Virginia, *68*
  Washington, D. C., *63*
Carnegie, Andrew:
  on beginning of steel industry, 236–237
  first enterprises of, 235–236
  gifts and bequests of, 259
  letter of gift to Carnegie Corporation, 261
  philanthropic principles of, 259
Carson, Kit, 146–149
Castillo de San Marco, *32–33*
Catlin, George, *148*
census figures, 169
"Champion," 355–356
Charlevoix, Pierre de, 46, 48
chemical research, *256*
Chesterton, G. K., 392
Chicago skyline, *206*
Churchill, Winston, 399
Civil War:
  Appomattox Courthouse, *283*
  Emancipation Proclamation, 118–119
  end of, 281
  Gettysburg, *281*
  Gettysburg Address, 280
  Greeley's open letter, 275–277
  Lincoln's reply to Greeley, 277
  Lincoln's war message, 274–275
  Pickett's Charge, 277–280
  statistics of, 266
  surrender of Lee, 281–282, 284–286
Clermont, the, *201*
cliff dwellings, *100*
clipper ships, 159
  Flying Cloud, 159, *162*
clover leaf highway, *253*
coal mine, *192*
college lecture hall, *325*
Columbia River, *143*
Columbus, Cristopher, *28,* 29–30
commencement procession, Harvard, *317*
Communism:
  Communist Control Act, 133
  recognition of Soviet Russia, 131–132
  Smith Act, 132–133
"Concord Hymn," 55
Connecticut, church at Litchfield, *89*
conservation:
  Holman, Eugene, on, 193–196

conservation (*cont.*):
  Osborn, Fairfield, on, 189, 193
  Pinchot, Gifford, on, 182–183
  Roosevelt, Theodore, on, 181
  Tennessee Valley Authority Act, 183
  Vogt, William, on, 183, 186–187
Constitution destroying the *Java,* the, *271*
Constitution of the United States, 62–64, 66
  comments on, 70–73
  text of, 401–407
contour farming, *179*
cotton gin, 198–199
Council of Four, the, *83*
"Country School, The," *306*
Crevecoeur, Hector St.-Jean de, 75
Cumberland Gap, *138*
Currier and Ives, *147, 155, 162*
Curry, John Steuart, 117

dairy farm, *190*
dance, the, 373–379
"Daniel Boone's First View of Kentucky," *139*
D-Day landing, 295
Declaration of Independence, 55–58
Declaration of the Causes and Necessity of Taking up Arms, 267–269
de Mille, Agnes, 373–374, 376–379
Dewey, John, 322–323
Dickinson, Emily, 340–341
Disney, Walt, 370, 372–373
Dodge, Grenville M., 164–167
"Domestic Manners of the Americans," 382–383
Duncan, Isadora, 374, 377
Dunham, Katharine, 378
Du Pont Company:
  chemical research of, *256*
  early days of, 254–255
  growth of, 256
  nylon, 258
  nylon parachutes, *257*
  research programs of, 257
dust storm, 187, *188,* 189

Eakins, Thomas, *204*
Edison, Thomas Alva, *208*
  on the electric light, 208
  model of first electric light bulb, *209*
education:
  Annapolis, *320*
  college lecture hall, *325*
  "Country School, The," *306*
  Dewey, John, on, 322–323
  Eliot, Charles W., on, 322
  Harvard College, 318
  Harvard University, 316, *317*
  high school, modern, 313
  Hutchins, Robert, on, 323–325
  Jefferson, Thomas, on, 313–315
  McGuffey Readers, 306–310, 312

Figures in italics denote illustrations.

education (*cont.*):
    Mann, Horace, on, 305–306, 322
    Massachusetts, school law of, 305–306
    Michigan State College, *324*
    Morrill Act, 315–316
    Mount Holyoke College, *324*
    Nock, Albert Jay, on, 319–320
    Penn, William, on, 321
    reading class, second grade, *311*
    school experience of Mary Antin, 312
    schoolhouse, early, *307*
    statistics on, 304
    West Point cadets, *321*
    William and Mary, College of, *302*
Eisenhower, Dwight D., 133–136
electric light, 208, *209*
electronic data processing machine, *231*
electronics, 230–232
Eliot, Charles W., 322
Emancipation Proclamation, 118–119
Emerson, Ralph Waldo, 55, 334, 337
emigration to America, 50–52
Ericsson, Leif, 27–29
"Evangeline," 332–333
Everett, Edward, 280

Fairless, Benjamin F., 240–241
Fantasia, *372*
Farewell Address, Washington's, 79–80
farm equipment, *180*
farms, *173, 177, 190*
Florida:
    Castillo de San Marco, *32–33*
    first permanent settlement in, 34
    Indians in, *31*
Flying Cloud, clipper ship, 159, *162*
football, 388
Ford, Henry, 247–250, *249*, 252–253
Ford Motor Company, *252*
    assembly lines of, *250–251*
    development of, 247–253
foreign policy:
    Monroe Doctrine, the, 80–82
    Washington's Farewell Address, 79–80
    Wilson's Fourteen Points, 82–84
    United Nations Charter, 84–85
Fourteen Points, Woodrow Wilson's, 82–84
Franklin, Benjamin, 51–52
free enterprise, 234–258
freedom of the press, 95–97
Frémont, John C., 146–149
frontier life, 146
Fulton, Robert, 199–200
fur trapping, 144–145, *145*

Gallows Hill, Salem, Massachusetts, *92*
Garfield, James A., 73–74
Garland, Hamlin, 306–308
Geer, Elizabeth Dixon Smith, 149–150
Gettysburg, *281*

Gettysburg Address, 280
ghost town, *158*
Gladstone, William, 62
Glasgow, Ellen, 351, 353
Goddard, Robert H., 225–228
Goethals, George W., 211–212
gold miners, *156*, 156–157
gold prospector, *157*
Gold Rush, 150–158
Golden Gate Bridge, *234*
Golden Spike ceremony, 165, *166*, 167
Gompers, Samuel, 127–129
Gone with the Wind, *371*
Good, Sarah, 94–95
Governor's Mansion, Charleston, West Virginia, *68*
Graham, Martha, 374, *376*, 377–378
Grant, Ulysses S., 282, *284*, 284–286
Greeley, Horace, 275–277
Griffith, David Wark, 368–370
"Gross Clinic, The," *204*
Guaranty Trust Building, *362*
Guggenheim, Harry F., 225

Hancock, John, 267–269
Harvard College, 318
Harvard University, 316, *317*
Hawthorne, Nathaniel, 330–331
Hernandez, New Mexico, *35*
high school, typical modern, *313*
Hokinson, Helen, *391*
Holman, Eugene, 193–196
Homer, Winslow, *306*
Hoover, Herbert, 71–72
"House of the Seven Gables, The," 330–331
Hubner, Baron von, 386, 388
Humphrey, Doris, 374, 377
Hutchins, Robert, 323–325

"I called it the gates of the rocky mountains," *141*
"Ichabod," 331–332
immigrant, *77*
immigration statistics, 169
Inchon, landing at, *300*
Independence Hall, *59*
Indians:
    census figures, 97
    Cheyenne Indian, *105*
    cliff dwellings, *100*
    dog dance, 375
    in Florida, *31*
    Joseph, Chief, *103*, 109–111
    La Farge, Oliver, on, 111–112
    Morgan, Thomas J., on, 97–98
    Navajo, *106, 107*
    plains Indians, *104*
    Pretty Hail, *102*
    Red Cloud, 99–100, *102*

Figures in italics denote illustrations.

Indians (*cont.*):
 Red Jacket, 98–99
 school for, *108*
 Seattle, Chief, 100, 109
 tepees, *104*
 Three Feathers, *103*
industry, American, 234–258
Irving, Washington, 328–330
"Israfel," 333–334

James, Henry, 348–349
James, William, 258, 344, 346
Jamestown church tower, *37*
Japanese attack on Pearl Harbor, *294*
Jefferson, Thomas:
 on agriculture, 172–175
 on architecture, 359
 on education, 313–315
 instructions to Lewis and Clark, 140–142
"John Brown's Body," 357–359
Johnson, Dr. Samuel, 382
Johnston, William G., 152, 154–155
Joliet, Louis, 45–46
Joseph, Chief, *103*, 109–111
journalism, 363–367

Keyserling, Hermann, 392
Korean War:
 American soldier, *399*
 landing at Inchon, *300*
 MacArthur's address to Congress, 299–300
 statistics of, 266
 Truman's war message, 298–299

labor unions, 127, 130
La Farge, Oliver, 111–112
Lal, Chaman, 390–391
Land Rush, Oklahoma, *169*
Lardner, Ring, 355–356
Lee, Robert E., 281–282, 284, *285*, 286
Le Moyne, Jacques, 31
Lewis, John L., *128*, 129–130
Lewis, Meriwether, 142
Lewis and Clark expedition, 140–144, *144*
Lexington, Massachusetts, *53*
Liberator bombers, *296*
Lincoln, Abraham:
 Emancipation Proclamation, 118–119
 Gettysburg Address, 280
 reply to Edward Everett, 280
 reply to Horace Greeley, 277
 second inaugural address, 286, 288
 war message, 274, 275
Lindbergh, Charles A., *221*
 barnstorming days of, 218–219
 flight to Paris of, 220–222
 Spirit of St. Louis, the, *220*
Litchfield, Connecticut, church at, *89*
Litvinov, Maxim, 131–132
Long, Dr. Crawford W., 203

Longfellow, Henry Wadsworth, 332–333

MacArthur, Douglas, 299–300
Macaulay, Thomas Babington, 72–74
McGuffey, William Holmes, 306–310, 312
McKinley, William, 288–290
Madison, James, 270–271
Maine, the, 290
Mann, Horace, 305–306, 322
Marbury versus Madison, 68–70
Marquette, Jacques, 45–46
Marshall, James W., 151–152
Marshall, John, 68–70
Maryland:
 tobacco cultivation, 42, 44
 toleration act, 88
Massachusetts:
 Gallows Hill, Salem, *92*
 Lexington, *53*
 Plymouth, *41*
 school law, early, 305–306
 settlement of, 39–40, 42
Masters, Edgar Lee, 357
Mather, Cotton, 93–94
Maurois, André, 397–398
Mayo, Joseph C., 277–279
Mayflower Compact, the, 42
Melville, Herman, 339
Mendoza, Francisco Lopez de, 34
Meuse-Argonne offensive, *293*
Mexican War:
 Polk's war message, 273–274
 storming of Monterrey, *272*
 statistics of, 266
Michigan State College, *324*
Mickey Mouse, *372*
"Miracle of America, The," 397–398
mission, California, *86*
Mission San Diego de Alcala, 48, *49*, 50
Mississippi River, 45, *345*
"Moby Dick," 339
Monroe Doctrine, the, 80–82
Monticello, *361*
Morgan, Thomas J., 97–98
Mormons, 112–113
Morrill Act, 315–316
Morton, Dr. William, 203, *204*
motion pictures, 367–373
Mount Holyoke College, *324*
Mount Vernon, *174*

Nation, Carry, 124–125, *125*
Navajo Indians, *106*, *107*
New England:
 settlement of, 39–40, 42
 town meeting, *67*
New Mexico, 34, *35*, 36
New Orleans, 46, *47*, 48
New York, *207*
newsstand, 365

Figures in italics denote illustrations.

Nock, Albert Jay, 319–320
North Pole, discovery of, 214–216
nylon, 258

oil industry:
  oil refinery, *246*
  oil transportation, *245*
  oil well, first, *242*
  oil wells, modern, *243*
  Standard Oil Company, 242–244
  Standard Oil (New Jersey), 244, 246
Oklahoma:
  Land Rush, *169*
  soil erosion, *189*
Oklahoma! 376
Oñate, Juan de, 34–36
O'Neill, Eugene, 353–355
open-hearth steel process, *239*
Oregon coast, *144*
Oregon Trail, 149–150, *153*
Osborn, Fairfield, 189, 193
Otis, Elisha, 207

Palou, Francisco, 48–50
Panama Canal, 211–212, *213*, 214
Peale, Rembrandt, *57*
Pearl Harbor, Japanese attack on, *294*
Peary, Robert Edwin, 214, *215*, 216
Penn, William, 321
Pennsylvania:
  early description of, 44
  farm in, *177*
  religious stipulations of charter, 90–91
philanthropy, 258–264
Pickett's Charge, 277–280
Pinchot, Gifford, 182–183
Plymouth, Massachusetts, *41*
Poe, Edgar Allan, 333–334
Polk, James K., 273–274
Pony Express, 162, *163*, 164
prairie schooner, *153*
Presidents, 76, 79
Preston, Thomas Randolph, 115–116
Priestley, J. B., 394
Prohibition, 124–125
"Puritan, The," *40*

Quakers, 44, 91

racial equality, 119, 121
racial segregation in public schools, 121
Rafferty, Thomas, 279–280
railroad, modern, *167*
ranch roundup, *191*
Ranney, William, *139*, *145*
reading class, *311*
Red Cloud, 99–100, *102*
Red Jacket, 98–99
Reed, Dr. Walter, 210–211

religious freedom, 88–91
Remington, Frederic, *163*
Revolutionary War:
  declaration of, 267–269
  statistics of, 266
Rhode Island, religious freedom chartered in, 90
Rickenbacker, Edward V., 223–225
"Rip Van Winkle," 328–330
Rockefeller, John D., 241, *260*
  philanthropic principles of, 262–264
  principal trusts of, 261
  on Standard Oil Company, 242–244
rocket, launching of, *229*
rocketry, 225–229
Rocky Mountains, *141*, 142
Roosevelt, Franklin Delano:
  recognition of Soviet Russia, 131
  war message, 294–296
Roosevelt, Theodore, 181
Ross, Alexander, 144–145
Russia, recognition of, 131–132
Ryder, Albert Pinkham, *326*

San Diego:
  bay of, 30–31
  Mission San Diego de Alcala, 48, *49*, 50
Sargent, John Singer, *260*
Sarnoff, David, 230–232
schoolhouse, early, 307
Seal of the President, *60*
Seattle, Chief, 100, 109
segregation, racial, in public schools, 121
"Self-Reliance," 334, 337
sequoias, *170*
Shenandoah Valley farm, *173*
Sherman Anti-Trust Act, 126–127
slaves, *119*
slavery:
  early protest against, 91, 93
  Emancipation Proclamation, 118–119
Smith, John, 36, *38*, 39
Smith Act, 132–133
Socialism, 127
soil erosion, *189*
Spanish-American War:
  McKinley's war message, 288–290
  the *Maine*, 290
  statistics of, 266
Spender, J. Alfred, 384, 386
Spirit of St. Louis, the, *220*
"Spoon River Anthology," 357
St. Denis, Ruth, 374, 377
Standard Oil Company, 242–244
Standard Oil (New Jersey), 244, 246
state governments, 66
Statue of Liberty, the, *400*
steamboat, Fulton's, 199–200, *201*
steel industry:
  Bessemer process, *238*
  Carnegie, Andrew, on, 236–237

Figures in italics denote illustrations.

steel industry (*cont.*):
  Fairless, Benjamin F., on, 240–241
  open-hearth process, *239*
  steel pipe, seamless, *240*
  steel suspension bridge, *234*
  United States Steel Corporation, 236
Steinbeck, John, 187–189
Stevenson, Robert Louis, 164
suffrage, women's, 121–123
suffragists, *122*
Sullivan, Louis Henry, 360
Supreme Court:
  decision on public school segregation, 121
  Marbury versus Madison, 68–70
Supreme Court building, *65*
surgery, 202–203, *204–205*
Sutter's mill, *151*

television studio control room, *233*
Tennessee Valley Authority:
  Act, 183
  Fontana Dam, *184*
  Fort Loudon Dam, *185*
Thanksgiving, the first, 42
Thoreau, Henry David, 337–338
tobacco, cultivation of, 42, 44
Tocqueville, Alexis de, 382
"Toilers of the Sea," *326*
"Tom Sawyer," 341–344
town meeting, *67*
transcontinental railroad:
  construction of, 164–167
  Golden Spike ceremony, 165, *166*, 167
  modern railroad, 167
"Trappers, The," *145*
Trollope, Frances, 282–283
Truman, Harry S.:
  report on atom bomb, 296–298
  war message, 298–299
Trumbull, John, *269*
"Turkey," *43*
T. V. A., *see* Tennessee Valley Authority
Twain, Mark:
  on Pony Express, 162–164
  "Tom Sawyer," 341–344

United Nations:
  charter of, 84–85
  General Assembly of, *85*
United States:
  Capitol, *63*
  census figures, 169
  citizenship requirements, 75–76
  Constitution of, *see* Constitution of the United States
  immigration statistics, 169
  presidents of, 76, 79
  Presidential Seal, *60*

United States (*Cont.*):
  recognition of Soviet Russia, 131–132
  statistics of wars, 266
  territorial growth of, 167–168
"Varieties of Religious Experience, The," 344, 346
Virginia:
  farm in, *173*
  Jamestown church tower, *37*
  Monticello, *361*
  Mount Vernon, *174*
  statute of religious liberty, 91
Vogt, William, 183, 186–187

wagon train, *150*, 152, 154–155
"Walden," 337–338
Waldseemüller, Martin, 30
War of 1812:
  Constitution destroying the *Java*, the, *271*
  Madison's war message, 270–271
  statistics of, 266
Warren, Joseph, 52–53,
Washington, Booker T., 119, *120*, 121
Washington, George, *78*
  on agriculture, 172, 173–175
  on the Constitution, 62
  Farewell Address, 79–80
Webster, Daniel, 70–71
Welch, Dr. William, 202
West Point cadets, *321*
Wharton, Edith, 349–351
wheat harvesting, *191*
"When Lilacs Last in the Dooryard Bloom'd," 338–339
White, William Allen, 364–367
White House, the, *64*
Whitman, Walt, 338–339
Whitney, Eli, 198–199
Whittier, John Greenleaf, 331–332
Wilde, Oscar, 383–384
William and Mary, College of, *302*
Williams, Roger, 88
Wilson, Woodrow:
  Fourteen Points, 82–84
  war message, 291–293
Winslow, Edward, 42
witches, *92*, 93–95
woman voting, *123*
women's suffrage, 121–123
Woods, Daniel B., 156–157
World War I:
  Meuse-Argonne offensive, *293*
  statistics of, 266
  Wilson's war message, 291–293
World War II:
  atom bomb, *297*
  D-Day landing, *295*
  Japanese attack on Pearl Harbor, *294*
  Liberator bombers, *296*
  Roosevelt's war message, 294–296

Figures in italics denote illustrations.

World War II (*cont.*):
  statistics of, 266
  Truman's report on atomic bomb, 296–298
Wright, Frank Lloyd, 360, *362*, 363
Wright, Joseph, *78*
Wright, Orville, 216
Wright, Wilbur, 217–218

yellow fever, 210–211
Yosemite Valley, 158–159, *160–161*
Young, Brigham, 112–113
Yutang, Lin, 393–394

Zenger, John Peter, 95–97

Figures in italics denote illustrations